Talking Back to the West

THE GEOPOLITICS OF INFORMATION

Edited by Dan Schiller, Amanda Ciafone, and Yuezhi Zhao

For a list of books in the series, please see our website at www.press.uillinois.edu.

TALKING BACK TO THE WEST

How Turkey Uses Counter-Hegemony to Reshape the Global Communication Order

BILGE YESIL

UNIVERSITY OF ILLINOIS PRESS
Urbana, Chicago, and Springfield

© 2024 by the Board of Trustees
of the University of Illinois
All rights reserved
1 2 3 4 5 C P 5 4 3 2 1
∞ This book is printed on acid-free paper.

Library of Congress Cataloging-in-Publication Data
Names: Yesil, Bilge, 1973– author.
Title: Talking back to the west : how Turkey uses counter-
   hegemony to reshape the global communication order /
   Bilge Yesil.
Description: Urbana : University of Illinois Press, 2024. |
   Series: The geopolitics of information | Includes
   bibliographical references and index.
Identifiers: LCCN 2023053702 (print) | LCCN 2023053703
   (ebook) | ISBN 9780252045899 (cloth) | ISBN
   9780252087998 (paperback) | ISBN 9780252056772
   (ebook)
Subjects: LCSH: AK Parti (Turkey) | Communication in
   politics—Turkey. | Mass media—Political aspects—Turkey.
Classification: LCC JA85.2.T9 Y48 2024 (print) | LCC
   JA85.2.T9 (ebook) | DDC 320.956101/4—dc23/
   eng/20240108
LC record available at https://lccn.loc.gov/2023053702
LC ebook record available at https://lccn.loc.gov/2023053703

For activists in Turkey who, despite immense risks, continue to talk back.

Contents

Acknowledgments　ix

Author's Note　xiii

Introduction　1

1　Battling against Western Media Imperialism: Domestic Crises and International Communication Initiatives　26

2　Legitimizing Turkey's Communication Model: Encounters with Foreign Media Organizations and Professionals　47

3　Restoring Justice to Muslims: Knowledge Production about Islamophobia and Erdoğan's Missionary Politics　70

4　Discrediting the West: Civilizationist Paradigm and Negative Visions of Europe and the United States　91

5　Promoting Turkish History and Civilization: Television Dramas and Muslim Audiences　114

Conclusion　136

Appendix　149

Notes　151

Bibliography　179

Index　225

Acknowledgments

Writing a book might appear to be a solitary undertaking, yet it is undeniably shaped by a diverse network of colleagues, friends, and family. I consider myself lucky to have learned from, conversed with, and been enriched by so many individuals. During the early stages of this project, my fellowship with the Committee on Globalization and Social Change at the City University of New York (CUNY) Graduate Center offered a nourishing intellectual environment. Weekly conversations with Herman Bennett, Susan Buck-Morss, Colette Daiute, Grace Davie, Michael Gillespie, David Joselit, Jane Marcus-Delgado, Zeynep Oğuz, Uday Singh Mehta, Julie Skurski, Joan Wallach Scott, and Gary Wilder helped me to refine my preliminary ideas.

I am also thankful for the opportunity to share earlier versions of this project at events hosted by Bilkent University, Georgia State University, George Washington University, New York University, University of Pennsylvania, and University of Washington. I extend my appreciation to Ayşe Brammer-Baltacıoğlu, Colleen Kennedy-Karpat, Marwan Kraidy, Matthew Powers, Maria Repnikova, Adrienne Russell, James Ryan, Guobin Yang, William Youmans, and Jing Wang for providing me with a platform. My thanks also go to Nabil Echchaibi, Aslı Iğsız, Reşat Kasaba, Selim Kuru, Melanie McAlister, Divya McMillin, Aswin Punathembekar, Natalia Roudakova, Ekin Yaşin, and many others for engaging with my arguments at these events.

During the later stages of my writing process, I had the good fortune of being introduced to the New Civilizationisms Project by Aslı Iğsız. I am grateful to her and to Thomas Blom Hansen and Srirupa Roy for welcoming me to this international community of scholars.

Stimulating conversations with colleagues at conferences, academic meetings, and other venues have been instrumental in honing my thesis. I thank Ozan Aşık, Burcu Baykurt, Clovis Bergere, Ergin Bulut, Stanislav Budnitsky, Yasemin Çelikkol, Paula Chakravartty, Jayson Harsin, Lisel Hintz, Stewart Hoover, Joe Khalil, Gholam Khiabany, Dani Madrid-Morales, Wazhmah Osman, Burak Özçetin, Lindsay Palmer, Reece Peck, Maria Repnikova, Mehdi Semati, Ceren Sözeri, Servet Yanatma, and Kate Wright for their constructive commentary and encouragement.

I discussed some of the ideas in this book in my "Media and Culture in the Middle East" seminar at the CUNY Graduate Center. My gratitude goes to my students in the Middle Eastern Studies program for their enthusiastic conversations. I also owe a debt to the faculty and staff at CUNY Middle East and Middle Eastern American Center, especially Beth Baron, Simon Davis, Dina Le Gall, and Christa Salamandra for making me a part of this wonderful community.

I express my deep appreciation to my interlocutors—media professionals and state officials—for providing much-needed information about the inner workings of various media organizations, government agencies, and ministries in Turkey. I cannot thank them by name as I must protect their identity, but their contributions have been vital to completing the manuscript.

Part of the research for this book was funded by the CUNY Academy Travel Award, Professional Staff Congress–CUNY Research Award, and College of Staten Island Provost Travel Award. At various stages of writing, Ergin Bulut, Louis Fishman, Joe Khalil, Wazhmah Osman, and David Weil read drafts and offered insightful commentary. I am also grateful to the anonymous reviewers of the manuscript for their detailed engagement with my arguments. Laura Portwood-Stacer's book proposal workshop served as the essential motivation for embarking on this project amid the pandemic. Beste Atvur, Kathleen Ryan, and Heath Sledge enhanced the text's readability and accuracy. The outstanding team at the University of Illinois Press made the editorial and production process a smooth one. I am particularly indebted to Daniel Nasset for his unwavering belief in this project and his guidance in bringing it to fruition. My gratitude also extends to Megan Donnan, Mary Lou Kowaleski, and Dustin Hubbart for their assistance.

My colleagues at the Department of Media Culture, College of Staten Island, provided me with a nurturing environment. I am grateful to Cynthia Chris, David Gerstner, Bang-Geul Han, Michael Mandiberg, Tara Mateik, Sherry Millner, Edward Miller, Reece Peck, Jason Simon, Valerie Tevere, and Cindy Wong. Rosemary Neuner-Fabiano and Gary Pizzolo have gone beyond providing administrative assistance; they have extended their friendship.

Sarolta Takacs, the dean of the Division of Humanities and Social Sciences, has always been a strong advocate. I also thank Dorothy Walsh at the College of Staten Library for her assistance.

My extended family in Turkey and friends across the globe may not be fully aware of their roles in helping me accomplish this project, but I am grateful for their presence: Mehmet Akın, Gunsel Aksü, Gürhan Aksu, Devrim Alparslan, Sue Asprocolas, Işilay Baran, Piraye Cemiloğlu, Paula Chakravartty, Sue Collins, Sibel Demirel, Ciğdem Emeksiz, Elçin Engin Atalay, Bahar Eris, Berna Gizer Zaimoglu, Birsen Gücer, Dalia Kandiyoti, Karin Karakaşlı, Victoria Khazan Pigault, Dilhan Kellenberger, Gholam Khiabany, Ebru Yalçın, Wazhmah Osman, MJ Robinson, Selma Şavas, Burcu Coka, Dilek Türkmen, Marion Wrenn, Cemile Yaltır Özkan, Aybike Yeşil, and Ender Yeşil. Finally, thank you, Katya, Jeffrey, and Victor for putting everything into perspective and reminding me what truly matters. And to my brother, Mustafa, and my parents, Sevim and Hakkı, I know you would have been proud.

Author's Note

This manuscript was completed before October 2023 when Hamas carried out its brutal attack and Israel proceeded with its genocidal campaign. Due to the publication timeline, I have not included a detailed analysis of Turkey and its communication entities' response to these events. Here, I share a few observations: Unsurprisingly, the Erdoğan government adopted an anti-Israel and anti-Western stance rooted in religious and ideological solidarity with Palestinians. In Turkish news media, initial condemnation of Hamas gave way to a strong rejection of Western imperialism and a fiery criticism of Israel, at times laced with anti-Semitic undertones. On the global communication front, AKP-backed initiatives lambasted Israel and the United States, emphasizing Turkey's humanitarian aid to Palestinians and hyping Erdoğan's role as a peacemaker. While their coverage may appear as a counterbalance to dominant Western narratives, they must be evaluated carefully, as argued in this book. Turkey's global communication organs rightly criticize Israel's apartheid regime, yet we must remember that Turkey has dispossessed, displaced, and subordinated its own Kurdish citizens for decades. Erdoğan's communication representatives rightfully point out the silencing of pro-Palestinian voices in Western media, culture, and academia, but we must acknowledge how they use these instances to conceal the AKP's suppression of dissent in all spheres of public life. Erdoğan and his proxies condemn the West for hypocrisy, yet we must pay attention to their silence regarding Turkey's ongoing trade relations with Israel amid the genocide. I hope this book serves as a reminder that whenever the Erdoğan government and its global communication apparatus condemn the West and emphasize Turkey's moral superiority, their actions are propelled not merely by advocacy for the oppressed, but rather by a power-driven, selective, and transactional agenda.

Talking Back to the West

Introduction

In November 2016 President Recep Tayyip Erdoğan of Turkey spoke at the official launch event of Turkish Radio and Television Corp.'s TRT World, the country's first English-language news channel. In his introduction, Erdoğan criticized what he called "the obstruction of truth by Western media," arguing that Western journalists ignored his government's achievements and presented a skewed version of news coming from Turkey.[1] He also condemned Western media for turning a blind eye to the plight of "the downtrodden and the oppressed," a reference he often uses to refer to Muslims and Global South publics.[2] Erdoğan ended his address by quoting his "favorite African proverb": "Unless the lions write their own stories, we will continue to listen to the hunters' stories."[3] Erdoğan's speech here signaled his government's intent to unsettle the Western domination of the world communication order, rectify misrepresentations of Turkey, and carve out a space for "the voiceless" peoples around the world.[4] *Talking Back to the West: How Turkey Uses Counter-Hegemony to Reshape the Global Communication Order* documents the processes behind this anecdote, examining Erdoğan government's global communication apparatus that claims to speak on behalf of the Global South and promotes Turkey as a rising power.

Since the latter part of the first decade of the 2000s, Erdoğan's ruling AKP government (Adalet ve Kalkınma Partisi, Justice and Development Party) has pursued an assertive foreign policy in the Middle East, Africa, the Balkans, and Central Asia, and government-sponsored outlets have ramped up their promotion of Turkey as a rising great power. In the early 2010s when international media began to criticize Erdoğan for his antidemocratic practices,

AKP officials mobilized both state-owned and loyalist commercial media to fend off such negative coverage. As a result of these intersecting motivations, the geopolitical and the promotional, Turkey has vastly expanded its global communication apparatus in English and other languages.

Today, the Erdoğan government's global communication apparatus comprises both state-controlled and commercially owned entities. The two main official state organizations are the TRT (Türkiye Radyo ve Televizyon Kurumu, Turkish Radio and Television Corp.) and AA (Anadolu Ajansi, Anadolu Agency). TRT runs television channels (TRT Arabi, TRT Kurdi, TRT World) and digital news sites (TRT Deutsch, TRT Français, TRT Russian, TRT Balkan, TRT Afrika). Its radio network, Voice of Turkey, broadcasts in thirty-seven languages.[5] Meanwhile, AA, Turkey's official news agency, provides wire services in thirteen languages via forty-one offices around the globe. The Directorate of Communications (İletişim Başkanlığı), which reports directly to Erdoğan's office, hosts regional and international media forums for foreign government representatives and media professionals. Commercial outlets sponsored by loyalist media tycoons include English-language newspapers (*Daily Sabah* and *Yeni Safak English*, both in Istanbul) and a 24/7 English-language online news channel (A News). Finally, SETA (Siyaset, Ekonomi ve Toplum Araştırmaları Vakfi, Foundation for Political, Economic, and Social Research), an AKP-affiliated international think tank, and Bosphorus Global, a loyalist communications entity, operate various websites and social media accounts to explain Turkey's values and vision to the world.

Although these organizations have different operational logics, they are run by a small coterie of Erdoğan loyalists who share similar long-term objectives and ideological premises. Across a wide spectrum of communicative activities (news, entertainment, conferences, awareness campaigns, development communication), they aim to position Turkey as a rising power and a leading humanitarian actor and disseminate the AKP's vision of Turkey-led Muslim internationalism. In pursuit of these objectives, they provide exultant coverage of Turkey's accomplishments both domestically and internationally while also criticizing its adversaries, particularly those from the West—Turkey's historical Other. Furthermore, they depict Turkey as a prominent actor capable of challenging Western hegemony and advocating for justice on behalf of "the voiceless" (that is, people, countries, and regions that have been victimized especially by the West). *Talking Back to the West* takes account of the foreign policy goals that motivate the government's external-facing communication program but does not analyze that program merely through the prisms of public diplomacy or soft power. Instead, it focuses on how these communication ventures are shaped by sociocultural vestiges and how, in turn, they instrumentalize religiously inflected identity politics.

In these efforts, AKP-aligned actors and entities do not fabricate falsehoods regarding Turkey or its adversaries. They bring attention to certain powerful truths (e.g., Islamophobia in Europe, colonialism in Africa, Western military interventions in the Middle East) but strategically obscure their complex underpinnings and implications, simplifying them into binary oppositions (e.g., East versus West, moral versus immoral). In their media and communication content, these actors and entities use facts within a framework that is aligned with the Erdoğan regime's preferred narratives while omitting those that do not. Their ultimate goal is to persuade global audiences that Turkey is reshaping the prevailing power dynamics and forging a "fairer world" on behalf of marginalized and oppressed peoples.[6] To maintain this projection, they intentionally exclude facts that could disrupt it, such as Erdoğan's authoritarianism and irredentist foreign policy. In light of this, *Talking Back to the West* proposes a theoretical perspective that emphasizes how AKP-directed communication entities utilize *strategic obfuscation*.[7] Strategic obfuscation involves the leveraging of authoritative truths and factual information while obscuring the intricate nature of the underlying phenomena beneath these truths. To clarify, strategic obfuscation doesn't revolve around disseminating falsehoods; rather, it focuses on accentuating specific facts, disregarding others, simplifying complex events into binary dichotomies, and thereby maintaining the capacity to shape public perception.

Turkey's outward-facing communication endeavors might be viewed as attempts to diversify and democratize the global communication landscape. This is, in fact, how Erdoğan's communication emissaries promote Turkey's international news channels and media assistance and journalism training programs: as tools to create inclusive spaces for politically, economically, and culturally marginalized communities; to give voice to "the voiceless"; and to create a more equitable world communication order. *Talking Back to the West* challenges this perception. It argues that the AKP-backed entities are not necessarily motivated by democratic and humanistic objectives but, rather, by the imperative to legitimize the domestic and foreign policy activities of a power-driven regime. It demonstrates that the Erdoğan regime's mobilization of counter-hegemony is underpinned by a selective and exclusionary notion of "the voiceless"—one that reflects its policy priorities as well as its nationalist-Islamist worldview. Last but not least, *Talking Back to West* documents how the AKP's external-facing communicative activities perpetuate East-West dichotomies, employ identity-based narratives, and cloak populist commentary as a critique of the West.

Research Agenda, Contribution, and Methods

Turkey's aforementioned outreach activities can be categorized under the umbrella of state-sponsored political communication, that is, the strategic targeting of foreign publics to attain certain political economic and cultural goals. Existing scholarship in this field has generally examined states' and elected governments' communication projects in the context of international relations, foreign policy, and war and conflict, viewing them as tools of propaganda, public diplomacy, and/or soft power.

Before proceeding, a concise overview of the terms "propaganda," "public diplomacy," and "soft power" is in order. "Propaganda" is the deliberate manipulation of beliefs by combining factual information with falsehoods, aiming to prompt specific actions from individuals or the public. Across various prominent definitions of propaganda, there is a focus on the manipulation of opinions, the objective of altering ideas or behaviors, and the deliberate nature of these activities.[8] "Public diplomacy," on the other hand, refers to a country's efforts to engage with foreign publics to foster understanding and build relationships. It encompasses various activities, such as cultural exchanges, educational programs, and international broadcasting.[9] As public diplomacy scholar Nicholas Cull notes, both propaganda and public diplomacy are about persuasion, but the former involves dictating a message and persuading the audience, while the latter entails listening to the other side and striving to develop a relationship. Also, propaganda often relies on deception and selective presentation of facts, while public diplomacy emphasizes ethical communication.[10] "Soft power," coined by political scientist Joseph Nye, refers to the ability of a country to influence others and achieve desired outcomes through attraction as opposed to coercion or force.[11] It includes cultural influence, economic strength, diplomatic relationships, technological advancements, and other factors that contribute to a country's ability to gain support.[12]

To go back to the literature on state-sponsored communication, an international relations framework has shaped most analyses of American, British, and German news organizations during World War I, World War II, and the Cold War.[13] The influence of this framework with its emphasis on foreign policy conflicts and global power struggles can still be observed in studies about contemporary news and information practices around the world.[14] Additionally, the scholarship on state-sponsored communication has expanded with the inclusion of Chinese, Russian, and Qatari case studies. Nonetheless, an international relations framework continues to influence the field. For example, countless edited volumes examine China's global news organizations and popular culture products as manifestations of the Communist Party's public diplomacy and/or soft power endeavors.[15] Russia's international communication enterprises are almost exclusively analyzed in terms of geopolitical conflicts between the Kremlin and the West, highlighting the (perceived) threats Russia poses to the Western democratic order.[16] Similarly, international relations concepts ground most analyses of Qatar-funded Al Jazeera network. These studies generally discuss Al Jazeera as a counter-hegemonic actor that challenges both regional state media and international Western news organizations or as a network that promotes democracy and sociopolitical progress in the Middle East.[17] Last but not least, the nascent literature on Turkey's external-facing communication program examines the Anadolu Agency, Voice of Turkey, TRT World, and other TRT channels through the lens of public diplomacy and as tools that the government uses to bolster its regional and international standings.[18]

Obviously, the aforementioned works provide important insights into the nexus of communication and international relations. While acknowledging these connections, *Talking Back to the West* does not examine Turkey's state-directed communication instruments purely in the context of public diplomacy or soft power, nor does it assess whether they generate legitimacy for the country among foreign publics. Although these are important research questions, this book adopts a cultural framework and examines the core ideas and symbols that organize the Erdoğan regime's global messaging. The book focuses on how Muslim identity politics, nationalist-Islamist ideology, and the specter of Western imperialism shape the regime's communication endeavors and with what implications on global communication writ large.

This emphasis on culture and identity invites several questions: What discursive strategies do Erdoğan's communication emissaries use to construct certain perceptions of the West, Turkey, Turks, and Muslims? To what extent are their communicative activities informed by the AKP's populist logic and anti-Western ideational framework? Which religious and identity-based tropes do they use to assemble Global South audiences? What drives the Erdoğan government to shed international attention on Muslim suffering? Why and how do AKP-backed outlets interrogate the West for not adhering to its own-professed values? What are their objectives in producing television shows that project Turkish Muslim civilization as superior to the West? How do they instrumentalize the debates that are taking place in Europe and the United States about post-truth and disinformation to promote Turkey's own communication policies? Why and with what tools do they engage in development communication in the Global South? And, what are the implications of all these initiatives on the global communication landscape?

Talking Back to the West addresses these and other questions through a discourse-historical analysis of a vast array of English-language audiovisual, print, online, and social media content. The discourse-historical approach allows researchers to integrate critical discourse analysis with the inquiry of social variables and historical knowledge of texts, actors, and institutions.[19] The representations of sociopolitical problems and the legitimation of dominant interests are embedded in history, and the discourse-historical approach helps to "triangulate analyses of the immediate texts under investigation; intertextual and interdiscursive relationships between utterances, texts, genres and discourses; social/sociological variables; and the broader sociopolitical and historical contexts."[20]

This book specifically examines English-language communication activities as opposed to those in other languages for a number of reasons. The AKP-affiliated legacy and digital communication outlets that operate in English target global audiences whereas those in Arabic, German, French, Russian, Balkan, and African languages have a specific national or regional focus. Since English is one of the most widely spoken languages around the world and is the lingua franca in diplomacy, business, and other fields, English-language operations allow the AKP-backed communication outlets to reach wider audiences around the world. Last but not least, it is via the English-language news operations that Erdoğan's communication emissaries can compete with established West-based organizations and present their alternative viewpoints on global events.

With this in mind, *Talking Back to the West* analyzes the following organizations and content categories:

- TRT World and its discussion programs, documentaries, and news coverage
- *Daily Sabah* and its news coverage and op-ed pieces
- Bosphorus Global, SETA, TRT World Research Centre, TRT World Citizen, and their communication and knowledge production activities
- TRT and AKP-affiliated commercial companies and their television dramas
- Directorate of Communications and Anadolu Agency and their various external-facing activities

Talking Back to the West does not offer a one-by-one analysis of each of the aforementioned organizations, nor does it review their entire output. Instead, it focuses on a number of topics that these entities cover consistently and extensively, examines the connections between such coverage and the AKP's nationalist-Islamist framework, and discusses the potential implications of such coverage on global communication. The process followed to select these topics is explained next.

Between 2015 and 2016, as I was finishing *Media in New Turkey: The Origins of an Authoritarian Neoliberal State*, I noticed a significant uptick in the AKP's external communication endeavors in English and began to monitor the activities of TRT World, Anadolu Agency, *Daily Sabah*, Bosphorus Global, and SETA. Later, I became intrigued by the establishment of the Directorate of Communications and its widening scope of international activities; the growth of Anadolu Agency's journalism training programs targeting media professionals in/of the Global South; and the rising popularity of AKP-sanctioned historical television series, especially among Muslim audiences worldwide. Over the next few years, I systematically followed Erdoğan's communication emissaries and state-run and loyalist media organizations, taking note of the core themes and ideas that underpin official statements, conferences, policy reports, and media output. Through this inductive process I identified the following narratives pushed forward by the AKP-backed entities as the focal point of my analysis: Turkey as a benevolent actor that is reshaping the global order, the West as morally bankrupt and dysfunctional, Muslims as victimized by Western hegemony, and Turkish Muslim civilization as exceptional.

I focused on a number of topics wherein these ideas were most vocally expressed. Media and communication content concerning Islamophobia, the refugee crisis, colonialism, and Ottoman history provided that opportunity. I chose to conduct in-depth textual analysis of news programs, documentaries, op-eds, and television series that tackle these topics. I intentionally refrained from conducting a quantitative analysis of social media accounts associated with the AKP-backed organizations. By doing this, I managed to go beyond quantitative assessments of whether these organizations share accurate information or how often they use (or not) particular arguments and ideas.

I complemented textual analyses of media output with an examination of policy documents government agencies published as well as official statements Erdoğan and his emissaries delivered. This allowed me to reveal how various state and nonstate entities' editorial policies and content production are shaped by Erdoğan's guiding principles. Lastly, I drew on expert interviews that I conducted with Turkish and foreign, current and former employees of TRT, TRT World, Anadolu Agency, and *Daily Sabah*, as well as officials from the Ministry of Foreign Affairs and the now-defunct Office of Public Diplomacy (Kamu Diplomasisi Koordinatörlüğü). I established contact with Turkish professionals and state officials using my personal connections in Turkey and gained access to foreign professionals via their colleagues at Al Jazeera, China Global Television Network (CGTN), and Deutsche Welle.

Throughout the book, I refrain from giving detailed information about my interlocutors' past and present employment statuses and the specific positions they occupy (or did) at state organs and AKP-backed outlets. I simply refer to them as "current/former, Turkish/foreign, employee/official" in order to ensure anonymity and protect them from potential government reprisals.[21]

Although the total number of interviews (twenty-one) may seem small, I want to remind readers that *Talking Back to the West* is not an ethnographic study of the AKP-backed communication entities. I use quotes from the interviews to enrich and contextualize my political economic, textual, and policy-related findings. Gaining access to individuals that work/ed at state and AKP-linked entities has been extremely challenging. For example, some foreign journalists and producers at TRT World declined my requests, citing that they did not have anything negative to say although I explained to them that my objective was not to dig dirt, so to speak. Those that agreed to talk to me did so only after they quit their jobs *and* left Turkey—a sign of their fear of government retribution. Many of the state officials at relevant ministries and Turkish media professionals at AKP-backed organizations that I approached did not want to talk to me at all. Some feared retaliation; others were ardent Erdoğan supporters who viewed me as an antigovernment activist.

The following sections first provide an overview of state-backed communication enterprises around the world and then trace the growth of Turkey's external-facing initiatives from the early twentieth century to present day.

Global Communications and the Proliferation of Non-Western Outlets

States and elected governments strategically target foreign publics in order to enhance their country's standing, garner support for their policies, and respond to critics. The earliest of these political communication programs emerged between World War I and the Cold War, when several countries developed regional and/or international radio stations to explain their policies to foreign audiences—stations that eventually expanded into vast networks, such as BBC World Service, Voice of America, Deutsche Welle, Radio Moscow, Radio China International, and others.[22]

The entry of commercial players into the 24/7 news market in English in the 1980s opened up a whole new arena for governments. CNN's live coverage of the events in Tiananmen Square in 1989 and of the Gulf War in 1991 led public broadcasters such as the BBC to follow suit, spawning a fast-growing international market.[23] This trend only intensified in the 1990s and 2000s, as both commercial and publicly funded broadcast outlets continued to proliferate due in part to advances in satellite and digital technologies, deterritorialization of communication, and deregulation and commercialization in national media markets.

Throughout the 2000s, several countries around the world increased their investments in international communication to reverse American and European dominance. China, which had already established a regional radio-TV apparatus in the 1980s and 1990s, began to develop a global network in order to explain its post-Mao era reforms to the world and to correct the negative Western narratives that dominated the airwaves after the Tiananmen Square massacre.[24] As the Chinese economy rapidly expanded in the first decade of the 2000s, so did the country's efforts to provide alternatives to Western framings of China. In response to President Xi Jinping's assertion that China should "give a good Chinese narrative and better communicate China's messages to the world," state-funded entities, such as CCTV (China Central Television), Radio China International, Xinhua News Agency, *People's Daily*, and *China Daily*, have rapidly globalized.[25] Today, China's global outreach extends into journalism training programs, investment in communication infrastructure development, and film and television production.

Qatar, another country of interest to scholars, entered the field of global communication in 1996, when its emir sponsored the launch of the Arabic-language Al Jazeera television to raise the country's profile regionally and internationally. A hybrid state-private entity, Al Jazeera transformed the state-controlled and heavily censored news landscape in the Arab world; it also provided alternative narratives to the dominant Western representations of the Middle East.[26] In 2005 Al Jazeera English began broadcasting; it described its mission as being "the voice of the voiceless" and started prioritizing reports about and from the perspective of marginalized peoples around the world. In 2011 Al Jazeera Balkans was launched, followed by Al Jazeera America in 2013 (though the latter only survived three years in the US cable market). The network's online news platform AJ+, born in 2014, provides social media content from its San Francisco office.[27] In addition to news, Al Jazeera offers several channels with Arabic-language programming, including beIN Sports, AJ Documentary Channel, AJ Children's Channel, and AJ Mubasher, a public-interest channel that broadcasts public events in real time, without editing or commentary. Al Jazeera also operates other communication-related entities: the Al Jazeera Centre for Studies, a research center that produces reports and policy briefs, and the Al Jazeera Media Institute, which provides training in communication and media sectors.

Russia is another country that has increased its presence in global communication. Following the adoption of the Doctrine of Information Security in

2000, it launched media and communication enterprises aimed at countering Western narratives.[28] In 2005 it inaugurated Russia Today, the country's first English-language news channel, in order to "represent Russia positively to the outside world."[29] In 2009 the channel was rebranded as RT; since then, its editorial strategy has been to invite audiences to "question more"—in other words, to interrogate the validity of news Western outlets disseminate. Unlike its Chinese counterparts, which primarily seek to disseminate positive narratives about the country, RT's key aim is to damage the image of liberal democracies and portray Western news media as willfully ignoring the social and political problems that afflict Western societies.[30] In 2014 Russia inaugurated Sputnik, a digital news service that replaced two state-run entities, the Voice of Russia radio network and the RIA Novosti news agency.[31] In addition to these outlets, Russia has also engaged in covert cyber operations to manipulate social media and influence public opinion around the world, especially in Europe and the United States. Since the 2016 US presidential election, Russian state agencies and hacker groups have been in the spotlight for their illicit media campaigns, which seek to meddle in foreign elections, spread disinformation, and digitally hack various institutions.[32] In March 2022 the European Union (EU) prohibited broadcasting content from RT's and Sputnik's English-language services, citing Russia's dis/misinformation campaigns in regards its attack on Ukraine. Major social media companies also blocked the sharing of content from RT and Sputnik on their platforms.[33] RT's and Sputnik's Spanish and Arabic services have not been affected by this ban and continue to reach audiences in Latin America and the Middle East.[34]

In addition to China, Qatar, and Russia, other states also seek to use television to their national advantage, including Iran's Press TV, Japan's NHK World, and Venezuela-based Telesur. The landscape of global news is, thus, a crowded one, examples of which include BBC World News, Euronews, CGTN, Channel News Asia, Deutsche Welle, France 24, NHK World, Press TV, RT, and Telesur. Some of these outlets also offer Arabic, French, or Spanish services.

In addition to television, there are also large international radio networks (BBC World Service, Voice of America, Radio France International, Deutsche Welle, Radio Sputnik, China Radio International, and NHK World Radio) with corresponding digital sites. Some states run international news agencies (the UK's BBC News, China's Xinhua, and Russia's TASS) and English-language newspapers (*China Daily*), as well. Last, but not least, state-run global communication is also moving online, as state officials and government representatives use social media sites to reach out to foreign publics and exert influence over other countries' political systems.[35]

In this ever-widening global communication landscape, non-Western outlets generally describe themselves as counter-hegemonic actors that bring alternative perspectives to global news, correct Western media's misrepresentations, and/or prioritize underreported countries and regions in their coverage. Turkey is making a place for itself within this field as it expands its roster of foreign language communication enterprises.

Growth of Turkey's External Communication Program

News Agency

Turkey's first foray into international communication can be traced back to the late nineteenth century, when its predecessor the Ottoman Empire founded its own national news agency. As chapter 1 details, this initiative was prompted by Ottoman officials' concerns about West-based news agencies' allegedly "hostile and malicious" coverage of the empire. Ottoman officials saw the commercial news agencies Reuters and Havas as mouthpieces of Great Britain and France and decided to counter them by establishing their own agency.[36] In 1909 they collaborated with a private individual to found the semi-official Ottoman Telegraph Agency. However, this entity was short-lived and ceased operations in 1914 due to the empire's entry into World War I.

After the war, in 1919, Havas and Reuters jointly founded a news agency in Istanbul, called L'Agence de Turquie. This agency, which included a representative from the Ottoman Ministry of Foreign Affairs, gave foreign journalists the exclusive right to report news about and from the empire. During the Turkish War of Independence (1919–23), prominent intellectuals recognized the need for a domestic news agency. Working closely with future Turkey's founder and first president, Mustafa Kemal, who was leading the war at the time, they created Anadolu Agency in 1920. Their goal was to inform domestic and foreign audiences about the War of Independence and to counter L'Agence de Turquie's allegedly biased coverage. In the beginning, then, Anadolu Agency was affiliated with the official circles that were engaged in the Turkish liberation movement.[37]

After Kemal's victory against the occupying forces and the founding of the Republic in 1923, the Turkish political establishment decided to make Anadolu Agency autonomous. In 1925 the AA was transformed into a joint stock company, controlled entirely by private shareholders. Over the years, however, due to a series of controversial capital augmentation and buy-back procedures, approximately half of the AA shares were reacquired by the Treasury, a development that eventually brought the agency under the control of ruling political parties.[38]

Under the AKP, the Anadolu Agency's budget has come to be entirely controlled by the Treasury and the Directorate General of Press and Information (Koordinatörlüğü Yayın Enformasyon Genel Müdürlüğü) and by proxy the office of the prime minister. In 2018 the AA was incorporated into the newly established Directorate of Communications, which centralizes all government communications under one roof and reports directly to Erdoğan. During the AKP era, Anadolu Agency expanded its services remarkably. In 2011 its wire service included five languages, with a daily output of 150 to 200 news items. Today, it operates more than thirty offices around the world, with wire service in thirteen languages. As chapter 5 discusses in detail, Anadolu Agency also offers an expansive roster of training programs via its News Academy to domestic and foreign journalists, especially those from the Middle East, Central Asia, Africa, and the Balkans.

Radio Network

Turkey entered the international radio broadcasting field in 1937 with its short-wave radio station, Voice of Turkey (VoT). Prompted by tense political relations with France that arose from the status of a province near the Syrian border, VoT sought to influence the local population in the area and shape the opinions of local decision makers to Turkey's advantage. Originally, the station broadcast in Arabic and was in operation only for an hour a day.[39]

Until the 1980s VoT operations were hampered by technological and economic impediments, and its broadcasts were limited to Arabic and English for a few hours a day. In the 1980s, thanks to developments in satellite technology and Turkey's opening to the Balkans and Central Asia, VoT introduced Chinese and Russian services; by 1995 it was broadcasting in seventeen languages.[40] After the AKP came to power in 2002, VoT grew at a rapid pace, and today it offers service in thirty-eight languages, ranging from Afghani to Turkmen, English to Swahili.[41] Websites in these foreign languages offer listeners access to live radio, archives of past programs, and podcasts.[42]

Television Outlets

Turkey embarked on international television broadcasting in the early 1990s to strengthen cultural ties with Turkish migrants in Europe and to draw post-Soviet Turkic republics into its orbit. Taking advantage of new satellite broadcasting capabilities, the Turkish Radio and Television Corp. (TRT) launched two transnational channels: TRT INT in 1990 and TRT Avrasya ("Eurasia" in English) in 1992. TRT INT targeted Turkish migrant workers in Europe and was explicitly designed to broadcast the "official cultural and political ideal of

Turkey" in the European public sphere with news, culture, and entertainment programming that projected the state-sanctioned version of Turkish identity.[43] The other channel, TRT Avrasya, targeted Turkic populations in Central Asia, seeking to reestablish the ethnic-cultural ties that were severed during the Soviet rule. TRT Avrasya was designed as a foreign policy tool to enhance Turkey's sphere of influence in this strategically important region. Together, the two channels sought to connect Turkish and Turkic populations dispersed across Europe and Asia to the homeland. For the Turkish government, they were important steps toward making TRT "one of the world's largest transnational media organizations—broadcasting from the Atlantic Ocean to the Great Wall of China."[44]

TRT's international expansion continued well into the 2000s. As chapter 3 details, the AKP government adopted an assertive foreign policy vision under Ahmet Davutoğlu, the former minister of foreign affairs. Accordingly, TRT began to inaugurate new regional channels one after another. In 2009 TRT Avaz ("voice" in Turkic languages) was launched to "develop bilateral and multicultural interactions" between Turkey and Turkic-speaking populations in Central Asia, the Caucuses, and the Balkans and to "support the common values" of these peoples.[45] The channel's programming included news, arts, music, and literature with a focus on Ottoman and Islamic history and culture.[46] Between 2017 and 2018, the channel was restructured to foreground the Turkish nationalist creed of "unity in language, mind and action" among the target communities.[47]

Also in 2009 TRT launched TRT 6, which broadcast in three Kurdish dialects (Kurmanji, Sorani, and Zazaki) as part of the government's attempt to reach out to Kurds in Turkey and in neighboring Syria, Iran, and Iraq. The channel was developed to compete with the Europe-based Kurdish satellite channel ROJ TV and to promote the AKP's Kurdish peace process. The channel had a mixed reception: it was praised for the AKP's recognition of Kurdish language and cultural rights (albeit politically motivated for EU membership) and criticized for disseminating the official Turkish perspective on the Kurdish issue. The channel was relaunched as TRT Kurdi in 2015.

In 2010 TRT launched TRT 7 al-Turkiyya, which targeted Arabic-speaking audiences in the Middle East. This channel used news and entertainment programming to promote Turkish tourism, businesses, and universities and to draw attention to Turkish economic projects in the region, disseminating an "image of Turkey as a friend of the Arabs and as a successful model to be emulated."[48] The channel was rebranded as TRT El Arabia 2015 and as TRT Arabi in 2019, which now presents news and analysis on regional and international events through the prism of Turkish foreign policy.

In 2015 TRT added TRT World to its roster, Turkey's first English-language news channel, which is discussed in detail in chapter 1. It also launched digital news sites TRT Deutsch and TRT Russian in 2020; TRT Balkan and TRT

Français in 2022; and inaugurated another digital news site, TRT Afrika, in 2023.

Last but not least, TRT launched an international streaming platform, called Tabii, in 2023 to present its family-friendly, conservative, and Turkish nationalist content to domestic and international audiences. In addition to mainstream series, Tabii features productions about historical Turkish Muslim warriors, scientists, and religious figures.

Aside from these outlets, other entities in the AKP's global apparatus carry out a range of public diplomacy, strategic communication, and public relations activities on behalf of the government. They include state organs, such as the Office of Public Diplomacy (now defunct) and the Directorate of Communications, and AKP-linked organizations, such as SETA and Bosphorus Global. The following section provides an overview.

Office of Public Diplomacy

Turkey's first-ever Office of Public Diplomacy (OPD, Kamu Diplomasisi Koordinatörlüğü) was founded in 2010.[49] With İbrahim Kalın (currently the director of Turkey's national intelligence organization) at the helm, and in line with Erdoğan's aspirations for global influence, the OPD's goals were to "ensure better coordination and cooperation between various public diplomacy actors in the country; improve Turkey's reputation; and increase its visibility and activity in international public opinion."[50] In practice, though, the OPD lacked the necessary resources to centralize existing public diplomacy activities that were carried out by numerous other entities under different ministries. Moreover, the OPD was primarily interested in assuring that foreign press corps received the official Turkish perspective on domestic and international developments and not so much in listening to and engaging with international publics.[51] As a result, the OPD's activities were limited to hosting foreign journalists for short-term visits in Turkey and holding monthly meetings with those who resided in the country. Its X (formerly Twitter) accounts in Turkish, English, and Arabic and its only Facebook page in Turkish produced little to no interaction with international audiences.[52] In 2018 the OPD was incorporated into the Directorate of Communications.

The Directorate of Communications

The Directorate was established in July 2018 as part of Turkey's transition from a parliamentary to a presidential system of government and is one of the several newly established offices that report directly to Erdoğan. The DoC comprises different departments, which oversee public relations, strategy development, public diplomacy, press management, and translation. In 2023 the DoC employed 694 permanent personnel and contractors, and its estimated budget for 2020–24 was $360 million.[53] Upon its founding, the DoC took control of the OPD and the Directorate General of Press and Information and, thus, became the central authority in managing relations between Erdoğan and the press, granting accreditation and residency permits to foreign journalists, and carrying out public diplomacy and international communication work on behalf of the AKP government.

The DoC undertakes a number of activities to promote Erdoğan, his government, and Turkey in a positive light, including but not limited to publishing op-eds in foreign newspapers under Erdoğan's name; publishing and distributing books on Turkey's foreign policy to foreign constituencies; organizing conferences, panels, and other events in Turkey and abroad; running social media campaigns in Turkish and foreign languages; and creating videos that celebrate Turkey's so-called glorious past and military might.[54] The DoC's current director is Fahrettin Altun, who has a PhD in communications from Istanbul University. Prior to assuming the director position, Altun served as the general coordinator of SETA's Istanbul office and later as SETA's deputy general. During this time, he also worked as an academic at private universities, penned op-eds for pro-government newspapers, and appeared on TRT as a commentator.[55]

SETA

SETA was founded in 2005 by a group of academics and businessmen with ties to the AKP, and it originally described itself as a nonpartisan, nonprofit research institute focusing on national, regional, and international issues. Its founding director was Kalın; its current director is Burhanettin Duran, a member of Erdoğan's Presidential Security and Foreign Policy Council.[56] Until 2013 SETA's main goal was to promote the AKP as the "leader of a democratic front of conservatives and liberals in Turkey" so as to garner support from the EU and the United States. Prominent liberals and leftist intellectuals, both Turkish and foreign, contributed articles to SETA's periodical, *Insight Turkey*, and spoke at SETA-organized panels and conferences. However, after 2013 SETA began to echo the AKP's argument that Gezi protestors constituted "a threat to the nation," openly toeing the government line.[57] Today, SETA seeks to disseminate favorable coverage of Erdoğan's domestic and foreign policies and to criticize rival countries via panels, periodicals, books, and online sites in English and other languages.

SETA has offices in Ankara and Istanbul, Turkey; Washington, DC, United States; Berlin, Germany; and Brussels, Belgium, and it employs about one hundred full-time staff, a third of whom occupy administrative posts.[58] SETA's research teams focus on domestic and foreign policy, economy, politics, society and media, security, law and human rights, strategy, energy, education, and social policies. Several of its research specialists are columnists for pro-government newspapers, and they also provide commentary on pro-government television channels and TRT's international channels. Over the years, some SETA researchers transferred to the Ministry of Foreign Affairs, the Anadolu Agency, and TRT; some even ran for public office under the banner of the AKP.[59]

Bosphorus Global

Bosphorus Global is a communications and public relations entity that was founded in 2015 by the pro-Erdoğan pundit Hilal Kaplan and her former spouse, Suheyb Ogut. Bosphorus Global describes itself as an independent nongovernmental organization (NGO); however, it is deeply imbricated with Erdoğan; his son-in-law Berat Albayrak, who served as the minister of treasury and finance; and Berat's brother, Serhat Albayrak, who owns *Daily Sabah*, A News, and several other domestic media outlets.

Bosphorus Global says it seeks to rectify the negative representations of Turkey in Western media and communicate accurate information about Turkey's adversaries to global audiences. It hosts foreign journalists and parliamentarians in Turkey and runs social media operations and so-called fact-checking websites, which chapters 1 and 4 further discuss.

Erdoğan's Communication Apparatus: Goals and Strategies

According to the director of communications, Fahrettin Altun, TRT's international channels, Voice of Turkey, and the Anadolu Agency comprise a "holistic communication strategy" that promotes "the real narrative, perception and recognition of New Turkey that stands on its own feet and has a say in the region and in the world." Altun asserts that these outlets inform global audiences of Turkey's "breakthroughs, values and esteemed civilization in every field."[60]

In addition to these state organs, commercially owned, English-language outlets contribute to the Erdoğan government's global communication work. As chapter 1 explains, these commercial outlets, namely the *Daily Sabah*, *Yeni Safak English*, and A News are owned by loyalist media tycoons, who receive a remarkable share of government contracts, state advertising, and cheap credit from state banks. Similar to state organs, these outlets seek to rebuke the allegedly duplicitous Western media coverage of Turkey, legitimize Erdoğan's security-oriented domestic policies, and garner international support for his foreign policy actions.

Although the instruments that make up Turkey's global communication apparatus all embrace the same guiding principles established by the Erdoğan government, they operate in quite different ways. For example, the Anadolu Agency functions like an official news bulletin, covering Turkey-related developments and world events strictly through the government's perspective. In contrast, TRT World uses formats and conventions inspired by CNN International, BBC World, and Al Jazeera, and during routine affairs its coverage is reminiscent of these news channels. However, during regional or international developments or breaking news that involves Turkey, it shifts to an entirely AKP-sanctioned content and perspective, featuring government officials and pro-government experts as commentators. *Daily Sabah*, *Yeni Safak English*, and A News also cover domestic and international news with a pro-AKP slant mimicking their Turkish-language parent organizations.

Whether under state control or guided by pro-Erdoğan loyalists, Turkey's global communication instruments are united by a shared set of objectives. One of their primary objectives is to legitimize Turkey's domestic and foreign policy actions and refute (potential) criticisms coming from Western leaders, policy circles, and news media. For example, when Turkey embarked on a military operation, code named Operation Peace Spring, in north Syria in October 2019, the AKP-aligned news outlets engaged in a days-long special coverage. TRT World featured expert interviews with government-friendly voices (e.g., the executive director of SETA, managing editor of *Daily Sabah*, representatives from an Islamic NGO) while the Anadolu Agency and *Daily Sabah* shared a steady stream of news reports, infographics, op-eds, and analysis pieces on their websites. AKP rank and file, pro-government troll accounts, and ordinary Erdoğan supporters shared these infographics and online news videos on X, using the hashtags #operationpeacespring, #BabykillerPKK and #BabykillerYPG, aiming to frame PKK (Partiya Karkeran Kurdistane, Kurdistan Workers' Party) and YPG (Yekineyen Parastina Gel, People's Defense Units) as terrorist organizations.[61] These English-language communication endeavors portrayed the operation as a legitimate security undertaking that sought to "neutralize" Kurdish PKK and YPG members in north Syria (the euphemism Turkish officials use instead of "kill"), to secure and rebuild the area, and establish a safe zone for the return of Syrian refugees.

Another significant instance of this legitimization effort is reflected in how the AKP's communication apparatus portrayed Turkey to international audiences following the February 2023 earthquakes. The devastating tremors affected the lives of more than fifteen million citizens across ten cities with the official death toll surpassing fifty thousand. Initially, the Erdoğan government's reaction was slow and inadequate. It did not fully utilize the military to coordinate rescue efforts, and its disaster management authority, AFAD (Afet ve Acil Durum Yönetimi Başkanlığı, Disaster and Emergency Management Presidency), was hindered by the country's highly centralized governance system.

As the government's slow response led to anger among the public, it became apparent that Erdoğan would not tolerate any form of criticism. Following a customary pattern, prosecutors aligned with the AKP initiated legal proceedings against journalists who offered critical coverage of the government's response and social media users that posted allegedly provocative content about the earthquake. The Radio and Television Supreme Council (RTUK, Radyo Televizyon Ust Kurulu) imposed monetary fines on television channels that highlighted government incompetence and corruption, and the Information Technologies and Communications Authority (Bilgi Teknolojileri ve İletişim Kurumu, BTK) throttled access to X (for about eight hours) to allegedly prevent the spread of disinformation.[62]

Meanwhile, the Directorate of Communications, AKP officials, the Anadolu Agency, and pro-government media outlets began utilizing the term "disaster of the century" to convey the notion that the seismic event was of such magnitude that no preventive measures could have effectively mitigated the destruction or that no government could have responded promptly to such a formidable challenge. The Directorate of Communications created an X account in Turkish under the handle @asrinfelaketi ("disaster of the century"), sharing videos documenting the intensity of the tremors. However, these efforts faced swift public criticism, and the X account was subsequently taken down.[63]

Regarding international communication efforts, TRT World, Anadolu Agency, the *Daily Sabah*, and SETA disseminated content that portrayed the earthquake as the largest and most destructive, covered in detail the government's relief efforts, and highlighted the resilience of the Turkish people and the widespread volunteer response. To strengthen these narratives, they often featured interviews with foreign scientists, aimed at confirming the "disaster of the century" refrain. Stories that showed ambulances airlifting survivors, deployment of container homes and field hospitals in the affected region, and rescues of individuals from beneath the rubble after prolonged periods were also included to convey a sense of hope and progress. Lastly, to showcase the government's perceived control over the situation, TRT World consistently provided live coverage of cabinet ministers and high-level state officials' press briefings.

Another primary objective of the Erdoğan regime's global communication apparatus is to shape a positive perception of Turkey and exert influence on a global scale. To this end, Turkey's media outlets promote the country's accomplishments across various domains, including the defense industry, health tourism, international education, technological innovation, and television exports. Additionally, these outlets emphasize Turkey's perceived significance in global governance, highlighting its contributions to conflict resolution, humanitarian aid, and development assistance. Through these coordinated efforts, their ultimate aim is to establish Turkey as a prominent player on the world stage. Some examples include but are not limited to the exultant coverage of Turkey's aid delivery to foreign countries during the COVID-19 pandemic, its mediation endeavors between Russia and Ukraine, and implementation of aid and development projects in Africa and Southeast Asia.

In accordance with the aforementioned objectives, the AKP's global communication outlets also seek to project Turkey's adversaries in a negative light, especially at times of foreign policy–related crises. To cite a few examples, in news coverage, conferences, and policy reports, these outlets criticize the United States for giving military support to Kurdish groups in north Syria, Greece and France for the objections they raise against Turkey's maritime expansion in the Mediterranean Sea, and Germany and Sweden for granting asylum to individuals the AKP government considers to be terrorists. At other times, they pay close attention to domestic developments that transpire, especially in Europe and the United States, and direct attention to topics such as Islamophobia, racism, and far-right extremism to question the Western model of progress and civilization. In conjunction with references to colonialism, slavery, the Holocaust, and the Srebrenica massacre, considered as part of the West's shameful past, the AKP's communication instruments aim to question the West's political and moral leadership. Simultaneously, AKP rank and file leverage instances of police brutality and rights violations in Europe and the United States to invalidate Western media and policy circles' criticisms of Turkey. In AKP-backed outlets' view, why should Turkey tolerate being lectured by Westerners who have a history of colonization, enslavement, and massacres and who continue to exert dominance through similarly unjust and morally questionable actions?

Islam, National Identity, and Anti-Westernism

Since this book focuses on how and why the Erdoğan government "talks back to the West," an overview of the role of the West in Turkish Islamist identity formation, politics, and discourse is in order. Turkey has been negotiating its relationship with the West since at least the nineteenth century, when the country's predecessor, the Ottoman Empire, launched a series of reforms aimed at reversing the decline of its military and political fortunes. In this period, the empire was represented as "the sick man of Europe" and was being threatened with imperial encroachments. In response, Ottoman statesmen undertook a series of modernization reforms to catch up with the West. They sought to depict the empire as a civilized power that was coeval with the West, yet politically and culturally independent from it; they framed the empire as a great Islamic, Eastern power that would civilize the rest of the Eastern world.[64] But in Islamist circles, these reforms were seen as "imitating the enemy," that is, the West, which for these groups was emblematic of moral degeneracy, materialism, and imperialism.[65] Islamists then saw history in Manichean terms, as "a struggle between two essentially different and inherently incompatible civilizations," and argued that the empire's decline could only be reversed by reconnecting with "the real culture and values of their own Muslim society."[66]

After the Ottoman Empire's losses in World War I, Islamists' calls for religious revival acquired an additional layer of Turkish nationalism. During the Turkish War of Independence, fought against the British, French, Greek, and Italian armies that occupied Istanbul and the Anatolian heartland, the ideological bonds between Islamism and Turkism strengthened. Yet after the Turkish Republic was established in 1923, many Islamists felt betrayed because of the top-down Westernization and secularization reforms the new ruling elites instituted.[67] The republican reforms were designed to civilize the Turkish society by eradicating those characteristics that the elites deemed "too Muslim and too Oriental," which they saw as hindering the country's development.[68] Throughout the 1920s and 1930s, these Westernization projects were repeatedly challenged by Islamist rebellions, which were all suppressed by the state.

Erbakan and the National Outlook Movement

In the post–World War II period, Islamism became increasingly imbricated with the Turkish right, conservatism, and anticommunism, bringing together a wide array of right-wing nationalist intellectuals, political parties, trade unions, and youth associations.[69] In 1970 Islamist actors entered into active politics with the founding of the MNP (Milli Nizam Partisi, National Order Party). The party was closed down in less than a year by the secularist establishment but was soon resuscitated as the MSP (Milli Selamet Partisi, National Salvation Party). The MSP was closed after the 1980 military coup, but it quickly sprang up again as the RP (Refah Partisi, Welfare Party). All three parties were founded by Necmettin Erbakan, who espoused an ideological framework known as Milli Görüş (National Outlook).

Erbakan advocated for industrialization. He had been educated in Germany and served as an academic in one of Turkey's top-ranking engineering schools in the 1960s, but he demonstrated a particular disdain for the West's putative materialism.[70] Erbakan saw the West as antagonistic to Islamic civilization, and at political rallies he described the International Monetary Fund (IMF) and the Organization for Economic Cooperation and Development (OECD) as modern incarnations of the "West's crusader mentality."[71] He warned Turkish politicians against joining the EU because it was a "Christian club" and would contaminate Turks' authentic culture.[72] In the late 1990s, during his term as prime minister as part of a right-wing coalition government, he helped found the Developing 8 as an alternative to the IMF and OECD. Known as the D8, the group consists of eight Muslim countries (Turkey, Bangladesh, Egypt, Indonesia, Iran, Malaysia, Nigeria, and Pakistan) and aims to increase multilateral political economic cooperation among them.

Erbakan also advocated anti-Semitic conspiracy theories, which claim that Zionists control the world economy and are collaborating with "Western powers" to destroy Turkey as "a country, nation, and community."[73] To ward off Western and Jewish encroachments, Erbakan argued that Turkey should return to its Islamic roots, unify Muslims around the world, and thus take back its historical leadership position in world politics.[74]

Erdoğan and the AKP

In the 1960s and 1970s a new generation of conservative political actors, including Erdoğan and other founding members of the AKP that would go on to hold national leadership roles, got their first taste of political activism in the Turkish-Islamist youth organization, Milli Türk Talebe Birliği (MTTB, National Union of Turkish Students). MTTB mobilized students from conservative, lower-middle-class backgrounds to promote political values that combined "hardline anti-communism and aggrieved religious nationalism."[75] Later, Erdoğan and would-be AKP members entered politics under Erbakan. In 1976 Erdoğan became a youth member in Erbakan's MSP where he displayed an anti-Western attitude and "mixed the nationalism of the developing world with declarations of Islamic identity."[76] In the 1990s he joined the party's next incarnation, the RP. There, he quickly moved up from district head to the inner circles of party management and in 1994 was elected the mayor of Istanbul—an event that set off shockwaves among Turkey's military-secularist establishment, given the RP's reputation as hardline anti-Western Islamists.

As the mayor of Istanbul, Erdoğan built a reputation as "a competent service provider" that could solve the various problems that had plagued the Istanbul municipality for years, such as garbage collection, public transportation, and budget deficits.[77] But in 1997 Erdoğan and the RP received a severe blow: Erdoğan was convicted by the secularist judiciary on charges of inciting religious hatred, sentenced to a ten-month prison term, and banned from politics.[78] The RP, which was part of a coalition government at the time, was forced out of office by the military for not observing the principle of secularism. It was later closed down by the Constitutional Court, the country's highest authority for constitutional review.

In 2001 Erdoğan returned to the political arena, cofounding the AKP with a group of prominent former RP members that made up the reformist wing of the party. The AKP sought to tap into voters' anxieties after the 2001 economic crisis, declaring that it would actively pursue neoliberal economic policies and a pro-EU agenda. To avoid conflict with the secularist military establishment and to increase its appeal to urban middle classes, the AKP also downplayed its conservative worldview.[79] To signal their departure from the core ideas of National Outlook (that is, anti-Westernism and Islamism), Erdoğan and his cofounders even announced that they had "removed their National Outlook robes." The AKP then defined its new political ideology as conservative democracy. In the 2002 general election, it won only 34 percent of the votes but, nonetheless, secured a majority in the parliament thanks to the proportional representation system.

During its first term in office (2002–7), the AKP vigorously implemented an IMF-sanctioned economic program that initiated a massive privatization scheme, incentivized foreign investment, and put in place employer-friendly labor laws. To satisfy the EU membership criteria, the parliament passed a series of legal reforms that enhanced freedoms of expression, religion, association, and assembly—at least on paper. However, the AKP's apparent embrace of Western democratic liberal norms was a strategic move aimed at dismantling Turkey's "tutelary regime" considered to be responsible for the "authoritarian practices of secularism" and the marginalization of pious Muslims.[80] In its second term (2007–11), the AKP launched the "Kurdish opening" (also referred to as the "Kurdish peace process"), said to be an attempt to find a solution to the decades-old armed conflict between the Turkish state and the PKK. Predictably, the so-called peace process was soon bogged down by mass arrests of Kurdish politicians, reoccurring clashes between Kurds and Turks, and Erdoğan's security-oriented policies.

During the EU membership negotiations and the Kurdish opening, Erdoğan and the AKP pragmatically adopted a public stance of neoliberal democratic governance, leading many observers to call the party "post-Islamist." However, as sociologist Cihan Tuğal notes, this period was in fact marked by the absorption of Islamism into the AKP's conservative neoliberal project.[81] When the Arab uprisings erupted, American and European policymakers and media circles applauded Turkey as a model country that had successfully married religion and market economy.

In its third term, the AKP eliminated potential military-secularist responses and assumed control of the judiciary and high state bureaucracy.[82] During this period, it also began to pursue a more openly conservative agenda in various fields of public life, expanding the religious public school system and increasing the budget of the Directorate of Religious Affairs (Diyanet İşleri Başkanlığı).[83] In foreign policy the AKP abandoned its early pro-Western liberal discourse and started to pursue a religiously framed strategy in the Middle East, supporting Hamas in Palestine, the Muslim Brotherhood in Egypt, Ennahda in Tunisia, and Sunni Islamist fighters in Syria.[84] As political theorist Halil İbrahim Yenigün reminds us, these ventures do not necessarily point to the AKP's top-down Islamization of society but to a "thickening of conservatism that deploys certain so-called 'Islamist' elements for its political platform."[85]

Outline of the Book

The central focus of *Talking Back to the West* is to explore the political economic mechanisms and ideational frameworks that shape the Erdoğan regime's global communication endeavors. Chapters 1 and 2 examine the regime's efforts to grow Turkey's influence and visibility in the global communication order in light of the domestic and foreign policy challenges it faced in the early-to-mid 2010s. Chapters 3, 4, and 5 present analyses of media and communication content disseminated by AKP-directed entities, demonstrating how these entities engage in strategic obfuscation and with what implications.

Chapter 1 offers a comprehensive overview of the communication challenges encountered by the Erdoğan government during the early to mid-2010s. It examines the Gezi protests in 2013 and the failed coup in 2016, shedding light on the government's efforts to legitimize its authoritarian policies in the eyes of the international community. The chapter focuses on the new English-language communication ventures the AKP and its allies established during this time (TRT World, the *Daily Sabah*, and Bosphorus Global). It examines the political economic and personal connections between these entities and Erdoğan while also placing them within the historical perceptions of Western media as a threat to Turkish sovereignty. Throughout the discussion, the chapter highlights how Erdoğan's communication emissaries strategically engage in debates about (Western) media imperialism to position Turkey as a resurgent counter-hegemonic force in global communication.

Continuing with the analysis of Turkey's attempts to project itself in a positive light, chapter 2 delves into the external activities of several key state organs, including the Directorate of Communications, TRT, and the Anadolu Agency, and analyzes how Turkish officials seek to grow Turkey's footprint in the global communication order. This chapter shows in detail how Erdoğan's emissaries appropriate ongoing debates on disinformation and post-truth, discredit social media companies, and advocate for digital sovereignty. Furthermore, the chapter uncovers a wide range of activities undertaken by these state organs to extend their communication vision to countries in Central Asia, Africa, the Middle East, and the Balkans. These activities include hosting regional and international media forums in Turkey, providing media assistance to foreign outlets, and conducting journalism training programs for foreign professionals.

Chapter 3 takes a deep dive into AKP-backed communication entities' portrayal of Turkey as a benevolent global power, particularly one that champions the rights of oppressed Muslims. It analyzes English-language communication and other knowledge production activities that address the perceived injustices Muslims face, with a specific emphasis on Islamophobia in the West. This chapter argues that while TRT World, SETA, the *Daily Sabah*, and similar entities rightly bring attention to anti-Muslim hatred, they strategically obfuscate the complexities involved, reducing Islamophobia to simplistic dichotomies of good versus evil.

Building upon these arguments, chapter 4 analyzes how and why the AKP-backed communication instruments construct negative depictions of the West. This chapter focuses on TRT World's and the *Daily Sabah*'s coverage of the refugee crisis, illustrating how their output essentializes Europe as shameful, immoral, and inhumane. Additionally, it explores how the AKP's communication emissaries, to signal the decline of the West, use social and political developments that have unfolded in Europe and the United States since 2016. To explain the roots of this emphasis on Western malaise, this chapter examines not only the strained relationships between Turkey and Europe and the United States but also the influence of Turkish Islamist thinkers of the mid-twentieth century in the production of Occidentalist images of the West.

Chapter 5 delves into the Erdoğan government's use of historical television dramas to promote Turkish history and civilization. The analysis primarily focuses on three shows—*Resurrection: Ertugrul, Establishment: Osman*, and *The Last Emperor*—which enjoy significant popularity among global audiences, especially Muslims. This chapter scrutinizes the political, economic, and sociocultural forces underpinning these shows, as well as the government's utilization of these programs to project the Ottoman Empire, Turks, and Turkey as civilizationally superior to the West. Through this analysis, it posits that the divisive and stereotypical portrayals of Christians, Jews, and, more broadly, the Western world within these shows perpetuate Samuel Huntington's clash of civilizations thesis.

The conclusion summarizes the objectives, political calculations, and ideological premises that define the Erdoğan regime's global communication apparatus. Additionally, it offers suggestions for future research, and draws attention to the efforts of Erdoğan's communication emissaries to engage with the Global South by employing the language of postcolonialism.

1

Battling against Western Media Imperialism

Domestic Crises and International Communication Initiatives

> International media look at Turkey not to discover the truth, but to find answers that already fit with their Orientalist perspective. Especially with the process that began after the Gezi Park incidents in 2013, our country has been exposed to grave injustices and double standards.
> —Recep Tayyip Erdoğan, 2020

Erdoğan often complains about the negative media coverage Turkey has received since the Gezi Park protests of summer 2013. These nationwide protests certainly seem to have taken the then prime minister by surprise: how, he might wonder, did a small environmental sit-in at Istanbul's Gezi Park turn into a massive antigovernment protest wherein a wide coalition of environmentalists, labor unions, Kurds, Turks, Alevis, feminists, progressive Muslims, and LGBTQ+ individuals called for his resignation? Yet, Erdoğan was equally, if not more, frustrated by the international media coverage of the protests. Images of Turkish police tear-gassing protestors and op-eds ringing alarm bells about Turkey's "slide into authoritarianism" became ubiquitous in major international outlets that summer, replacing the glowing coverage the AKP had received throughout the first decade of the 2000s.[1] Where were all the Western journalists that had praised Turkey's prodemocracy reforms and economic progress?[2] What about those who had held up Turkey as a model country for Arab nations during the uprisings only a few years ago?[3]

As protestors sat in parks and marched in city streets across the country, Erdoğan spoke at a rally in Istanbul to mobilize his supporters to unite against the protestors. At one point, he addressed the international news media directly: "There is something called journalistic ethics. Be honest. Be fair. You shamelessly say 'First the Arab Spring, now the Turkish Spring.' Look at this crowd [of AKP supporters]. Go ahead and dare not to report it. Go ahead, BBC! Go ahead, CNN! Go ahead, Reuters!"[4]

According to Erdoğan, Western media hyped a nonexistent Turkish Spring as part of a larger campaign by the West to create chaos in Turkey and overthrow his government.[5] Indeed, one staunch pro-Erdoğan daily newspaper claimed that Reuters, the Associated Press, and CNN International rented live-broadcast equipment well before the protests had even started, implying that these organizations played a part in organizing the "Gezi rebellion."[6] As Erdoğan accused "the interest-rate lobby [an anti-Semitic reference to Jewish bankers] and international media outlets" of stirring up trouble, pro-AKP newspapers began to ask why Western news organizations were covering the protests live.[7]

Although the protests wound down by the end of the summer, critical coverage of the AKP in international media did not. The Gezi protests of 2013 were only the beginning of a series of domestic and regional crises for the government, all of which would be vigorously covered by international news media. In December 2013 shocking evidence of corruption that involved Erdoğan, his family, and cabinet ministers became public, unravelling the decade-long alliance between the AKP and Fethullah Gülen, a cleric who at the time ran a wide network of conservative entrepreneurs, schools, charities, and media companies in Turkey and abroad.[8] Meanwhile, Sunni fighters in Syria, which the AKP supported, failed to topple the Bashar al-Assad regime, followed by an unprecedented influx of Syrian refugees into Turkey. Between 2015 and 2016, the Kurdish peace process collapsed, a series of deadly ISIS (Islamic State of Iraq and Syria) attacks on Turkish soil claimed hundreds of lives, and Kurdish cantons emerged across the Syrian border leading the AKP government to engage in military operations in north Syria.

Among these developments, the Erdoğan government's support for the Muslim Brotherhood and Sunni fighters in the Middle East, and securitization of the Kurdish issue, received increasing criticism in international news media.[9] However, according to the AKP cadres, this was all "black propaganda" that aimed to undermine Erdoğan because he stood up against Western powers' "hegemonic plans" in the Middle East.[10] Erdoğan himself intimated that Western "imperial powers" had set up a "trap" to drag Turkey into the war in Syria, and he used the term "the mastermind" to refer to this so-called shadowy group.[11]

Why did Erdoğan and his supporters view the international news landscape as a battlefield in the ostensible conflict between Turkey and the West and continue to do so? Why do they portray Western news organizations as a threat to Turkey's sovereignty? What connections do they see between media and imperialism? How do they seek to counter Western media and the alleged imperialist ploys they serve? How is their notion of Western media as an agent of imperialism articulated with historical grievances? The answers to these questions comprise the analysis in this chapter. They reveal the sociocultural vestiges and historical legacies that underpin the AKP's global communication apparatus and help to explain why it expanded so rapidly after 2013.

As the introduction has recounted, when the AKP took power in 2002, it inherited a number of foreign-language outlets from previous administrations, and it developed new regional television channels in Arabic and Kurdish to expand its sphere of influence. In the early to mid-2010s, the Gezi Park protests and the geopolitical shifts in the Middle East, especially those concerning Syria, Kurds, and ISIS, prompted the AKP government to counteract the critical narratives in Western media. To this end, the AKP worked with its allies in media and civil society to develop different arms of a globally oriented, English-language communication apparatus: a print and digital newspaper (*Daily Sabah*), a 24/7 television news channel (TRT World), and a digital communications and public relations entity (Bosphorus Global). This chapter begins with an analysis of each of these entities, paying special attention to the political economic structures and ideational frameworks that underpin them. Then examined is the Erdoğan government's relapse into another communication crisis in the wake of the 2016 coup attempt when party officials and supporters lamented Western media's biased coverage and amplified their negative attitude toward Western journalists. Lastly, the chapter situates the AKP's global communication endeavors within the context of Turks' long-standing fears of Western imperialism and skepticism toward Western media.

The Birth of the *Daily Sabah*

When the AKP came to power in 2002, it did not have enough people qualified to carry out international communication work, so it recruited actors linked to Gülen. Gülen and his followers had been packing key state organs with conservative actors since the 1970s in order to weaken Turkey's military-secular establishment, and they were obvious allies for Erdoğan, who was also striving to reduce the military's hold over politics and move marginalized Muslims from the periphery to the center of Turkish politics.

During the first decade of the 2000s the AKP had benefited handsomely from the Gülenists serving in law enforcement and the judiciary, and the dishonest tactics they used to remove secularists from state institutions. The AKP also used to its advantage the English-language newspaper *Today's Zaman*, published by a Gülen-affiliated media company, which reported positively on Erdoğan and his government without sounding like a crude mouthpiece. Some of this newspaper's executives had been educated in journalism schools in Europe and the United States, and its reporters were familiar with Western-style reporting and public messaging. *Today's Zaman* also had a large roster of op-ed writers that hailed from different ends of the political spectrum, which helped to project an image of itself (and the AKP) as valuing diversity and plurality. This partnership seemed to be ideal for meeting the AKP's international communication needs.

However, in December 2013 the overall AKP-Gülen alliance collapsed in a spectacular fashion. Gülenists exposed a massive corruption network within the AKP that reached all the way to the top, implicating Erdoğan, his family, and some cabinet ministers. In response, Erdoğan began to purge Gülenists from state institutions, leading to a profound reshuffling in state organs that were heavily stacked with Gülenists: law enforcement, the judiciary, and intelligence services.[12] The repercussions were also felt in media and public diplomacy fields. Overnight, *Today's Zaman* and its sister Turkish-language print and television outlets turned into ardent critics of the AKP, and Erdoğan retaliated by removing Gülen-affiliated personnel from international communication and public diplomacy institutions.[13]

Already reeling from the negative international coverage of the Gezi protests, the AKP now found itself faced with highly critical reporting from *Today's Zaman*. An English-language newspaper that would explain the AKP's side of the story was now of vital importance. Turkuvaz Media Group, co-owned by Serhat Albayrak (whose brother, Berat Albayrak, is married to one of Erdoğan's daughters), stepped up to the task and launched the *Daily Sabah* in February 2014. As one of my interlocutors, a former journalist with the paper told me, the Albayrak brothers were personally involved in the development of the *Daily Sabah*, which was intended to be a "counter force" against "the West's propaganda campaigns" and "*Today's Zaman*'s attacks."[14] They envisioned the paper as a tool for explaining Erdoğan's foreign and domestic policies to "diplomats, journalists, and the political elite" in Europe and the United States, to elicit the support of these groups and also to drown out the voices of Gülenist journalists in the international arena. In addition to the Western elite decision makers, the paper also targeted the expatriate community in Turkey. Serdar Karagöz, the founding editor in chief of the *Daily Sabah*, argued that foreign newspapers generally engaged in manipulative coverage concerning Turkey, and he added that the *Daily Sabah* would "help expats to thoroughly understand the country."[15] But, as chapters 3 and 4 discuss in detail, the *Daily*

Sabah is more than an innocuous guide for expats, diplomats, and foreign journalists residing in Turkey. Its editorial line is so unabashedly aligned with the Erdoğan government that, according to another former journalist with the paper, "If you want to know what the government thinks about an issue or what it is planning to do, then take a look at *Daily Sabah*."[16]

Daily Sabah's Links to Erdoğan

The publisher of the *Daily Sabah*, Turkuvaz Media Group, was established in 2007 as the media arm of Çalık Holding, a large conglomerate with business interests in energy, mining, construction, finance, and telecommunications. In 2008 Çalık Holding acquired one of the largest newspaper and television outlets in the country (*Sabah* and ATV), thanks to a cheap loan from state-owned banks. It is no coincidence that Berat Albayrak was Çalık Holding's CEO at the time; this acquisition was an early move in Erdoğan's plan to cultivate a loyalist press.[17] In 2013 Turkuvaz Media Group was sold to Kalyon Group, another pro-Erdoğan conglomerate that has risen to become one of the biggest players in construction, energy, and real estate in Turkey thanks to the lucrative state contracts it receives. Currently, Turkuvaz Media Group owns two national newspapers, two television channels, eleven radio stations, and eighteen periodicals.

Many of the *Daily Sabah*'s senior managers and prominent op-ed writers hold positions at other AKP-sponsored entities and/or have close relationships with the Erdoğan family. For example, Karagöz is a high school friend of one of Erdoğan's sons, Bilal. In 2018 after four years at the helm of the *Daily Sabah*, Karagöz became the editor in chief of TRT's international news channels. In 2021 he was appointed as the director general of the Anadolu Agency. Similarly, Meryem Ilayda Atlas, *Daily Sabah*'s former editorial coordinator and now a board member of TRT, attended the same high school as Bilal Erdoğan. One of the witnesses at her wedding was Erdoğan's daughter, Sumeyye.[18] Before joining the *Daily Sabah*, Atlas had worked as a researcher at the pro-Erdoğan think tank SETA. *Daily Sabah*'s most prominent op-ed columnists, Burhanettin Duran and Kılıç Buğra Kanat, currently serve as directors at SETA. Another well-known op-ed columnist, Hilal Kaplan, has close relationships with Erdoğan and the Albayrak brothers.

Daily Sabah's Editorial Policy

As noted above, the *Daily Sabah* was launched in the aftermath of the Gezi protests and the collapse of the Erdoğan-Gülen alliance. The rationale behind it was (and still is) to "prevent foreign media organizations based in countries that have issues with Turkey" from "telling lies, spreading disinformation, and engaging in manipulation."[19] Since its founding, the *Daily Sabah* has sought to legitimize the AKP's foreign policy decisions, such as Turkey's military incursions into north Syria, securitization of the Kurdish issue, and purchase of Russian missile defense systems, all of which have strained the relations with the United States and the European Union. Its print version in English is distributed to foreign consulates and diplomatic missions, and it also has an Arabic digital edition.[20] Until March 2017 the *Daily Sabah* was distributed to members of the European Parliament in Brussels, but then it was banned upon a Dutch lawmaker's complaints about its editorial line and spreading of hate speech.[21] The complaint was based on an op-ed that recounted a diplomatic tension between Turkey and Germany and the Netherlands and accused the latter two countries of fascism (see chapter 4 for a detailed discussion). In response to the ban, the *Daily Sabah*'s editorial team argued that the European Parliament was intolerant toward different opinions and was attacking press freedoms.[22]

Turkey's First International News Channel: TRT World

In the post-Gezi period, the AKP began to develop the second arm of its external communication apparatus and moved into the international television news field with the launch of TRT World in 2015. Although the idea for a 24/7 English-language channel goes back to the late 2000s and early 2010s when Turkey was reformulating its foreign policy, according to one of my interlocutors, the AKP moved up the channel's planned launch in response to the Gezi protests and the geopolitical shifts taking place in the Middle East at the time, especially the rise of Kurdish cantons across the Syrian border.[23] Government officials saw TRT World as a vehicle to "protect Turkey's interests and image" against "international actors and their influence operations."[24] Carlos van Meek, who was hired from Al Jazeera English to launch TRT World and served as its director of news until his departure in 2016, described the channel's goal as counteracting the "underrepresentation and misrepresentation of Turkey" and putting "the Turkish side of the story out there."[25]

Similar to its counterparts in the English-language news arena, TRT World covers politics, business, sports, arts, and culture. Its live and recorded news bulletins incorporate in-studio and on-the-ground reporting from around the world with Western and non-Western presenters and reporters—a strategy that other international news channels also use to "appeal to the greatest number of viewers around the world and also make [the channel] culturally proximate."[26] TRT World broadcasts documentaries and in-depth analysis and discussion programs, such as *The Newsmakers*, *Nexus*, *Africa Matters*, *Across the Balkans*, *Strait Talk* (the channel's only show dedicated to matters concerning Turkey), *Roundtable* (presented out of London studios), *Inside America*, and *Bigger Than Five* (both presented out of Washington, DC, studios).[27]

According to TRT's 2022 annual report, the channel is available in 190 countries via 12 satellites.[28] It is also viewed via cable and streaming platforms, its YouTube channel, and proprietary apps on mobile devices. TRT World has partnerships with hotel chains in thirty-one countries and with a major in-flight live-TV service provider.[29] TRT World, like its Chinese and Russian counterparts (the CGTN and RT, respectively), does not provide information about actual audience numbers.[30] Nonetheless, TRT's annual reports provide some general data about the channel's social media following. In 2020 TRT World registered 3.7 billion content clicks, 615 million video views, and 105 million interactions, and its Facebook account grew by 20 percent; Twitter account, 25 percent; YouTube account, 34 percent; and Instagram account, 65 percent.[31]

TRT World's Editorial Policy

TRT World dedicates a significant amount of time to Turkey's activities in global governance, humanitarian aid, defense, energy, technology, education, health care, and tourism. This type of content is generally delivered via news stories, documentaries, one-on-one interviews with government officials, and live coverage of official events. At times of political, economic, or diplomatic crises between Turkey and a foreign country, TRT World features news stories, documentaries, debate, and analysis programs that take a critical approach toward the foreign country's government or political leader. When it comes to pivotal events inside Turkey, the channel provides news and commentary strictly through the government's perspective and gives an international platform to AKP officials and their proxies to legitimize Erdoğan's policies.

According to AKP cadres, the founding of TRT World has been "a natural extension of Turkey's ascendance" in the Middle East and around the world. They argue that the channel is a manifestation of Turkey's "civilizational values and historical responsibility to humanity" and its "all-embracing, all-inclusive" foreign policy, which they weigh against the "rising xenophobia, anti-immigrant sentiments, and radical political groups in Europe."[32] They see the channel as speaking for "the forgotten ones" that the West and its "global media order" have ignored.[33] According to government officials and channel executives, this is what sets apart TRT World from its counterparts in the crowded landscape of international television news: its "humanitarian perspective" and incorporation of voices and stories of "the downtrodden," such as "the children [who are] bombed in Gaza, civilians massacred in Syria, elected politicians toppled by the army in Egypt."[34]

Obviously, AKP officials and TRT World executives are not the first ones to criticize international news channels for their coverage of global affairs. Despite the growing number of non-Western media outlets, domestic and foreign affairs in/of the West continue to be covered more regularly and extensively compared to those in other countries that receive media attention only during crises or in the context of their relations with Western powers.[35] For example, as Lilie Chouliaraki notes, in the case of humanitarian emergencies in the Global South, international news outlets generally put out shorter segments and report from the main newsroom without any local correspondents.[36] In another study of satellite news, Chouliaraki underscores how people who suffer from crises in the West are humanized "as if they were 'us,'" while non-Westerners are dehumanized as if "their pain or death were not relevant to our moral consciousness."[37] Examples of this were manifest in West-based media representations of Syrian refugees as "illegal migrants" versus that of Ukrainians as "just like us"[38] and the disproportionate amount of airtime dedicated to the deadly submersible accident in the North Atlantic versus the capsizing of a refugee boat in the Mediterranean Sea.

To go back to TRT World executives: while they are correct in pointing to the unbalanced representation of the Global South in international news, their answer to the problem, that is, TRT World's "humanitarian coverage," is not very convincing. As chapters 3 and 4 show, TRT World does indeed foreground voices and stories from the Global South, but in a selective manner as per the AKP's geopolitical economic priorities. The channel's references to being the advocate of "the voiceless" are not novel, either. They parallel Al Jazeera's self-description as being the "voice of the voiceless."[39] As communication scholars Mona Elswah and Philip Howard show, TRT World's style guide resembles that of Al Jazeera so much so that it has been described by a longtime TRT employee as "plagiarism."[40] Additionally, TRT World's digital department and research center mimic AJ+ and Al Jazeera Centre for Studies, respectively.[41] TRT World also hired many of its senior producers, editors, and presenters from the Qatari network, including but not limited to van Meek and Soraya Salam (part of the launch team), Imran Garda (presenter), David Foster (presenter), Ghida Fakhry (presenter), Riyaad Minty (director of digital operations at TRT), and Andrew Hopkins (diplomatic correspondent).[42]

TRT World's Political Economic Structure

According to İbrahim Eren, former director general of TRT, who oversaw the launch of TRT World, the channel is a "balanced news outlet and a public broadcaster," not a "state bulletin." In the words of Eren, TRT World follows the principles of "truthful, honest, and objective reporting" and is only "pro-Turkish as much as BBC is pro-British."[43] A channel executive I interviewed also echoed this description and said that TRT World is an "independent public service broadcaster" and a "credible and objective" news organization.[44] A foreign producer who worked at TRT World from its inception until 2020 explained to me how recruiters for the channel told job applicants that TRT is similar to BBC, that is, it is funded by tax fees and operates as a public service broadcaster.[45]

But these descriptions ignore the long history of the politicization of TRT and its domestic and international channels. Although TRT was founded as an autonomous public institution in 1964, it fell under the control of government officials and the military-bureaucratic establishment in the 1970s.[46] Since then its staffing and programming decisions have consistently been subject to the whims of politicians, and its budget has remained under the control of state auditors. TRT's main source of revenue is taxes and fees collected by the state: according to its 2019 report, 56 percent of TRT's revenues came from tax fees imposed on electronic goods, 35 percent from electricity bills, and 10 percent from advertising.[47] Like its parent company, TRT World is neither financially nor politically independent. According to media reports, the channel's initial budget was US$250 million in 2015; the source of this funding is unknown.[48] Industry analysts who spoke to the *Financial Times* in 2016 estimated the annual operating costs as being somewhere between US$77 and US$155 million, depending on the size of the channel's international operations.[49] Opposition parties in Turkey filed queries about the operating budgets of both TRT and TRT World, but AKP officials never responded to them.

TRT's politicization has reached new heights during the AKP era. Between 2007 and 2014, approximately three hundred personnel were transferred from various state institutions to TRT as part of the AKP's attempt to build a loyalist team at the network.[50] As one of my interviewees who used to work at TRT told me, during the first decade of the 2000s, numerous media professionals were hired from Gülenist newspapers and television channels to pack the organization with pro-government employees when the AKP-Gülen alliance was running smoothly. In the wake of the 2016 coup attempt, employees that were known or suspected to have Gülenist links were summarily dismissed from TRT and its international channels and replaced by party loyalists.[51] In 2018 TRT further purged the ranks: it incentivized eighteen hundred of its personnel to retire early based on claims of "surplus staff" but quickly hired fourteen hundred new personnel. According to Haber-Sen (Basın Yayın, İletişim ve Posta Emekçileri Sendikası, Press, Communication, and Postal Workers Union), Turkey's leading union within the relevant sectors, this was a move to replace experienced, professional journalists with AKP-affiliated third parties that have little professional journalistic training and little compunction about pro-government reporting.[52] In 2019 union representatives also found out that TRT World instituted a new hiring system that gave preferential treatment to candidates from pro-AKP groups, such as graduates of religious vocational high schools and graduates of the same high school that Erdoğan's son attended.[53]

Although there is no existing analysis of TRT World employees' direct or indirect links to the AKP, a quick survey of its senior staff shows the extent to which party loyalists control the channel. Some have personal connections to the Erdoğan family; others have previously worked at pro-government news outlets. For example, Eren, TRT's deputy director general between 2013 and 2017 and director general between 2017 and 2021, used to work as the deputy general manager of ATV, which is owned by Serhat Albayrak's Turkuvaz Media Group. Karagöz, editor in chief of TRT World, TRT Arabi, and TRT Deutsch between 2018 and 2021, used to work at *Sabah* and then went on to launch *Daily Sabah*, also owned by Turkuvaz. Both Eren and Karagöz are high school classmates of Erdoğan's son, Bilal. Bora Bayraktar, who currently serves as a director at TRT World, held the position of general manager at CNN Türk from 2018 to 2019. During his tenure, the channel underwent a significant editorial transformation after being acquired by a pro-Erdoğan conglomerate. Yusuf Ozhan, before he became a content manager at TRT World, was in charge of digital operations at TürkMedya, another pro-Erdoğan outlet.

The close links between TRT World and the AKP government came under scrutiny by US officials when the administration of President Donald J. Trump began to force certain international media outlets to register under the Foreign Agents Registration Act (FARA). In 2017 the Justice Department determined that TRT World, like RT, Sputnik, CGTN, Xinhua, and Al Jazeera, is engaged in "political activities" and serves as a "publicity agent" and an "information-service employee" on behalf of its sponsoring government. Although TRT World representatives argued that the channel was financially and editorially independent, US officials concluded that TRT World is controlled by the AKP government in regards its "leadership [structure], budget and content."[54]

As Elswah and Howard note, in its early days, TRT World strived to operate like "a public service broadcaster" and "a public diplomacy project" and presented itself as such but eventually hired AKP loyalists in managerial positions and succumbed to censoring stories that seemingly clashed with the AKP government's preferred narratives.⁵⁵ To this day, TRT World executives take great pains to position the channel as an independent public service broadcaster that abides by journalistic norms of professionalism and objectivity. However, as shown above, the channel is deeply imbricated with the Erdoğan government on various levels from funding structure to hiring practices. Chapters 3 and 4 discuss how in its coverage TRT World follows the government's talking points.

Digital Communication Initiatives and Bosphorus Global

The third arm of the AKP's post-2013 communication strategy is digital media. In addition to the *Daily Sabah* and TRT World, the AKP also invested in English-language digital communication projects, albeit indirectly. Bosphorus Global was founded in 2015 by the pro-AKP pundit Kaplan and her then spouse Suheyb Ogut to carry out social media work on behalf of the Erdoğan government.

Bosphorus Global's Political Economic Ties to Erdoğan

As noted in the introduction, Bosphorus Global self-identifies as an independent NGO, but its personal and financial ties to the Erdoğan government are too deep to ignore. Kaplan is a staunch Erdoğan supporter who writes op-ed columns in the *Daily Sabah* and its Turkish-language counterpart *Sabah*. She is also a frequent guest on political talk shows on pro-government channels, where she defends AKP policies and attacks opposition figures. Kaplan accompanies Erdoğan on international trips and attends press conferences held with foreign leaders. In July 2021 she was appointed as a board member of TRT.

The seed money for Bosphorus Global was put up by Berat Albayrak. According to leaked emails, Ogut requested 400,000 Turkish liras (approximately US$133,000 at the time) from Berat Albayrak in September 2015 to cover the first month of operations and 120,000 Turkish liras per month thereafter (approximately US$40,000).⁵⁶ Ogut also sent Albayrak an email with information about a waterfront villa in Istanbul. Ogut later rented the villa at approximately US$6,700 per month to serve as the headquarters of Bosphorus Global.⁵⁷

Social Media Activities

Bosphorus Global is not the AKP's and its allies' first foray into digital communication operations. During the Gezi protests, AKP cadres were alarmed to see that activists and dissidents were using X to communicate, organize, and mobilize, and that the general public was getting its news about the protests mainly from X rather than partisan news media.[58] A furious Erdoğan declared X to be "the worst menace to society" and accused it of harboring "all sorts of lies." Government officials announced that they would place restrictions on X and other social media sites in order to maintain public safety, and twenty-five X users were arrested for "spreading false information" and "inciting people to join the demonstrations."[59]

In September 2013, after the protests ended, the AKP recruited a team of six thousand "volunteers" to "promote the party perspective and monitor online discussions."[60] Predictably, these pro-government accounts began to intimidate journalists and academics that expressed critical opinions about Erdoğan and the AKP, and thus came to be known as AK Trolls.[61] AK Trolls is not a homogeneous group, and their relationship to the AKP has never been formally acknowledged. However, existing research has verified connections among AK Trolls, government officials, and pro-AKP pundits.[62] According to a network analysis, a major node on X producing "AK Troll discourse" is none other than Bosphorus Global and Kaplan.[63] In June 2020 Bosphorus Global's X account was restricted as part of X's takedown of a Turkish influence operation network of 7,340 accounts. Researchers at the Stanford Internet Observatory found that the network, linked to the AKP's youth wing, circulated pro-government narratives and impugned opposition figures in the Turkish online sphere.[64]

Digital Projects

In its mission statement concerning its English-language websites, Bosphorus Global says that "subaltern groups" have been alienated from the "international public sphere" and that their "opinions, [demands,] and representations" have been "stigmatized."[65] Bosphorus Global promises to rectify this by "eliminat[ing] dominant discourses produced by the mainstream [international] media" and "generat[ing] publicity for political and social actors" that have been marginalized by "official discourses and institutions."[66]

Bosphorus Global presents its activities as being primarily concerned with creating spaces to enable subaltern subjects to speak out against hegemonic Western news media. To this end, it operates a fact-checking site that monitors the "factual accuracy of various news and claims about Turkey."[67] Known as Fact-Checking Turkey (FCT), this initiative (with a corresponding X account, @FactCheckTR) was developed in response to international media's negative representations of Turkey. However, FCT does not meet the standards of legitimate fact-checking. Legitimate fact-checking initiatives provide information about their methods, criteria, and team members, and they follow the protocols of the International Fact-Checking Network.[68] FCT does none of these things. In addition, it fact-checks only news articles that are critical of Erdoğan and the AKP, and it allegedly debunks these articles not with publicly available and verifiable information but with biased and unverifiable sources: statements from AKP officials and unverified reports from state-run and pro-AKP media outlets.[69] FCT primarily nitpicks extraneous details rather than address core issues, and it is known to engage in political offensives against Erdoğan's enemies. Therefore, it is safe to say that FCT operates more like an agent of the Erdoğan government than an independent and legitimate fact-checking organization.

Bosphorus Global's other English-language websites, the Chronicles of Shame (with corresponding Twitter account @ShameChronicles) and the Crackdown Chronicles (@CrackdownReport) spotlight racism, Islamophobia, and rights violations in the West in an attempt to expose Western governments' double standards and hypocrisy. By recycling news stories that are originally published in international media about police brutality, human rights violations, media censorship, and the weakening of the rule of law in the United States and in European countries, both projects aim to frame Western governments as morally corrupt (see chapter 4 for a detailed discussion).

Countering Western News Organizations after the Failed Coup

So far, this chapter has traced the developments that explain why the AKP and its allies launched new communication organs in response to various crises that transpired in the early 2010s, and revealed the political economic connections and editorial alignment between these new entities and the Erdoğan government. This section turns to how and why the AKP had to redouble its communication efforts once again in 2016 when a bloody coup attempt shook the country.

On the night of July 15, 2016, a faction of the army linked to Gülen attempted an uprising—a last ditch effort in their years-long power struggle with Erdoğan. The failed insurgency left behind it more than two hundred dead civilians, bombed government buildings, and abandoned military tanks on the streets of major cities. In the immediate aftermath of the coup attempt, the AKP government declared a state of emergency and dismissed military officers, law enforcement personnel, civil servants, academics, and education personnel—anyone it suspected of affiliation with Gülen and his vast network of businesses, schools, NGOs, and media outlets. Under the pretext of national security concerns, the AKP seized the opportunity to expand the purge to other perceived enemies, especially the Kurds and leftists. In a matter of months, more than ninety thousand civil servants were dismissed, and more than forty thousand were in pretrial detention.[70] The purges did not spare the media: twenty journalists were arrested, and dozens of newspapers, periodicals, television, and radio outlets were shuttered based on their alleged ties to Gülen, the PKK, and other declared terrorist organizations.[71]

Pro-AKP media outlets celebrated the defeat of the coup as the triumph of Turkish democracy, ignoring the negative implications of Erdoğan's declaration of emergency and his overenthusiastic use of the additional powers it granted. In contrast, international news media and human rights organizations sharply criticized the AKP's disregard for rule of law and due process and published allegations of torture and mistreatment of coup planners at detention centers.[72]

To deflect criticism of its postcoup security measures, the AKP followed those well-trodden paths of public messaging for damage control. Turkish diplomats and representations around the world carried out twelve thousand diplomatic engagements, gave three thousand interviews, and published six hundred op-eds in international outlets in order to persuade foreign publics that the AKP's postcoup security measures were legitimate and necessary.[73] Erdoğan gave interviews to international outlets ranging from CNN to *Le Monde*, trying to convey to global audiences the impact of the abortive coup and seeking to rationalize the AKP's subsequent security measures. In his interview with *Le Monde*, he pointedly noted:

> When Mr. Putin called me to present his condolences [after the coup attempt], he didn't criticize me on the number of people who had been dismissed from civil service. But all the Europeans asked me [about it]. A state has the right to hire and dismiss its civil servants as it wishes. It is up to us to decide who we want to work with and who we want to dismiss. We are struggling against a coup attempt, against terrorists. The Western world must understand what we are dealing with.[74]

This alleged lack of understanding toward Turkey soon became a focal point in pro-Erdoğan actors' criticisms of Western media. The state-run Anadolu Agency shared online a fact sheet in which it criticized Western outlets for "trivializing the coup attempt." The fact sheet singled out quotes from Fox News, the *New York Times*, *Foreign Policy*, and the *Guardian* to demonstrate that "Western media organs use the coup attempt to lash out at Turkey's president and government, while ignoring Turkish people's embrace of democratic ideals."[75]

The frustration with Western media coverage was also the reason a group of pro-Erdoğan civilians started @VoicesofJuly15 on X a week after the coup attempt. The group identified its primary objective as "taking on the foreign press" and "sharing the noble struggle for democracy by the people of Turkey" with audiences worldwide: "Voices of July 15 is comprised of the youth from all walks of life . . . [that] aim to spread true and trustworthy information on the events of July 15. We are voices which are unheardable [sic]. We want to announce our voice ourselves."[76]

To counter the allegedly false news spread by Western media, the account circulated memes, infographics, and videos in English that explained the role of Gülen in the coup attempt, complained about Western governments' embrace of Gülen as an exiled cleric, and commemorated those who lost their lives fighting the coup plotters.[77] In one of its hashtag campaigns, #WhatWouldYouDo, it asked international publics how they would react if the London Bridge was bombed or tanks rolled over civilians on the streets of New York City. In another campaign, #TurkeyIsNotAChicken, the group invited its followers to tweet their criticisms of Western media coverage by mentioning @ForeignPolicy, @guardian, @FoxNews, @Independent, @NYTimes, @SputnikInt, and @Telegraph—the same outlets included in the Anadolu Agency's fact sheet.[78] In countless tweets, @VoicesofJuly15 lamented the "irresponsible, inaccurate, and downright malicious reporting by Western media outlets" calling it a "media coup."[79]

Turkish diplomatic corps also used X and started their own hashtag campaign, #1507mfa, to label Gülen as a terrorist mastermind, legitimize the dismissals and arrests of Gülenists, and applaud civilians for their role in thwarting the coup.[80] AKP's preferred narratives were also disseminated by nonstate actors that, too, opened new accounts and launched hashtag campaigns in English.[81] Like the diplomatic corps members, these interlocutors portrayed Gülen as a terrorist mastermind, legitimized the postcoup measures, and challenged the Western media coverage. These accounts and campaigns, which were not officially linked to the AKP, were, nonetheless, promoted by government officials, partisan journalists and pundits, and Turkish diplomats, ensuring widespread circulation.[82]

Anti-Gülen messaging was blasted across social media by other actors, as well. Shortly after the coup attempt, a narrative began circulating on 4chan (an anonymous bulletin board) accusing US presidential candidate Hillary Clinton and the Central Intelligence Agency (CIA) of conspiring with Gülen to topple Erdoğan. According to *Buzzfeed*, the users making these posts were "extremely likely" to be AK Trolls although there is no evidence that confirms this. These 4chan posts were picked up by American right-wing media outlets *Breitbart* and the *Daily Caller*, both of which published their own stories about alleged connections between Gülen and the Clinton Global Initiative.[83]

Subsequent pieces on *Breitbart* and the *Hill* expanded these claims, asserting that "Gülen's vast global network" was a "cult" and a "dangerous sleeper terror network." These pieces were penned by none other than Robert Amsterdam, AKP's attorney in the United States, who was working to extradite Gülen from the United States, and by Michael Flynn, Trump's national security adviser, who received payments at that time from an AKP-affiliated businessman.[84]

Certainly, there is ample room for criticism when it comes to Western news organizations' coverage of the coup attempt, particularly their limited understanding of the true nature of the Gülen network and its alliance with the AKP. However, this flawed coverage should not be attributed to a deliberate plot against Turkey, as claimed by AKP rank and file. Instead, the flaws stem from various factors that affect the overall coverage of international developments by Western news media. These factors include financial pressures leading to downsizing of international staff and the closure of foreign bureaus, a lack of journalists well-versed in sociocultural dynamics and historical contexts of the country they are covering, as well as the preference for presenting international news in simplified frameworks rather than complex ones for easier consumption. It is likely that Erdoğan's communication emissaries are either unaware of these underlying reasons for the subpar quality of international news reporting or they willingly disregard them to deflect attention away from their own actions and blame Western media instead.

Hostility toward Western Journalists

As discussed above, the AKP government and a constellation of state and nonstate actors undertook a feverish communication campaign pertaining to the coup attempt in 2016, criticizing Western news media for turning a blind eye to the havoc Gülenists wreaked on July 15. They implied that the negative slant of this coverage confirmed their fears about Western media being part of a larger ploy against Turkey. Soon, government officials began to target foreign journalists and correspondents, directly and indirectly. Erdoğan used the term "agent-terrorist" to refer to Deniz Yücel, a Turkish-German journalist working for *Die Welt*, because of his reporting on the coup attempt. Yücel was charged with spreading "terrorist propaganda" and spent a year in prison in solitary confinement. He was later released and returned to Germany but was sentenced in absentia to a three-year prison term for his alleged links to Gülen and the PKK.[85]

Other foreign journalists and correspondents were also arrested, deported, and/or harassed, some for reporting on Gülen and others for reporting on the Kurdish issue, the Syrian civil war, and ISIS. For example, in December 2016, an X user with links to Bosphorus Global targeted the *Wall Street Journal*'s Turkey correspondent, Dion Nissenbaum. The tweet called on the Turkish National Police to deport Nissenbaum immediately because he had shared a screenshot of an ISIS video in which a Turkish soldier was burned alive.[86] A week later, Nissenbaum was detained for three days without access to his family or lawyers. Upon his release, he immediately left Istanbul.[87] Another journalist accused of treason by Erdoğan and attacked by pro-AKP media was Ceylan Yeginsu, the *New York Times*'s Istanbul correspondent. Yeginsu was subject to intimidation and death threats on social media because she reported on ISIS's recruiting of Turkish citizens in the capital city of Ankara. She eventually had to leave the country and relocated to England.[88]

The Erdoğan government's antagonism toward international news media is extensively documented in a 196-page report that was published by SETA in 2019. Titled *The Extensions of International Media Outlets in Turkey*, the report analyzes Turkish-language services of Deutsche Welle, BBC, Voice of America, Euronews, the *Independent* (London), Sputnik, and China Radio International.[89] It is worth noting that the Turkish word for "extension" (*uzanti*) conjures up the word "tentacles," making a thinly veiled reference to infiltrations or insidious operations. The report gives background information about the said news organizations, examines their coverage of important developments in Turkey (e.g., the coup attempt, arrests of Kurdish parliamentarians, Turkey's military operations in north Syria), and accuses them of anti-Turkey bias.[90] Oddly, though, the report does not support its argument via a detailed analysis of news reports published by the aforementioned organizations. Instead, it comments on personal backgrounds and political views of the journalists that work for these organizations, cherry-picking excerpts from their social media accounts and work histories and insinuating that they have secret ties to Western actors.

Upon its release, the report was widely condemned by Turkish and international journalism associations that saw it as blacklisting journalists. İsmail Çağlar, the report's lead author, rejected the criticisms, arguing that the report was based on a "scientific approach" and that SETA's interest in "international media operations in Turkey" was not different than US-based think tanks' interest Russian influence operations in the United States.[91]

Another episode of this hostile attitude transpired in July 2021, this time concerning Western-funded news organizations in Turkey. An op-ed columnist at *Sabah* wrote that a US-based private charity, Chrest Foundation, has been funding independent online news sites in Turkey since 2001.[92] Although the list of recipients and grant amounts was publicly available on the foundation's website, *Sabah* and other pro-government newspapers called the funding a scandal and started a smear campaign against the outlets that received foreign funds.[93] Prominent independent news sites in Turkey, such as Bianet, Medyascope, and P24, were soon labeled as "*fondas*" in Turkish, a blend of the words "*fon*" ("fund" in English) and "*yandas*" ("partisan"). These sites have never hidden the fact that they received grants from Chrest or other foreign organizations. As a matter of fact, they list on their websites both the institutional grants and the individual donations they receive. Nonetheless, pro-Erdoğan pundits discredited these independent outlets as "political hitmen" weaponized by the United States and CIA against Turkey.[94] Soon, the AKP government chimed in, and Erdoğan's communications czar, Fahrettin Altun, claimed that foreign funding is a tool that "some foreign leaders [use] to [intervene in] Turkish politics."[95]

Western Media as Agents of Orientalism and Imperialism

Both the SETA report and the "*fondas* media" allegations are premised on the notion that Western media and Western NGOs act as instruments of the states from which they come, spreading false stories about Turkey and/or collaborating with local actors to oust Erdoğan. This threat discourse is a consequence of Turks' long and complicated relationship with the West, as recounted in the introduction. Since the Ottoman Empire's slow demise in the late nineteenth and early twentieth centuries, the Turkish psyche has been scarred with long-standing fears of Western aggression and contoured by antagonisms between Muslim Turks and the Judeo-Christian West. To this day, the nationalism produced by this historical antagonism and the refrain of "the survival of the Turkish state" play important roles in Turkey's domestic politics and its international affairs.[96]

In addition to these fears, the AKP's hostility toward Western media can be understood as a reaction to (real or perceived) Orientalist representations of Erdoğan and Turkey. For example, op-ed writers in the *Daily Sabah* accused "Western intellectuals and politicians" of supporting anti-Erdoğan activists during the Gezi protests "as if they were their colonial big brothers."[97] A SETA report noted that "Western media's typical Islamophobic" approach to Turkey was built on "long-standing Orientalist framings of Muslim societies."[98] Eren imputed the growing "anti-Turkey coverage in Western media" to Orientalism:

> Western media appropriated concepts of equality and justice, whose roots can actually [be found in our own civilization] and pretended they existed

in the West. Western media never really saw the big picture. It only saw the parts that concerned [the West]. It looked at the Middle East through an Orientalist lens. It looked at Africa differently. It always had a West-centric approach and covered the world from the perspective of the West. Now, Western media started an all-out campaign against Turkey. They don't know Turkey at all, they don't bother to learn, and they knowingly put out false [stories].[99]

These op-eds, reports, and statements quoted above and many others invoke Edward Said's seminal work, *Orientalism*, and seek to critique, however crudely, Western journalists' representations of Turkey.[100] In *Orientalism*, Said shows how Western artistic, cultural, and scientific works represent non-Western peoples as backward, stagnant, violent, irrational, and ultimately inferior to the West and argues that these works have an inherent political function: to facilitate Western-directed modernization programs and/or justify Western control and intervention in the so-called Orient. Fundamentally bound up with colonial discourse and imperialist projects, Orientalist representations and the justifications they provide for Western domination endure to this day. For example, as media studies scholar Wazhmah Osman notes, the US occupation of Afghanistan was rationalized in part by the "imperial gaze" directed at the country after September 11 and the flawed representations disseminated by international media.[101]

In the case of Turkey, there is much to be criticized about international news outlets' coverage of Turkish politics, society, and culture. With a few exceptions, it is not uncommon to see foreign journalists reduce Turkey's complex dynamics to oft-cited dichotomies, such as modern versus traditional, secular versus conservative, urban versus rural. Notwithstanding such problematical coverage coming from West-based outlets, it is important to note that the AKP cadres intentionally conflate reasonable criticisms of Erdoğan and his government with modern day Orientalism. They automatically label any critical piece published in international news media as Orientalist and Islamophobic in order to shield Erdoğan from criticism and deflect attention away from his dangerous policies. However, as elaborated on below, the notion of Western powers launching attacks against Turkey through their media outlets and portraying the country in an Orientalist manner is not a recent phenomenon but, rather, has its roots in the late nineteenth century.

During the late nineteenth century, there were widespread speculations in the European press regarding the decline of the Ottoman Empire, often portrayed as the "sick man of Europe." This was also a period when the mass circulation of newspapers and magazines experienced remarkable growth throughout Europe, and Ottoman statesmen began to attach greater importance to the management of press affairs. As historian Houssine Alloul and foreign affairs specialist Roel Markey show, Ottoman authorities were acutely aware of the "Orientalist fantasies about the Empire" prevalent in European newspapers, and they vehemently objected to articles that portrayed sultan Abdulhamid II, the ruler at that time, as a tyrant and a despot.[102] They also expressed concerns regarding the dominance of news agencies based in Europe. They accused Havas and Reuters of engaging in "hostile and malicious reporting" against the empire, contending that these agencies served the interests of the French and British states in which they originated.[103] To counteract these narratives, the Ottoman authorities established offices to monitor the coverage of the empire in European daily newspapers.[104] They provided Ottoman diplomats with press releases to counter rumors and falsehoods about the empire, actively demanded corrections from European newspapers, and even inserted disclaimers in papers that were considered sympathetic to the empire's cause.[105] Additionally, in an effort to exert greater control over news about the empire and its representation, they established a semi-official Ottoman news agency. However, its existence was short-lived.[106]

These efforts to manage the press were, at bottom, efforts to manage the image of the empire in Europe, which the Ottoman authorities knew was vital to their survival.[107] Not only did Ottoman officials seek to control the European press coverage of the empire but they also established permanent diplomatic corps in Europe, sent representatives to international organizations, and joined major international exhibitions, all intended to present the empire as the leader of the Islamic world and, at the same time, a "modern member of the civilized community of nations."[108] These image management activities were part of the empire's modernization and reform movements, which emerged in response to Europe's military and technological superiority as well as to the Great Powers' encroachments on Ottoman provinces in the Balkans and the Middle East. Understandably, Ottoman officials were alarmed by the European vision of a backward, crumbling empire that was ready to be colonized.[109]

Approximately 150 years later, Erdoğan and his emissaries continue to view critical Western media coverage as a prelude to an attack against Turkey. An opinion piece penned by Yusuf Özkir, a board member of the Anadolu Agency, provides a window into this worldview. In his column, Özkir raises questions about a collaborative YouTube channel that Deutsche Welle, France 24, BBC, and Voice of America launched targeting Turkish-speaking audiences in Turkey and abroad.[110] That these four major Western broadcasters partnered up for the very first time in history has raised eyebrows among the pro-AKP circles. Özkir writes that "these media outlets" are, "in a very sophisticated manner, plac[ing] undue emphasis on Turkey's social problems with the intention of creating a vulnerability."[111] Özkir then reminds his readers of the "similar treatment" endured by the late nineteenth-century Ottoman ruler Abdulhamid II at the hands of the European press:

> When Sultan Abdulhamid II was ousted ... the European capitals were very happy. They saw Abdulhamid as an obstacle to their goal of disintegrating the Ottoman Empire, but they hid this goal skillfully in their public statements. After the toppling of Abdulhamid, Western media ran the headline "End of the Sultanate" with immense joy. Another obstacle to reaching their goal was thus removed.[112]

The AKP cadres and supporters find a powerful symbol in Abdulhamid II.[113] They see him as the "last proudly Islamic sultan that stood up against Europe," working to unite Muslims around the world.[114] They draw parallelisms between Abdulhamid II's and Erdoğan's struggles against foreign powers (see chapter 5 for a detailed analysis).[115] Accordingly, they use the so-called unfair treatment of Abdulhamid II by European newspapers to bolster the claim that Western media organizations are once again colluding with Western governments to destabilize Turkey and curb its rise to a great power status. In 2015, when Erdoğan criticized the *New York Times*'s coverage of Turkey, he even drew a parallel between himself and Abdulhamid II: "This newspaper had once called the Ottoman Sultan an 'absolute monarch.' And today it directs to the Republic of Turkey and myself the same hate that it once directed to the Ottoman state."[116]

Today, Turkey is not faced with territorial loss or imminent collapse. Nonetheless, the AKP cadres assert that the survival of the nation is at stake and that every precaution must be taken against the so-called Western enemies. Fueled by pugilistic nationalism, they describe Turkey's new communication ventures as part of their honorable fight against the West and the unjust global order it has created. The following chapter examines how the Erdoğan government struggles against West-based media companies, seeks to improve the global communication order, and ultimately grow Turkey's presence and influence in this realm.

2

Legitimizing Turkey's Communication Model

Encounters with Foreign Media Organizations and Professionals

Turkey is subject to relentless attacks from the "global fake news industry," according to Fahrettin Altun, the director of communications.[1] In Altun's view, media companies based in the West, irrespective of their legacy or digital nature, engage in influence operations against Turkey and provide a platform for terrorists. But Altun's concerns transcend Turkey's borders and encompass broader ramifications of communication technologies worldwide. He laments the global spread of disinformation and hate speech and assigns culpability to social media companies for exacerbating these problems:

> [They] have been complicit in many of the street protests, acts of violence, and [online] lynchings that took place in recent years. Their endless ambitions and desire for profit, and ability to set artificial [news] agendas via algorithms threaten democratic politics, debate culture, and the public sphere. Moreover, these companies act arbitrarily and irresponsibly when it comes to data collection and are not transparent about their data sharing policies. Their interference in the Brexit referendum and the 2016 presidential elections in the United States has been debated and criticized around the world.[2]

Another point of contention for Altun is "the hegemony of a handful international media companies" and their disregard for truth: "Despite their dominant position, these companies do not function as the voice of truth or the mirror of reality. Instead, they continue to [publish and broadcast] as per the interests of the global order of exploitation, the global order of oppression."[3]

In response to these problems, Altun advocates for implementing robust national and supranational regulations, tempering "internet freedoms with national security concerns," and redefining the "professional and moral principles of the press."[4] Collectively, these propositions constitute Turkey's Communication Model (Türkiye İletişim Modeli), which Altun describes as a "strong bulwark against the crisis of truth" and a means of fighting against "lies, disinformation, terrorist propaganda, digital fascism, media imperialism, and cyber bullying."[5]

The propositions put forth by Altun may appear necessary and beneficial within the global communication context, unless one is acquainted with the systematic suppression of Turkey's media landscape under the very regime Altun represents. Throughout the 2010s, the AKP deployed legal and financial measures to gain control over mainstream news outlets, penalize dissenting voices, and cultivate a loyal media apparatus supportive of Erdoğan.[6] Presently, nearly 90 percent of print and broadcast news media is owned by companies that have political and economic affiliations with the AKP, and forty journalists are behind bars for their work.[7] In addition to curtailing traditional media, the AKP has also imposed stringent controls on digital communications and has expanded state surveillance of online users.[8] Today, over four hundred thousand websites are blocked in Turkey; social media companies are obligated to share user data with the government; and journalists, activists, and ordinary citizens live in fear of prosecution for their online activities.[9] Unsurprisingly, Turkey ranks 149th out of 180 countries in the World Press Freedom Index,[10] with its internet freedom status assessed as "not free" by Freedom House, a nonprofit organization known for its political advocacy work.[11]

Despite the bleak circumstances, the Erdoğan regime presents a contrasting narrative. Altun asserts that the AKP has "expanded and secured freedoms of press and speech in incomparable ways" in regard to previous Turkish governments and that Erdoğan is the only world leader who is "crusading for truth."[12] Furthermore, Altun and his associates undertake various international activities to expand Turkey's footprint in the global communication order. The Directorate of Communications (DoC) organizes regional and international meetings in Turkey, inviting communication professionals and government representatives from abroad to discuss prevailing issues concerning media and communications. Other state organs, such as TRT, TRT World, and the Anadolu Agency, conduct training programs for journalists and provide technical resources to radio and television channels located outside Turkey, with the aim of rectifying imbalances in global communication flows. Since these activities primarily target professionals and organizations in the Global South, Altun and his associates assert that Turkey is opening spaces for marginalized voices in global public sphere.

How, then, can one reconcile these external-facing activities, seemingly dedicated to improving the global communication environment, with an increasingly restrictive one at home? To address this and other related questions, this chapter offers an analysis of Turkish officials' narratives and activities that seek to legitimize and diffuse their vision of communication, foster relationships with foreign media professionals and government representatives, and increase Turkey's profile in global communication networks. The first section delves into Altun and his colleagues' attempts to justify Turkey's restrictive communication policies that prioritize national security over free flow of information. Unveiled are the key tactics employed in this pursuit, such as appropriating current debates about post-truth and disinformation, strong-arming foreign media companies that operate inside Turkey, and advocating for digital sovereignty. The subsequent section focuses on the international activities conducted by DoC, the Anadolu Agency, and other state organs, which encompass media and communication-related forums, journalism training programs, and media assistance projects specifically tailored for the Global South. Through a discussion of official statements and publicly available information pertaining to these initiatives and through expert interviews, this chapter elucidates how the regime emissaries "diffuse [their own] knowledge, norms, and ways of thinking" in order to grow Turkey's presence in the global communication environment.[13]

Co-opting Current Debates about Disinformation and Post-Truth

Authoritarian regimes are known to engage in a number of activities to justify their repressive actions, avoid delegitimization, and present themselves favorably to the global community. To spread their preferred narratives, ruling elites in these regimes use official statements and press releases while leveraging regime-friendly news outlets and undertaking international activities.[14] But they do not invent their justification strategies from scratch; instead, they find "sources of inspiration" in the international context.[15] First and foremost among these sources is the predominant "international discourse"—that is, the prevailing debates and narratives about a given issue at a particular moment. For example, in the context of online communications, authoritarian regimes such as those in China, Iran, and Russia exploit the international consensus surrounding issues of hate speech, online bullying, data security, or defamation. These countries strategically utilize these concerns as a framework to legitimize their censorship and surveillance schemes, positioning them as indispensable tools for thwarting the propagation of false information, countering foreign interference, and upholding public order. By conflating legitimate concerns about disinformation and data security with restrictions on online speech, they aim to rationalize their control mechanisms.[16]

In this regard, current debates about disinformation and post-truth in Europe and the United States have especially proven advantageous for authoritarian actors. Although these problems have been manifest in various forms in other national contexts, it was not until the Brexit referendum and the election of Trump in 2016 that they gained prominence within academic and policy circles in the Global North.[17] Subsequently, there has been a surge in scholarly literature pertaining to dis/misinformation, the crisis of journalism, media polarization, and other related challenges in Global North contexts. This exponential growth has prompted certain analysts to attribute blame to malicious foreign actors, social media companies, or the technology itself as underlying factors contributing to these phenomena.[18] Academic and professional organizations have engaged in fact-checking initiatives and led projects aimed at countering disinformation to demonstrate their commitment to tackling the contemporary epistemic crisis. Legislators in Europe and the United States began to pay close attention to social media giants, such as Facebook, X (formerly Twitter), and Google, particularly, in relation to their activities during election periods.

Taking advantage of this growing attention on disinformation and post-truth, Turkish officials have redefined these concepts as per their political objectives and used them to justify existing or future media legislation. For example, Altun consistently stresses the need for effective control mechanisms (i.e., government regulation) to prevent disinformation. By utilizing globally significant examples of disinformation campaigns, such as those during the invasion of Ukraine and the COVID-19 pandemic, Altun calls on states, civil society, and traditional and social media companies to join forces in combatting disinformation.[19]

In contrast to his generally mild statements aimed at international audiences, Altun adopts a more assertive tone when communicating with domestic constituents inside Turkey. In his definition of post-truth, he (rightly) points at "subjective beliefs and emotions taking over objective facts" but also adds that post-truth is largely the outcome of "malicious" activities undertaken by outside actors against a country's sovereignty.[20] He describes disinformation as the "distort[ion of] information and the mislead[ing of] society" but also combines it with "evil politics" that is allegedly designed to "cause harm to a country and society."[21] By pointing to so-called evil actors and their malicious activities, Altun reiterates conspiratorial narratives about Western media attacks against Turkey and lays the groundwork for future restrictions on media and communications.

In addition to observing the international environment and co-opting the prevailing discourse on a given topic, authoritarian regimes also use the policy decisions of other states to "alter the costs and pressures" associated with similar policies they might be introducing at home. The AKP rank and file often use internet and social media laws in Germany, France, and the United States as examples of Western countries' own attempts to regulate the online sphere. An illustrative instance can be observed in the case of Germany's implementation of the Network Enforcement Act (NetzDG) in 2017, designed to combat online hate speech. Despite the numerous criticisms leveled against NetzDG within Germany, AKP officials, similar to their counterparts in Russia, Malaysia, the Philippines, Singapore, and Venezuela, seized upon it as a justification for their own stringent measures.[22] In 2022, when the Turkish parliament passed the disinformation law, an AKP lawmaker claimed that he talked to American authorities who affirmed the similarities of the disinformation laws of the United States and Turkey.[23] Obviously, there is no government legislation concerning disinformation in the United States, but this does not seem to have stopped the AKP parliamentarian from making false statements.

Discrediting and Strong-Arming Foreign Media Companies

Another strategy that Turkish officials use to justify their communication policies is to discredit social media companies based on their commitment to democratic principles and the protection of free speech. (This approach parallels the strategy discussed in chapter 4, which entails the questioning of Europe's civilizational values.) During 2019 and 2020, Erdoğan's emissaries began to disseminate negative narratives concerning X and YouTube, prompted by these companies' actions to block specific accounts or content associated with the AKP government. In October 2019 X temporarily blocked the account of TRT World because of a potentially sensitive content it posted about the ongoing Turkish military operation in north Syria at the time. Serdar Karagöz, the then editor in chief of TRT's international channels, questioned whether X was a "credible platform for free speech" at all. Because TRT World's post was about a Turkish military operation that targeted Kurdish fighters in the region, Karagöz argued that X was embracing a pro-Kurdish ideology just as other social media companies and the American government were doing.[24] In a subsequent development in 2020, Turkish officials once again expressed their displeasure toward X as the platform dismantled a substantial network of over seven thousand accounts that had been actively disseminating pro-AKP narratives. According to a report published by the Stanford Internet

Observatory, this network, primarily comprising bot accounts, was responsible for generating millions of tweets that endorsed Erdoğan's policies and criticized opposition parties. Altun slammed the report as being "unscientific, biased, and politically motivated" and claimed that the takedown decision proved that X was "not merely a social media company, but a propaganda machine with certain political and ideological inclinations."[25]

The recurrent pattern of portraying social media companies as ideologically biased against Turkey came to the forefront in 2021, as well. This time, the focus shifted to YouTube, as the platform removed a video in which Altun delivered a speech about the assassination of Turkish diplomats by the Armenian Secret Army for the Liberation of Armenia (ASALA) in the 1970s and 1980s. YouTube justified its decision by citing violations of its hate speech policies. In response to the removal of the video, Altun took to X to express his dissatisfaction. In a series of tweets, he shared a direct link to the video, emphasized his stance against YouTube's alleged "double standards and hypocrisy," and said, "YouTube considers what we said ... [to be] a hate crime, [but ignores] the hate speech directed at Islam and Muslims, and readily opens space for terrorist organizations' black propaganda."[26] In protest of YouTube, he concluded with his trademark refrain, "Long live the truth!"[27]

It was during these spats that Erdoğan's communication emissaries also sought to undermine social media companies' credibility, as evidenced by Altun's characterization of them as purveyors of "digital fascism." In scholarly literature and media discourse, digital fascism is generally used to denote the social media practices of neo-Nazi or far-right groups. However, Altun employs this term as yet another instrument to criticize Facebook, X, and YouTube for what he perceives as their double standards. According to Altun, these platforms exhibit leniency toward terrorist organizations and morally questionable groups while censoring content disseminated by representatives of the Turkish nation.[28] Altun also employs terms such as "digital colonialism" and "cyber imperialism." In academic and policy domains, these terms are often used to underscore the dominant position of US-based technology companies. However, Altun and his colleagues adopt a different perspective, asserting that these companies knowingly employ their platforms to undermine Turkey's sovereignty, national unity, and moral values.

It is no coincidence that Erdoğan's emissaries began to utilize the aforementioned narratives at a time when the AKP was tightening its grip over social media. This convergence was apparent in the establishment of the Digital Platforms Commission in the Turkish parliament in July 2020. The commission was initially tasked with addressing issues related to internet safety, cyberbullying, and online privacy. However, it swiftly turned its attention toward drafting an amendment to the existing internet law, which would enforce a requirement for social media companies to designate a local representative.[29] The commission worked to force social media companies with more than one million daily users in Turkey to store user data locally and comply with content removal requests issued by Turkish authorities. In cases of noncompliance, social media platforms would face a twenty-four-hour blocking period, accompanied by escalating fines ranging from one million to three million euros. Subsequent measures would involve advertising bans and bandwidth throttling up to 90 percent. Previously, Turkish authorities could only submit removal requests to the headquarters of social media companies, which are based in the United States and operate under US jurisdiction. According to transparency reports released by Google, Facebook, X, and YouTube, every year tens of thousands of posts, tweets, and videos are already removed upon Turkey's request. With the new law, however, the AKP and its proxies in the judiciary would be able to block "more content, and faster" without having to apply to any foreign headquarters.[30]

The commission set a deadline requiring social media companies to appoint local representatives by November 2020, stipulating repercussions for noncompliance. While VKontakte, the Russian social media company adhered to the deadline and designated a local representative, Facebook expressed its refusal to comply with the new requirements. Google, X, and YouTube remained conspicuously silent on the matter.[31] Advocates for human rights and freedom of speech urged social media companies not to yield, cautioning them about the potential role they may assume as a tool for Turkish state censorship.[32] Following the expiration of the deadline, the Erdoğan government initiated the imposition of financial penalties on various platforms, including Facebook, X, Instagram, and TikTok.[33] Faced with the imminent threat of bandwidth throttling, a measure that would render the platforms practically unusable within Turkey, social media companies eventually succumbed to the mounting pressure and expressed their intention to establish local representation. By September 2022 Facebook, X, Instagram, and YouTube all opened local offices in Turkey with registered addresses but lacking genuine legal affiliation with their parent companies.[34]

In October 2022 the Erdoğan government solidified its legal, administrative, and financial pressures on social media companies by passing the disinformation law.[35] As per the provisions of the law, social media companies are now required to establish separate legal entities in Turkey that bear financial, administrative, and criminal liabilities. Failure to establish the mandated legal entity within a six-month period can lead to advertisement bans and throttling of up to 90 percent of bandwidth capacity. Furthermore, the law also requires popular messaging apps, such as WhatsApp, Signal, and Telegram, to officially register local offices in Turkey. These companies will be required to provide regular updates on various aspects, including the number of active users and data related to voice and video calls, as well as instant messages.[36]

The Erdoğan regime has not only targeted social media companies but also foreign media organizations that provide Turkish-language services. In April 2021 it put RTUK (Radyo ve Televizyon Ust Kurulu, Supreme Board of Radio and Television) in charge of monitoring internet media. This move had an unforeseen consequence: media outlets operating from abroad and providing news to audiences in Turkey were suddenly classified as broadcast television entities and required to obtain licenses from RTUK and comply with its regulations. RTUK put its new powers to use in November that year when Deutsche Welle's Turkish service aired a documentary that triggered a backlash from the AKP's spokesperson. RTUK first issued a warning to Deutsche Welle, and when the channel failed to obtain a license as demanded, RTUK implemented an access ban in July 2022.[37] Voice of America's Turkish service also found itself entangled in this access ban due to its failure to secure the required license. Both DW and VoA contended that acquiring a license would have granted the AKP government the power to censor editorial content.[38]

The aforementioned government pressures on foreign media companies have faced substantial criticism, primarily focusing on their domestic ramifications—that is, the bolstering of state authority in the digital realm, monitoring of user activity, and suppressing dissenting viewpoints. However, it is crucial to acknowledge that these policy actions also serve as a demonstration of the Erdoğan regime's external power projection. Through the enactment of these laws, the regime seeks to portray Turkey as a formidable actor capable of exerting influence over foreign media companies. Investigations, fines, and restrictions all serve to showcase that Turkey has the authority and the ability to assert control over prominent social media and broadcasting companies operating within its jurisdiction irrespective of their scale and market influence. Such oppositional grandstanding can also be found in Turkish officials' efforts to establish digital sovereignty.

Advocating for Digital Sovereignty

In 2021 the director of the presidential office of digital transformation, Ali Taha Koc, questioned why the Turkish government should trust Western tech giants for safeguarding the country's "data security and digital sovereignty." Koc continued: "You can't talk about freedoms and democracy when these companies have so much data. In that sense, data safety is as important and urgent as the security of our borders. Russia and China created local alternatives to GAFAM [Google, Apple, Facebook, Amazon, and Microsoft]. The world is bigger than GAFAM."[39]

While Koc's attempt to evoke Erdoğan's famous refrain ("The world is bigger than five") may be seen as an attempt to flatter his boss, it is still noteworthy because it sheds light on Turkey's aspirations for digital sovereignty and its perception of China and Russia as successful exemplars in this regard.

The term "digital sovereignty" refers to the "exercise of state power within national borders over digital processes such as the flow of online data and content, surveillance and privacy, and of the production of digital technologies."[40] It is about the creation of nationally bounded internet segments and the shifting of global internet governance toward a state-centric model. Promoted by China since the 1990s, digital sovereignty emerged out of concerns with the pioneering role the United States and Europe had played in establishing and regulating core internet infrastructure. Additional arguments stemmed from Chinese authorities' fears about the transmission of West-based information into China and potential political instability.[41] Thus, digital sovereignty came to be rhetorically linked with cyber and national security and shaped China's digital policies over the years. Today, foreign companies that deal with "critical information" in China are required to establish domestic joint ventures with Chinese firms and to store data on local, government-owned servers.[42] To fortify digital sovereignty, Chinese authorities also incentivize local innovation and digital services.[43] To advocate its preferred model of state-centric internet governance, China has increased its involvement in global internet governance forums via both governmental and private sector participation and began to host international forums to promote itself as the leading actor in internet policy.[44] One of the notable forums for discussing these issues is the World Internet Conference, an event that China has organized since 2014. At these events, Chinese officials alert other countries, especially the developing ones, to the inadequate representation of non-Western actors in international organizations and to the United States' "cyber-hegemonic" position, and ultimately raise questions about why the rest of the world should be required to observe online freedom of speech and other "Western values."[45]

The concept of digital sovereignty and the associated policy recommendations, which seek to challenge Western hegemony, have also been promoted by Russia. Similar to Chinese efforts, Russian officials have employed various measures since the 1990s, such as data localization laws to enhance their authority over internet usage within their national boundaries. Additionally, they have expressed a desire to reshape the existing global internet governance framework, which is currently dominated by US-based NGOs, in favor of a new model that prioritizes states' own interests.[46] By advocating for these changes, Russian authorities aim to assert greater control over the digital realm and reduce the influence of Western actors in global internet governance.

In order to foster the global acceptance of digital sovereignty as a guiding principle, Russia has initiated annual gatherings with BRICS (Brazil, Russia, Indonesia, China, and South Africa) countries and members of the SCO (Shanghai Cooperation Organization) and signed bilateral agreements with them pertaining to communication infrastructure and organizations. The SCO serves as a platform for both Russia and China to coordinate digital communication policies among member nations and establish novel international standards concerning the internet.[47] Through these collaborative efforts, Russia and China seek to promote a shared vision of digital governance that aligns with their respective notions of sovereignty and emphasizes the need for greater autonomy in the digital realm.[48]

Several other nations have also embraced the principle of digital sovereignty. Iran has undertaken measures to establish a "national" or "clean" internet framework, aiming to safeguard the nation against external interferences, such as cyberattacks, cyber espionage, and harmful online content.[49] These efforts involve enhancing the technical capabilities of internet and telecommunication infrastructures within Iran, prioritizing domestic websites over foreign counterparts, and developing indigenous alternatives for social media platforms, email providers, and search engines.[50]

The Erdoğan government for its part has recently begun to advocate for digital sovereignty. Following the coup attempt in 2016, the Erdoğan government introduced a decree law aimed at incentivizing social media companies to establish local data centers, offering them favorable terms concerning land use, corporate taxes, and energy bills.[51] In 2017 the minister of communications announced plans to establish Turkey's own data centers, emphasizing the importance of storing user data within the country's borders to facilitate "comprehensive analysis of online communications," a euphemism for state surveillance.[52] The government also highlighted data localization in its National Cyber Security Strategy and Action Plan (2020–23), asserting that state authorities can effectively prevent antistate activities if they have access to user data of individuals suspected of terrorism.[53]

In addition to advocating for data localization, the AKP government also endorses the development of domestic social media platforms, search engines, and email services as viable alternatives to foreign technology companies. Within the AKP ranks, there is a concerted effort to encourage users to transition from popular platforms like WhatsApp and X to locally developed applications like BiP and Yaay. This push is driven by concerns over data security and (perceived) violations of Turkish citizens' privacy rights by foreign companies. For instance, when WhatsApp announced changes to its data-sharing policy that would apply to Turkey and not to EU countries, Altun characterized the decision as "tyrannical."[54] He cautioned Turkish citizens against trusting WhatsApp and other foreign social media companies in matters concerning the right to privacy. Several government officials also took this opportunity to promote the use of locally developed apps, publicly announcing on X their decision to close their WhatsApp accounts and transition to BiP.

Turkish officials' emphasis on national security and user privacy serves to legitimize current and future initiatives to expand state authority over online communications. The government's attempts to establish digital sovereignty, while less developed compared to China, Iran, and Russia, are nonetheless influenced by similar conceptual frameworks. Like Chinese and Iranian authorities, the Erdoğan government is motivated by the belief that the internet has the potential to destabilize the country and introduce allegedly harmful values to the younger generation. Turkish officials' discourse surrounding digital sovereignty also bears resemblance to that of their Russian counterparts. In both countries, there persists a deep-seated suspicion regarding the intentions of Western governments, which can be attributed to historical experiences of defeat and perceived humiliation at the hands of the West (Turkey following World War I, and Russia after the Cold War).[55] In the realm of media and communications, both Turkish and Russian officials view Western news organizations, social media companies, and tech giants as threat sources and use hyped-up concerns about national unity and sovereignty as a pretext for their surveillance and censorship schemes.

Preferential Treatment of Chinese and Russian Media Organizations?

Thus far, this chapter has examined how Turkish officials seek to rationalize their restrictive communication policies, discredit and strong-arm West-based social media companies, and call for Turkey's digital sovereignty. Turkish state officials' confrontational attitude toward these companies then raises the question: What is their approach to non-Western media entities operating within Turkey, such as the Turkish language services of Russia's Sputnik and China's Xinhua News Agency, China Radio International, and *China Today*? As scholar of Turkey-China relations Çağdaş Üngör points out, while Turkish officials view Western media critically and maintain confrontational relationships, Chinese news outlets are rarely targeted and are perceived as relatively harmless.[56] For example, while the SETA report, discussed in chapter 1, criticized Western news outlets for their alleged biased coverage of Turkey, it nonetheless commended China Radio International for maintaining an impartial stance in its coverage of sensitive topics, such as the Kurdish issue and Turkey's Syria policy.[57] It is also worthwhile to note that the Turkish edition of *China Today* is published by Turkuvaz Media, whose owner Serhat Albayrak is the brother of Erdoğan's son-in-law, Berat Albayrak (see chapter 1). Turkish officials have also treated Russian media activities inside Turkey differently in comparison to Western ones. For example, in 2015 when Sputnik's Turkish edition published critical pieces regarding a rumored oil deal between Turkey and ISIS, AKP officials refrained from accusing Russia of carrying out disinformation campaigns against Turkey, as they typically do with Western media.[58] During Turkey's 2023 presidential elections when Erdoğan's opponent accused Russia of election meddling, not only did Turkish officials who usually decry influence operations remain silent but the minister of foreign affairs also called these accusations "false and unfair."[59]

These instances then shed light on the confrontational stance Turkish officials adopt when dealing with Western media companies, juxtaposed with a comparatively subdued approach toward their Russian and Chinese counterparts. Furthermore, as mentioned earlier, the endeavors of Russia and China to establish digital sovereignty are favorably perceived by Erdoğan's communication emissaries. The differing approaches of Turkish officials toward American and European media organizations in contrast to Russian and Chinese ones can be understood in the context of deteriorating relations with the West, Turkey's historical grievances toward Western powers, and Erdoğan's pursuit of closer geopolitical economic ties with Russia and China.

Diffusing Turkey's Communication Norms and Practices

While Turkish officials openly criticize and exert pressure on Western media companies, their interactions with media and communication entities in the Global South take on a distinctly different tone. For example, the DoC hosts forums that bring together foreign government representatives and media practitioners; TRT and Anadolu Agency offer training programs for journalists from Central Asia, Africa, the Middle East, and the Balkans; and TIKA (Türk İşbirliği ve Koordinasyon Ajansı Başkanlığı, Turkish Cooperation and Coordination Agency) undertakes material assistance projects to support media outlets in these regions. This section examines these initiatives, and asks: What strategies are employed to position Turkey as a counterweight to Western hegemony in the global communication arena?

How do the international initiatives undertaken by Turkish officials align with the government's foreign policy objectives and priorities in the Global South?

To address these questions, I examined the meetings DoC has organized for foreign media professionals and government representatives, including but not limited to Stratcom (Strategic Communication) summits. I conducted a thorough analysis of the DoC and Stratcom websites for information about these gatherings and watched all publicly available videos. In the case of the Anadolu Agency's and TRT's journalism training programs, I relied on publicly available data from the respective institutions' websites and social media accounts.

Media and Communication Forums

In recent years, the DoC has hosted an increasing number of media and communication-related meetings in Turkey, attracting the attendance of foreign government officials, academics, and experts. Organized under the label of Stratcom, these events provide opportunities for AKP officials and pro-Erdoğan media professionals to project a positive image of Turkey's communication landscape and forge alliances that promote their policies.[60]

The DoC held its inaugural Stratcom summit in Istanbul in December 2021, which comprised panel discussions on nation branding, digital diplomacy, media planning, political communication, digital journalism, and artificial intelligence.[61] Among the 118 speakers that took the floor over the two-day summit were government officials, journalists, academics, and practitioners from thirty countries, as well as communication experts from the European Union, North Atlantic Treaty Organization (NATO), United Nations Children's Fund (UNICEF), United Nations Development Program (UNDP), United Nations Environment Programme (UNEP), and International Atomic Energy Agency (IAEA). By inviting foreign experts from various countries, including notable speakers such as Simon Anholt, the leading authority on nation branding, DoC aimed to add a sense of credibility to the summit. Meanwhile, by giving a platform to Turkish speakers from the Ministry of National Defense, Turkish Red Crescent (the country's leading humanitarian organization), TIKA, Anadolu Agency, TRT, *Daily Sabah*, and SETA, it also promoted the AKP government's own communication endeavors.[62]

The DoC held its second Stratcom summit in Istanbul in December 2022. Despite its smaller scale, the event convened fifty speakers, including foreign experts, Turkish government officials, and representatives from the private sector. The summit focused on current topics such as post-truth, hate speech, government communication, and ethical obligations of technology companies.[63] Like its predecessor, the summit provided an opportunity for media professionals aligned with the Erdoğan regime to share their insights.

In May 2022 the DoC organized the youth edition of Stratcom, known as Stratcom Youth. This event served as a gathering point for university students, attracting approximately one hundred participants from different countries to Antalya, a city located on Turkey's Mediterranean coast. Spanning a duration of six days, the program offered training sessions and interactive workshops on strategic communication, public diplomacy, disinformation, crisis communication, and public relations.[64] But Stratcom Youth was more than a training program that was generously funded by the Turkish government (all transportation and accommodation costs were covered). As noted on its website, its broader objective was to promote Turkey's Communication Model to local and foreign university students.[65] Notably, the lineup of speakers at Stratcom Youth predominantly comprised individuals affiliated with the state apparatus: officials from the Ministry of Youth and Sports and prominent figures occupying leadership positions at the DoC, TRT, the Anadolu Agency, and the *Daily Sabah*. In addition, representatives from public relations departments of Turkish Airlines and the Turkish Red Crescent, as well as those from pro-government media outlets were also present, thereby reflecting a concentrated effort to disseminate the AKP's communication policies.[66]

In addition to Stratcom events, the DoC also organizes meetings that are specifically targeted at state officials, media professionals, and/or civil society representatives from Central Asia and Africa. Turkey has focused on these regions as per its foreign policy agenda since the 1990s, and during the AKP era, endeavors to strengthen political economic and cultural ties with countries in Central Asia and Africa have intensified, resulting in multifaceted collaborative initiatives across various domains (see chapter 3 for a detailed analysis). For its part, in 2021 the DoC convened approximately five hundred foreign individuals, including high-ranking state officials, media professionals, academics, and students from Azerbaijan, Kazakhstan, Kyrgyzstan, Turkey, and Uzbekistan, which are member countries of the Organization of Turkic States (OTS) founded in 2009 to increase cooperation among the nations. During the same year and extending into 2022, the DoC hosted other media-focused events exclusively for OTS members, such as the meeting of the ministers and high officials in charge of media and information, the media coordination committee meeting, and the social media training program.[67] In relation to Africa, the DoC orchestrated the Turkey-Africa Media Summit in Istanbul in 2022. This two-day gathering brought together a diverse group of eighty diplomats, academics, media professionals, and NGO representatives from forty-five African nations. Among the speakers were officials from the DoC, TRT, Anadolu Agency, SETA, and the Ministry of Foreign Affairs, as well as executives representing Turkish energy, defense, and construction companies that maintain business engagements in Africa. This assortment of speakers underscores how events organized by the Erdoğan government serve multiple objectives, spanning the realms of public and private interests, politics, and commerce.[68]

These international events afford an opportunity for the Erdoğan government to disseminate its narratives and practices concerning media and communications. By hosting these events in Turkey, Turkish officials gain an advantageous position to shape the meeting agendas in accordance with their political objectives. They promote Turkey's foreign policy agenda in a positive light and convey their core ideas about media-state relations to attendees. Opening and closing remarks are typically delivered by Altun himself, who disseminates the view that states must urge social media platforms to "give up providing propaganda opportunities to terror organisations" and announces Turkey's readiness to share its "institutional capacity, legislative expertise and practical experience" with other countries.[69] Occasionally, Erdoğan himself attends these events to deliver the keynote address either in person or through video link. During his speeches, Erdoğan directs attention to how social media platforms, once vehicles of freedom of speech, are now threatening democracies.[70] These international events also dedicate special sessions to the Ministry of Defense or the Ministry of Foreign Affairs so they can present on Turkey's fight against terrorism and its broader foreign policy. Participants in these forums are gifted with publications about Turkey, its politics, and culture.[71] Last but not least, they engage in cultural tours, where they learn about Turkish history, culture, and values while experiencing the hospitality of their Turkish hosts. These activities obviously help Erdoğan's emissaries to cultivate bonds with foreign media professionals and government officials and help to expand their networks.

Material Assistance and Training Programs

To present the country as a benevolent actor that reshapes the global communication order on behalf of the marginalized and to foster stronger ties with media organizations and professionals in the Global South, Turkish state organs also undertake material assistance and training programs. In line with the country's foreign policy agenda, they extend support to media outlets operating in Central Asia, Southeast Asia, Africa, the Middle East, and the Balkans and provide training programs for journalists from these regions.

Technical equipment assistance and capacity-building programs are typically implemented by TIKA in collaboration with Turkish embassies on the ground. TIKA runs a special program, known as the Program for the Improvement of the Technical Infrastructure of Media Organizations. This program offers tangible support to radio stations, television channels, and film studios in numerous countries, such as Afghanistan, Pakistan, Lebanon, Libya, Kenya, Namibia, Uganda, Tanzania, Tunisia, Azerbaijan, Kyrgyzstan, Turkmenistan, Montenegro, and Serbia.[72] An important point to note here is that such assistance is predominantly directed to state-run organizations in these countries, rather than independent outlets or civil society associations. For instance, TIKA's technical equipment donations between 2012 and 2018 in fourteen African countries exclusively benefited state-affiliated news agencies, television channels, and radio stations.[73] TIKA also contributes to the establishment of television and film studios, digitization centers, and digital design laboratories at universities in these countries aiming to assist local students in their media-related endeavors.

Training programs are offered by the Anadolu Agency, TRT, TIKA, and YTB (Yurtdisi Türkler ve Akraba Topluluklar Baskanligi, Presidency for Turks Abroad and Related Communities), either individually or in collaboration with each other. The Anadolu Agency News Academy (Anadolu Ajansı Haber Akademisi), established in 2012, offers comprehensive training programs as well as specialized sessions in war and conflict coverage, finance and economy journalism, energy journalism, and diplomacy journalism.[74] In 2020 the AA News Academy trained over eight hundred journalists hailing from fifty different countries. In 2022 that number rose to approximately twenty-five hundred.[75] Similar to TIKA's geographic focus, the News Academy also targets journalists in Central and Eastern Europe, the Balkans, Africa, and the Middle East with the aim of fostering the development of a "new generation of journalists."[76]

These regions have also been the primary target of TRT's Media Academy Program (MAP) during its operation period between 2009 and 2017. In its most recent training program in 2017, TRT MAP convened a diverse cohort of 162 participants from Central Asia, Southeast Asia, Africa, the Middle East, and the Balkans. The program encompassed a wide range of courses, including content production, radio and TV broadcasting, news media, and broadcast technologies.[77] Although the MAP has been discontinued since 2017 for reasons undisclosed, TRT remains committed to providing training opportunities through its affiliated entities.

In 2017 TRT World Citizen, the philanthropic branch of TRT World, initiated a project known as Journalism for Juniors (J4J). Initially, J4J targeted Syrian refugee students residing in Turkey.[78] As part of the program, TRT

World and TRT Arabi staff carried out eleven workshops for Syrian students, teaching them about mobile journalism, field production, and storytelling. At the time J4J described its goal as to enable Syrian refugees "to tell their own stories and share their voice with the world" and "to empower them to take control of their own narratives."[79] In 2021 the J4J project was officially established as TRT Journalism for Juniors, and since then it has organized training programs for high school students both in Turkey and abroad. These training programs cover a range of essential skills in the field of journalism, including mobile journalism, storytelling, digital journalism, and field production. An integral aspect of J4J's approach is to equip students with the knowledge and techniques required to become a journalist using nothing more than a phone and to encourage them to engage in journalism with "a human first mentality."[80] For its training programs outside Turkey, TRT Journalism for Juniors collaborates with TIKA, the Yunus Emre Institute, and the Turkish Maarif Foundation.[81] As of May 2023 Journalism for Juniors offered training programs at high schools in Afghanistan, Albania, Austria, Bulgaria, Georgia, Iraq, Kirgizstan, North Macedonia, Moldova, Romania, Tajikistan, Tanzania, and Tunisia.[82]

In regards the geographic focus of Turkey's media training initiatives, Africa is particularly significant. Between 2013 and 2019 TIKA, in partnership with TRT and the Anadolu Agency, conducted sixteen training programs in different countries across the continent, focusing on areas such as war journalism, radio broadcasting, media ethics, and diplomacy journalism.[83] In 2019 TRT, YTB, and the Anadolu Agency jointly organized the inaugural Africa Media Representatives Training Program (AFMED) in Ankara to promote collaboration, knowledge sharing, and best practices among early and mid-career media professionals.[84] During the three-week-long program, broadcast professionals from Ethiopia, Morocco, Kenya, Libya, Mali, Niger, Nigeria, Somalia, Tanzania, Tunisia, Chad, Liberia, and Senegal attended classes, went on city tours, and traveled to Istanbul to participate in the TRT World Forum.[85] The second and third editions of AFMED took place virtually in 2021 and 2022 with the participation of twenty journalists from Africa on each occasion.[86]

Turkey's training programs not only aim to impart practical skills to participants but also serve as a platform for advancing the official narratives of the government in relation to its domestic and foreign policies. This approach was evident in the first AFMED, where participants had the opportunity to engage with officials from the Ministry of Foreign Affairs, SETA, and humanitarian aid organizations affiliated with the AKP. During these meetings, participants received information about Turkey's anti-terrorism campaigns against PKK and ISIS and Turkey's humanitarian initiatives.[87] And since this program coincided with Turkey's military operation in north Syria, code-named Operation Peace Spring, this first AFMED was also an opportune platform to inform African journalists about Turkey's Syria policy. The president of the YTB expressed this sentiment: "I am confident that the participants will learn about Operation Peace Spring and Turkey's foreign policy. And when they go back to their countries they will disseminate this information [to African audiences]. Therefore, we can think of [AFMED] as an endeavor to explain Turkey's position concerning Operation Peace Spring."[88]

As a former official who used to work at the Ministry of Foreign Affairs told me, state organs do in fact utilize these training programs to inform foreign journalists about the AKP's foreign policy objectives with the hope that they will embrace a pro-Turkish vision in their professional work:

> After the 2016 coup attempt, the government was really concerned with Africa and the Balkans. Because these were the two regions where Gülen was running schools, charities and businesses. As you know, [the AKP] had to convince these countries [in Africa and the Balkans] to shut down Gülen's schools. And it was successful. Many of the schools are no longer owned by Gülen's people. To go back to your question, about training programs: whenever there is a journalism program, [state officials] also use it as an opportunity to tell African journalists that Gülen is a terrorist. They give [participants] booklets [that are published by the AA] that explain who Gülen is, what his followers did during the coup, why they are dangerous to Africa, too. And they do the same thing about PKK and YPG. [Turkish organizations] explain Turkish military operations against PKK and YPG, explain why they are necessary.[89]

It is important to note that Turkey's external activities in the field of communication also serve as platforms for state officials to engage with foreign journalists and persuade them about Turkey's foreign policy actions. According to an official familiar with AA training programs for African journalists, participants are carefully selected based on their professional standing in their respective countries to ensure their ability to effectively present Turkey to their audiences back home. In other words, these programs are not solely intended to empower African journalists to share their own stories, as state officials often claim, but also to have them disseminate "Turkey's story" to African audiences.

Strategic Collaborations

To enhance Turkey's global influence in the field of communication and garner support for its communication policies, Erdoğan's emissaries also sign cooperation agreements and spearhead the establishment of joint entities with foreign governments. For example, RTUK led the creation of regional bodies focused on broadcasting regulation, namely, the Black Sea Countries Broadcasting Regulatory Authorities Forum (BRAF) and the Organization of Islamic Cooperation Broadcasting Regulatory Authorities Forum (OIC-IBRAF). BRAF was founded in Istanbul in 2008; its secretariat is based in RTUK offices in Ankara, and its secretary general is also a RTUK member. BRAF brings together broadcasting regulatory authorities from Albania, Armenia, Azerbaijan, Bulgaria, Georgia, Greece, Moldova, Romania, Russia, Serbia, Turkey, and Ukraine with the aim of facilitating dialogue and cooperation.[90] Similarly, the OIC-IBRAF was established in Istanbul in 2011, with its secretariat located in Ankara and operating under the leadership of RTUK. OIC-IBRAF aims to promote dialogue and collaboration among broadcasting regulatory authorities of member countries of the Organization of Islamic Cooperation.[91]

In 2022 the Anadolu Agency announced plans to establish the Turkic News Agencies Association, a joint entity to be headquartered in Istanbul. Karagöz, the director general of AA, emphasized the agency's commitment to delivering accurate news reporting and thus its status as a role model for news agencies in Turkic republics in Central Asia. AA is set to assume a leadership role within the association to foster collaboration among news agencies and offer training programs.[92] AA has also been actively signing cooperation agreements with numerous news agencies worldwide, expanding its global network and aiming to strengthen its reputation as a trusted news agency.

A New Player Development Communication?

With the aforementioned training and media assistance programs, Turkey is but one of the many countries that is actively engaging in development communication. Development, a hallmark of modernization theory, emerged after World War II at a time when "wealthier nations invested in rebuilding areas devastated through conflict." As a "transnational enterprise," development builds on the assumption that "technology and knowledge will transform suffering communities into more modern, democratic nation-states."[93]

An integral component of development projects today comprise media and communications. It was Daniel Lerner who during the Cold War contended that "exposure to media cultivates empathy, which inspires democratic and entrepreneurial participation." His argument resonated with American policymakers, convincing them that media had the potential to catalyze advancement in developing nations.[94] Since then, American and European governments, national aid agencies, foundations, and donor organizations have provided media assistance and training programs around the world as part of their democracy-building activities. In the 1960s the International Press Institute and the Ford Foundation offered long-term training programs in Anglophone Africa to enshrine the Western journalism model in newsrooms and universities as a means of improving democracy and forestalling Soviet influence.[95] In the 1990s the US government and American and European foundations sponsored journalism training programs in Central Asian states to replace Soviet-style journalism with West-based models and, by proxy, to facilitate these countries' transition from communism to liberal democracy.[96] After September 11, the United States and its European allies turned their attention to the Middle East and Afghanistan and funded local radio and television outlets and improved telecommunications infrastructures in the hopes of generating West-friendly media content, developing a robust civil society, and ultimately rooting out extremism.[97]

Today, there is a long list of governments, national aid agencies, NGOs, and international donors that carry out a wide array of development communication projects around the globe. Previous paradigms of development have come under criticism, and Cold War–era approaches to development communication have also changed. Development agencies and donor organizations now incorporate local actors into their projects, taking into consideration the complexities of social and political change.[98] Meanwhile, non-Western actors have also begun to undertake their own development communication projects in an effort to expand their political, social, and cultural influence worldwide, in competition with Europe and the United States. Notably, China has significantly bolstered its investments in communication infrastructure in Africa through initiatives such as the Forum on China-Africa Cooperation (FOCAC), as well as in other developing nations via the Belt and Road Initiative (BRI).[99] However, it is important to note that China's assistance is primarily directed toward state-run media entities, rather than commercial media outlets or civil society organizations.[100] China also conducts training programs for journalists from numerous countries, which not only offer skills-based training but also include visits to Chinese companies, guided tours, and insights into Chinese culture, history, and politics.[101] As scholar of China-Africa relations Lina Benabdallah observes, China has established people-to-people networks as a means to legitimize its governance, development, and security practices. Benabdallah emphasizes the significance of cultural and diplomatic exchange initiatives, as well as professional training programs, orchestrated by China for the benefit of African officials and professionals. These platforms serve as channels for "knowledge production and skills transfer," allowing Chinese authorities to portray China and its relationship with Africa in a positive light. Moreover, these spaces contribute to the production of Chinese expertise in fields like journalism, development, and security, thus enabling the dissemination of Chinese values within these domains.[102]

Turning to Turkey, the Erdoğan government also aims to expand the country's presence in the world communication order through international forums, training programs, and technical assistance. These endeavors are still in their early stages and cannot be compared to those undertaken by European countries, the United States, or China in terms of their reach, scope, and consistency. According to a state official with knowledge of these activities, Turkey's communication outreach to foreign media professionals lacks a comprehensive and enduring strategic vision. Various entities seem to be organizing similar training programs and government-level meetings without a cohesive and coordinated strategy in place.[103] Nevertheless, these initiatives seek to engage foreign communication professionals and state officials from the Global South as allies and are rapidly expanding.

Turkish officials characterize their journalism training and media assistance initiatives as endeavors directed toward creating a more equitable communication framework. They present them as tangible examples of Turkey's commitment to empowering "the voiceless," which in this context refers to government representatives and media professionals from the Balkans, Middle East, Africa, and Southeast Asia who often find themselves marginalized within the international media landscape. In this context, the narratives put forth by the Erdoğan government bear similarities to the ideals of the New World Information and Communication Order (NWICO), which emerged in the 1960s and 1970s within the broader context of postcolonial movements. During this period, newly independent nations voiced their concerns about the dominant position held by European and American news agencies, the Western powers' disregard for the cultural sovereignty of developing nations, and the one-sided flow of news, entertainment, and culture from the North to the South. Consequently, in the late 1970s member countries of the Non-Aligned Movement (NAM) presented proposals aimed at establishing a more equitable communication and information framework. These proposals encompassed structural and organizational changes related to telecommunications infrastructure, the allocation of radio frequencies, the regulation of transnational corporations, the facilitation of regional news exchanges, and the development of journalist training programs.[104]

In 1976 NAM countries presented their proposals to the United Nations Educational, Scientific, and Cultural Organization (UNESCO). At UNESCO the International Commission for the Study of Communication Problems was established to conduct comprehensive studies and explore potential solutions to the existing flaws in the global communication system.[105] In its 1980 report the commission put forward several recommendations: democratization of access to communication, establishment of self-reliant communication systems in Third World countries, enhancement of international news gathering, and advancement of international cooperation.[106] Regrettably, the realization of a new communication order faced obstacles due to a blend of ideological disputes among UNESCO members, strong resistance from the United States and Great Britain regarding the commission's suggestions, and the prevailing 1980s mindset that favored market-driven remedies over political interventions.[107]

Turkey, although not a formal member of NAM, had a presence at the commission meetings through the participation of Turkish journalist Hıfzı Topuz. Unfortunately, there is a lack of comprehensive analysis regarding Turkey's official stance on the NWICO apart from Topuz's personal recollections of the commission meetings.[108] The executives I interviewed from TRT World and the Anadolu Agency did not indicate any awareness of the NWICO movement. Additionally, I have not encountered any mentions of the NWICO or the UNESCO commission in statements made by Altun, Karagöz, Eren, and Erdoğan's other communication emissaries. Unfortunately, my attempts to secure interviews with these officials have gone unanswered, posing a difficulty in directly probing their viewpoints on the NWICO. Nonetheless, it is safe to argue that while Turkish officials' criticisms of the global communication order are, in general, accurate, they lack a nuanced comprehension of the complex power-knowledge dynamics at play. Their perspective tends to oversimplify the intricate network of relationships among governments, regulatory bodies, media and technology companies, and audiences. At the same time, they assert that Turkey's outreach to communication professionals and organizations from the Global South can easily rectify the inequities in the global communication order. It's crucial to emphasize that the Erdoğan government is primarily driven by the aspiration to bring these Global South actors into Turkey's orbit and have them convey Turkey's narrative to their respective audiences in their home countries, all while adopting a paternalistic approach toward them, reminiscent of their claims to guardianship of oppressed peoples.

In conclusion, this chapter has delved into the strategies employed by the Erdoğan government to legitimize its communication vision. Erdoğan's communication emissaries actively work to erode the credibility of Western media organizations, leveraging ongoing debates about disinformation, post-truth, and digital sovereignty. They employ coercive tactics to enforce compliance with Turkish regulations, aiming to bring Western media companies in line with their prescribed standards. At regional and international gatherings hosted in Turkey, they advocate for communication policies that prioritize national security over the free flow of information. State organs, such as TRT, the Anadolu Agency, and TIKA, utilize media assistance and journalism training programs as means to establish partnerships with foreign governments and media professionals, particularly those in the Global South. Through cooperation agreements, Anadolu Agency seeks to expand its global presence and amplify the dissemination of news content that aligns with the AKP's perspective. In parallel, the establishment of regional regulatory bodies by RTUK serves the purpose of promoting regulatory harmonization while advancing a specific understanding of media-state relations that aligns with Turkey's preferences. Collectively, these activities are aimed at growing Turkey's visibility and influence as a resurgent actor that contributes to the improvement of the global communication order while conveniently ignoring the AKP government's detrimental communication policies inside the country.

3

Restoring Justice to Muslims

Knowledge Production about Islamophobia
and Erdoğan's Missionary Politics

In September 2019 Erdoğan held a trilateral meeting with Pakistan's and Malaysia's prime ministers on the sidelines of the United Nations General Assembly in New York City. Afterwards, the three leaders announced plans to launch an international television channel dedicated to "combating Islamophobia" and "setting the record straight on Islam."[1] In May 2021, at the first International Media and Islamophobia Symposium held in Turkey, Erdoğan reiterated the need for a "strong communication network" to fight against Islamophobia—the "cancer that is spreading rapidly in many parts of the world, especially in the West."[2] Speaking at the same event, Serdar Karagöz, Anadolu Agency's director general, announced plans to set up a special "monitoring unit" to track Islamophobic incidents around the world.[3]

Intended to be part of an Istanbul-based media center, the said international television channel and the Anadolu Agency's Discrimination Line have yet to materialize.[4] But according to Karagöz, Turkey's existing global communication outlets, TRT World, the Anadolu Agency, and the *Daily Sabah* are already at the "forefront of fighting Islamophobia."[5] Although there is no independent research demonstrating their effectiveness, these news organizations do indeed cover Islamophobia extensively. The *Daily Sabah* features a special Islamophobia section on its website, giving readers direct access to all the news reports and editorial content on the topic. TRT World and the Anadolu Agency cover anti-Muslim hatred and its various manifestations in news reports, online news videos, documentaries, and/or special reports. Another AKP-backed entity, SETA addresses Islamophobia in its English-language reports and in conferences it organizes in Western capitals.[6]

With this in mind, this chapter examines the AKP-backed entities' communication and knowledge production activities concerning Islamophobia.

Among the key questions are: Why do the AKP's global communication instruments draw attention to Islamophobia? How are their communicative activities articulated with the notion of Muslim victimhood that undergirds much of the AKP's Islamist politics? Which cases of Islamophobia warrant international media attention from the AKP's communication apparatus, and which ones don't? What are the implications of these practices on the conceptualization and communication of the relations between Muslims and the West? To address these questions, this chapter presents an analysis of Erdoğan's and his communication emissaries' official statements; news coverage, and documentaries from TRT World; news coverage and op-eds from the *Daily Sabah*; and reports, conferences, and awareness campaigns from SETA, TRT World Research Centre, and TRT World Citizen.

First, this chapter provides a comprehensive overview of the AKP's integration of Muslim identity within its foreign policy, along with the corresponding aid, development, cultural, and educational initiatives specifically aimed at Muslim populations across the globe. This overview is warranted since the Erdoğan government portrays itself as the champion of disadvantaged Muslims and as a virtuous actor striving to restore justice to them within the global order. Next examined is how the AKP-backed outlets communicate Islamophobia to audiences and the connections between their output and Erdoğan's missionary politics. Throughout this analysis, the chapter highlights specific examples of content from TRT World, the *Daily Sabah*, and SETA where they are of representative relevance. Lastly, the chapter focuses on the selective and transactional nature of the AKP's instrumentalization of Islamophobia.

Incorporation of Muslim Identity into Foreign Policy

During the late 2000s, Turkey's long-standing Western-oriented foreign policy underwent a major transformation.[7] Under the leadership of Ahmet Davutoğlu, who first served as an adviser to Erdoğan, then as the minister of foreign affairs (2009–14) and as prime minister (2014–16), the AKP formulated a foreign policy agenda that sought to leverage Turkey's historical, cultural, and religious ties to countries in the Balkans, Middle East, Central Asia, and Africa. According to Davutoğlu, Turkey could earn its rightful place as a great power on the world stage by embracing its imperial past and "venturing outwards with confidence and assertiveness" to form new alliances in the aforementioned regions. In addition to accruing strategic benefits to Turkey, these new partnerships would help to unify Muslims in the Middle East who had been separated from each other after the collapse of the Ottoman Empire.[8] To achieve pan-Islamic unity, Davutoğlu did not necessarily prescribe to replace modern nation-states with a new transnational entity. In his mind,

Turkey's cultivation of deep relationships with Muslim-majority countries would be sufficient to render the territorial borders "*de facto* meaningless" and bring together dispersed Muslims—under the leadership of Turkey, of course.[9]

As per Davutoğlu's strategic depth doctrine, the AKP government embarked on several foreign policy initiatives in the 2010s to build an Ottoman-like greatness in its own neighborhood and beyond.[10] The inspiration drawn from the ascendance of China, India, Russia, and Brazil in world affairs and the impulse to use Arab uprisings to flex Turkey's regional power also played a role in the shaping of this new foreign policy.[11] As such, the AKP strengthened diplomatic and economic relations with several Arab countries, acted as a peace broker in regional conflicts, and even attempted to influence internal politics in Iraq and Syria by lending support to Sunni groups.[12] In the Balkans it focused its attention on cultivating political, economic, and cultural relationships with countries with visible Muslim populations, such as Albania, Bosnia, and Kosovo. It improved existing joint projects in energy, trade, and transport with Central Asian republics while expanding its cooperation with Azerbaijan in military-technical, trade, and energy fields.[13] Last but not least, it made a remarkable pivot to Africa, increasing the number of Turkish embassies in the continent, growing trade volume, and undertaking development assistance projects in Muslim-majority countries.[14]

These foreign policy moves were not entirely novel but partly a continuation of previous governments' endeavors. In the 1990s Turkey had signed economic and technical cooperation agreements with at least a dozen countries in Africa and provided assistance to the newly independent Turkic republics in Central Asia (Kazakhstan, Kyrgyzstan, Turkmenistan, and Uzbekistan). During the AKP era, however, diplomatic, cultural, educational, and trade engagements with the Balkans, Middle East, Central Asia, and Africa have expanded considerably, not to mention the increase in humanitarian aid and development assistance provided to these regions. To garner public support for these costly engagements and instill a sense of ethnic-national pride at home, Erdoğan and the AKP rank and file have constructed Turks as the grandchildren of Ottomans, and Turkey as an inherently great power restoring its rightful place in the world.[15] Erdoğan and his supporters constantly make references to Turkey's so-called glorious past and frame Turkish foreign policy as reviving the lost connections among brotherly Muslim communities.

Because of its emphasis on building an Ottoman-like influence in politics, economy, and culture in the geographical areas over which the empire once reigned, the AKP's policies are described as neo-Ottomanist. In domestic politics, neo-Ottomanism provides the ideological component for Erdoğan's New

Turkey, one that "continues the traditions across the imperial and republican forms of rule, upholds Muslim identity as a fraternal force that could counter Kurdish separatism, and defends a more visible and effective role of religion in public life."[16] In foreign policy, neo-Ottomanism is implicated with Turkey's self-representation as the bearer of a "moral mission and a civilizational duty" toward Muslims, discussed in detail below in the section "Muslim Victimhood and Erdoğan's Missionary Politics."[17]

Turkey's Outreach to Muslims

It is not an exaggeration to state that the Erdoğan government funnels its foreign aid and development assistance primarily toward Muslims.[18] Turkey's aid and development agency, TIKA was founded in 1994 with the specific task of providing development aid to post-Soviet Turkic states in Central Asia and rekindling ethnic and cultural ties with them. During the AKP era TIKA has grown exponentially and has gone beyond its original remit in Central Asia. It is now active in 150 countries, especially in the Balkans, Middle East, Central Asia, and Africa.[19] In projects such as providing water, sanitation services, food aid, and emergency assistance to those in need, TIKA coordinates with Islamic nongovernmental organizations (NGOs) that are directly or indirectly affiliated with the AKP.[20] It coordinates with youth organizations that have organic ties to the AKP and assists their members to carry out aid and relief work in Muslim-majority countries. Members of these organizations view their international aid work as a reflection of "a great nation helping the ummah [the collective community of Muslims]."[21]

An interesting component of TIKA's work is its focus on keeping alive the Ottoman Muslim heritage around the world via restoration of Ottoman-era tombs, mosques, and other historical buildings. For example, between 2017 and 2019 TIKA carried out fifty-seven such restoration projects in numerous countries from Albania to Iraq.[22] Last but not least, TIKA plays a leading role in the construction of new mosques, such as those in Maryland in the United States (the largest in North America), Cambridge, England (billed as the world's first "eco-mosque"); Cologne, Germany (the largest in Europe), and Albania, Ghana, and Kyrgyzstan (the largest in their respective regions) and thus helps to forge Turkey's image as a superior state in the international system and in the eyes of the world's Muslims.[23]

The religious inflection of Turkey's global outreach can also be observed in activities carried out by another state entity, the Diyanet (the Directorate of Religious Affairs). Founded in 1924 as a state entity to provide Islamic religious services and manage places of worship, the Diyanet expanded considerably during the AKP era both in terms of its mandate and budget. Having gone beyond its original remit, it is now an integral player in the AKP's educational, cultural, family-oriented public services with a budget surpassing those of several cabinet ministries.[24] In addition, the Diyanet is also active in the international arena via the Diyanet Foundation, which runs Quran schools, trains preachers, equips places of worship, and carries out charity work in numerous countries. As per the government's aspirations to leadership of the so-called Muslim world, the Diyanet also organizes summits in Turkey for Muslim leaders from Africa and Latin America.[25]

Other state entities that are oriented toward Muslims and/or Muslim Turks are AFAD (Afet ve Acil Durum Yönetimi Başkanlığı, Presidency of Disaster and Emergency Management), YEE (Yunus Emre Enstitüsü, Yunus Emre Institute), and YTB (Yurtdışı Türkler ve Akraba Topluluklar Başkanlığı, Presidency for Turks Abroad and Related Communities).

AFAD was established in 2009 to carry out risk reduction and disaster-management work under the Ministry of the Interior. In addition to such activities at the domestic level, AFAD is also engaged in international humanitarian aid campaigns. Since 2018 it has organized fundraising campaigns to address humanitarian emergencies in Myanmar (aid to Rohingya Muslims), Palestine, Somalia, and Syria. According to its director, AFAD's international activities are a natural outcome of the "conscientious heritage granted to our noble nation through history" and demonstrate that "faithful Turks are here to help."[26]

YEE is Turkey's leading cultural diplomacy organization, whose mandate is to "enhance [the country's] recognition, credibility and prestige in the international arena." To this end, YEE offers Turkish language classes, art, and culture activities via its sixty-three offices around the world. According to its website, the institute, founded in 2007, is named after Yunus Emre, the Sufi poet who strived for the creation of a "more peaceful world."[27]

Similar to YEE, YTB also provides cultural and educational services but focuses on Turks in diaspora and "related communities"—that is, people of Muslim Turkish heritage. YTB was founded in 2010 to rekindle the "common values" between Turkey and its "brotherly communities" in the Balkans and Central Asia. Among YTB's projects are those that pertain to cultural heritage, history, and Turkish-language education. YTB offers scholarships to students who wish to study in Turkey and, as noted in chapter 2, organizes training programs for young journalists and media professionals from Africa, Central Asia, the Balkans, and the Middle East.

The AKP government, following Davutoğlu's prescription for making Turkey a great power, has incorporated Muslim identity and Ottoman heritage into its initiatives in foreign aid, development assistance, and cultural-educational diplomacy work. Although Davutoğlu himself was forced to resign in 2016, his ideas continue to shape the work of TIKA, AFAD, Diyanet, YEE, and YTB—all primarily oriented toward Muslims in an effort to pull them into Turkey's orbit. For its part, the communication leg of the AKP's global outreach program presents Turkey as a leading humanitarian actor that looks out for the well-being of fellow Muslims. TRT World, Anadolu Agency, SETA, the *Daily Sabah*, and other entities give extensive and critical coverage to topics that are of interest to Muslims, Islamophobia first and foremost among them. The following section analyzes in detail how the AKP-sponsored entities communicate and produce knowledge about Islamophobia.

Islamophobia and the Erdoğan Government

Islamophobia is the fear, hatred, and prejudice toward Islam and Muslims at individual and institutional levels and is manifest in hate speech, physical attacks, discrimination, civil rights violations, and large-scale persecution campaigns.[28] Islamophobia is a form of racism because its targets also include non-Muslims (e.g., Christian Arabs, Hindu Sikhs) that share clothing, skin color, or language usually associated with Muslims.[29] It is fomented by "existing Eurocentric and Orientalist" power structures and is therefore enmeshed with racial politics worldwide.[30]

Islamophobia is not a new development. Nor is it merely entrenched in religious opposition. Beginning with Muslim expansion into Europe in the eighth century and extending to the rise of the Ottoman Empire in the fifteenth, European rulers and the Roman Catholic Church constructed Islam as a source of threat and enmity in order to justify their military and political projects.[31] Modern nation-states have used the "dread of Islam" to rationalize violence against internal and external threats in the name of state-building.[32] In the eighteenth and nineteenth centuries, European and American imperialisms framed Muslims and the East as being inferior to the West, thus concealing their capitalist, expansionist agendas behind modernization theories and development projects.[33] In contemporary United States, Islam has been conflated with terrorism since at least the Iran hostage crisis, shaping American foreign policy and national political identity in important ways. Needless to say, anti-Muslim politics in the United States has gained traction after September 11 and reached new heights during the Trump presidency. Meanwhile, in Europe, deep-rooted Orientalist and racist ideologies have recently resurfaced alongside far-right movements, and depictions of immigrants and refugees from the Global South—the majority of whom are Muslims—as civilizational threats have become commonplace. In China, India, and Myanmar, ethnic nationalists and religious hardliners have also subjected Muslims to large-scale, state-sanctioned persecution campaigns.

Islamophobia is an important topic for the Erdoğan government, which projects itself as a virtuous actor that redresses the injustices Muslims face. AKP-backed entities consistently report on the EU's discriminatory policies against migrants that arrive from Muslim-majority countries, the Narendra Modi government's crackdown on Muslims in India, Myanmar's forced displacement of Rohingya Muslims, and Israel's attacks against Palestinians. AKP-backed communication entities also remind audiences of past persecution campaigns against Muslims, such as the Srebrenica massacre wherein thousands of Bosniak Muslims were killed by Serbian forces. The following sections offer an analysis of the AKP government's communication and knowledge production activities about Islamophobia in news coverage, documentaries, reports, conferences, and awareness campaigns.

Islamophobia in the News

In their news coverage, TRT World and the *Daily Sabah* take a factual approach and provide information about the who's, where's, and when's of anti-Muslim hatred and its manifestations (e.g., verbal abuse, physical assault, vandalism, and arson; passage of anti-Muslim legislation; violation of Muslims' civil rights).

A considerable volume of news coverage is devoted to Islamophobia in non-Western contexts, such as anti-Muslim legislation in India, repression of Muslims in Kashmir, and persecution of Rohingya Muslims in Myanmar and of Uighur Muslims in China. Still, as can be seen in table 3.1, the volume of newsfeed on Islamophobia in Western contexts surpasses non-Western ones, which can be attributed to the potentially high(er) number of Islamophobic incidents in Europe, North America, and Oceania.[34] Nonetheless, the quantitative tilt toward Western contexts works well with the Erdoğan regime's strategy, which uses Islamophobia to criticize the West and to assemble Muslim publics through their affective grievances toward Western powers.

In his speeches, Erdoğan acknowledges that anti-Muslim discrimination is "observed in different geographies" but emphasizes that it is "an ideological fanaticism that is spreading like poison ivy, especially in Western countries."[35] In the aftermath of high-profile developments in the West (e.g., the passing of an anti-radicalism bill in France, the Christchurch mosque attacks in New Zealand), Erdoğan and AKP rank and file quickly issue statements calling out Western hostility toward Muslims but generally remain silent on other instances of discrimination and violence against Muslims in

Table 3.1 Countries mentioned in Islamophobia-related news coverage between January 1 and October 1, 2021

	TRT World online videos (n 92)	Daily Sabah new reports (n 197)
Australia	3	7
Belgium	2	4
Bulgaria	2	3
Canada	2	4
China	9	15
Czechia	1	5
Denmark	3	7
France	7	13
Germany	9	18
Greece	4	8
India	8	15
Ireland	1	3
Myanmar	2	7
Netherlands	4	11
New Zealand	5	9
Poland	2	5
Serbia	1	5
Sri Lanka	3	9
United Kingdom	8	21
United States	16	28

non-Western contexts (more on this later in the section "Instrumentalization of Islamophobia").

The association of Islamophobia with the West is seen in statements delivered by Erdoğan's emissaries that occupy top communication positions, as well. According to Serdar Karagöz, the Anadolu Agency's director general, Islamophobia "has been produced by the Western ruling elites [during] the establishment of the Western hegemony.... It is an indispensable [tool] for [Western] hegemons, [because] it lays the ground for [their anti-Muslim] security policies."[36] Fahrettin Altun, the director of communications, argues that "Europe's hostility towards Muslims ... is inseparable from the increasingly widespread hostility towards Islam, Turkey, and our president."[37]

How do these statements about anti-Muslim hatred as a specifically Western phenomenon shape TRT World's and the Daily Sabah's coverage then? One of my interviewees, a former foreign producer at TRT World, said the channel gives more attention to anti-Muslim hatred in the West than in other national or regional contexts:

> TRT World is well-aligned, or you could even say it's integrated with the government's attitude towards Europe and the United States. Islamophobia [in these countries] gets more attention than [that in] India and China. When there's a major Islamophobic attack like the one in New Zealand church attack, it gets more airtime in hourly news bulletins and in debate programs. There is even a few documentaries [on TRT World] about the Christchurch attack, for example. Islamophobic attacks in India are also covered, and there are news reports about [Muslim] Uighurs in China. But these are mostly [in the form of] short videos on [TRT World's] YouTube channel.[38]

The *Daily Sabah* also covers anti-Muslim attacks that transpire in different parts of the world but foregrounds those in the West by mourning them on its front page and/or by publishing op-eds that specifically criticize the United States and European countries. Similar to TRT World's editorial line, the *Daily Sabah*'s coverage of and commentary on Islamophobia is also tilted toward the West. According to a former *Daily Sabah* journalist I interviewed, this selective attention serves two purposes:

> Erdoğan uses these Islamophobic attacks [in the West] to mobilize his voters at home. Remember how he showed the video of the Christchurch attack at one of his rallies? He was basically telling his supporters, "Look, this is how Westerners treat us Muslims." On the other hand, he brings up Islamophobia in Europe to slam European leaders whenever he has a political feud with them. For example, when Turkey and France had a dispute over gas drilling in the Mediterranean Sea, Erdoğan was attacking [French president Emmanuel] Macron for passing the anti-Muslim legislation. And [the *Daily Sabah*] really harped on this.[39]

The above quotes do not necessarily point to direct managerial influence on TRT World and *Daily Sabah* journalists but, rather, illustrate how their editorial policies and consequent news coverage are guided by Erdoğan's rhetoric and actions.[40] The journalists I interviewed for this study said they and their colleagues were already familiar with TRT World's and the *Daily Sabah*'s editorial lines concerning the West, in general, and with Erdoğan's discourse on Islamophobia in the West, in particular. A foreign news producer at TRT World offered the following explanation:

> Turkish journalists [at TRT World] are already primed to reproduce this discourse [on Islamophobia.] This is not surprising, because they are mostly

political hires; they are generally plucked by loyalist [Turkish] executives from the AKP circles. And they have this sense of duty to spread Erdoğan's message to the world. Then there are those young junior journalists that usually come from Muslim countries. Some from Pakistan, some from [Muslim] diaspora in the U.K. And you can tell that they really buy into the narrative that TRT World is acting as the voice of Muslims. And they consider it an urgent task to cover Islamophobia, as their duty to the Muslim world, to make their suffering known.[41]

How do official government narratives about Islamophobia shape the news coverage then? According to media and public affairs scholar Robert Entman's "cascading network activation model," news frames diffuse from top government officials to "networks of news organizations and within and across them; to the networks of journalists; on to the textual networks of connected and repeated keywords, themes, and visual images and symbols published in media texts."[42] There is also ample research on journalists' socialization into the organization's norms, values, policies, language, and discourse and the reproduction of institutionally favored narratives.[43] Notwithstanding the fact that newsrooms can also be sites of contestation, there is a process of adaptation to the organization's news culture and a process of negotiation whereby journalists end up modifying their work.[44] In those cases, journalists are usually driven by a number of factors that range from "direct managerial influence" to "feelings of obligation, mobility aspirations, and absorption in the day-to-day tasks of collecting news" with "little time [left] to reflect on bigger, policy questions."[45] Economic and cultural rewards (i.e., gaining experience, education, skills, reputation) also play a role in journalists' embracing of the parameters set by the news organization they work for.[46] For example, in their study of Russia Today (RT), the Kremlin-backed news channel, Elswah and Howard show that monetary incentives and job promotions play a role in the socialization of young, inexperienced foreign journalists into the RT's news culture.[47] The journalists I interviewed at TRT World did not necessarily bring up economic rewards but discussed the importance of gaining journalism experience and fulfilling a moral duty to fellow Muslims. This is how a foreign journalist that works at TRT World put it:

> [TRT World] is opening its doors to young Muslim journalists like me. It's giving me a chance to do important work. You know how Muslims are covered in the West. As terrorists or reactionary people. We are trying to correct it. We want to make sure Muslims are not seen as terrorists. Actually, it's the opposite. Muslims are the victims. Especially, in Europe and America. They are the victims of hate speech and violent attacks. I see it as my duty to tell this truth to our viewers.[48]

Although the number of journalists I interviewed at TRT World and *Daily Sabah* is limited (due to reasons discussed in the introduction), the above quotes nonetheless contextualize the AKP-backed outlets' coverage of Islamophobia. That is, TRT World and the *Daily Sabah* cover anti-Muslim hatred wherever it transpires, but that which occurs in the West gets further attention via op-eds, front-page news, special reports, awareness campaigns, and documentaries in line with the government's preferred narratives.

Islamophobia in Documentaries

In addition to news reports, TRT World also addresses Islamophobia via documentaries and in regard to different manifestations of anti-Muslim hatred. For example, *Muslims in Britain: Unheard Voices* (2019), *Another America: The First Muslims in America* (2019), and *The Last Prayer: Surviving Christchurch* (2019) all investigate anti-Muslim hatred in everyday life in Western contexts. *Muslims in Britain* recounts how British Muslims from all walks of life are seen as "outcasts" and "terrorists" and are pressured to "prove their humanity" on a daily basis. *Another America* sheds light on the intersection of religious and racial injustices in the United States, focusing on the marginalization and stereotyping of Black Muslims. *The Last Prayer* covers the aftermath of terrorist attack that killed fifty-one worshippers in New Zealand from the perspective of the Muslim community and their lived experiences of discrimination in New Zealand.

TRT World documentaries also examine other manifestations of Islamophobia, that is, military attacks and police violence against Muslims. *Unwanted: The Rohingya Exodus* (2017) tells the story of Rohingya Muslims fleeing the Myanmar military and Buddhist nationalists; *The Face of Hate: Anti-Muslim Violence in Sri Lanka* (2018) investigates hardline Buddhists' attacks against Muslims; and *Kashmir: Fault Lines in the Valley* (2019) offers a look at the physical and emotional toll of Hindu nationalists' persecution of Muslims.

Last but not least, TRT World documentaries bring attention to anti-Muslim hatred in the context of Europe's discriminatory migrant policies. One of the common frames that runs across these documentaries is concerned with Europe's alleged lack of humanity. *Beaten by the Border* (2019), *Transit* (2018), and *Hopes Denied: An Aegean Tragedy* (2021) all investigate European authorities' direct and indirect attacks against refugees and migrants, framing the attacks as a battle between compassion and inhumanity (Chapter 4 details these documentaries that focus on the refugee crisis).

Although the facts of marginalization, exclusion, and persecution of Muslims cannot be disputed, the discursive strategies used to mediate them are worthy of discussion. Through strategic obfuscation (as discussed in the introduction), these documentaries establish binary oppositions, such as the oppressed versus the oppressor, peace versus violence, compassion versus inhumanity, justice versus injustice. They offer a cursory description of the problem while ignoring the historical and structural conditions that have produced it. For example, *Kashmir, Unwanted*, and *The Face of Hate* tell us how many Muslims were killed, injured, and/or displaced in India, Myanmar, and Sri Lanka but fail to acknowledge the postcolonial histories and socioeconomic dynamics that fuel Islamophobia in these countries. Likewise, *Muslims in Britain* and *Another America* mention the racialization of Muslims but do not examine the moral panic about Islam in Europe and the United States that skyrocketed especially after September 11 and then again during the refugee crisis. *Beaten by the Border, Transit*, and *Hopes Denied* rightly criticize the EU's discriminatory border policies but ignore how right-wing, nationalist politicians and sensationalist mass media exploit nativist and anti-immigration views in Europe and thus worsen existing anti-Muslim sentiments. And because these documentaries frame Islamophobia as a battle between good and evil, they implicitly link the elimination of anti-Muslim hatred to the rise of a benevolent and just power.

Islamophobia in Reports, Conferences, and Awareness Campaigns

Other AKP-backed organs that pay a significant amount of attention to Islamophobia include SETA, TRT World Research Centre, and TRT World Citizen. For its part, SETA organizes webinars and roundtables on the topic in Washington, DC, Brussels, and other European capitals.[49] It covers Islamophobia in its monthly periodical *Insight Turkey* and in its digital publication *Politics Today*, both of which feature contributions from Turkish and foreign analysts on global affairs.[50] Since 2015 it has also published annual *European Islamophobia Reports* that investigate anti-Muslim racism in approximately thirty European countries across various fields, such as employment, education, politics, media, and legal systems. Funded by the EU and penned by foreign analysts (a sign of how SETA and the AKP deploy non-Turkish experts to lend legitimacy to their narratives), these reports document the "central figures in the [local] Islamophobia network" in each country and make policy recommendations to European governments.[51]

SETA's reports are symbolically important for the Erdoğan government for they are seen as examples of counter-hegemonic knowledge production. They are viewed as defiant rejoinders to Western governments and/or West-based organizations (e.g., Amnesty International, Human Rights Watch, Freedom

House) that publish annual reports about human rights violations, free speech issues, and other instances of democratic failures around the world. According to Turkish officials, Western actors calling out other countries' shortcomings while wilfully ignoring their own is a sign of their hypocrisy. The words of Mevlüt Çavuşoğlu, Turkey's former minister of foreign affairs (2014–23), are a clear illustration of this posture: "The European Union and the United States publish reports on Turkey and other countries, but from now on Turkey is produc[ing] its own reports on acts of Islamophobia and racism—for the good of humanity."[52]

Another entity that addresses anti-Muslim hatred in the West via reports, policy papers, and conferences is the TRT World Research Centre. The center makes sure to address Islamophobia at its flagship event, TRT World Forum, which brings together international policy makers, academics, civil-society leaders, and journalists in Istanbul on a yearly basis. Since the first forum it held in 2017, the center has made sure to devote at least one session to Islamophobia-related topics, such as the post-September 11 counterterrorism measures, rise of racist and far-right populist movements in the West, and Western media's negative portrayals of Muslims.[53]

Muslims' plight is also highlighted by TRT World Citizen, which aims to amplify the voices of those impacted by humanitarian crises around the world.[54] To this end, it creates social media content, hosts events, and organizes annual signature campaigns. TRT World Citizen's first campaign in 2017, Am I Not a Child? examined the sexual exploitation and trafficking of unaccompanied refugee children in Europe.[55] In 2018 the Women of War campaign focused on the suffering of women in Syria, Myanmar, Bosnia, Kashmir, and South Sudan—all of which are home to significant Muslim populations.[56] The 2019 campaign Hello Brother was inspired by the last words of a Muslim man killed in the mosque attack in Christchurch, New Zealand, and it invited audiences to rally against anti-Muslim violence and to share their "own stories of hope, unity and love" via short videos.[57] TRT World Citizen's 2020 campaign, Dignity without Borders, highlighted the human rights abuses suffered by Afghan, Syrian, Rohingya, and Kashmiri Muslim immigrants in Europe.[58]

Thus far, this chapter has discussed how AKP-directed entities report on and produce knowledge about anti-Muslim hatred and/or Muslim suffering. The following sections examine how these activities are complemented by those that point to Turkey as a viable actor that can ameliorate these injustices.

Turkey as the Advocate of Oppressed Muslims

Every year at his address to the UN General Assembly, Erdoğan brings up the allegedly most egregious feature of the global order, that is, the domination of the UN Security Council by only five countries and its lack of Muslim representation. And every year, he concludes his speech with his motto, "The world is bigger than five."[59]

The use of this motto on the international stage can be traced back to 2014 when a front organization for the AKP, known as Genç Siviller (Young Civilians) launched a promotional campaign on behalf of Erdoğan.[60] At an event held on the sidelines of the annual UN General Assembly, Genç Siviller announced that they had placed ads with the tagline "The world is bigger than five" in *Le Monde*, the *Guardian*, and the *Washington Post*, prominent newspapers in three member countries of the Security Council.[61] (*China Daily* and *Moscow Times*, however, had declined to publish the ad.) At the same event, Genç Siviller screened a music video produced to promote The World Is Bigger Than Five campaign. In the video, Black, Brown, and White actors in traditional clothing sing a soft rock tune and declare that they are not American, British, Chinese, French, or Russian (a reference to the five members of the Security Council):

> They will not force us
> They will not control us
> They will stop degrading us.[62]

A few years later, an English-language music video *The World Is Bigger Than Five* delivered a similar message of defiance, albeit in a more tearful tone. Conceived by an AKP parliamentarian, the video leaves uncovered no topic that is central to Erdoğan's message: the refugee crisis in Europe, wars in Syria and Iraq, oppression of Palestinians, and economic underdevelopment of Muslims. And it explicitly blames the UN for the suffering of Muslims:

> The world is blind
> The UN is deaf
> Five states decide on the world's state
> With one veto, the UN watches the oppressed.

These lyrics are accompanied by images of war-torn cities, refugees waiting behind fences, children in Africa receiving food aid, and a Palestinian teenager being blindfolded by Israeli police. When the lyrics point to Erdoğan as the savior of the oppressed peoples ("The world is bigger than five / The sun will rise over the night"), we see images of Turkish aid convoys in Africa, schools and hospitals built by TIKA, and Muslims praying at Al Aqsa Mosque in Jerusalem—all of which serve as references to Muslim salvation. Based on the tropes of oppression and salvation, the music video exemplifies Erdoğan's missionary politics and his government's description of Turkey as a benevolent Muslim power.

In addition to these campaigns and music videos, there are other English-language communicative activities inspired by Erdoğan's motto. On X (formerly Twitter), the Directorate of Communications, Ministry of Foreign Affairs, diplomatic corps, and rank-and-file AKP members use the hashtag #WorldIsBiggerThanFive to promote Turkey as a peace mediator, defender of human rights, and a great power that is pursuing justice on behalf of the oppressed peoples.[63] The hashtag #TheWorldIsBiggerThanFive was also used by Lindsay Lohan, the Hollywood actor, in 2017 when Bosphorus Global invited her to tour the refugee camps in Turkey and meet with Erdoğan and his wife at the presidential palace. Following her trip, Lohan posted pro-Turkey messages on Instagram and X.[64]

Bigger Than Five is the name of a global affairs program on TRT World that bills itself as one that "brings in-depth reporting to global justice issues ... in a rapidly changing world [where the] traditional influence of the five permanent members of the U.N. Security Council is being challenged by new emerging forces." Last but not least, it is the inspiration beneath *A Fairer World Is Possible: A Proposed Model for a United Nations Reform*, a book published in 2021 under Erdoğan's name.[65] The book describes Turkey's "quest for global justice" in the face of "the refugee crisis, international terrorism and Islamophobia," and makes calls for reforming the UN so that "injustice, discrimination and double standards" toward Muslims will be remedied.[66]

Coupled with the media coverage of and knowledge production about Islamophobia, the AKP government's global messaging rests on highlighting the plight of Muslims and portraying Turkey as a virtuous actor (indeed, the only one) that can undo the injustices Muslims suffer from. To assemble Muslim audiences based on shared grievances, especially those that originate from the West, Erdoğan and his communication emissaries resort to deploying victimhood tropes. What are the sociocultural underpinnings of the Erdoğan government's discourse of victimhood and injustice? How can one then make sense of their preoccupation with Muslim victimhood? These are the questions the following section addresses.

Muslim Victimhood and Erdoğan's Missionary Politics

Political leaders often use victimhood to gain sympathy from voters, consolidate their base, or legitimize their positions at home and abroad. They present themselves as victims of some form of wrongdoing (Donald Trump spreading false information about electoral fraud after the 2020 presidential elections), obfuscate unfavorable historical facts (Victor Orban representing Hungarians as helpless victims of Nazism and communism), or distort the truth to rationalize their foreign policy decisions (Vladimir Putin claiming that Russia is the victim of Ukrainian neo-Nazi groups). Aside from these manipulative tactics, politicians also tap into actual examples of how particular ethnic, racial, and religious groups have been marginalized so as to present themselves as the champion of those groups. Aside from political leaders, states that are engaged in nationalist rhetoric also turn to victimhood tropes to justify their actions.[67] Victimhood and trauma can also be used to legitimize exclusionary projects or military aggression toward the Other and to shore up popular support on the world stage.[68] Finally, ethnic, racial, and religious minorities mobilize experiences of suffering and collective trauma to bolster group identity, maintain self-understanding, and build solidarity networks.[69]

The Erdoğan regime directs attention to historical and contemporary manifestations of Islamophobia, especially those occurring in the West, and uses the plight of Muslims to portray Turkey as their advocate. But the deployment of Muslim victimhood in Turkish politics is not new or specific to the AKP. It has been used by various right-wing nationalist and Islamist actors since at least the early twentieth century.[70] As cultural studies scholar Özlem Savaş explains, nationalist Islamist thought in Turkey has for decades been permeated by the narrative of "undeserved suffering" that flows from "the religious mythology of Islam" and its parables of oppression and injustice.[71] Savaş shows how Turkish Islamist thinkers have generated a deep-rooted, expansive category of Muslim victimhood by combining "the suffering of Mohammed and the first Muslims" with the suffering experienced after the fall of the Ottoman Empire, the end of the caliphate, and the Turkish Republic's top-down Westernization program.[72]

Among the most ardent purveyors of the "Islamist victimology" in Turkey is Necip Fazıl Kısakürek, a revered figure among nationalist-Islamist circles in Turkey, not to mention Erdoğan and the AKP.[73] As political scientists Birol Başkan and Ömer Taşpınar note, Kısakürek "told and retold the personal hardships some religious figures experienced in the early years of the Republic," contributing to the formation of a narrative that views pious Muslims as victims relegated to the peripheries of political, economic, social, and cultural life by the Westernizing elite (more on Kısakürek in chapter 4).[74] Likewise, communications scholar Nagehan Tokdoğan emphasizes how the notion of Muslim victimhood in Turkish politics is interwoven with concepts of loss, persecution, and injustice, all of which constitute integral components of the AKP's populist politics.[75]

Since coming to power in 2002, the AKP has repeatedly framed itself and its supporters as victims in a never-ending conflict with the West. As discussed in detail in chapter 1, especially in response to the domestic and foreign policy failures and the recurring episodes of economic downturn since 2013, AKP cadres have "redefined or expanded the notion of the corrupt elite" to include international institutions, leaders of other countries, and foreign journalists.[76] Today, the Erdoğan government recounts various international actors from governments to journalists as threat sources against the survival of the Turkish nation-state and the Muslims it protects. Erdoğan's emissaries have extrapolated this anti-Western rhetoric to the international plane and now promote Erdoğan as "the voice of a deprived global Muslim community."[77]

Obviously, such religiously inflected narratives are calculated to accrue political power to Turkey on the world stage, but they are also epiphenomenal with Turkish Islamists' long-standing mission to end the persecution and humiliation of Muslims (think of the lyrics "They won't degrade us" in the AKP's music video discussed earlier). This form of politics, centered on "a moral community struggling [against] conspiratorial enemies, and engaged in a mission toward redemption and salvation," is what political scientist José Pedro Zúquete refers to as "missionary politics."[78] Missionary politics is driven by the idea of a crisis, which is both material and spiritual and "has existed for years and centuries, affects all areas of life, and has the potential to affect the survival of the community."[79] It is powered by an antagonism between the community and "sinister groups," a historical awareness of the "decisive struggle for survival," and the promise of salvation.[80] As political scientist Bilge Yabancı explains, in the domestic context of Turkey, the AKP's missionary politics imagines the survival of the nation and the people's justice and dignity to be under continuous threat, and promises to replace humiliation with recognition and respect.[81]

On the international plane, this missionary politics frames the world's Muslims as oppressed and victimized, alerts them to their survival being at stake, and promises to save them. This is why Turkey's communication outlets use Islamophobia (and other examples of Muslim suffering) to signal that the West is a threat source against Muslims worldwide and to present Erdoğan as a defiant Muslim leader that stands up to Western powers. As discussed in this chapter, AKP-backed entities communicate and produce knowledge about Islamophobia via news, documentaries, reports, conferences, and awareness campaigns. In doing so, they not only seek to inform international audiences about Islamophobia but, more importantly, to convince Muslims worldwide that Turkey is bringing attention to their suffering and thus advocating on their behalf. However, as discussed next, although the Erdoğan government projects itself as the champion of Muslims, its advocacy is selective and conditional depending on its geopolitical economic calculations.

Instrumentalization of Islamophobia

Islamophobia and, more broadly, political economic and sociocultural marginalization of Muslims are indeed genuine problems enmeshed with long-standing racial politics in Europe and the United States. Anti-Muslim hatred affects the well-being of hundreds of millions of Muslims around the world, not to mention the threats they pose to peace and security at regional, national, and global levels. As such, Islamophobia does warrant sustained and critical attention from media organizations. Of vital importance are reports and analyses that shed light on the connections between Islamophobia and far-right, White supremacist, racist, and/or ethnoreligious nationalist politics.

With that being stated, I maintain a critical stance toward the communication and knowledge production endeavors undertaken by AKP-backed entities in relation to Islamophobia and other instances of Muslim suffering. My critique arises from the observation that these entities obscure the intricate dynamics that underlie Islamophobia, simplifying them into dichotomies of Muslims versus the West, victims versus oppressors, and good versus evil. Through such strategic obfuscation, they promote the notion that Turkey alone possesses the capability to counteract Islamophobia, redress grievances faced by Muslims, and facilitate the triumph of good over evil. These political assertions, while implicit, essentially advocate for Turkey's rise to prominence and superiority over the West as the ultimate remedy to combat Islamophobia.

Second, Islamophobia-related communicative activities from AKP-directed entities are politically motivated and transactional, rather than principled. The AKP government selectively emphasizes instances of Islamophobia in particular countries, notably focusing on Western nations, while its advocacy for Muslims remains contingent. A pertinent illustration of this is Erdoğan's conspicuous reluctance to criticize China's persecution of Uighur Muslims, who share ethnic ties with Turks. Despite his previous labeling of China's policies as genocidal in 2009, Erdoğan has since maintained his silence regarding the plight of Uighur Muslims. Analysts attribute this shift in stance to the $3.6 billion loan provided by China to Turkey in 2018 during a period of considerable depreciation of the Turkish lira. Additionally, Turkish officials' aspirations to attract Chinese investors and tourists to the country further contribute to this change in Erdoğan's approach.[82] During a visit to Beijing in 2019 aimed at fostering economic cooperation, Erdoğan made remarks suggesting that the "Uighur issue" was being exploited by those that were "behaving emotionally" with the intention of undermining the bilateral relations between Turkey and China.[83] Erdoğan's tentative alignment with China has resulted in various challenges for Uighurs who have sought refuge in Turkey in recent times. This includes significant difficulties in obtaining residency permits for Uighurs residing in Turkey, as well as the looming threat of arrest and subsequent deportation to China for prominent Uighur activists.[84]

Another illustrative instance that underscores the contingent nature of the Erdoğan government's advocacy for Muslims pertains to the Palestinian cause, which occupies a significant position within Islamist politics in Turkey. Erdoğan does not hesitate to publicly condemn Israel for its policies, the most notable episode of which occurred at the World Economic Forum in Davos in 2009. During a panel discussion alongside then Israeli president Shimon Peres, Erdoğan openly criticized Israel's offensive actions in Gaza, remarking to Peres, "When it comes to killing, you know very well how to kill. I know well how you hit and kill children on beaches."[85] Subsequently, Erdoğan left the podium, vowing never to return to Davos. His remarks were hailed by his supporters in Turkey and certain parts of the Arab world as a symbol of his championing of the Palestinian cause. However, there are also instances when Erdoğan opts for silence or even extends gestures of goodwill toward Israel, driven by concerns over political and economic interests. Following the killing of Turkish aid volunteers by Israeli forces aboard the *Mavi Marmara* aid flotilla in 2010, diplomatic relations between Turkey and Israel remained stagnant until 2016. At that point, Erdoğan made the decision to rekindle relations and publicly announced that Turkey would not pursue legal action against Israeli soldiers for the killing of Turkey's citizens. A few years later, Erdoğan even voiced criticism toward the organizers of the aid campaign for not consulting with him beforehand.

Erdoğan's conditional advocacy of Muslims provides insights into the differential treatment exhibited by TRT World, the *Daily Sabah*, and SETA concerning Palestinians and Uighurs in comparison to Muslims residing in Europe. For example, TRT World reports on specific events, such as Israel's air strikes in Gaza and police violence at Al Aqsa mosque, along with pertinent political and diplomatic developments. However, it refrains from producing critical documentaries that scrutinize Israel's actions. Similarly, with regards to Uighur Muslims, AKP-affiliated entities avoid direct and critical coverage of the actions undertaken by Chinese authorities, instead choosing to report on the international condemnation of China by human rights organizations. SETA does not produce annual reports on China or Israel, and TRT World Citizen does not initiate awareness campaigns focused on the plight of the Uighurs or Palestinians.

Finally, the Erdoğan regime's self-representation as a champion of oppressed peoples warrants careful consideration for another reason. AKP-backed communication entities portray Turkey as a defender of human rights on the international stage, yet these narratives obscure the pervasive repression and marginalization experienced by various communities within Turkey, such as the Kurds, Alevis, and LGBTQ+ individuals. Regarding the Kurds, the AKP initially supported the Kurdish peace process but in 2015 abandoned this stance. Subsequently, it has employed disproportionate measures against Kurdish politicians and activists under the guise of antiterrorism laws, leading to their arrests, trials, and dismissals from public office. Protestors and civilians in predominantly Kurdish provinces have also been subject to excessive use of force by Turkish police and military, while Kurdish voices in media and civil society have been stifled under the pretext of national security. Similarly, Alevis, who adhere to a different branch of Islam than Turkey's Sunni majority, have faced repression for decades, compounded by their historical persecution under Ottoman rulers. Although the AKP has made overtures to the Alevis during election periods, the social exclusion of this community, consisting of approximately twenty million individuals, continues. Threats and attacks against their religious centers persist as manifestations of this marginalization.[86] The LGBTQ+ community also endures escalating harassment, violence, and discrimination in Erdoğan's Turkey. In 2014 riot police deployed tear gas and rubber bullets to disperse participants of the Pride March in Istanbul. Since then, the government has consistently denied permission for peaceful marches and targeted LGBTQ+ organizations and events. Inadequate legal protections and discrimination in employment, healthcare, and housing were already prevalent issues faced by LGBTQ+ individuals, which have been further exacerbated. Erdoğan, along with his political allies and supporters, now openly vilifies LGBTQ+ individuals. During his 2023 reelection campaign, Erdoğan referred to LGBTQ+ individuals as "a poison injected into the institution of the family," amplifying concerns within the community regarding their well-being.[87]

In sum, the Erdoğan government's portrayal of itself as a compassionate actor is problematic on multiple fronts. Its approach to Muslim advocacy is characterized by selectivity and transactionalism, lacking a consistent commitment to genuine support. Furthermore, the government deliberately obscures its own repressive actions at home. Communication entities supported by the AKP present Turkey as a benevolent power to international audiences, exploiting Islamophobia and in other instances Muslims' plight to enhance the country's profile. However, it is imperative not to lose sight of the fact that these entities effectively conceal the true nature of a repressive regime that systematically marginalizes diverse groups inside Turkey.

4

Discrediting the West

Civilizationist Paradigm and Negative Visions of Europe and the United States

In *The Well-Protected Domains: Ideology and the Legitimation of Power in the Ottoman Empire, 1876–1909*, historian Selim Deringil documents the Ottoman ruling elite's efforts to project an image of the empire as the only great Muslim power of its time and at the same time a member of the "club of civilized powers."[1] Deringil highlights an interesting instance where the perspectives of the Ottoman statesmen found their way into the local press, specifically disseminating negative portrayals of the West. A notable periodical, *Servet-i Fünun* (Wealth of Sciences) frequently published human interest stories from the West in order to expose the "degenerate and violent nature of the Western world." Within its pages, readers found vividly illustrated stories about "'cruelty to blacks in the United States,' 'a tram robbery in the middle of Paris,' and 'appalling living conditions of Chinese coolies in San Francisco.'"[2]

Human-interest stories were not all that *Servet-i Fünun* published. The magazine also covered political developments of the period, such as the Balkan Wars (1912–13), which brought an end to the Ottoman rule in the region. Along with other notable publications, *Servet-i Fünun* paid extensive attention to the suffering of the local Muslim population in the Balkans. As historian Doğan Çetinkaya shows, the Ottoman press covered the atrocities Bulgarian, Greek, Serbian, and Macedonian soldiers committed against Muslims, sometimes in shocking detail. They published stories about Muslim girls being raped, Muslim men being arrested, and religious practices being banned by Christian soldiers, describing these attacks as "shameless, nasty, rude, and vulgar."[3] This coverage was aligned with the activities of Ottoman statesmen and nationalist civic associations that sought to persuade domestic and foreign public opinion that the empire was fighting for the welfare of Muslims.[4]

Looking ahead about a century, one can observe a parallel where Erdoğan, AKP officials, and loyalist media engage in similar criticisms of Turkey's Western adversaries. During the peak of the refugee crisis in 2015 and 2016, Erdoğan called European leaders shameless and immoral for not fulfilling their humanitarian obligations.[5] Pro-government newspapers questioned whether the Western civilization could still be upheld as a model for the rest of the world, given what they saw as Europe's barbaric treatment of refugees. In the aftermath of the Brexit campaign and Trump's election in 2016, the AKP's global communication apparatus capitalized on the sense of malaise that permeated European and American politics. They covered the challenges afflicting the Western liberal democratic order (e.g., racism, far-right extremism, income inequality) while also strategically reminding audiences of the historical transgressions committed by the West (e.g., colonialism, Nazism, the Holocaust) thus interrogating the perceived superiority of the West.

In light of these negative constructions of the West, several crucial questions arise: What are the underlying dynamics, both foreign and domestic, that drive Erdoğan's communication emissaries to disseminate such images? What are the historical legacies and religiocultural factors that contribute to morally inflected criticisms of the West? Additionally, how do these attempts to discredit the West align with Turkish Islamist thinkers' civilizationist paradigm, and can one evaluate them as genuine humanist critiques of the West?

To address these questions, this chapter begins with a discussion of how the Erdoğan government's relations with the West guided the country's international messaging in the early to mid-2010s. Focusing on the coverage of the refugee crisis, the chapter shows how TRT World's and the *Daily Sabah*'s outputs have been influenced by Erdoğan's moral framework, portraying Europe as shameful and inhumane. Next discussed is how and why AKP-backed entities have directed attention to certain developments that transpired in Europe and the United States in the post-2016 era, such as racial justice protests and the rise of far-right movements. Finally, the chapter discusses Turkey's attempts to discredit the West in the context of civilizationist paradigm and points to the importance of religiocultural elements and historical legacies in the construction of Occidentalist narratives.[6]

Foreign Policy Developments and Media Attention toward the West

In the early 2010s the AKP government took bold steps in international affairs, buoyed up by its institutional hegemony in domestic politics, the country's economic growth, and Western policymakers' endorsement of Turkey as a model for emerging democracies in Middle East and North Africa.[7] It strengthened Turkey's political economic ties with Muslim-majority countries in Africa, Central Asia, and the Balkans and burnished the country's image as a leading humanitarian actor.[8] According to İbrahim Kalın, foreign policy adviser to Erdoğan at the time, these developments were signs of Turkey's "growing soft power" and "rising international profile in foreign policy, healthcare, technology, art, and humanitarian assistance."[9] Kalın lamented that despite its achievements, Turkey was still "misunderstood in the international environment. Some think of it as a backward Middle Eastern country, and others think that it blindly imitates the West and has no identity or roots of its own." He added that he would assume the directorship of the newly established Office of Public Diplomacy (OPD), which would specifically tackle this issue and "tell Turkey's new story—a story that is dynamic, multi-faceted and exciting."[10]

Unfortunately, this "new story" encountered significant challenges as a result of interconnected domestic and regional upheavals that transpired during the early to mid-2010s. Erdogan's crackdown on Gezi protestors in 2013 and his subsequent consolidation of political power transformed Turkey's image from that of a model country to one perceived as veering toward authoritarianism. As European and American policymakers voiced concerns about the state of Turkish democracy, Erdoğan's response grew increasingly confrontational. Amidst the Gezi protests and faced with criticisms of his government, Erdoğan proclaimed, with evident exasperation, "Turkey is much freer than almost all of the E.U. member countries." By highlighting instances of demonstrations occurring in Europe, he redirected the attention toward his critics:

> Now you're talking about the Gezi Park incidents. Why do you ignore the incidents that took place in Frankfurt, Germany? Just recently, incidents took place in Hamburg. Why don't you see the incidents in Hamburg? You have seen what the police have done there. In France, I see Roma people being chased away and deported. Is this democracy? I see that there is no respect for personal freedom of belief in France at the moment.[11]

Around the same time as Gezi protests, another significant development unfolded with the Egyptian military's removal of the Muslim Brotherhood government from power. Erdoğan seized the opportunity to castigate Western governments, asserting that European and American leaders failed to promptly denounce the event as a coup: "I am surprised by the West. They cannot even say this was a coup. What happened to their democratic ideals?"[12] And he queried the whereabouts of Western leaders who advocate for the adherence to democratic principles in other nations: "Where are those who go around giving lessons in democracy?"[13]

The following year, Erdogan's dissatisfaction with the West escalated upon the United States' decision to extend support to the Kurdish YPG in their combat against ISIS. This sentiment intensified in 2016 when European and American officials criticized Turkey for implementing stringent security measures following the failed coup attempt (see chapter 1). Within the AKP ranks and among right-wing nationalist voters, there was widespread belief that the United States was actively involved in facilitating the establishment of a Kurdish mini-state along the Turkey-Syria border. Drawing from the Muslim Brotherhood's experience, it was also speculated that had the coup plotters succeeded in Turkey and removed Erdoğan from power, Western governments would not have objected at all. AKP officials made efforts to convince their Western counterparts that both the YPG and the Gülenists are terrorist organizations posing significant threats to Turkey's security, but their attempts proved futile. Expressing his disillusionment, Erdogan lamented, "The Western world does not understand us, and they never will. We are aware of this. They have not been honest with us."[14]

As Erdoğan adopted an increasingly anti-Western discourse, the sense of frustration among Turkish diplomatic corps was becoming palpable. As a former state official, who served at the Ministry of Foreign Affairs during that period, told me:

> They were tired of not being able to convince Brussels and Washington, DC, about Turkey's position. They knew that Obama was not going to end America's partnership with the YPG. And they knew that [America] was never going to extradite Gülen. Europeans saw Erdoğan as an autocrat and that wasn't going to change. This was the sentiment among a lot of folks in the Ministry. [They were thinking,] "We explain [Turkey's] position over and over, but they [Europe and the United States] don't even listen to us."[15]

Officials engaged in public diplomacy and international communication work were also experiencing a sense of resignation. As conveyed by a current official serving at the Ministry of Foreign Affairs:

> Especially after [the coup attempt], a lot of people thought, "We couldn't explain ourselves to the West. We couldn't explain our stance [regarding Gülen]." But they still continued to hope or they wanted to believe that, "If we do a better job, then the West will understand us. They will support us." If you ask me, our president [Erdoğan] knew very well that the problem wasn't about us. He knew that it wasn't going to make a difference in the West. No matter what we did. No matter how well we used diplomacy. I think he was very clear about this. That it's not our fault. The West just doesn't listen. They don't want to listen. They have a specific mindset about Turkey. It's not going to change.[16]

While the AKP government was mired in the aforementioned domestic and regional quandaries, trying to tackle the communication crises they triggered, drastic transformations were taking place at the international level. As political scientists Mustafa Kutlay and Ziya Öniş note, China and Russia were growing their political, economic, and/or military presence around the world, coinciding with the perceived decline of Euro-American hegemony in international affairs. The West-led global order was seemingly eroding as result of the continuing repercussions of the 2008 financial crisis, Brexit and uncertainties surrounding the future of the European Union, election of Trump and the United States' subsequent withdrawal from its commitments to liberal democracy, and the resurgence of ethnonationalist movements on both sides of the Atlantic Ocean. Together, these developments presented "Turkey and other countries in the Global South with new possibilities to assert themselves more proactively" on the world stage.[17] For the AKP cadres, the potential emergence of a post-Western world order was an opportunity to be exploited. According to one of my interviewees who used to work at the Office of Public Diplomacy:

> Europe was still trying to recover from the financial crisis, then there was Brexit. There were a lot of questions about the EU's future, the economy, the politics. Mainstream parties were threatened by extreme, right-wing politicians everywhere. In Italy, Hungary, Austria. Then there was Trump. People could not believe how Americans could elect this man as president. What was wrong with American people? What happened to American democracy? These events in the Western world were a great opportunity for Erdoğan. [His advisers] argued they could now turn the table and say [to the West]: "You have been telling us to protect democracy, but look at yourselves. Look what's happening to your democracies." I can say there was a great sense of vindication amongst them [*laughs*].[18]

How then did the Erdoğan government's communication instruments report on various crises unfolding in the West? To address this question, the following section examines the coverage of the refugee crisis as a case study, since this particular development in Europe has been central to Turkey's self-representation as morally superior to the West.

The Refugee Crisis and Its Centrality to Turkey's Self-Image

The influx of refugees fleeing ethnic and military conflicts in the Middle East, Africa, and Southeast Asia and seeking refuge in Europe began in 2014 and escalated to unparalleled levels by 2015. Between 2015 and 2016 an estimated one million refugees embarked on a perilous journey to Europe. Turkey's active involvement in the refugee crisis arose from its geographic position bridging Europe and the Middle East. Turkey served as a starting point for hundreds of thousands of Syrians, Iraqis, and Afghans who sought to continue their journey to Greece through the Aegean Sea or via land routes to the Balkans.

In 2016 Turkey's involvement acquired a political dimension when the AKP government entered into an agreement with the European Union aimed at curbing the flow of refugees.[19] According to this agreement, commonly known as "the migrant deal," Turkey would prevent refugees from crossing into EU territory and take back those who had already done so.[20] As part of the agreement, the European Union committed to the reciprocal resettlement of Syrian refugees from Turkey on a one-to-one basis. Additionally, there was a pledge to ease visa restrictions for Turkish citizens and to revive Turkey's EU accession process.[21] In addition, the European Union promised to provide financial aid to Turkey to defray its refugee-related expenses in health, education, and humanitarian assistance.[22] After the signing of the agreement, the number of refugees arriving in Greece dropped from approximately eight hundred thousand to thirty thousand. Since then, the European Union has committed six billion euros (approximately US$6.4 billion) to Turkey for humanitarian assistance, infrastructure improvement, education, and health services.[23]

At the time the agreement was signed, Turkey had already established itself as the largest host of refugees worldwide, with 2.5 million Syrians residing within its borders. This was a result of the AKP government's open-door policy in the early phases of the Syrian civil war, operating under the belief that the Assad regime would swiftly be overthrown, and refugees would eventually be repatriated. At the time AKP officials and pro-government media depicted Syrian refugees as "our Muslim brothers in need" and Turkey as a safe haven for victims of war. Pro-government newspapers painted a positive picture of inclusion and cultural exchange and asserted that Turkey, a "merciful and mighty" nation, was protecting its "victimized guests" from harm.[24]

Today, Turkey is host to around 3.6 million Syrian refugees, constituting a significant portion of the local population in southeastern provinces while also being concentrated in inner-city districts of Istanbul and Ankara. Many of the Syrians residing in Turkey contribute to the local economy through employment, whether formally or informally, and some even operate small businesses.[25] The initial warm reception they received has faded away over the years. Cultural conflicts, working-class rivalries, and Turks' misconceptions regarding government support for Syrians have contributed to violent tensions in certain provinces, leading to acts of vandalism targeting Syrian homes and businesses.[26] As public opinion polls reveal, there are notable levels of racism and xenophobia toward Syrians. According to a poll, conducted in Istanbul, which is host to the highest number of refugees in Turkey, 64 percent considered Syrians to be a source of burden for the country.[27] Another survey, also conducted in Istanbul, found that 49 percent of the city's residents believed Syrians belong to an inferior race, while 36 percent expressed doubts regarding Syrians being victims of war.[28]

Despite these tensions, the AKP government persists in its benevolent rhetoric claiming that it aims to "embrace" Syrian refugees as opposed to "kicking them out" of the country.[29] During the general election of 2023, opposition parties pledged to repatriate Syrian refugees and hardened their nationalist rhetoric, and Erdoğan, too, voiced his intent to start talks with the Assad regime and resettle Syrian refugees voluntarily.[30]

Shaming Europe

Since the beginning of the refugee crisis, the AKP's global communication instruments have strategically ignored the tensions between Turks and Syrians and, instead, emphasized the government's humanitarian efforts highlighting the favorable living conditions in refugee camps, as well as the educational and vocational programs offered to Syrians. This positive coverage is reinforced by reports, policy papers, and panel discussions undertaken by TRT World Research Centre, TRT World Forum, and SETA, all of which echo the government's narrative of Turkey as an exemplar of humanitarianism.[31] As discussed below, this international messaging regarding the refugee crisis is not simply centered on Turkey but also on Europe.

To rationalize their policies, interests, and values on the world stage, all governments and states use strategic narratives that are based on the country's role in the international order.[32] Inasmuch as these narratives are used to shape the preferred identity of the country in question ("who we are"), they also seek to influence of the perception of rival countries and their identities ("who they are").[33] This section examines the strategic narratives spread by Turkey's global communication instruments about Europe and who Europe is. The findings presented here are based on textual analyses of documentaries and discussion programs on TRT World and on opinion pieces in the *Daily Sabah*, and come from representative examples. I chose these documentaries, discussion programs, and op-eds instead of plain news coverage because these types of content go beyond the mere reporting of factual information; they draw upon a combination of information, commentary, and opinion and thus offer insights into the Erdoğan government's narratives.[34]

To begin, it is crucial to acknowledge that there are undeniable realities that form the basis of the negative portrayals of Europe. Many European countries have indeed failed in their institutional and humanitarian responses toward refugees. As an example, over three thousand refugees have tragically lost their lives during perilous crossings across the Mediterranean and Aegean Seas, with tens of thousands of others enduring difficult conditions in camps and makeshift settlements in Italy, Greece, and France.[35] My intention in this section is not to ignore these facts but to demonstrate how the AKP's communication tools have effectively utilized them to denounce Europe based on its moral values while asserting Turkey's perceived superiority.

Moral frames are used by all politicians to shape public perception of certain issues and to present them as "matters of right and wrong."[36] This approach often involves employing binary and "uncompromising" reasoning, leaving "little room for alternative perspectives." As such, it evokes strong emotions among audiences, diminishes tolerance for disagreement, and contributes to heightened political polarization.[37] Whenever Erdoğan addresses the refugee crisis, he consistently categorizes European governments and institutions as immoral while positioning Turkey as a virtuous actor that "opens its heart and doors" to refugees.[38] Erdogan's narratives, as discussed in chapter 3, cascade down to editors, producers, writers, journalists, and researchers working at various AKP-sponsored communication outlets. For example, during the height of the refugee crisis, the *Daily Sabah* opinion writers mimicked Erdoğan and compared Turkey's benevolence to Europe's lack of humanity.[39] For example, when the lifeless body of Alan Kurdi, a three-year-old Syrian boy was found on a beach in Turkey after a fatal journey across the Aegean Sea, a *Daily Sabah* op-ed piece announced, "Europe failed the humanity test."

The piece was written by İlnur Çevik, a veteran journalist and one of Erdogan's advisers. Çevik said: "[Refugees] are drowning in the Aegean, they face hell on the Greek islands, and those who manage to make their way to the Balkans encounter racial animosity from Serbian hordes." In comparing these responses from European nations, Çevik continued:

> Turkey has set up excellent camps for the Syrians near the border and allowed more of them in to stay in cities all across the country. Today Turkey hosts about 2 million Syrians, which is a record for any country in the world that faces a similar situation. Turkey has spent $6.5 billion in taxpayers' money for these people who are living in relatively decent conditions. Many international organizations and governments have acknowledged the incredible sacrifices Turkey has made for these people.[40]

A similar comparison was drawn by Melih Altinok, another prominent opinion writer for the *Daily Sabah*, who emphasized the hypocritical and self-centered attitudes of European governments. Altinok posed a rhetorical question, asking who the "real barbarians" were, the East or the West:

> Welcoming these helpless civilians [Syrian refugees] without hesitation, [Turkey] has spent nearly $4 billion so far. . . . So, how does the West, which accuses Middle Eastern countries of being barbaric and claims to [own the notions of] social harmony, modernity and human rights, exhibit its difference? [They boast] the signatures they have under the Universal Declaration of Human Rights, [but] European countries and the U.S. did not even open their borders for 4,000 or 5,000 of these refugees. They are trying to choose engineers or doctors from the [pool of] refugees [that apply for asylum]. In other words, even at such a hard time for humanity, the West still pursues its own interests and tries to benefit from the helpless people instead of providing assistance. We call such opportunism "[grave] robbery" in the Middle East.[41]

While these and other op-eds in the *Daily Sabah* resonated with Erdogan's moral framework in such strong terms, similar negative perspectives could also be observed on TRT World, albeit in a more subdued manner. This is primarily because op-eds in the *Daily Sabah* are translated versions of articles initially published in the *Sabah*, which are crafted with a deliberate inflammatory tone to mobilize Turkish readers. But even when the *Daily Sabah*'s editorial team pens original pieces for foreign readers, they do not shy away from using the same caustic language. During an interview, one of my sources, who previously worked as a reporter at the *Daily Sabah*, shed light on why the publication is comfortable employing such "angry" rhetoric:

> Writers and editors usually don't care if their messages come across as angry. I mean, they don't care if they are turning away the foreign readers with their angry tone. Actually, they *want* to write in this angry tone. So they can prove to the owner of the paper that they are doing their job, which is carrying Turkey's message to the world. And they can also show the readers, the foreigners, and the expats that this is the New Turkey, and it will not sit and wait quietly. It will not be lectured by Europe. As Erdoğan always says, it will give the Western world the answer it deserves.[42]

In contrast to the *Daily Sabah*, TRT World produces original programs specifically tailored for international audiences, without repackaging any Turkish-language content from TRT. Furthermore, it consciously avoids utilizing provocative content and style, aiming to present itself as a public service broadcaster that operates independently from the AKP government. However, similar to other state-run news organizations, TRT World strategically selects and emphasizes specific events, narratives, and values in line with the priorities of its sponsor. As demonstrated below, its current-affairs programs and documentaries align closely with the Erdoğan government's moral framework, albeit in a more restrained manner compared to the *Daily Sabah*.

During the refugee crisis, TRT World's flagship current affairs and discussion programs, namely, *The Newsmakers* and *Roundtable*, directed their focus toward European countries' contentious actions. They extensively covered topics such as police brutality at the refugee camp in Calais, France; physical assaults by Croatian border guards against refugees; missing refugee children across Europe; and other topics related to the refugee crisis.[43] In an effort to project editorial independence, *The Newsmakers* and *Roundtable* invited foreign guests instead of relying solely on government-approved Turkish voices. Yet, they still adopted the government's approach of criticizing European countries as being shameless, immoral, inhumane, and calculating. This inclination was apparent in the titles of episodes and opening statements, where the hosts referenced Europe's disregard for human rights and raised questions about its approach to the refugee crisis. For instance, in "Did Europe Turn Its Back on Syria?" an episode of *Roundtable*, the host rhetorically questioned if Europe was "immune to shame."[44] In an episode of *The Newsmakers*, titled "What's a Refugee's Worth in the EU?" it was suggested that Europeans were being strategic and motivated by self-interest. The episode covered the European Union's plans to provide financial support to non-EU countries with the expectation that they would manage the refugee problem on behalf of the union.[45]

TRT World also covered the refugee crisis in its documentaries, invoking similar moral frames centered around humanity, compassion, and shame. For instance, the documentary *Beaten by the Border* (2019) explores the plight of refugees who experienced physical assault and had their belongings confiscated by Croatian border guards. It contrasts Croatian authorities' "inhumanity" with Bosnian villagers' compassion (for they provide food and shelter to refugees) and ultimately brands the Croatian border "Europe's border of shame" where "European values of freedom, human rights and dignity are too often ignored."[46]

Morally framed comparisons are more prominently highlighted in other documentaries, namely, *Transit* (2018) and *Hopes Denied: An Aegean Tragedy* (2021). *Transit* commences with interviews with smugglers and refugees in the Turkish port city of İzmir, following the refugees' journey to Lesvos, Greece. It depicts the unsanitary and inhumane living conditions at this refugee camp in Greece while featuring firsthand accounts from refugees: "This camp is not for people. This camp is for the animals"; "Where is the humanity? Where is the peace that Europe talks about? Europe has to be ashamed of that'" and

"We fought to death and came here to at least experience some humanity. Is this the value of humans?"

On the other hand, *Hopes Denied* begins with real-time footage of a rescue operation conducted by the Turkish Coast Guard in the Aegean Sea, followed by interviews with refugees that were just rescued from the water, visibly shivering:

> They don't know what humanity is. They don't treat us like humans. There were twenty-eight of us on the journey. We all got off the boat and ran. They said we would be taken to camps. They, instead, brought us back to shore and started beating us. Then they put us on another boat and checked our pockets for money and phones. They beat us and pushed the raft out into the sea.

The documentary then sheds light on who "they" are: Greek officers who violated international laws by forcibly pushing back over nine thousand refugees into the sea in 2019 alone. Subsequent interviews with refugees are interspersed with visuals of the Turkish Coast Guard conducting rescue operations, providing food, and administering medical checkups to the refugees. When the documentary proceeds to show piles of trash and ramshackle tents in the refugee camp in Lesvos, Greece, the contrast between the two countries is made clear: one that cares and saves lives, and the other that doesn't. In the closing scene, a refugee shares his testimony, "We were supposed to go to Europe where human dignity is respected. They said we could seek refuge there. We are dismayed. There's none of that."

Capitalizing on the Western Malaise

Thus far, analysis has centered on the morally inflected narratives used by the *Daily Sabah* and TRT World concerning European countries' response to the refugee crisis. Aside from this coverage, AKP-supported entities have also focused on other critical developments that transpired in Europe and the United States in order to portray them in a negative light. Among these developments are the resurgence of far-right extremism, anti-Muslim hate attacks, racial justice protests, and socioeconomic inequality in Europe and the United States. Serdar Karagöz, the former editor in chief of TRT's international channels and the current director general of Anadolu Agency, explained the rationale behind this approach: "Western media always broadcasts tragedies that take place in the East. TRT World instead focus[es] on problems, tragedies, and dilemmas of the West. It [aims to] reverse Western media's gaze that has been trained on the East."[47]

Karagöz reiterated a similar perspective when describing the editorial policy of TRT Deutsch, the German-language digital news platform that was launched in January 2020. He asserted that German media outlets fail to cover Germany's political, economic, and social problems in a critical manner and positioned TRT Deutsch as an outlet that would reveal "the far-right [movements], Islamophobia, income inequality, and half-finished infrastructure projects" that plagued Germany.[48]

TRT World's programs focusing on the United States exhibit similar approaches. For instance, *Inside America with Ghida Fakhry*, a political talk show aired weekly from TRT World's studios in Washington, DC, purports to "uncover some of the *underreported* stories across the United States," such as gun ownership, racial injustice, domestic terrorism, deteriorating infrastructure, and foreign policy shortcomings (emphasis added).[49] Although these topics are indeed covered extensively and critically by American and international news media, *Inside America* claims to bring a new critical approach to analyzing American politics, economy, and foreign policy. From time to time, the program includes appearances by intellectuals and political figures known for their sharp criticism of the United States, such as Noam Chomsky, Cornel West, Ilhan Omar, and Seymour Hirsh, among others.

TRT World offers additional programs exclusively dedicated to the United States, namely, *My America* and *The Crossroads,* both of which are online video series aimed at providing insights into American society. *My America* embarks on a journey across the United States to explore "the social, cultural and political stories that often go *unnoticed* by the mainstream media" (emphasis added).[50] In each approximately fifteen-minute episode, it covers such topics as White supremacy, anarchist militia groups, systemic racism, and gun violence, which, indeed, receive considerable coverage from American news organizations. On the other hand, *The Crossroads* delves into identity, religion, culture, and race within the American context. Episodes, each spanning twelve to fifteen minutes, explore topics including anti-Asian hate, Ukrainian immigrants, Muslim communities, and homelessness in the United States. Aside from these programs, TRT World has also produced several documentaries shedding light on various issues afflicting American society, such as gun violence (*The U.S. and Their Guns: An American Story, Gunning for Change*), racism (*The Color of Justice, The Price of Protest, Deadly Racial Disparity, Black and Blue: Policing the Police*), migration (*Undocumented in America*), and social divisions (*America Divided*).[51]

Although the aforementioned programs do not overtly endorse a moral framework or explicitly denounce the United States as morally degenerate, their purpose resides in drawing attention to the internal predicaments of the country and accentuating its myriad challenges and perhaps even signaling its decline. Returning to Karagöz's comments about TRT World's role in the international media landscape and the state officials' remarks about American democracy discussed earlier, these programs serve as instruments through which Turkey can redirect attention away from itself and toward its adversaries in the West.

An illustrative instance of this can also be seen in the efforts of Bosphorus Global, the pro-Erdoğan entity, which aims to expose the "inner political contradictions" and "hypocrisies" of the West.[52] To this end Bosphorus Global operates two English-language websites, Chronicles of Shame and Crackdown Chronicles, accompanied by their respective X accounts. These websites present themselves as repositories documenting human rights violations, racism, and discrimination in the United States and European countries.

The home page of Chronicles of Shame features an interactive world map with blinking red dots, indicating instances of human rights violations, racism, and discrimination in various countries (except Turkey, of course).[53] Clicking on a country on the map directs users to a dedicated page containing dozens of news articles on Islamophobic incidents, mistreatment of refugees, racist attacks, sexual harassment, and domestic violence. Although Chronicles of Shame does not exclusively focus on the West, the number of news articles from Europe and the United States significantly outweighs those from non-Western nations. It is also worth noting that Chronicles of Shame does not conduct independent research but, rather, shares articles published by international news media, particularly West-based outlets, without proper referencing. The irony lies in the fact that the website plagiarizes from the very same Western media organizations that its sponsor, the Erdoğan government, accuses of exhibiting biased coverage toward Turkey.

Bosphorus Global's other website, Crackdown Chronicles, exclusively concentrates on the West, with the intention of exposing various dysfunctions within Western democracies. On the website, users are provided with a drop-down menu where they can select a country (for example, "European countries," "the United States," "Israel," "Australia") to gain insight into how they "monitor and censor the media, respond to protests with police violence, arbitrarily designate [individuals] as terror suspects under extensive terror laws, and [violate] their rights." Alternatively, users can explore various topics, including "crackdown on media," "police violence," "crackdown on academics," "anti-terror policies," and "defamation laws."[54] It is noteworthy that these topics correspond directly to those areas for which the AKP government regularly faces criticism from Western governments and human rights organizations.

While these websites copy and paste news articles from international news media, their social media accounts on X (@ShameChronicles and @CrackdownReport) provide additional commentary, often infused with sarcasm. For instance, a news story regarding the FBI's surveillance of Muslims is accompanied by the caption, "Illegal surveillance from the USA, land of freedom"; a video depicting Canadian police beating protestors is accompanied by the comment, "Democracy, human rights, civilization. All in Canada!"; and an article addressing anti-Black racism in Switzerland is accompanied by the remark, "One of the 'most livable' countries in the world!"[55]

Obviously, events in Europe and the United States, be they domestic or foreign policy related, carry implications that resonate worldwide, prompting thorough coverage by all international news organizations. And since Turkey has decades-long political, economic, trade, and defense ties with Europe and the United States, it is expected that Turkish media outlets cover major developments in these countries in detail. As noted at the beginning of this chapter, the challenges that threaten Western liberal democracies have become prime opportunities for Erdoğan's communication emissaries to deflect attention from Turkey's own democratic backsliding and contentious foreign policy decisions. The developments in Europe and the United States have also provided ample material to scrutinize the dominant position of the West in the global order and portray it as an ailing hegemonic power. Racism, xenophobia, Islamophobia, political polarization, social justice issues, and labor protests in Europe and the United States are not only topics to be covered in news reports; they are also the vehicles that the AKP cadres use to signal the decline of Western hegemony. Across a wide range of communicative practices, from official statements to news and commentary, AKP officials and their proxies assert that the West doesn't live up to its own democratic ideals, Western civilization is deeply flawed, and emerging powers, such as Turkey, present alternative models in political and moral leadership.

As part of this strategic approach, the Erdoğan government consistently reminds Western powers about the atrocities they committed throughout history, including but not limited to colonialism, slavery, Nazism, the Holocaust, and the Srebrenica massacre. It emphasizes that Turkish history remains untarnished by such stains, thus asserting Turkey's superiority to the West. For example, in 2019, when Italy and France publicly acknowledged the Armenian Genocide, then minister of foreign affairs Mevlüt Çavuşoğlu not only denied the genocide but also resorted to whataboutism: "We are proud of our history. [Turkish] history has never had any genocides. And no colonialism exists in our history. France is the last country which can lecture Turkey on genocide and history. France should mind its own dark history in Rwanda and Algeria."[56]

Likewise, on the Armenian Genocide Remembrance Day in 2022, İbrahim Kalın posted the following tweet about the long list of crimes committed by Western powers: "Oh you modern barbarians who led millions [of people] to their death, started world wars, produced weapons of mass destruction, dropped the atom bomb, traded slaves. Our history is free from genocides, ethnic cleansing and the Holocaust. Look at yourselves in the mirror."[57]

AKP officials also employ Nazism and the Holocaust as a means to shame Europe. A notable example of this tactic took place during a diplomatic crisis that unfolded in 2017, involving Turkey, Germany, and the Netherlands. Two ministers from the AKP government were on their way to attend rallies in Europe to garner support from the Turkish diaspora for the approaching constitutional referendum in Turkey. When Dutch and German authorities canceled the rallies for security reasons and blocked the ministers, Erdoğan called them "Nazi remnants and fascists" because they had allegedly violated free speech rights of the Turkish government and the Turks.[58] The following day, the *Daily Sabah*'s editorial team echoed the same refrain in a piece titled "Fascism Consuming Europe":

> The Netherlands appears to be going through a sort of mass psychosis. It is disconcerting to witness a full-blown Nazi revival across the continent. What's even worse is the total silence that has descended on the capitals of Europe at a time when one country after another is surrendering to fascistic forces.... The mainstream politicians in Germany and the Netherlands are trying to appease the rising racist tendencies among their population, once again adopting anti-Turkish rhetoric and acts to placate the extremist forces.[59]

Likewise, when the French president Emmanuel Macron proposed a plan to fight "Islamic radicalism" in 2020, Erdoğan once again mentioned Europe's "crimes against humanity" and compared not just France but all of Europe to the Nazis:

> Relocations, inquisitions and genocides toward members of different religions is not a practice that is foreign to Europe. The crimes against humanity committed against Jews 80 years ago, the acts against our Bosnian siblings in Srebrenica just 25 years ago, are still in the memory. You are in a real sense fascists. You are in a real sense the links in the chain of Nazism.[60]

This wasn't the first time Erdoğan referenced the Srebrenica massacre of 1995 to strike back at European governments. During the aforementioned diplomatic crisis with Germany and the Netherlands, he brought up the role of the Dutch peacekeeping forces and said: "We know the Netherlands and the

Dutch from the Srebrenica massacre. We know how rotten their character is from their massacre of 8,000 Bosnians there."[61] TRT World, the *Daily Sabah*, and SETA commemorate the Srebrenica massacre annually through special programming, reports, and extensive coverage. TRT World has produced several documentaries shedding light on the Bosnian war and the atrocities committed against Bosnian Muslims by the Serbian army, including titles such as *Justice Denied*, *Srebrenica: Unwinding Memories*, and *Undeniable*. Additionally, TRT has collaborated in the production of the acclaimed film *Quo Vadis, Aida?* which focuses on the Srebrenica massacre. The Bosnian war and its aftermath are also depicted in the television series *Dayton*, available on TRT's streaming platform, Tabii.

How do AKP's global communication entities capitalize on systemic racism, socioeconomic inequality, anti-immigrant, and far-right movements in the West and align with the strategies Chinese and Russian state media outlets employ? Both China and Russia strategically use instances of political, economic, and social crises in the Euro-American bloc to "affirm, contest and reshape" perceptions of Western power, hegemony, and global leadership.[62] For instance, Russia utilizes its state-supported international media outlets and the social media posts of its governing elites to disseminate disparaging narratives concerning the US-led global order. Using both legacy and digital media, it conveys a message of the breakdown of democratic institutions, particularly within the Euro-Atlantic bloc, while portraying itself as a resurgent great power.[63] For example, the state-owned RT television network, in its reporting on the 2020 US presidential election, fostered doubt regarding American democracy by magnifying narratives surrounding civil unrest, cultural divisions, and allegations of electoral fraud.[64] Sputnik, the state-run news agency, in its coverage of the Black Lives Matter (BLM) protests, portrayed American society as one that is beset by chaos and social divisions.[65] RT's Arabic service, which caters to viewers in the Middle East, also seized the opportunity the BLM protests presented to depict the United States as an unstable nation on the verge of civil war.[66] Similarly, China's English-language newspaper *Global Times* and official news agency Xinhua took advantage of the BLM protests to highlight systemic racial and economic disparities in the United States, portraying Americans as "brewing in rage."[67] Chinese state officials even trolled their American counterparts on X, posting messages of support and solidarity with African Americans, using hashtags like #ICantBreathe and #JusticeForGeorgeFloyd.[68]

Existing scholarly research often attributes anti-Western narratives found in state media outlets of Russia and China to the geopolitical rivalries between these countries and the Euro-American bloc.[69] Global power struggles are also used to explain critical portrayals of the West that are disseminated by Turkey's international communication outlets. As mentioned earlier in this chapter, the Erdoğan government's foreign policy challenges during the mid-2010s have, indeed, guided these negative depictions. However, Turkey's attempts to discredit the West are not merely targeted at European and American audiences but also, and more important, at Muslims worldwide. The Erdoğan regime strategically capitalizes on Turkey's Muslim identity, projecting an alleged inherent benevolence while contrasting it with the perceived corruption and immorality of the West and tapping into the moral values of Muslim audiences. Its aim is to win support from Muslims who, due to their historical and contemporary experiences of Western imperial projects, military interventions, and political, economic, and cultural marginalization, are more receptive to these narratives. Therefore, it is essential to investigate the origins of the negative images of the West in connection with Turkish Islamist thought, particularly, a specific strand that emphasizes the superiority of Islamic civilization.

Critical Visions of the West and the Civilizationist Paradigm

In the Turkish context, criticisms of the West began to surface in the late nineteenth century, a time of decline and encroachments coming from European imperial powers. Ottoman intellectuals voiced their disapproval of European powers, accusing them of disregarding their own professed standards of civilization due to their imperialistic ambitions. These intellectuals also perceived the policies of European powers toward the Muslim world as driven by a "Crusader, Christian agenda."[70] Meanwhile, others acknowledged some positive aspects of European civilization, such as science and technology, but, nonetheless, criticized Europe's "decadent, immoral, vice-prone and ugly side."[71] Yet another group of intellectuals directed attention to European Orientalism and its misrepresentations of the Ottoman Empire and Islam and sought to correct the racist portrayals of Turks and Muslims in their novels, poems, political commentary, and literary criticism.[72]

These criticisms surged after the Ottoman Empire lost massive territories in North Africa and the Balkans between 1911 and 1913, and reached a peak during the Turkish War of Independence between 1919 and 1923 when the Turkish people fought to protect Anatolia from occupation by the British, French, Greek, and Italian armies. One of the influential Turkish Muslim critics of the West during this period, the poet Mehmet Akif Ersoy, describes Western civilization in one of his poems as a "single-fanged monster" and asserts that it could never extinguish the Islamic faith.[73] According to Ersoy, Islamic civilization was "virtuous" compared to the Western civilization because it was based on justice, not power and interest.[74]

Following the establishment of the Turkish Republic in 1923, there were warnings that Europe was still "harboring evil intentions, eternal animosity, and corrupt feelings" toward the Turks.[75] Meanwhile, some thinkers reacted strongly to the top-down modernization project that promoted Western civilization as superior and sought to eradicate all things Ottoman and Islamic. Among them were Necip Fazıl Kısakürek and Nurettin Topçu, who emerged as notable figures for their criticism of the West and greatly influenced Turkish Islamist thought from the 1950s onwards. Both Kısakürek and Topçu had studied philosophy at Sorbonne University with prestigious scholarships from the Turkish state, and thus they were highly familiar with the internal debates taking place in Europe regarding modernity and its associated crises.[76]

Kısakürek identified Western civilization as being in a state of crisis due to its adherence to materialistic values over spiritual ones. According to his analysis, the two world wars were indicative of this crisis. Kısakürek contended that neither capitalism nor communism could address the "spiritual malaise" afflicting Western societies, as these ideologies were merely the two sides of the same civilization. He proposed a remedy that highlighted the civilizational superiority of Islam and advocated for the revival of the Grand East as an alternative to the West.[77] *Grand East* was also the title of the magazine (Büyük Doğu in Turkish) Kısakürek published intermittently from 1943 to 1978, echoing his concerns about the various crises faced by Western civilization and disseminating his vision of "spiritual, social, economic and political unity of different Islamic nation-states against the West."[78] Similar to Kısakürek, Topçu also cautioned his readers against the perils of blindly imitating the West and emphasized that the Turkish nation would lose its "creative cultural spirit" and become enslaved by "a soulless civilization" driven only by technology.[79] He proposed that the solution lay in reviving the Turkish nation as a cultural and moral community with a particular focus on the Turkish interpretation of Islam.[80]

Another intellectual who has been influential on the formation of Turkish Islamist thought, Sezai Karakoç, also focused on civilizational dualities between East and West. Karakoç acknowledged the significant wounds inflicted upon the Islamic world by Western hegemony, but he firmly believed that Islam would eventually revive the "civilization of humanity," bringing an end to the perceived "cruelty and barbarism of the West."[81] He had observed the independence struggles of Tunisia and Algeria during the Cold War era and argued that the decolonization movements would lead to the restoration of dignity in the Muslim world and the East. Karakoç proposed the "civilizational resurrection of Islam" as an alternative to socialism and capitalism and a remedy for the crises plaguing the modern world.[82]

Kısakürek, Topçu, and Karakoç all have exerted immense influence on Turkish Islamist thought and conservative circles, including the AKP cadres. Their critical perspectives on the West and vision of a resurgent Islamic civilization have left a lasting impact on conservative politics in Turkey.[83] Thus, their ideas provide valuable insights into how and why the AKP government and its communication instruments construct negative visions of the West. Their influence is readily apparent in a multitude of activities undertaken by Erdoğan and his government. Erdoğan frequently incorporates Kısakürek's poetry into his speeches and makes references to Topçu's teachings.[84] Since 2017 the Ministry of Culture and Tourism has presented awards to writers and poets in honor of Kısakürek. The Ministry of Education has given Topçu's name to numerous public high schools across the country. Karakoç, on the other hand, has received literary prizes from both the Ministry of Culture and Tourism and the president's office. Additionally, his life and work have been featured in a documentary produced by the state broadcaster TRT.

The influence of Kısakürek, Topçu, and Karakoç on the AKP rank and file extends beyond these acts of public recognition. Erdoğan and other leading AKP figures began their political careers as members of the Milli Türk Talebe Birliği (MTTB, National Union of Turkish Students), which drew inspiration from Kısakürek's ideas for many years. Abdullah Gül, a founding member of the AKP and former president, is known for his admiration for both Kısakürek and Karakoç. The impact of these intellectuals' civilizationist thinking is also evident in the writings of Ahmet Davutoğlu, the architect of the AKP's foreign policy agenda (see chapter 3), and Kalın, current director of Turkey's national intelligence organization.[85] Considering their significant past roles within SETA, the Office of Public Diplomacy, and the Ministry of Foreign Affairs, it is essential to examine the perspectives held by these two individuals regarding Turkey's relationship with the West.

Davutoğlu, in his book *Civilizational Transformation and the Muslim World*, criticizes Western societies for their consumerism and perceived immorality and argues that some civilizations, such as the Islamic one, can successfully resist Western hegemony around the world.[86] In his other works, Davutoğlu positions Turkey as the focal point of such a civilizational revival, assigning the Ottoman Empire the role of an intercivilizational "basin."[87] Kalın, on the other hand, takes issue with defining civilization solely with references to European culture and history, and criticizes those who consider non-Western societies as inherently uncivilized. In *Barbar, Modern, Medeni*

(Barbaric, Modern, Civilized), Kalın offers a critique of the prevailing mindset during the eighteenth and nineteenth centuries, where civilization was predominantly defined by advancements in science, technology, and industry and used as a tool to justify Western colonialism.[88] In this book, Kalın also discusses Islamic notions of ontology, harmony, aesthetics, and community to present Islamic civilization as a viable alternative to its Western counterpart.

Although not a direct continuum, there are important similarities between the civilizationist thinking advocated by Kısakürek, Topçu, and Karakoç, on the one hand, and the arguments put forth by Davutoğlu and Kalın, on the other. One shared aspect is the argument that Western societies prioritize power and self-interest over humanistic values, while Islam and Islamic civilization are viewed as possessing inherent solutions to crises spurred by modernity. Additionally, there is a strong resistance against the idealization of Western civilization whether by European intellectuals or the modernizing elites in Muslim-majority countries. Finally, there is consensus on the revival of Islamic civilization as a means to counter Western hegemony on the international stage and challenge Eurocentric modernization projects at home.

Huntington's Thesis and the AKP's Civilizationist Discourse

Such a focus on civilizational exceptionalism inevitably evokes Samuel Huntington's thesis on the clash of civilizations. In an article he published in 1993, Huntington argued that conflicts in the post–Cold War era would stem from civilizational differences rather than ideological, political, or economic power struggles.[89] He identified seven civilizations (Chinese, Japanese, Hindu, Muslim, Latin American, African, and Western), assigning unique identities to each one, associating the Islamic civilization with violence and presenting it as diametrically opposed to the Western one.[90] Since then, Huntington's thesis has received criticism on several grounds. One major critique pertains to his methodology, specifically, his portrayal of civilization as a cohesive unit with well-defined territorial boundaries.[91] For instance, Huntington treats Western civilization as a homogeneous entity, neglecting the distinctions among different European and North American nations. Similarly, the inherent differences within Muslim-majority countries resulting from colonial legacies, political trajectories, levels of development, and various ethnic, class, educational, and sociopolitical complexities are also obscured.[92]

An additional area of contention arises from Huntington's assertion that Western civilization is superior due to its perceived alignment with democratic ethos, culture, and political values. Within Huntington's "Euro-centric culturalist" perspective, other civilizations, particularly Chinese and Islamic ones, are portrayed as incompatible with democracy.[93] This characterization stems from the belief that religious factors inherent in these civilizations breed hostility toward concepts such as individual liberty, the rule of law, human rights, and cultural freedom. As Edward Said astutely notes, this analysis falls into the realm of Orientalism. Its "bellicose statements" not only revive the Cold War–era opposition between "the West and the rest" but also mobilize "primitive passions" and "fortify boundaries . . . between past and present, us and them."[94]

Following the events of September 11, Huntington's thesis gained traction among Western policymakers, despite its limitations and divisive rhetoric. During the early part of the first decade of the 2000s, the AKP had presented Turkey as a panacea to the "clash of civilizations" that so permeated political discourse. In an interview with a British newspaper, Erdoğan said: "Turkey is a catalyst to make sure we have harmony of civilizations. It is a bridge between the Islamic world and the rest of the world. [To have] a country like Turkey, where the cultures of Islam and democracy have merged together . . . will bring harmony of civilizations."[95] In 2006 Turkey became a cosponsor of the UN's Alliance of Civilizations initiative with Spain, pledging to promote "dialogue among cultures, civilizations and religions."[96] Under a national action plan, it developed approximately seventy projects in the fields of arts, culture, and education aiming to "demonstrate how different religious groups . . . co-existed peacefully in the Ottoman Empire" and do so in modern Turkey. But as historian Cemil Aydin notes, "neither the AKP leaders nor the intellectuals close to them" were able to clarify what they actually meant by Turkey's unique role in reconciling civilizations and thus could "not go beyond the superficial harmony-themed slogans."[97]

During the 2010s the AKP's "alliance of civilizations" approach underwent a noticeable shift as Erdoğan adopted a more confrontational stance toward the West. This shift, as explained in previous sections, can be attributed to the interplay of domestic and foreign policy developments that took place in the 2010s and has manifested itself in the negative media images of the West.[98] Today, the Erdoğan government actively propagates the superiority of Turkish Islamic civilization—an idea shaped by Kısakürek, Topçu, and Karakoç and incorporated into Turkey's foreign policy by Davutoğlu. It is important to acknowledge that while Huntington's framework is divisive and perpetuates Orientalist images of Muslims, the Erdoğan regime is engaging in a similar practice, albeit from the opposite perspective. As discussed next, the negative portrayals of the West as inhumane, immoral, shameless, and dysfunctional should not be mistaken for a progressive or humanist critique, nor do they intend to foster constructive dialogue for positive transformation. Instead, they reinforce an essentialist dichotomy between Islam and the West, falling into the category of Occidentalism.

In its broadest definition, Occidentalism refers to critical representations of the West. It is not a simple hatred of the West but a response to the West's "historical power and ability to construct and impose images of alien societies."[99] Nevertheless, despite this noble objective, Occidentalism is not exempt from inherent challenges. As anthropologist and historian Fernand Coronil explains, Occidentalist representations compartmentalize the world into distinct and bounded units, thereby reinforcing the dichotomy between the West and the Rest. In doing so, they often overlook the intricate and interconnected histories that have shaped the relationship between the two units.[100] Ultimately, both the West and the Rest are reduced to homogeneous entities that are characterized by stereotypical frameworks, preconceived explanations, and fixed identifiers.[101]

Another crucial aspect to consider is that the Occidentalist reification of the West does not stem from a lack of understanding. In the words of social anthropologist Nadje Al-Ali, Occidentalist thinkers seek to "gain symbolic advantages for 'the self' and to handicap 'the other'" and consequently leverage these advantages over their adversaries for domestic and foreign political purposes.[102] As sociologist Meltem Ahıska warns us, such oversimplified and negative portrayals of the West are often intricately tied to political endeavors that aim to "consolidate hegemony in line with [one's] pragmatic interests" at home and on the international stage.[103]

All of these issues are evident in the actions of the Erdoğan regime. First, domestically, Erdoğan accuses his political opponents, particularly those aligned with Kemalist ideology, of collaborating with Western powers (see chapter 1) and insinuates that if the AKP were to be ousted from power, it would mean a loss of Turkish independence. In his 2023 presidential election campaign, Erdoğan referred to the opposition bloc as "subcontractors of imperialists" and asserted that his government has been combating imperialists ever since assuming power in 2002: "We said 'stop' to the imperialist colonial order. We objected to the global system established by the imperialists."[104]

Second, at the international level, the Erdoğan government strategically employs the negative portrayals of the West to contest the prevailing global order and validate its own power-driven and expansionist foreign policy agenda. For example, from 2016 to 2020 Turkey carried out military operations in northern Syria, subsequently assuming governance over three specific areas. Within these areas, Turkey provides crucial infrastructure and health and education services while ensuring a pro-Turkey demographic dominance of

Sunni Muslims.[105] In 2020 the AKP government extended military assistance to the Government of National Accord in Libya with the aim of safeguarding its economic and geopolitical interests in North Africa. This move also sought to leverage Libya as a gateway for enhanced economic involvement in the Sahel and sub-Saharan Africa regions.[106] Last but not least, Turkey has pursued a policy of challenging maritime boundaries with Greece and Cyprus and simultaneously established new economic zones in the Eastern Mediterranean.[107]

In an effort to legitimize these expansionist endeavors and preempt potential criticisms from other regional actors, Erdoğan highlighted the historical association of Syria, Libya, and the Mediterranean Sea with the Ottoman Empire, emphasizing Turkey's kinship ties with the peoples in these regions: "We are not looking for adventures in Syria, Libya, or the Mediterranean. Above all, we have no imperial ambitions. Our eyes are not blinded by the greed for oil and money. Our only goal is to protect the rights and the future of ourselves and our brothers."[108] Erdoğan consequently framed Turkey's endeavors beyond its borders as motivated by altruism and highlighted how they are different from the "self-serving practices of Western powers."[109]

As this chapter has shown, Erdoğan and his communication emissaries portray the West as morally corrupt, hypocritical, and in decline to bolster Turkey's image as civilizationally superior. During the refugee crisis, for instance, AKP-aligned entities circulated negative images of Europe, emphasizing its failure to adhere to principles of equality, dignity, and human rights. Similarly, they capitalized on social and racial justice protests in the United States and far-right movements in Europe to question whether Western societies could still be seen as the arbiters of democracy and human rights for the rest of the world. It is essential to note that while these negative representations identify the problems afflicting Europe and the United States, their circulation is solely aimed at concealing Erdoğan's own expansionist foreign policy and suppression of human rights at home. The Occidentalist representations discussed in this chapter serve only to promote Turkey as a "generous patriarch," to criticize the AKP's internal and external adversaries, and to legitimize Erdoğan's power-driven regime, not to offer a genuine critique of Western modernity.[110] The following chapter explores how the AKP's global communication apparatus reinforces the dichotomies between Turkey and the West through historical television dramas.

5

Promoting Turkish History and Civilization

Television Dramas and Muslim Audiences

In July 2019 an Islamic charitable foundation in Pretoria, South Africa, organized a Turkish Day offering children's activities, an archery course, and Turkish food. The main attraction at the event—the most prominent feature on the flyers—was a presentation titled "History of Ertuğrul and the Legacy of the Ottoman Empire."[1] Why did the organizers use a presentation about Ertuğrul, a thirteenth-century Turkish historical figure, and the Ottoman Empire to attract South African Muslims to this fundraising event? The answer to this question is found in *Resurrection: Ertuğrul*, a Turkish historical drama about the namesake leader of a Turkish Muslim tribe considered to be the forefather of the Ottoman dynasty. *Resurrection* was produced for Turkey's state broadcaster TRT and endorsed by the Erdoğan government for its positive depiction of the country's history and civilization. It has been wildly popular among international audiences and spawned similarly themed historical dramas that also have gained popularity at home and abroad.

This chapter discusses the Erdoğan government's deployment of historical dramas as part of its global messaging, specifically the framing of Turkey as a benevolent power that is poised to return Muslims to their glorious past. The focus is on *Resurrection: Ertuğrul* (*Diriliş: Ertuğrul* in Turkish), *Establishment: Osman* (*Kuruluş: Osman* in Turkish) and *The Last Emperor* (*Payitaht: Abdulhamid* in Turkish), all of which are produced by commercial companies with personal and political economic ties to the AKP and are easily accessible outside of Turkey via streaming platforms, fan websites, and/or TRT's foreign-language YouTube channels. Set in pre-, early, and late Ottoman eras, respectively, all three shows espouse a Turkish Muslim sensibility by articulating binary oppositions between Turks and the West and presenting the former as civilizationally superior. The central figure in all these shows is the archetypal Muslim man, who is "self-assured, calm and strong" and has an "unshakable faith, and power and authority to guide others,"[2] be it in military or political battles against foreign powers.[3]

This chapter begins by locating these government-sanctioned dramas within the context of Turkish television series' growing popularity since the 2010s and analyzes the political economic and sociocultural dynamics that undergird them. Next, it focuses on how the Erdoğan government has used these historical dramas as part of its global messaging. Lastly, examined are specific textual and discursive elements that make these dramas so appealing to Muslim viewers in the Global South. Among the questions addressed are: What histories and knowledges of the Ottoman Empire, Islam, and Islamic civilization do these shows communicate? How are they informed by the AKP's cultural and political goals at home and utilized as part of its outreach activities abroad? In what ways do these texts serve as alternatives to those produced by creative industries in the Global North? How do Muslim audiences respond to them in the context of rampant Islamophobia around the world?

Global Popularity of Turkish Content

Since the early 2000s, Turkish television series (*dizi* in Turkish) have become increasingly popular on a global level.[4] These weekly rags-to-riches stories, crime dramas, and literary adaptations are generally produced and distributed by commercial broadcast channels and privately held companies in Turkey.[5] The first Turkish series to make a splash outside the borders of Turkey was *Gümüs* (*Noor* in Arabic), which became a huge hit with Arab audiences in 2008. *Gümüs* was followed by *Binbir Gece* (*A Thousand Nights*), *Muhteşem Yüzyıl* (*Magnificent Century*), *Fatmagül'ün Suçu Ne?* (*Fatmagul*), and countless others, all of which attained high ratings first in the Balkans and Middle East and later in Latin America. Since the 2010s Turkish content has made inroads into African markets as well. In Ethiopia, Somalia, and South Africa, Turkish series have surpassed the traditionally popular Bollywood productions.[6] In sub-Sahara, they have their own exclusive channel, launched by one of Africa's leading pay-television companies;[7] and in West Africa, they run on a channel dedicated to Turkish and Latin American content.[8] Turkish series are also becoming increasingly popular in Asia. They first gained attention in India, Pakistan, and Indonesia, then in Malaysia, Vietnam, and the Philippines. In India they are available on a dedicated channel on Zindagi TV, a subsidiary of Zee Entertainment Enterprises.

It is no surprise, then, that Turkish television exports rose steadily over the years. In 2013 they brought in $100 million in foreign revenues; $500 million in 2020,[9] and they were projected to cross the $1 billion mark in 2023.[10] In 2017 Turkey also became the second-biggest exporter of television series after the United States, accounting for 25 percent of all imported fiction content around the globe.[11] Turkish producers now sell remake rights to their American, Belgian, German, and Japanese counterparts and create exclusive content for Netflix's global audiences.[12]

Rise of AKP-Sanctioned Historical Dramas

All of the early Turkish series that became global hits during the early 2010s were produced and distributed by privately owned companies and/or commercial channels. While these series enthralled international audiences, those produced by the state broadcaster TRT were conspicuously lacking in global success. Although TRT aired a number of series on its flagship channel TRT 1, it achieved neither the domestic nor the foreign success of its commercial counterparts. As media studies scholar Josh Carney notes, the state broadcaster did not seem bothered by this disparity until *Magnificent Century* (2011–14) became a ratings phenomenon, first in Turkey and then around the world.[13] *Magnificent Century* is an Ottoman-era costume drama that recounts intrigue and betrayal in the Ottoman harem during the sixteenth-century reign of Sultan Suleiman. The show caused a great deal of controversy among conservative circles in Turkey because of its focus on the private life of the sultan. Although it was fictionalized, it often showed him drinking and enjoying intimate moments with his concubines, activities that were deemed unacceptable since Ottoman sultans also claimed the title of the caliph and were seen as successors to the Prophet Mohammad. Due to these allegedly offensive representations, conservative viewers filed complaints with Turkey's broadcasting regulator. Erdoğan himself condemned the show for portraying Suleiman as an "indulgent harem-lover" instead of the "proud conqueror" he was and even called for penalizing the channel that aired it.[14]

In response to these complaints, TRT provided a direct counterpart to *Magnificent Century*. In 2012 the state broadcaster embarked on its own costume drama that narrated Ottoman history from an AKP-sanctioned perspective.[15] Titled *Bir Zamanlar Osmanlı: Kıyam* (Once upon a Time in the Ottoman Empire: Rebellion), the series recounts a mob uprising in eighteenth-century Istanbul. According to Carney, despite its star actors and prominent directors, *Rebellion* received low ratings and was cancelled after two seasons.[16] However, TRT remained unwavering in its attempt to present an alternative retelling of history as per the AKP's cultural, political agenda. İbrahim Eren, then deputy director general of TRT, invested in a new series that would "strengthen the nationhood sentiment of the Turkish people by teaching how the Turkish state came into existence."[17] He recruited Mehmet Bozdağ to produce it. Bozdağ was then a novice in the television sector, but he had the right connections and the preferred Turkish Islamist ideological outlook. He was experienced in documentary production as well as historical film and television work. Back in 2004 Bozdağ had been part of a team that produced a documentary under the auspices of the Ministry of Tourism and Culture. The documentary narrated the life of Necip Fazıl Kısakürek, the prominent Islamist poet idolized by conservative circles and the AKP (see chapter 4 for a detailed discussion). Later, Bozdağ joined Tekden Film, a production company founded by Kemal Tekden, an AKP parliamentarian at the time. At Tekden Film, Bozdağ wrote the docudrama *Ustalar, Alimler, Sultanlar* (Masters, scholars, sultans), which focuses on prominent Ottoman sultans and Islamic scholars.[18]

Given Bozdağ's conservative credentials, TRT's new historical drama was in good hands, ideologically speaking. The show, *Diriliş: Ertuğrul (Resurrection: Ertuğrul)*, tells the story of Ertuğrul Ghazi, the father of Osman Ghazi, who would later found the Ottoman dynasty. *Resurrection* focuses on Ertuğrul's time as the leader of the thirteenth-century nomadic Turkish Muslim tribe known as the Kayı. The show features high production values, well-choreographed action scenes, and, most important, a narrative arc that focuses on Turks' heroic battles against the Mongols, Knight Templars, and the Crusaders during their westward settlement in Anatolia. In its first season, 2014–15, the series became a huge hit with Turkish audiences. Over the next five seasons, it received high ratings, generally earning a market share of 25 to 30 percent and breaking a record with a 40 percent share in 2017.[19] By 2017 *Resurrection* became one of Turkey's most successful television exports; it was sold to sixty countries.[20] When Netflix included it in its 2016 roster (with English subtitles), *Resurrection* became a global phenomenon, eventually labeled by viewers and critics as the "Turkish *Game of Thrones*."[21]

Resurrection is a far cry from *Magnificent Century*. As Carney shows, it does not violate the sacred status of the historical figure it focuses on but glorifies the (proto-) Ottoman past in alignment with the AKP's cultural, political vision. It bears noting that *Resurrection* is liberal in its interpretation and re-creation of Ertuğrul's deeds. Again as Carney notes, it takes advantage of the fact that in this period in Turkish history there are "no historical records from Ertuğrul's lifetime," and the "few accounts that relate his life emerge approximately a century after his death and are of questionable accuracy."[22] Indeed, Bozdağ, the show's creator, acknowledges the near-absence of historical records from the thirteenth century, saying in an interview, "There is too little information about that period, maybe four, five pages. Even the names are different in different sources." But he notes, "History has a spirit, and it is the spirit of the thirteenth century we are recounting [in *Resurrection*]."[23]

The protagonist of *Resurrection* is Ertuğrul Ghazi (Ghazi means "holy warrior" in Turkish), who embodies bravery, valor, righteousness—and, most important, piety. When he is not on horseback or in hand-to-hand combat with enemies, Ertuğrul is seeking guidance from his spiritual mentor, the renowned Muslim poet, mystic, scholar, and philosopher Ibn Arabi. Ertuğrul and his fellow Kayı people are often seen praying, reciting from the Quran, and quoting Prophet Mohammad's sayings. Indeed, Ertuğrul's piety sets the tone for the entire show: the opening scene of the first episode features him uttering the phrases, "Allah is alive! Allah is one and only!" as he and a blacksmith forge a sword. Needless to say, *Resurrection* contains no sexually suggestive material, and it firmly limits romantic relationships to verbal expressions of warmth and tenderness.

According to Bozdağ, *Resurrection* was born out of the need for "an accurate history" of "our own past," from which, he says, Turkish society has been alienated during the country's Republican-era projects of Westernization and secularization.[24] Bozdağ contends that his main objective in creating popular culture texts is first and foremost to "earn God's mercy," and his secondary aim is to reestablish the "lost connections between contemporary Turkish society and our own history and identity . . . without hurting our ancestors' souls," unlike *Magnificent Century*, which in the conservative view desacralized Sultan Suleiman.[25] Bozdağ's expression of the show's goals, with emphasis on cultural alienation is testament to his alignment with the AKP's political vision, which seeks to restore to Turks their history that has been distorted by the Westernizing elites.

As such, *Resurrection* has been promoted by the AKP as a pivotal step toward establishing its cultural hegemony inside Turkey. Erdoğan has made several public statements lamenting that his government has not yet been able to attain this goal. In 2017, for example, he said he welcomed "the increasing interest in preacher schools and new course offerings about the Quran" but regretted that "we still have several shortcomings in regards raising the new generation of our dreams."[26] A year later he elaborated on his vision of this new generation: "pious [and] good people that have respect for their history, culture and values."[27] Given *Resurrection*'s potential role in this conservative cultural reeducation, Erdoğan has publicly endorsed the show, visited the set, and flown with the series' creator and lead actor on a state visit to Kuwait. The series' theme song is regularly played at AKP rallies and official state events, and members of the cast often participate in annual celebrations of the conquest of Istanbul.[28] The AKP government, thus, not only supports but also takes advantage of *Resurrection*, using it to mobilize its base.

In the wake of *Resurrection*'s success in Turkey and abroad, there has been a marked increase in new productions that play on themes of Turks' struggle against Western powers, their guardianship of the ummah, and embodiment of Islamic civilization.[29] In 2017, when *Resurrection* was in its third season, TRT 1 began to broadcast *The Last Emperor* (*Payitaht: Abdülhamid*), which focuses on the trials and tribulations of the late nineteenth-century Ottoman sultan Abdülhamid II.[30] Then came *Mehmetçik Kut-ül Amare*, the story of the Ottoman army's victory against the British in a World War I battle. In 2019 the stringently pro-government channel ATV aired *Establishment: Osman* (*Kuruluş: Osman*), which is considered to be a sequel to *Resurrection* because it tells the story of Ertuğrul's son Osman and his founding of the Ottoman dynasty. The latest incarnations of this genre include *The Great Seljuks: Guardians of Justice* (*Uyanış: Büyük Selçuklu*), *Barbarossa: The Sword of the Mediterranean* (*Barbaros: Akdeniz'in Kılıcı*), *Barbarossa: Sultan's Edict* (*Barbaros Hayreddin: Sultanın Fermanı*), and *Epic* (*Destan*). TRT continues to commission content that focuses on Turkish Islamic civilization, religious figures, and warriors from the past and/or the Turks' battles against the West. Among these shows are *Rumi*, *Gilani the Ascetic*, *Akif*, *Young Ibn Sina*, and *Golden Apple: The Grand Conquest*, which are exclusively available on Tabii, TRT's global streaming platform. According to a report in the Turkish press, many of these series are produced by companies owned by Bilal Erdoğan's high school friends and/or other pro-AKP companies.[31]

As table 5.1 shows, a handful of companies dominate this niche market of government-friendly historical dramas. Tekden Film is owned by a former AKP parliamentarian; Bozdağ Film was founded by Bozdağ after his departure from Tekden Film; Akli Film previously produced documentaries and promotional videos for TRT; and ES Film is owned by Yusuf Esenkal, who is Bilal Erdoğan's friend. Furthermore, all of these dramas are sold to TRT or ATV, the pro-government channel that has close ties to the Erdoğan family (see chapter 1).

One could then argue that the post-*Resurrection* boom in historical dramas has been made possible by clientelist relationships among commercial producers, pro-government channels, and the state broadcaster. Production companies are well aware of the direct and indirect financial and promotional support they will receive from TRT and loyalist commercial channels in return for churning out ideologically friendly content. In the meantime, by contracting and including these dramas on their primetime lineup, pro-government

Table 5.1. Government-sanctioned historical dramas, 2014 to 2023

Original Title in Turkish	Title in English	Production Company	Years of Seasons	Number of Episodes
Broadcast on ATV				
Destan	Epic	Bozdag Film	2021–22	28
Kuruluş: Osman	Establishment: Osman	Bozdag Film	2019–23	127
Broadcast on TRT 1				
Barbaros Hayreddin: Sultanın Fermanı	Barbarossa: The Sultan's Edict	ES Film	2022–23	20
Barbaroslar: Akdeniz'in Kılıcı	Barbarossa: The Sword of the Mediterranean	ES Film	2021–22	32
Uyanış: Büyük Selcuklu	The Great Seljuks: Guardians of Justice	Akli Film	2020-21	34
Mehmetçik: Kut-ül Amare	Little Mehmed	Bozdag Film	2018–19	33
Diriliş: Ertuğrul	Resurrection: Ertugrul	Tekden Film	2014–19	150
Filinta	Filinta: Dawn of the Millennium	ES Film	2014–16	56
Payitaht: Abdülhamid	The Last Emperor	ES Film	2017–21	154
Yunus Emre: Aşkın Yolculuğu	Yunus Emre: Journey of Love	Tekden Film	2015–17	44

Note: Number of episodes is those broadcast on Turkish channels. On foreign streaming platforms or television channels, these numbers would be considerably higher, because the episodes are modified from the original 120 to 150 minutes to 40 to 60 minutes. For example, 150 episodes of *Resurrection* correspond to 448 episodes on Netflix.

channels do their part in helping the AKP to achieve its political, cultural objectives and providing symbolic support for Erdoğan.

Historical Dramas as Tools of Political Communication

AKP-sanctioned historical dramas are illustrative of memory politics through which public opinion leaders, political movements, and/or state actors aim to "establish a certain perspective of history in the public sphere."[32] As discussed above, the AKP and its ideological allies find in television the means to overturn the country's so-called distorted history, *resurrect* the accurate one, and accordingly institute their own understanding of "the self and the other" along the axes of ethnic, national, and cultural identities.[33] In regard to memory politics, scholars note that "historical myth-making and idealized constructions of the national past" play an integral role in the production and circulation of a particular ideology. For example, the glorification of "a harmonious, civilized society" that supposedly existed in the past is among the important tools far-right movements in Europe use as they seek to elevate an "ethno-national community model" over the cosmopolitan model and its so-called afflictions.[34]

In Turkey, the AKP government uses television series to convey particular ideas about the past and to generate "religious cohesion, collective identity and moral renewal" in the public.[35] This investment in the mythology of the Turkish-Ottoman past serves not only domestic but also international objectives, in this case, the forging of a Turkey-led international Muslim solidarity. Through historical dramas, the Erdoğan government presents the Ottoman Empire as a harmonious entity under which Muslims lived in peace and enjoyed the benevolence of their Turkish rulers. In deploying these dramas, the government aims to communicate that the so-called golden age of Muslim unity can be achieved under the rightful leadership of Turkey, and current predicaments of the ummah (sectarian divisions, political economic marginalization, absence of a leader) can be easily resolved.

How did the Erdoğan government begin to use television series to deliver its preferred narratives to foreign publics then? It bears noting that the AKP did not set out on this course with a specific plan in mind. *Resurrection* was originally created for domestic audiences, and it was only after its international success that the AKP recognized the potential use of this and other historical series to project a positive image of Turkish history to foreign audiences. Even well before *Resurrection*, mainstream dizis had become widely popular around the world and thus prepared a favorable environment for the reception of Turkish content. In other words, the AKP's political deployment of historical dramas was not by design but a byproduct of economic (program sales) and popular dynamics (interest in Turkish culture) that had been in place since the mid-2010s. A programming executive at TRT confirmed this point to me:

> You remember the large numbers of tourists [coming to Turkey] from the Middle East when shows like [*Magnificent Century*, *A Thousand Nights*] were popular? That was about ten years ago. And now, I think for the past five to six years, there are sightseeing tours in Istanbul organized for dizi

fans coming from places like America. Then there were a Mexican couple and an American man, I think, that converted to Islam after watching [*Resurrection*]. People [in Pakistan] naming their babies Ertuğrul. All of that. So [the government] realized that these shows have a potential and zeroed in on them.[36]

The government's treading on the heels of the marketplace can be seen in the timeline of TRT's foreign-language offerings. For example, it was only in 2019 when TRT made available on YouTube dubbed and/or subtitled versions of *Resurrection*, *The Last Emperor*, *Filinta*, and *Yunus Emre* (see table 5.2).

Likewise, it was in 2019 and 2020 that TRT and TRT World opened X accounts dedicated to *Resurrection* and other shows (@trtdrama_en, @trtdrama_ar, @TRTErtugrul_AR, @TRTErtugrul_EN) to promote them to English- and Arabic-speaking audiences. By then, these series were already available on Netflix and/or other streaming platforms and on websites, such as Kayi Family TV, Historical Fun TV, and Osman Online.[37] Dozens of Facebook groups had already been active for a while (see table 5.3), where fans of *Resurrection, Establishment*, and *The Last Emperor* discuss characters and storylines, share tips about traveling to Turkey, and spar over politics and Islamic teachings.[38] In sum, Erdoğan's communication emissaries at TRT trailed, not

Table 5.2 TRT's YouTube channels featuring historical dramas in foreign languages, 2019 and 2020

YouTube Channel	Date of Creation	Featured Series	Dubbing Language	Subtitle Language
TRT Drama Arabic	March 2019	The Last Emperor, Filinta, Yunus Emre, Resurrection	Arabic	(none)
TRT Drama English	October 2019	The Last Emperor, Filinta, Yunus Emre, Resurrection	(none)	English
TRT Drama Russian	April 2020	Yunus Emre, Resurrection	Russian	(none)
TRT Drama Spanish	December 2019	Resurrection	Spanish	(none)
TRT Ertugrul by PTV	April 2020	Resurrection	Urdu	(none)
TRT Ertugrul Arabic	March 2019	Resurrection	Arabic	(none)
TRT Originals Urdu	April 2020	The Last Emperor, Resurrection, Yunus Emre	Urdu	(none)
TRT Resurrection	March 2019	Resurrection	(none)	English

Table 5.3 English-language Facebook fan pages for historical dramas, May 2023

Facebook fan page	Number of members	Date of creation
Kuruluş Osman and Ertugrul with English Subtitles	293,000	January 2018
Kayi Family TV International	58,000	May 2018
Dirilis Ertugrul, Kuruluş Osman, and *Uyaniş Beyuk Seljuklu Lovers**	377,000	July 2018

* The group name was changed in February 2021 to include the series, *The Great Seljuks*.

preceded, the international fandom that had already coalesced around these shows.

Symbiotic Narratives in Popular Culture and Political Communication

To understand the government's deployment of historical dramas as part of its global communication program, it is important to examine the affinities between the plotlines of these series and the AKP's preferred narratives. In both cases, Turks are presented to be fighting against foreign powers, which aim to curb their rise to greatness or encroach on their sovereignty. Turks are also promoted as benevolent guardians of Muslims working to unite them and guaranteeing their welfare.

In *Resurrection* and *Establishment*, Ertuğrul and Osman lead their armies in fierce but righteous battles against the Crusaders, Byzantines, and Mongols, as well as traitors from within. In both shows, Christianity and Tengrism (a shamanistic religion practiced by Mongols) constitute the religious Other vis-à-vis Islam. In *The Last Emperor*, the main threat source comprises Western imperial powers and their internal collaborators (Greek and Armenian subjects of the Ottoman Empire, the reform movement of Young Turks, and Zionists). The enemies in these dramas are the same enemies that Erdoğan and his proxies blame for inciting the Gezi protests, the coup attempt, and other alleged political, financial attacks against Turkey that have taken place since the 2010s (see chapter 1). The conspiratorial narrative that underlies *The Last Emperor* is often reiterated by the AKP and its voter base, that is, Jews and Zionists played an active role in the collapse of the Ottoman Empire, and they continue to work with Western powers to weaken Turkey.

In addition to military and political battles, another overarching theme found in these series is related to the virtues of Turkish Islamic civilization and the concept of justice. In *Resurrection* and *Establishment*, Ertuğrul and Osman are portrayed as true embodiments of "*ghaza*," a term that technically means military raids, Islamic holy war, or a combination of both.[39] But ghaza also invokes the end of oppression and institution of justice, which, in Islamic teachings, is linked with just governance, benevolence, mercy, and compassion. As discussed in detail in chapters 3 and 4, these are the same themes that the AKP government reiterates via its humanitarian aid and development assistance targeted at Muslims in the Global South and its communication activities that shed light on the suffering of Muslims.

Whereas *Resurrection* and *Establishment* recount the glory days of Turco-Ottoman expansion, *The Last Emperor* tackles the decline of the Ottoman Empire in the late nineteenth century—its massive territorial losses and economic and technological inferiority to Europe. Despite its focus on a period of retrenchment, the series, nonetheless, portrays sultan Abdülhamid II as a wise statesman who maintains order in his empire and unifies his dispersed Muslim subjects even as Europeans and Zionists conspire to weaken his rule. In *The Last Emperor*, justice is achieved not via conquest (after all, this is the story of the empire's dissolution) but by Abdülhamid II's benevolent and fair treatment of his Muslim and non-Muslim subjects.[40]

This same specific intertwining of Turkish rule with the Islamic concepts of justice and benevolence is evident in Erdoğan's public statements that seek to rationalize his government's geopolitical ventures in Africa, the Middle East, and the Balkans, which some critics have described as neo-imperialist.[41] According to Erdoğan,

> In our civilization, conquest does not mean occupation or plunder ... but the elimination of oppression and in its stead the institution of justice as demanded by Allah.... Our ancestors built infrastructure, provided welfare services, and practiced cultural and religious tolerance in the lands they conquered. [Like them] we, too, build infrastructure, establish justice, and assert the rule of law ... in all the territories we set foot in.[42]

Ever careful to dissociate the Ottoman past and his government's geopolitical (and at times military) engagements from Western imperialism, Erdoğan here sets binary oppositions between plunder and civilization, oppression and justice, occupation and "setting foot."[43] Likewise, when Turkish officials discuss Turkey's pivot to Africa, they contrast their own geopolitical economic engagements in the continent with the "disgraceful history of European colonialism."[44] As they tell it, Turkey is pursuing a "win-win policy" in Africa, striving for a mutually equal and beneficial relationship with African governments and working to "eliminate the [ongoing] slavery and colonization" of the continent.[45] This same attempt to separate Turkey's geopolitical economic ambitions from Western imperialism is also evident in the AKP's legitimization of its cross-border military operations in north Syria. In some foreign policy circles, these operations, which took place between 2016 and 2019, were criticized as "invasion" or "near-annexation," but AKP officials described them as humanitarian initiatives, claiming that that their objective was simply to "facilitate the safe and voluntary return of displaced Syrians" and to liberate "Kurds, Arabs, Christians and others [in the region] who have been suffering under the [Kurdish terrorists]."[46] These justifications are illustrative of the AKP's civilizational discourse for they emphasize how Turkey builds schools, hospitals, and sports facilities in towns that are ravaged by war and thus uplifts the local populace.[47]

Another important point is related to how the Erdoğan government touts its foreign aid and development works in the Global South for their purely humanitarian and civilization-building potential while ignoring the fact that many of its infrastructure projects are contracted to pro-AKP businessmen. Loyalist news media organizations in Turkey explicitly connect the infrastructure development projects in predominantly Muslim countries to similar projects undertaken by Ottoman sultans, pointing at the historical continuity of Turks' civilizational mission toward Muslims. In *The Last Emperor*, subplotlines show Abdülhamid II personally designing transportation projects in order to unify Muslims, only to be hampered by scheming Europeans. Harping on the historical continuity between Ottoman statesmen and AKP officials, pro-government media in Turkey do not shy away from portraying Erdoğan as Abdülhamid II's spiritual successor, because he overcomes the alleged meddling from the West and "realizes [the sultan's] dreams."[48]

In this regard, the AKP's political use of history is more than a simple glorification of the past; it is also about making a promise to Muslims about the future. Through historical dramas, humanitarian aid, and development assistance, the AKP communicates to Muslims that the golden age of unity and prosperity can be achieved once again, under the leadership of Turkey. It promises Muslims a break from their present predicament (economic underdevelopment, political and cultural marginalization, wars, and occupations) by intimating that a proud Muslim community can be *resurrected* under the guidance of Turkey and its faithful leader, Erdoğan.

Muslim Audiences' Responses to AKP-Sanctioned Dramas

As discussed in chapter 3, Turkey undertakes numerous outreach projects in Africa, Southeast Asia, Central Asia, the Balkans, and the Middle East via its embassies, aid and development organizations, and cultural centers.

It also actively utilizes historical dramas to promote Turks' contributions to Islamic history and civilization and to position Turkey as the rightful leader of Muslims worldwide. In this regard, especially *Resurrection* and *Establishment* are considered to be contributing to the country's public, educational, cultural diplomacy activities in Africa and Southeast Asia. As a representative from Anadolu Agency who is familiar with the government's outreach work in these regions told me:

> They complement our other endeavors [in these regions]. Think about the fact that TIKA builds roads and schools, and YEE [Yunus Emre Enstitüsü, Yunus Emre Institute] gives Turkish language classes in Africa. Diyanet builds mosques and sends preachers to these countries. When people watch our shows, they become interested in Turkish culture and go to YEE's activities. Or maybe during the day, they go to a mosque that was built by TIKA, then they watch *Resurrection* in the evening. They know how we [the Turks] support our Muslim brothers. By watching these shows, they learn how we did this in the past during the Ottoman Empire. And then they see how we continue this tradition [of helping Muslims] in real life. For example, when they receive help from Turkish government after a disaster.[49]

A similar point was made by a TRT executive who is familiar with foreign programming and underscores the role of the channel in promoting Turkey's growing presence in the aforementioned regions: "These series are very popular in Pakistan, Afghanistan, Bangladesh, and countries in Africa. At TRT, we hope that people in these countries have a positive opinion of Turkey. In terms of what Turks did in the past, during the Ottoman Empire by bringing together Muslims under one roof. We hope that these shows deliver this message."[50]

Indeed, the idea that Turkish television series facilitate positive attitudes toward Turkey has been in circulation for more than a decade. Since the early 2010s when commercially produced dizis began to attain international popularity, analysts have argued that Turkish content creates cultural affection and sociopolitical attachment and, thus, helps to grow the country's soft power.[51] Likewise, Turkish government officials and AKP-backed media outlets have endorsed television exports both for the economic revenue they bring in and the capacity to wield soft power in the Middle East and beyond.[52] TRT World, the Anadolu Agency, and the *Daily Sabah* frequently report on how Turkish series, in general, generate soft power for Turkey and how *Resurrection*, in particular, inspires Muslim viewers in the Global South.[53]

Meanwhile, scholarly analyses have been more cautious in regard to the power of Turkish content and showed that the reception of Turkish series in certain parts of the world can be quite mixed. For example, communication studies scholars Zafer Yoruk and Pantelis Vatikiotis note that although

Turkish series are popular among audiences in Greece, they are also viewed by television industry representatives as "invading the national airwaves" and by ethno-nationalist groups as "contaminating the pure Hellenic culture."[54] In Guinea, as global media scholars Marwan Kraidy and Clovis Bergere argue, viewers are "dazzled" by the "ostentatious consumer lifestyles" they see in mainstream Turkish series and make positive associations with Turkey, but they also express negative opinions about actual Turkish commercial investments in their country.[55]

In light of the fact that existing audience studies focus on mainstream Turkish dizis (not the AKP-sanctioned historical dramas), it is necessary to examine the responses to *Resurrection*, *Establishment*, and *The Last Emperor* and their underlying political messages about Turkey's role vis-à-vis the Muslim world. To this end, I conducted in-depth interviews with Muslim viewers and asked them why they, as Muslims in or of the Global South, find these historical dramas appealing, what they think about on-screen portrayals of Muslims, Turks, and the West, and if they map any connections between these dramas and Turkey's outreach initiatives.[56]

Positive Portrayal of Muslims

Muslim viewers I interviewed (male or female, living in the Global South or in diaspora) all watch and admire the three historical dramas in question because they are "set in the Muslim world, with Muslim characters like us."[57] In the post–September 11 world, where Muslims are more often than not associated with terrorism in entertainment and news media, these dramas provide Muslim viewers with solace. As one research participant said, in these dramas "Muslims are not the terrorists. They are the heroes. It's nice to see Muslims as heroes for once."[58] Echoing this, another participant noted that "unlike in Hollywood movies, Muslim men are not portrayed as terrorists. They are leaders, scholars, and they are fighting for justice. They are honorable men."[59] Female viewers also expressed their appreciation of the portrayals of Muslim women because they counteract the conventional stereotypes about their obedience to male authority and their perceived victimization at the hands of men. They noted how female characters in *Resurrection* and *Establishment* are "not just wives or mothers, but strong women."[60] They are not "your typical Muslim women in hijab taking care of dozens of babies like in Hollywood movies."[61] They "know how to use a knife and protect themselves. They give political advice to men and participate in state affairs."[62]

Viewers also noted that these shows' positive depictions of Muslims offer a viable alternative to both Hollywood and Bollywood productions—the traditionally dominant sources of entertainment in South Asia. According to participants from Afghanistan and Pakistan, where skepticism of "Western media imperialism" is high because of the colonial histories of the region, Turkish historical dramas are considered counterforces against the "damaging effects" of American film and television. Turkish dramas do not "offend Muslims and Islamic culture" or "poison our youth with scenes of sex and drugs."[63] Complaints about Hollywood (a stand-in for US media and popular culture), thus, centered on inappropriate and indecent content. In contrast, Bollywood productions were criticized for their portrayals of Muslims as "invaders and tyrants." A viewer from Pakistan noted, Turkish historical dramas "make us proud of being Muslim. We are not ashamed like we are when we watch Muslims as bad guys that only kill people and nothing else."[64]

These viewers also admired the depiction of governance and social life in "the Muslim world." As one participant commented, these dramas portray Muslims as the "kind, honest people" they are; the characters maintain good neighborly relationships, as their faith and traditions dictate.[65] Another participant mentioned that *Resurrection* and *Establishment*, set in beautiful natural environments, "show audiences the ideal Muslim society,"[66] and another participant said *The Last Emperor* shows "a well-developed, well-functioning society."[67] These positive representations stand in stark contrast to the stereotypical Orientalist depiction of Muslims as "a bunch of terrorists running around in dusty, dirty Third World villages."[68]

All of the participants noted that in these shows, Islam is accurately depicted as a source of good, as a peaceful religion; once again, the shows are seen as counteracting negative representations of Islam in Western media. As one viewer commented, "*Resurrection* and *Establishment* give us a sense of hope at a time when the Islamic civilization is in decline. We get to see the old days of Muslim glory and the Islamic way of life. We see how Muslim societies are built on respect and honor, not materialism. Helping the poor and showing justice to everyone. These are the differences of Islamic civilization from the Western civilization."[69]

Indeed, the majority of participants compared Islamic and Western civilizations in terms of moral values, such as respect to spirituality, mercy, compassion, and justice. One participant said, "*Resurrection* and *Establishment* show us how the Ottoman Empire was fair to non-Muslims living under their rule, how Muslim leaders were ethical [leaders] and cared about human rights."[70] Another viewer who immigrated to the United States approximately twenty years ago directed attention to these dramas' emphasis on "social justice issues" and added: "They tell us that you don't just live for yourself, but you think about your tribe, too. Islam tells you to look for the old and the poor. This is what's lost here in the U.S."[71] Yet another viewer praised Muslims of the twelfth and thirteenth centuries as "the true progressives" of their era.[72]

In light of the above findings, one can then conclude that Muslim viewers find satisfaction in watching these series mainly because of the positive portrayals of Islam, Muslims, and Muslim societies. In addition to these representations that counter Western stereotypes, they also appreciate the foregrounding of Islamic values of justice and compassion, which they then use to draw comparisons between East and West.

Muslims' Plight in Real Life

Binary oppositions between East and West were especially pronounced when viewers discussed how the three series depicted the protagonists' defiant attitude against Western powers and their defense of Muslims from imperialist ploys. As one participant put it, "Ertuğrul, Osman, and Abdülhamid, they all spoke up against the West, and they took action. They were not submissive to the West when they saw their fellow Muslims suffering."[73] Some participants made connections between the series and how Muslims were facing similar oppressions and attacks in real life, with some viewers criticizing "Arab countries" for "choosing to remain silent in the face of Islamophobia and poverty in the Muslim world" and others bemoaning Muslim leaders that "collaborate with Europe, U.S., and even Israel" to attain personal power.[74]

The topic of the oppression of Muslims in Palestine, India, Europe, and the United States was a key vector where participants made connections between the series and real life. Some discussed the plight of Palestinians, mentioning Israeli forces' assault on Gaza in June 2021, and others brought up Indian nationalists' killing of Muslims in Kashmir.[75] One participant lamented the disastrous consequences on Muslims of the US occupation of Iraq and Afghanistan.[76] In discussing these contemporary world affairs, all participants, without exception, pointed fingers at the United States for meddling with the Middle East and knowingly unleashing wars and poverty on Muslims. One participant remarked that *The Last Emperor* was able to "teach us about how a few families and certain groups in the West manipulate the East"—an articulation of many of the anti-Western, anti-Zionist plotlines of the show: "We learn about how Jews, Armenians, and Western powers attacked the Ottoman Empire in the nineteenth century." He noted that "similar attacks are ongoing against Muslim nations today." Adding a caveat that it was "not all but only some Jews and Armenians that created strife," this viewer said Muslims should watch *The Last Emperor* to learn "what's hidden in history books."[77]

One important theme that emerged from the interviews had to do with the role of religion in state affairs. Participants noted that Ertuğrul, Osman, and Abdülhamid II were always aided by Islamic scholars and philosophers. In *Resurrection*, the spiritual guide to Ertuğrul is Ibn Arabi, and in *Establishment*, Osman's guide is Sheik Edebali, the influential leader of a Sunni brotherhood. These spiritual figures tell parables about the Prophet Mohammed and quote his sayings while dispensing political and military advice. In *The Last Emperor*, Abdülhamid II is himself portrayed as the mature, wise, spiritual sultan, and so he is the one that shares stories and quotes from the prophet. Nonetheless, all three series depict the importance of the religious ethos in state affairs. As one participant noted, "Osman, Ertuğrul, and Abdülhamid show us how to find inner peace when you are fighting against enemies, even when you are fighting against your own brothers. They find peace in their faith. It's because Allah guides them. And they are successful because they work together with religious leaders."[78]

Portrayals of Non-Muslims

Despite the aforementioned positive reception, these historical dramas are not entirely immune from criticism. At least two participants, one living in the United States and the other in the United Kingdom, noted the binary oppositions that *Resurrection*, *Establishment*, and *The Last Emperor* depict between Muslims and the West, good and evil, virtuous and immoral. These viewers lamented the reductive nature of these representations, one noting that "Christians [in *Resurrection* and *Establishment*] are always the bad guys. They are always drinking. For example, Nicola, the Byzantine commander [in *Resurrection*] always has a drink in his hand. And he is shown as romantically involved with another man. Drinking Christians, gay Christians . . . These are easy targets."[79] The other participant added, "In Western media, Muslims are always the terrorists. In [*Resurrection* and *Establishment*], Christians are always the bad guys. All the time! I don't want to see this. It shouldn't be too extreme in terms of the representations of Christians. [Writers and producers] can be more moderate."[80] The one-dimensional representations that these viewers pointed out are grounded in Islamic teachings that prohibit alcohol consumption and homosexuality, capitalizing on (at least some) Muslims' aversion to these allegedly sinful behaviors. Interestingly, while these two viewers criticized the depictions of Christian characters' personal lives, they did not voice similar complaints about these series' political messages; that is, they did not seem to be troubled by the portrayals of Christians and Jews as cunning figures determined to destroy Turks and Muslims. The sympathy the participants extended to Christian characters in regards their personal lives did not transfer to their political activities. When asked why, both mentioned that there are ongoing "coordinated attacks against Muslim nations" around the world undertaken by "Americans and powerful Jewish circles."[81]

Another strand of criticism was related to the prevalence of depictions of violence, especially in *Resurrection* and *Establishment*. As a female viewer put it, these series "are too violent. Everyone says you can watch them with your kids because there is no sexuality, but I am worried about all that bloodshedding."[82] This point was echoed by another participant, a male, who expressed concern about the conflicting messages these dramas communicate: that "on one hand, Islam is a religion of peace and Muslims are not terrorists, and on the other, Muslims are beheading Christians."[83]

Influence of Ottoman Rule on Audience Responses

Does the generally positive reception mentioned above result in approval of Turkey's proposed leadership of Muslims worldwide? Does it raise awareness of Turkey's outreach efforts in predominantly Muslim countries in the Global South? The individuals I interviewed did not explicitly express any cultural or political endorsement of Turkey (or Erdoğan) along these lines. This lack of endorsement can be attributed to the fact that these viewers primarily interpret these dramas through a religious lens rather than that of national identity. As evident from the aforementioned comments, they perceive the main characters primarily as Muslim rather than Turkish. When comparing the storylines and real-life events, they tend to view the contrast between Muslims and the West rather than between Turks and the West. Consequently, the overshadowing of Turkish identity by religious identity can help elucidate why these dramas do not automatically generate immediate approval of Turkey as the leader of Muslims.

Furthermore, the viewers I interviewed displayed limited awareness of the outreach activities undertaken by the Erdoğan government in Africa and Southeast Asia, unless their respective countries receive(d) Turkish humanitarian aid and development assistance, host(ed) Turkish cultural and educational organizations, or witness(ed) a surge in Turkish business investments. In this context, only three participants from Ethiopia, Somalia, and South Africa expressed positive views regarding Turkey's presence in their countries.

Finally, the audiences I interviewed for this study were predominantly from countries that were not historically part of the Ottoman Empire (see the appendix). This was not a deliberate selection on my part but, rather, a result of the recruitment process, where no viewers from the Middle East or the Balkans volunteered to participate. This raises a couple of interesting questions: Are the AKP-sanctioned historical dramas better received in regions where viewers have no historical connection to the Ottoman Empire? Conversely, do audiences in countries that were once part of the Ottoman Empire tend to offer more critical responses to these dramas?[84] To answer these questions, in-depth audience studies are required to ascertain the extent to which the historical experience of Ottoman rule, or lack thereof, influences audience reception. Nonetheless, there is already a certain level of negative reaction to the AKP-sanctioned dramas in the Middle East and the Balkans—two regions ruled by the Ottoman Empire for centuries. This sentiment is especially evident in the Middle East where regional actors often clash with the Erdoğan government. In 2018 the Dubai-based satellite network MBC Group announced the suspension of all Turkish series, without providing a specific reason. Although privately owned, MBC maintains political connections with the Saudi royal family. Erdoğan's aspirations to revive Turkey's historical position as the leader of the global Muslim community have long been viewed as a source of contention by Saudi Arabia and its allies. Therefore, analysts interpreted MBC's decision as politically motivated, aiming to "curb Turkey's soft power" and exert pressure on Erdoğan to alter his Middle East policy.[85] After MBC's announcement, Egypt followed suit, banning all Turkish content in the country. Egypt's Dar Al-Iftaa al-Misriyyah, one of the oldest and most influential bodies responsible for issuing religious edicts across the Arab world, accused Turkey of trying to create an "area of influence" for itself in the Middle East. It issued a fatwa that specifically targeted *Resurrection* because it allegedly aimed to revive the Ottoman Empire and "regain sovereignty over Arab countries."[86]

In 2019 Saudi Arabia and the United Arab Emirates (UAE) financed a television series to reveal the "hypocrisy and cruelty of the Ottoman Empire towards the Arabs." They poured US$40 million into producing *Mamalik el-Nar* (Kingdoms of Fire) that was later broadcast on MBC. According to its producer, the fourteen-episode drama aimed to show the audiences that the Ottoman Empire was "not the zenith of Muslim unity, but a dark time for the Arabs." Criticizing Erdoğan's policies in the Middle East, the producer said: "The Arab world entered into darkness because of the Ottoman invasion. After all of the criminal actions of the Ottomans in the area, some people present them as the protectors of Islam. And now, these neo-Ottomans [a reference to the AKP cadres] say they will restore grandeur to the Islamic nation. We had to respond to this."[87] In 2023 MBC aired another series *Safar Barlik* based on Arab characters that revolt against the Ottoman Empire's conscription orders during World War I. Across twenty episodes, *Safar Barlik* (literally translated as "military mobilization") portrays Turks as ruthless colonialists that torture and kill Arabs.[88] That the show aired during the holy month of Ramadan when TV viewership spikes across the Middle East is a testament to Saudi Arabia's determination to remind audiences of the "horrifying days of the Ottoman Empire" in the region and undercut Turkish dramas' appeal.[89]

Turkish series have also elicited negative responses in the Balkans, a region ruled by the Ottomans for nearly five hundred years. In the early 2010s religious and nationalist groups in the Balkans campaigned against *Magnificent Century*, and a Greek Orthodox bishop even declared that the very act of watching the show was "tantamount to telling [Turks] that we've surrendered."[90] In 2012 a nationalist Serbian group launched a campaign against *Magnificent Century* because of its alleged representation of "[the Ottoman sultan] Suleiman as a positive historic personality," which contradicted the Serbs' view of Ottomans as harsh rulers that subjugated Balkan communities.[91] Viewers in Kosovo reacted against *The Last Emperor* because it depicted Abdülhamid II as a "virtuous leader" and the Ottoman Empire as a "positive force."[92]

Countering Stereotypes and Unintended Consequences

This chapter has examined the narratives presented in *Resurrection*, *Establishment*, and *The Last Emperor*, which depict military and political conflicts between Turks and their adversaries. All three dramas revolve around courageous, devout, and honorable Muslim men who confront external (mainly Western) powers and internal traitors. The storylines intertwine military battles and political intrigues with religious rituals. These rituals serve to emphasize an Islamic ethos and convey notions of hope, unity, mercy, salvation, and sacrifice. By doing so, these series position Islamic civilization, particularly as embodied, preserved, and defended by Turks, as superior to the purportedly immoral, oppressive, and unjust West—a recurring theme in Erdoğan's global messaging, as discussed in chapters 3 and 4.

Muslim audiences find gratification in positive portrayals of Islam and Muslims these series offer, especially against the backdrop of the realities of the post–September 11 world. As global media scholar Wazhmah Osman notes, since September 11, there has been a spike in the negative portrayals of Arabs, Muslims, and, more broadly, people from the MENASA region (Middle East, North Africa, South Asia) in Global North media and popular cultures.[93] These representations, whose roots can be traced back to early twentieth-century Hollywood films, have cemented the notion that people from the MENASA region are "despotic and barbaric" and/or "Islamic extremists and terrorists" and thus "in need of punishment, intervention, and saving" by the US security apparatus. Countless films and television shows have circulated these representations (and continue to do so), thus "reinforc[ing] the hierarchy of imperial power."[94] In contrast, AKP-sanctioned historical dramas provide alternative and positive perspectives on Islam and Muslims, as highlighted by the audiences I interviewed. This then raises the question of whether these series can be seen as counter-hegemonic responses to the prevailing stereotypes found in American and European popular culture texts. While the initial answer to this question leans toward affirmation, it is crucial to also consider these series' political functions and implications.

The influence of Turkish historical dramas extends beyond depicting Muslims in a positive light. These AKP-sanctioned narratives intertwine the so-called Islamic golden age with the Ottoman imperial past while labelling Turkish Islamic civilization as distinct and superior to its Western counterpart. Regrettably, a side effect emerges when these historical dramas employ a method of Othering, similar to what Western media and popular culture industries do in their representations of Muslims. These series perpetuate civilizational dualities between Muslims and the West, portraying the latter as oppressive, scheming, and deceitful (sometimes incorporating latent or explicit anti-Semitic content) and thus perpetuating Huntington's "clash of civilizations" thesis (see chapter 4).

As social scientists Sebastian Haug and Supriya Roychoudhury note, Turkey portrays itself as a compassionate and paternal figure, assuming the role of "the world's conscience," a term frequently used by the AKP rank and file. Government officials present Turkish altruism as deeply rooted in the civilizational framework of Islamic charity and solidarity, based on a favorable interpretation of the Ottoman Empire. It is important to acknowledge that while these assertions disseminate exultant narratives about the Turks, they also promote a sense of Othering. As discussed earlier, AKP-sanctioned dramas sharply align Muslim Turks with justice, compassion, mercy, and generosity, and Christians and Jews with deceit, hypocrisy, and backstabbing. In this regard, they very much invoke the narratives utilized by ethno-nationalist political movements in other parts of the world, albeit from the other side. In Europe the prevailing civilizational framework accentuates Christianity as a culture that aligns with values such as "human rights, tolerance, gender equality, and support for gay rights" while labeling Islam as a threat to Europe and its civilization.[95] In the United States the religious right expresses concern about the alleged persecution of Christianity and its associated civilizational principles. This sentiment was dangerously echoed by Donald Trump, who called upon Europeans and Americans to safeguard Western civilization from internal or external forces that "come from the South or the East [and] that threaten to erase the bonds of culture, faith and tradition that make us who we are."[96] In India Hindu nationalists use civilization-based identity markers to portray Muslims as "others" who offend Hindu values while presenting the country's "millennium-old traditions of eastern spirit" as the source of its cultural and moral superiority.[97]

Considering the fact that similar practices of Othering, albeit from the opposite side, permeate the AKP-approved historical dramas, the broader implications of these popular cultural texts must be carefully assessed. Given the reasons outlined above, it is imperative not to simply perceive them as righteous counter-hegemonic responses to Western portrayals of Muslims. Instead, one must firmly acknowledge the existence of divisive narratives within these shows.

Conclusion

Talking Back to the West has presented an analysis of Turkey's global communication apparatus, focusing on its expansion, objectives, and strategies. It has examined the development of its various components in light of intersecting domestic, regional, and international developments and dissected the political economic structures and ideational frameworks that define their activities.

In the early 2010s the AKP used its newly established Office of Public Diplomacy, the government-aligned think tank SETA, and the state-run channels TRT Arabi and TRT Kurdi to promote Turkey as a rising power in the Middle East and a reliable partner of the Western alliance. Capitalizing on Western policymakers' (albeit misguided) portrayals of Turkey as an exemplary combination of democracy, market economy, and Islam, the AKP enjoyed a favorable position on the world stage. However, by the mid-2010s the tide turned dramatically for both the AKP's and the country's image. Erdoğan's consolidation of political authority, securitization of the Kurdish issue, and support for Sunni factions in Syria drew extensive scrutiny from Western media and policy circles, and the AKP officials found themselves compelled to rectify Turkey's deteriorating image.

To counteract the negative coverage in Western media, generally perceived as deliberate attacks against Turkey, the AKP and its allies undertook concerted efforts to expand the country's presence in the global communication order. The removal of Gülenist actors from international communication and public diplomacy spheres had left a void, further fueling the AKP's concerns about public messaging. Moreover, the ambitious geopolitical economic agenda that the government was pursuing in the Global South necessitated effective engagement with international audiences. In 2015 the Erdoğan government launched TRT World to communicate its policies, values, and vision to English-speaking audiences around the world. Existing organizations, such as the Anadolu Agency and SETA, played their parts by echoing the government's preferred narratives in their news coverage and policy reports, respectively. Erdoğan loyalists joined in these efforts by launching the newspaper the *Daily Sabah* and the digital communication and public relations venture Bosphorus Global. The AKP and its allies have continued to grow this globally oriented network, subsequently launching digital news platforms in languages other than English.

In addition to these news and information-related endeavors, state organs, such as the Directorate of Communications, TRT, the Anadolu Agency, and TIKA, have all been working to expand Turkey's influence and visibility in the global communication order. These entities undertake various initiatives such as organizing international media forums, spearheading regional collaborations, and offering journalism training programs and material support to media outlets in the Global South.

Whether under state control or run by pro-Erdoğan loyalists, these entities share a set of common objectives as discussed in detail in the introduction. One of their primary goals is to shape a favorable perception of Turkey and create global influence. These entities actively promote Turkey's accomplishments and present the country as a prominent actor in conflict resolution, humanitarian aid, and development assistance. Additionally, they strive to validate Turkey's domestic and foreign policy choices, particularly those that are prone to attracting scrutiny from international media and policy circles. Important events in Turkey, such as presidential elections, as well as contentious foreign policy initiatives, such as military operations in northern Syria, represent pivotal moments when the AKP-directed communication instruments allocate substantial resources to validate the government's actions, all the while overlooking any missteps.

In connection with this legitimation work, another objective of Turkey's global communication apparatus is to criticize foreign adversaries in accordance with the government's geopolitical economic agenda. The topics that generate disapproving coverage from AKP-backed outlets include but are not limited to the United States' support for the YPG in northern Syria, Greece's and France's objections to Turkey's expansion of maritime zones, Syrian President Assad's atrocities against civilians, and Germany's and Sweden's granting refuge to Gülenists and PKK members. AKP-aligned communication entities also monitor domestic developments within Europe and the United States, aiming to accentuate their internal crises. By addressing Islamophobia, far-right extremism, antirefugee policies, rights violations, and police brutality in these countries, they portray the West as morally flawed, hypocritical, and in decline. Concurrently, they project Turkey as the champion of "the voiceless" (i.e., those who experience political economic, social marginalization at the hands of Western powers) and as a rising great power capable of challenging Western hegemony and creating a more just global order. This portrayal of Turkey as a benevolent force pursuing justice and human rights under Erdoğan's leadership constitutes a pivotal component of the AKP's global communication activities.

Beneath the efforts to discredit the West lies a deeper agenda of interpellating Muslims and rallying them under Turkey's purportedly altruistic leadership of the ummah. The depiction of the West as immoral, power-driven, and dishonest serves as a strategic tool for the Erdoğan regime to position itself as the guardian of Muslims while portraying its geopolitical economic ventures in the Global South as righteous endeavors aimed at forging a fairer world on behalf of all oppressed peoples. This vision positions Turkey's foreign policy actions as evidence of its resolute defiance toward the West—a clever tactic employed by the AKP to appeal to the Global South, which has long suffered from Western (neo)colonialism. Across a wide range of communicative activities from news reports and documentaries to conferences and television dramas, AKP-backed outlets reinforce the notion of civilizational dualities between Turkey and the West, such as just versus unjust, moral versus immoral.

In light of the aforementioned observations, it is evident that these negative portrayals of the West are not solely driven by journalistic intentions to report noteworthy events. They are also rooted in political calculations and ideological principles. *Talking Back to the West* has unveiled the multifaceted factors that contribute to the Erdoğan regime's global messaging, from contemporary foreign policy objectives to the deeper cultural and identitarian dynamics. It has thus shown how the Erdoğan regime instrumentalizes a discourse that revolves around human rights and justice in order to rationalize its antidemocratic measures within its own borders and its power-oriented geopolitical economic agenda in the Global South.

A New Communication Order? A Postcolonial Critique?

Erdoğan's emissaries present their communication activities as crucial steps aimed at disrupting Western media imperialism and rectifying the power imbalances within global communication flows. Their perspective is largely influenced by their interpretation of Western journalists, news organizations, and social media companies as collaborators with foreign governments in a concerted effort to destabilize Turkey. As discussed in chapters 1 and 2, the

AKP cadres perceive Western media as a source of threat to the survival of the state, echoing the anxieties of Ottoman officials regarding the dominant position of the European press and news agencies in the late nineteenth century.

They accuse Western news organizations and social media companies of displaying bias in their coverage of Turkey and launching disinformation campaigns, all of which they assert are part of a larger imperialistic scheme. Consequently, they frame Turkey's global communication endeavors as a counteroffensive against the West and as representative of their efforts to redress the imbalances in global communications. A noteworthy illustration of this perspective can be found in Fahrettin Altun's speech during the launch event for TRT Français in 2022:

> We are faced with the dominance, the hegemony of a handful international media companies. Despite their dominant position, these companies do not function as the voice of truth or the mirror of reality. Instead, they continue to [publish and broadcast] as per the interests of the global order of exploitation, the global order of oppression. TRT's new initiative [TRT Français] is the rejection of this international hegemony. It's an attempt to offer an alternative. Just as TRT World and TRT's other channels do. [It] is an illustration of Turkey's objection to global injustice. It is a reflection of our Esteemed President's motto, "The world is bigger than five" and "A fairer world is possible."[1]

Similar to TRT, the Anadolu Agency is also portrayed as an example of Turkey's commitment to eradicate the "injustices in global information flows," in the words of Yusuf Özkır, board member of the Anadolu Agency. According to Özkır, the Anadolu Agency is a catalyst in Turkey's endeavors to transition from being a passive recipient of news to an active producer and distributor. This transformation is viewed as an integral part of Turkey's broader aspiration to challenge the prevailing dynamics of global order and exert greater control over the narratives that shape international perceptions: "The Anadolu Agency is now competing with global news agencies. It now has a share in this market that is dominated by foreign agencies. It is working to reverse their unidirectional, West-centric news flows. Changes in information flows can lead to an equitable [information] order."[2]

There are parallels between Turkish officials' narratives and the objectives of the NWICO movement (see chapter 2). Erdoğan's emissaries articulate the necessity to challenge the privileged position of Eurocentric knowledge and information systems and consistently emphasize the importance of empowering those who have been silenced. Echoing various arguments put forth by postcolonial thinkers, these emissaries exhibit a recurring focus on power dynamics and inequality, agency and resistance, voice and representation. While it is not my intention to provide an exhaustive point-by-point analysis of the resonances between postcolonial criticism and Turkish officials' arguments, it is, nonetheless, important to briefly acknowledge some prominent postcolonial thinkers whose ideas are repurposed by Turkish officials. In terms of power hierarchies that exist in knowledge production and dissemination, one notable work is Walter Mignolo's manifesto on "epistemic disobedience."[3] Mignolo contends that prevailing knowledge systems, predominantly based on Western epistemology, have systematically marginalized and oppressed alternative forms of knowledge, especially those originating from colonized societies. He proposes "epistemic disobedience" as a means of raising questions about who generates knowledge and where this knowledge is generated, changing the content of knowledge systems and the "terms of the conversation" between dominant and marginalized groups.[4] In a similar vein, Dipesh Chakrabarty questions the notion of Europe as the original site of modernity and criticizes the disproportionate prominence given to European social and political thought. He argues that Eurocentric notions of capitalism, history, and time are not inherently universal but were constructed and imposed as such through processes of imperialism and various nationalisms.[5]

In regard to voice and representation, one needs to mention Gayatri Spivak, who in her influential essay "Can the Subaltern Speak?" raises critical questions about the challenges of representation, power dynamics, and the complexities of giving agency to marginalized groups within oppressive systems.[6] Spivak notes that the subaltern's voice is often silenced and distorted and that attempts at representing the subaltern or giving them a voice may inadvertently reinforce the very systems of power they seek to challenge and lead the marginalized people to rely on Western intellectuals to speak about their experiences. Spivak also criticizes "epistemic violence," that is, the projection of Eurocentric norms and knowledges on developing countries while ignoring the political interests of the creators.

In light of the Erdoğan government's calls to decenter the West and to reorient Turkey and Muslim publics from "passive to active, inert to sovereign, represent*ed* to represent*er*" (to use Deniz Kandiyoti's words),[7] can we assess Turkey's global communication efforts within the context of postcolonial resistance? Can we interpret the regime emissaries' activities to disrupt the Orientalist gaze as genuinely counter-hegemonic? Are Turkey's international communication and knowledge production activities representative of an epistemic emancipation? Do the AKP-aligned communication instruments undertake a genuine humanist critique of the West? Do they offer an affirmation of universal norms and values about human rights? No, is the brief response to these inquiries. Now, let me elaborate further.

To begin, regime emissaries' criticisms of the global communication order (although generally correct) do not comprise a nuanced understanding of the intricate power-knowledge relationships. Their perspective relies on simplistic notions that portray Western media organizations and professionals either as minions at the service of their respective governments or as inherently Orientalist and biased against Erdoğan (see chapter 1). They reduce the complex web of relationships among governments, regulatory bodies, media and technology companies, and audiences to a narrative about the West meddling in Turkey's internal affairs (see chapter 2). An illustrative example of this pattern occurred during TRT World's special coverage of Turkey's presidential elections in May 2023. On the day of the runoff, May 28, TRT World aired a segment that analyzed how international news media covered the Turkish elections. The segment singled out the *Economist*, *New York Times*, *Washington Post*, *Guardian*, *Politico*, and *Foreign Policy*, arguing that their coverage showcased a clear desire to see Erdoğan removed from office. In another segment aired on the same day, Klaus Jurgens, one of TRT World's foreign analysts, suggested that Turkey's success and influence in recent years had led to an increase in negative coverage by Western media. Jurgens lamented that editorial boards of Western media organizations were singling out Erdoğan as an object of hatred, thereby exacerbating divisions within European societies.[8]

This skeptical view of Western media doesn't merely stem from a limited comprehension of the intricate interplay between media and politics. As Nadje Al-Ali aptly points out, overly simplified depictions of the West aren't exclusively born out of misunderstanding or ignorance. Rather, they are integral components of broader political agendas: "Blaming the West for most evils in the world is generally paralleled by a passionate and uncritical embracing of one's own primordial group without paying too much attention to the social, cultural, economic and political realities inside one's nation."[9]

In this regard, it is crucial to explore how the actions of the Erdoğan government are primarily motivated by self-interest and a deliberate disregard for their own errors, rather than a sincere commitment to advancing the democratization of global communication. As demonstrated throughout this book, the Erdoğan government strategically expanded its global communication tools during the early to mid-2010s to justify its authoritarian policies within Turkey as well as its irredentist foreign policy agenda in the Middle East and North Africa. Since then AKP-aligned communication entities have strived to confer legitimacy upon Erdoğan's domestic and foreign policy moves and, ultimately, to accrue (more) power to his personalized regime.

Examining several parallel developments provides a greater clarity on this matter. As the Erdoğan government has expanded its political economic and cultural outreach activities in the Global South, it has opportunistically utilized Islamophobia and other instances of Muslim suffering to portray itself as a champion of justice and a defiant actor speaking truth to power. As it escalated Turkey's political and military involvement in Syria and Libya, it has amplified the humanitarian aspects of its foreign policy. As it consolidated its grip on media outlets in Turkey, it has positioned Turkey as an actor aiming to dismantle Western media hegemony and as an advocate of media professionals and organizations based in the Global South.

The Erdoğan government's utilization of such counter-hegemonic arguments serves to legitimize Turkey in the eyes of the global community. Nora Fisher-Onar, an international studies scholar, aptly articulates this phenomenon as a result of the "moral injury" that Turkey (and other postimperial states such as Russia and China) experienced vis-à-vis the West in the nineteenth and twentieth centuries.[10] Military defeats, political setbacks, and near colonization by Western powers left enduring scars on these successor states. Moreover, these states' efforts to elevate their status in the post-empire era within a Western-dominated international system have given rise to additional anxieties. To reaffirm their ontological security, postimperial states construct fresh narratives that emphasize specific glories and traumas from their imperial past. These narratives invoke a sense of world-historic grandeur and play a crucial role in positioning the successor states as resurgent great powers offering alternative viewpoints to Western universalism. In addition to portraying the West as an adversary, these narratives also scrutinize the role of Western powers as norm-setters within the international system. Simultaneously, they aim to convince their Global South interlocutors that imperialism is an exclusively Western phenomenon, even as they themselves pursue postimperial projects in their neighboring regions.

Talking Back to the West has detailed the utilization of such narratives by the Erdoğan government, shedding light on the profound cynicism that accompanies them, especially in light of Turkey's pursuit of antidemocratic and irredentist goals—at home or abroad. It has argued that the AKP-backed initiatives have a detrimental impact on the global communication landscape because they strategically obfuscate complex social, political, cultural phenomena; reinforce binary identity constructs; and perpetuate civilizational dualities between Muslims and the West. In an era defined by post-truth where the proliferation of dis/misinformation poses significant threats to democracy, the Erdoğan government's global communication apparatus should not be regarded as an exemplar of counter-hegemony or merely as an extension of Turkey's public diplomacy efforts. Instead, it should be recognized as a venture carried out by an undemocratic and power-driven regime, one that is shaped by long-standing religious and cultural grievances.

Suggestions for Future Research

Talking Back to the West has examined Turkey's English-language communication activities undertaken by state-run organizations and loyalist actors in media and civil society aligned with the Erdoğan regime's foreign policy and ideational frameworks. It has emphasized that at the heart of the regime's communication strategy lies a highly instrumentalized counter-hegemonic approach. Given its scope, *Talking Back to the West* has deliberately set aside a number of questions. This section reviews some of these questions, aiming to stimulate future research in the fields of journalism, global media, and political communication.

To begin with, scholars of journalism can study the extent and characteristics of government intervention within news organizations supported by the AKP. Compared to their Russian and Chinese counterparts, Turkish state-backed media outlets, such as TRT World and the Anadolu Agency, have not received adequate attention with regard to questions about editorial independence, internal tensions that stem from government interference, or journalists' handling of top-down directives in their everyday work.[11] As of 2023, only Elswah and Howard analyzed how the Erdoğan government exercises control over TRT World.[12] Based on interviews with journalists, Elswah and Howard show that TRT World managers, handpicked from among Erdoğan loyalists, ensure a government-friendly tone in the channel's output and that the government control has increased sharply after the coup attempt in 2016. These points have also been confirmed by channel executives and employees I interviewed for this book. According to two of my interviewees, top-down editorial direction during and in the wake of the coup attempt became more pronounced; Turkish executives received "talking points" from Erdoğan's advisers and shaped the coverage accordingly. Although foreign journalists had always known that they were supposed to cover certain issues as per Turkish state narratives (for example, one cannot use the word "genocide" in reference to the 1915 killings of Armenians), political interference in the postcoup period became too extreme to tolerate and led to the departures of approximately three dozen foreign employees (out of the entire two hundred workforce) in the summer of 2016. Eren, the then director general of TRT, rejected the claims about government control and imputed this exodus to foreign employees' general "security concerns."[13]

TRT World employees I interviewed shared other stories about government influence on the channel's editorial line and day-to-day practices, as well.

For example, foreign journalists working on a story about Turkey's mayoral elections in 2019 were told by a local executive not to announce the AKP candidates' losses until they got the greenlight from senior management. On another occasion, a foreign producer found out that a segment of his show would be edited out because of a political comment made by one of the on-air guests. Although the said comment was from several years ago and not even directly related to Erdoğan, AKP, or Turkey, it was, nonetheless, interpreted by a senior manager as risky.

While chapters 3 and 4 discuss how government narratives cascade from high-ranking state officials down to executives and editors, further in-depth analyses are still necessary to understand quotidian tensions, negotiations, and collaborations in newsrooms at TRT World, the Anadolu Agency, and the *Daily Sabah*. For example, how do Turkish executives responsible for ensuring pro-government coverage navigate their interactions with foreign staff members who desire to exercise a certain level of agency? Are there instances of tension or negotiation between these parties? What is the perception of local and foreign staff members within these organizations regarding their organizations' links with the Erdoğan government? Do they view it as collaborative, adversarial, or a mix of both? How do these perceptions shape their professional conduct and decision making? How do local and foreign staff members perceive the impact of the Erdoğan government's crackdown on the media landscape in Turkey? Does it affect their trust in the credibility and independence of the organizations they work for? These are important questions that would help scholars to gain a comprehensive understanding of the media-politics framework within and beyond these organizations.

In addition to examining the interplay between structure and agency within news organizations, researchers can also investigate the political and economic factors influencing the recruitment and retention of personnel at TRT World, the Anadolu Agency, and the *Daily Sabah*. Through my interviews with current and former employees of TRT World and the *Daily Sabah*, it became apparent that local editors, producers, and journalists are predominantly selected from AKP loyalists, with specific emphasis placed on their past or present affiliations with Gülenists—a factor that renders them ineligible for employment. Of course, different criteria are employed when it comes to selecting foreign staff members. In its early days, TRT World made a deliberate effort to hire renowned journalists and producers primarily from Al Jazeera English, both to give the channel a head start and to enhance its credibility. But when numerous foreign employees resigned in the wake of the coup attempt in 2016, TRT World made the decision to fill those positions with media personnel from Turkey and/or the Global South. As per one of my interviewees, the recruitment of young journalists of Global South descent had already been underway prior to the coup attempt, in order to ensure "Turkey-friendly" coverage and to gradually replace "Westerners."[14] This strategic shift was also motivated by cost considerations, as "Westerners" incurred higher expenses for the channel (e.g., higher salaries paid in foreign currency as opposed to Turkish lira, rent assistance, private school tuition for children). Once TRT World evolved into a fully operational channel, it became feasible to substitute the Western journalists with Turkish and other non-Western journalists.[15] This was also confirmed to me by a former TRT executive:

> [TRT World] had two different hiring systems for foreigners. One for Westerners and others who came from Al Jazeera, Deutsche Welle, and CGTN. Another one for non-Westerners. This second group was mostly young journalists from Pakistan and South Africa. Some of them were second-generation Muslims in Europe. Their salaries were lower than the Westerners and ex–Al Jazeera people. They didn't have the same extras, like housing assistance. This was known as the "Paki package." [TRT World managers] thought [these young reporters] could learn from experienced Westerners and Al Jazeera journalists, and then take their place in the future.[16]

Undoubtedly, this hierarchical hiring system is deeply troubling on multiple fronts. It perpetuates inequality, exhibits racist tendencies, and showcases a profound level of cynicism, particularly when juxtaposed with TRT World and the AKP's self-proclaimed roles as advocates for marginalized Muslims. However, this tiered recruitment-and-retention approach is not exclusive to non-Western staff but also extends to Turkish individuals. As a foreign producer at TRT World told me:

> Foreign staff that came from Al Jazeera, like presenters, news directors, producers, department heads.... They are paid huge salaries in US dollars. Their rents for luxury apartments in Istanbul and private school fees for their children are all covered. For Turkish employees, it is different. They don't have that preferential treatment. And I think they were resentful. I don't know, maybe some of them were even happy when [foreign staff] quit after the coup attempt.[17]

Given the dynamics within newsrooms, further research is imperative to examine the hiring schemes employed by TRT World and other media outlets supported by the AKP. Such investigations would provide valuable insights into the tensions that may arise between Western, non-Western, and Turkish staff members, shedding light on these intricate dynamics.

Apart from the aforementioned inquiries within the field of journalism studies, there are additional avenues of exploration for scholars of global media, such as similarities and differences between Turkish and other state-backed communication activities. There is extant literature that shows how states and elected governments engage with foreign publics to cultivate a favorable image, promote their ideas and policies, and extend their sphere of influence at regional or global levels.[18] Turkey's state-run news organizations share similarities with those operated by China and Russia in terms of motivations and strategies. A notable common factor is the sponsoring states' grievances toward the global media order, particularly the belief that their respective countries receive biased treatment from Western media outlets.[19] For example, Chinese authorities were frustrated with the Western news coverage of the Tiananmen Square massacre, and Russian officials strongly criticized the Western focus on the Color Revolutions.[20] As chapter 1 shows, the AKP was alarmed with foreign news reports about the Gezi protests and with the portrayal of Erdoğan as an autocrat. These instances highlight the discontent experienced by China, Russia, and Turkey toward the Western perspective (i.e., the focus on human rights and democracy) and help to explain why these countries decided to establish their own English-language news channels: to provide an alternative approach to global news coverage, present their own perspectives, and, ultimately, influence global public opinion in their favor. The launch of international news channels, news agencies, newspapers, or news sites by Russia, China, and Turkey can also be viewed as an attempt to challenge the Anglo-American monopoly on news and foster greater diversity in global information flows.[21] This goal of balancing the information flows between the Global South and the North is also shared by Al Jazeera English, which aims to report overlooked stories from the standpoint of "the voiceless"—representing the Global South, the marginalized, and the oppressed.[22]

Apart from the aforementioned motives, TRT World also exhibits similarities with RT and CGTN in terms of strategies. Similar to RT, TRT World generates critical narratives regarding the West and fosters "doubts about its media, agenda and values" but without openly endorsing anti-Western conspiracy theories.[23] Like CGTN, TRT World aims to rectify Western misrepresentations of the country, explain its stance and values, and promote its achievements.[24]

Considering these similarities, scholars of global communication can delve into the impact of sociocultural encounters between Russia, China, Turkey, and dominant Western powers. As noted in the previous section, culturally informed analyses of postimperial states' interactions with the West can add invaluable insights into studies of Russia's and China's global communication activities.[25] In these analyses, scholars can also observe the utilization of civilizationist narratives by postimperial states that seek to bolster their legitimacy while also aiming to reshape the global order. Some potential questions to address in this regard would include the following: What are the central themes and narratives within Russia's and China's civilizationist discourse, and how do they shape their global communication efforts? Are there specific historical or cultural references that are frequently highlighted in these global communication efforts? How do civilizationist narratives change in response to evolving international or domestic events?

Another promising area for research involves Turkey's external communication activities in languages other than English. While the focus of *Talking Back to the West* has been on English-language content, there is a need for in-depth analyses of TRT's other television channels (TRT Kurdi and TRT Arabi) as well as digital news platforms (TRT Balkan, TRT Français, TRT Deutsch, TRT Russian, and TRT Afrika). Additionally, exploring the foreign-language editions of the *Daily Sabah* and Anadolu Agency would be worthwhile. Conducting longitudinal studies on the content of TRT Arabi and TRT Kurdi can provide insights into how these channels' coverage of the Middle East has evolved in line with the AKP's changing relationships with Egypt, Israel, Saudi Arabia, Syria, and the Kurdish political movement in Turkey. TRT Afrika is worthwhile to study since it complements Turkey's pivot to Africa in terms of diplomacy, trade, humanitarian aid, cultural and educational exchange, and development communication.

Due to its scope, *Talking Back to the West* has knowingly eschewed an analysis of Voice of Turkey, but it is, nonetheless, important to acknowledge the significant role that radio plays as a source of news and entertainment around the world. Consequently, Voice of Turkey warrants further attention from scholars. Researchers can investigate its expansion since the first decade of the 2000s, examining its political and cultural significance in the Balkans, Central Asia, and Africa. Additionally, there is a need to explore whether and how Voice of Turkey fills the void left by Western governments' closure of their long-standing radio services (e.g., BBC World Service) in these regions.

Last but not least, it is essential to examine how Turkey's global communication content is perceived by foreign audiences and whether it generates legitimacy and influence for the Erdoğan government. This inquiry is crucial in understanding the role of global communication as a mechanism for legitimization, particularly, for authoritarian actors like Erdoğan, who are consistently concerned with maintaining their regime's stability. Currently, there is a lack of audience research specifically focused on AKP-backed outlets. Although the popularity of TRT World, the Anadolu Agency, and other entities can be measured to some extent by way of their social media statistics, the focus on social media popularity may not be representative of their overall influence. To comprehensively assess whether these outlets contribute to legitimizing and exerting influence on behalf of Erdoğan, scholars would need to conduct qualitative audience analyses. This approach would provide valuable insights into the reception of Turkey's global communication efforts.

Appendix

Table A1. Research Participants Interviewed for Chapter 5

Research Participant	Country of Origin	Gender
1	Afghanistan	Male
2	Afghanistan	Male
3	Afghanistan	Female
4	Bangladesh	Male
5	Bangladesh	Female
6	Bangladesh	Female
7	Indonesia	Female
8	Indonesia	Male
9	Indonesia	Male
10	Indonesia	Female
11	Indonesia	Male
12	Malaysia	Male
13	Malaysia	Male
14	Malaysia	Female
15	Malaysia	Female
16	Pakistan	Female
17	Pakistan	Male
18	Pakistan	Male
19	Pakistan	Male (lives in the UK)

Research Participant	Country of Origin	Gender
20	Pakistan	Female
21	South Africa	Male
22	South Africa	Female
23	South Africa	Male (lives in the United States)
24	South Africa	Female
25	South Africa	Female
26	Sri Lanka	Male
27	Sri Lanka	Male

Notes

Introduction

1. Presidency of the Republic of Türkiye, "TRT World's Cameras."
2. The term "Global South" obviously goes beyond geographic connotations. Although the term does not have a single straightforward definition, in this book I use it to refer to a "transnational political subjectivity" of peoples and spaces who have been negatively impacted by contemporary capitalist globalization and who have experienced the "humiliation, racism, genderism" caused by coloniality. See Mahler, *From the Tricontinental to the Global South*, 32; Mignolo, "Global South and World Dis/Order," 185. The term also evokes the dominated peoples' agency and their attempts to transform the "colonial matrix of power" in politics, economy, or knowledge production. See Dirlik, "Global South," Mignolo, "Global South and World Dis/Order."
3. Presidency of the Republic of Türkiye, "TRT World's Cameras."
4. A caveat is in order about how I use the terms such as "the West" and "Western." For the AKP and broader nationalist Islamist circles in Turkey, "the West" is an imagined homogenous entity, which primarily refers to European countries, the United States, and Israel, as well as Canada, Australia, and New Zealand. "The West" and related terms, such as, "Western powers," "Western media," "Western journalists," are deeply embedded in Turkey's social, cultural, and political vocabulary. For this and stylistic reasons, I use these terms without quotation marks throughout the book and ask the readers not to interpret it as a sign of essentialization.
5. TRT, *Faaliyet Raporu 2022*, 315.
6. The Erdoğan regime uses the term "a fairer world" to reiterate that the existing global order is not fair and, therefore, must be rebuilt. It is also the title of a book allegedly penned by Erdoğan himself—*A Fairer World Is Possible: A Proposed Model for a United Nations Reform* (Istanbul: Turkuvaz Kitap, 2021).
7. I am grateful to one of the anonymous reviewers for suggesting the term "strategic reductionism," which ultimately inspired my use of "strategic obfuscation."
8. Bernays, *Propaganda*; Ellul, *Propaganda*; Laswell, *Propaganda Techniques*; Jowett and O'Donnell, *Propaganda and Persuasion*.

9. Cull, *Public Diplomacy*, 1.
10. Cull, *Public Diplomacy*, 13.
11. Nye, "Soft Power."
12. For a critical and comparative analysis of the concept, see Baykurt and de Grazia, *Soft Power Internationalism*.
13. Cull, *Selling War* and *Cold War*; Jenks, *British Propaganda*; Herf, *Nazi Propaganda*; Rawnsley, "Introduction."
14. Livingston, *Terrorism Spectacle*; Entman, *Projections of Power*; Snow and Kamalipour, *War, Media, and Propaganda*; Briant, *Propaganda and Counter-Terrorism*; Miskimmon, O'Loughlin, and Roselle, *Strategic Narratives*; Brady, "Authoritarianism Goes Global"; Jamieson, *Cyberwar*; Pomerantsev, "Authoritarianism Goes Global"; Bastos and Farkas, "'Donald Trump Is My President"; Fisher, "Demonizing the Enemy"; Moore and Colley, "Two International Propaganda Models."
15. Wang, *Soft Power in China*; Thussu, *Communicating India's Soft Power*; Gao, Ingram, and Kee, *Global Media and Public Diplomacy*; Zhang, Wasserman, and Mano, *China's Media and Soft Power*; Thussu, "Globalization of Chinese Media"; Zhu, Edney, and Rosen, *Soft Power*.
16. Van Herpen, *Putin's Propaganda Machine*; Boyd-Barrett, *RussiaGate and Propaganda*; Jankowicz, *How to Lose the Information War*; Kreps, *Social Media and International Relations*.
17. Lynch, *Voices of the New Arab Public*; El Nawawy and Iskandar, *Al Jazeera*; Seib, *Al Jazeera Effect*; Cherribi, *Fridays of Rage*.
18. Goksu, "Return of the War on Terror"; Sim and Göksu, "Comparative Discourse Analysis"; S. B. Çevik, "Discursive Construction"; Baritci and Aydeniz, "Kamu Diplomasisi Aracı Olarak Medya"; Elswah and Howard, "Where News Could Not Inspire Change."
19. Wodak, "Politics as Usual," 529.
20. Wodak, "Discourse-Historical Approach," 69, and "Politics as Usual," 529.
21. All necessary procedures regarding anonymity, confidentiality, and privacy were followed during the recruitment, interview, and transcription stages, and necessary approvals were obtained from the City University of New York's Human Research Protection Program.
22. Rawnsley, "Introduction," 42–44; Yablokov, "Conspiracy Theories," 301–5; Rawnsley, "To Know Us Is to Love Us"; Jenks, *British Propaganda and News Media*; Cull, *Cold War*.
23. Volkmer, *Global Public Sphere*; Rai and Cottle, "Global Mediations."
24. Rawnsley, "To Know Us Is to Love Us."
25. Thussu, "Globalization of Chinese Media."
26. Cherribi, *Fridays of Rage*; El Nawawy and Iskandar, *Al Jazeera*; Seib, *Al Jazeera Effect* and *Al Jazeera English*; Zayani, *Al Jazeera Phenomenon*.
27. Youmans, *An Unlikely Audience*.
28. Rawnsley, "To Know Us Is to Love Us," 275.
29. Birge and Chatterjee-Doody, "Russian Public Diplomacy," 174.
30. Yablokov, "Conspiracy Theories"; Birge and Chatterjee-Doody, "Russian Public Diplomacy."
31. Rawnsley, "To Know Us Is to Love Us," 278.

32. Boyd-Barrett, *RussiaGate and Propaganda*; Kreps, *Social Media and International Relations*.
33. Deutsch, "RT, Sputnik Content Officially Banned."
34. Myers and Frenkel, "How Russian Propaganda Is Reaching."
35. Miskimmon, O'Loughlin, and Roselle, *Strategic Narratives*; Manor, *Digitalization of Public Diplomacy*; Kreps, *Social Media and International Relations*.
36. Yanatma, "Dominance, Collaboration, and Resistance," 5–9.
37. Yücetürk, "Tanzimat'tan Cumhuriyet'e Haberleşme."
38. Turk, "Anadolu Ajansi"; Yücetürk, "Tanzimat'tan Cumhuriyet'e Haberleşme"; Bengi, "Tarihsel Süreç İçinde Anadolu."
39. TRT, "Kilometre Taslari."
40. TRT, "Kilometre Taslari."
41. For a full list, see TRT, "External Services Department."
42. To access these websites, see TRT, "External Services Department," https://trtvotworld.com, and click on a language.
43. Aksoy and Robins, "Thinking across Spaces," 348; Karanfil, "Continuities and Changes."
44. Aksoy and Robins, "Thinking across Spaces," 346.
45. "TRT Türk Dünyasına Avaz Avaz Seslenecek."
46. Ertekin, "Uluslararası Sistemde," 339.
47. Parim and Cetin, "Bir Kamu Diplomasisi Aracı," 35.
48. Al-Ghazzi and Kraidy, "Neo-Ottoman Cool 2," 2354.
49. In the realm of nation branding, the AKP government embarked during its initial term in office on several initiatives to enhance trade, investment, and tourism. One such undertaking was the Turquality campaign introduced in 2004, aimed at enabling Turkish companies to establish their brand recognition in global markets. Nas, "Branding and National Identity," 205. Throughout the 2010s, the Ministry of Culture and Tourism, in collaboration with diplomatic missions in the Middle East, executed modest-scale branding endeavors in the region, with a focus on cultural and religious affinities. Tecmen, "Relations between Public Diplomacy and Nation Brands," 28. Concurrently, branding campaigns were targeted at European audiences. Aligned with the AKP's aspirations for European Union (EU) membership, the Brand Turkey campaign portrayed the country as an "economic and security partner" of the EU, a "cradle of civilization and religion," and an "intercultural bridge" connecting the East and West. Tecmen, "Relations between Public Diplomacy and Nation Brands," 28. In 2014 the AKP collaborated with the Turkish Exporters Assembly for a branding initiative, Turkey: Discover the Potential. This campaign sought to showcase Turkey's historical legacy, cultural richness, industrial prowess, quality service sector, human resources, and artistic heritage. Rumelili and Süleymanoğlu-Kurum, "Brand Turkey," 558. For a comprehensive examination of these campaigns during the first decade of the 2000s, refer to the works of Nas, Rumelili and Süleymanoğlu-Kurum, and Tecmen. Additionally, for a critical analysis, see Iğız, "From Alliance of Civilizations to Branding the Nation."
50. Sevin, "Bridge No More?" 2; Tecmen, "Relations between Public Diplomacy and Nation Brands."
51. Sevin, "Bridge No More?"
52. Sevin, "Bridge No More?" 2.

53. Özer and Özçetin, "Rewriting History in Contemporary Turkey."
54. Özer and Özçetin, "Rewriting History in Contemporary Turkey."
55. Directorate of Communications, "Biography."
56. Özkan, "SETA."
57. Özkan, "SETA," 235.
58. Gurpinar and Aydin, "Uniformization of Think Tanks," 9.
59. Gurpinar and Aydin, "Uniformization of Think Tanks," 8.
60. Directorate of Communications, "Director's Message."
61. The PKK was founded in 1978 with the goal of establishing an independent Kurdish state. Since the 1980s, it has been involved in armed conflicts with Turkish armed forces in pursuit of greater Kurdish autonomy and political rights. On the other hand, the YPG, established in 2011 by Syrian Kurds, has primarily focused its efforts on combating ISIS (Islamic State of Iraq and Syria) in northern Syria. It is also involved in overseeing the governance of autonomous Kurdish cantons within the region. The AKP government regards both organizations as terrorist entities that pose a threat to Turkey's sovereignty.
62. "How Government Attacks on the Press."
63. Tuncer, "'Asrın Felaketi' Propagandası."
64. Deringil, *Well-Protected Domains*; Makdisi, "Ottoman Orientalism."
65. Makdisi, "Ottoman Orientalism," 787; Lord, *Religious Politics in Turkey*, 211; Çınar, "Turkey's 'Western' or 'Muslim' Identity," 182.
66. Çınar, "Turkey's 'Western' or 'Muslim' Identity," 182.
67. Lord, *Religious Politics in Turkey*, 214.
68. Ahıska, "Occidentalism."
69. Lord, *Religious Politics in Turkey*, 216.
70. Uzer, "Turkey's Islamist Movement and the Palestinian Cause," 25.
71. Genc, "Erdoğan's Way," 26.
72. Uzer, "Turkey's Islamist Movement and the Palestinian Cause," 25.
73. Cornell, "Erbakan, Kisakurek, and the Mainstreaming of Extremism," 13.
74. Uzer, "Turkey's Islamist Movement and the Palestinian Cause," 27.
75. Karaveli, "Erdoğan's Journey."
76. Insel, "Becoming a World Economic Power," 189.
77. Aytaç and Onis, "Varieties of Populism."
78. The charges stem from a poem Erdoğan read at a public demonstration. "Erdoğan 24 Yıl Sonra Aynı Yerde." The verses that especially irked the secularist establishment are:

> The mosques are our barracks
> The domes our helmets
> The minarets our bayonets
> and the faithful our soldiers.

79. Atasoy, *Islam's Marriage with Neoliberalism*; Altinordu, "Political Incorporation."
80. Çınar, "Turkey's 'Western' or 'Muslim' Identity," 182.
81. Tuğal, *Passive Revolution*.
82. Lüküslü, "Creating a Pious Generation"; Z. Yilmaz, "AKP and the Spirit of the 'New' Turkey."
83. Altinordu, "Uncivil Populism in Power," 84.

84. Yenigün, "New Antinomies of the Islamic Movement," 240.
85. Yenigün, "New Antinomies of the Islamic Movement," 243.

Chapter 1. Battling against Western Media Imperialism

1. Kristianasen, "Turkey's Ailing Sultan"; "After Protests, Evaluating Turkey's Role as a Democracy"; "Prime Minister Erdoğan's Strongman Tactics."
2. Purvis, "Recep Tayyip Erdoğan"; "Surprisingly European."
3. "Hard Act to Follow"; Burns, "Rise of Turkey." As I discuss in *Media in New Turkey*, the positive coverage of the AKP in international media during the first decade of this century was largely misguided. The AKP's commitment to democratic norms had been fragile well before the Gezi protests, yet it was largely ignored in West-based media and policy circles. This was mainly because the narrative of a democratic Muslim country in the post–September 11 era had a certain appeal among American and European policymakers. See Yesil, *Media in New Turkey*, 10–12, 127–31.
4. Hacaloğlu, "Başbakan Erdoğan'dan Batı Medyasına Eleştiri."
5. Conspiracy theories about foreign enemies and internal traitors working against Turkey and the Turks are neither new nor specific to Gezi protests. In the early twentieth century, there were anti-Semitic conspiracy theories that blamed the dethronement of the Ottoman sultan Abdulhamid II on "secret Jews" in the higher echelons of the state. This and other anti-Semitic conspiracy theories were later entrenched by Turkish anti-Zionists between the 1920s and 1950s. See Baer, "Enemy Old and New." During the Cold War era, right-wing, conservative circles claimed that leftist youth and labor movements in Turkey received instructions from the Soviet Union and its Jewish co-conspirators. See Bora, "Komplo Zihniyetinin." Anti-Semitic and other conspiracy theories about Europe and Israel aiming to destroy Turkey have persisted throughout the 1990s and the first decade of the 2000s. See Yılmaz, "Euroscepticism in Turkey," and Cornell, "Erbakan, Kısakurek, and the Mainstreaming of Extremism."
6. "Dış Basın Cephe Savaşı Veriyor."
7. Kurban, "Basbakan Erdoğan"; Daloğlu, "Atalay Claims."
8. For a detailed analysis of Erdoğan-Gülen alliance, see Hendrick, *Gülen*.
9. "Turkey's Erdoğan Tightens His Grip"; "Arrogance Undoes the Turkish Model"; Kessler, "Autocrat-and-Mouse Censorship Game"; Traub, "Déjà Vu and Paranoia"; Shafy, "Rise and Fall of Erdoğan's Turkey."
10. Oruc, "President Erdoğan as a Target"; Dağı, "Batı Medyasının."
11. Akyol, "Middle East 'Mastermind.'"
12. Tugal, "Towards the End of a Dream?"; Tas, "History of Turkey's AKP-Gülen Conflict"; Martin, "Allies and Enemies."
13. Later in 2016, the AKP appointed a government administrator to run *Today's Zaman* and other Gülenist outlets and eventually shut them all down. See Yesil, "Authoritarian Turn or Continuity."
14. Former *Daily Sabah* journalist, interview with author, July 3, 2020.
15. Aldinç, "Türkiye'yi Dünyaya."
16. Former *Daily Sabah* journalist, interview with author, December 16, 2021.
17. Yesil, *Media in New Turkey*.
18. "DS Editorial Coordinator Atlas."

19. "4'üncü Yaşında 4'üncü Dil."

20. *Daily Sabah* has a sister organization called A News, an online news channel. Launched in April 2017, A News delivers English-language content online and strictly through the prism of the Erdoğan government. At the time of its founding, the head of its news department described the mission of A News as such: "Western media disseminates news that defames Turkey. They broadcast anti-Turkish news reports. We launched A News to give an accurate portrayal of what is happening in Turkey and our region to help people learn about the facts. We want the facts to be heard around the world in response to the [influence] operations against Turkey. A News will be the voice of Turkey and it will provide a voice for the oppressed communities that have little chance to make their voices heard." "A News."

21. "European Parliament President Bans Distribution."

22. "With Daily Sabah Ban."

23. Former TRT World executive, interview with author, March 20, 2021.

24. "TRT World Türkiye'nin Mesajını Dünyaya İletecek."

25. Srivastava and Mance, "Turkish TV Station Aims."

26. Jirik, "CCTV News and Soft Power," 3544.

27. "Bigger Than Five" is titled after Erdoğan's motto, "The world is bigger than five," which criticizes the domination of the UN Security Council by five countries and not including the voices of Muslims. See chapter 3 for a detailed discussion.

28. TRT, *Faaliyet Raporu 2022*, 158.

29. Kington, "TRT World's Live Broadcast"; TRT World, "Hotels."

30. Both CGTN and RT assert that they reach tens of millions of viewers and online subscribers, but there is little data to support these claims. See Rawnsley, "To Know Us Is to Love Us."

31. TRT, *Faaliyet Raporu 2020*, 273; TRT, *Faaliyet Raporu, 2022*, 347.

32. "TRT World Test Yayınına Gecti"; "TRT World Türkiye'nin Mesajını Dünyaya İletecek."

33. "TRT World Test Yayınına Geçti."

34. "TRT World Test Yayınına Geçti."

35. Tunstall, *Media Were American*.

36. Chouliaraki, *Spectatorship of Suffering*.

37. Chouliaraki, "Symbolic Power of Transnational Media," 344.

38. Szeto, "Former Syrian Refugee Cries Foul"; Newman, "Right Kind of Refugees."

39. Boyd-Barrett and Xie, "Al-Jazeera, Phoenix Satellite Television," 213.

40. Elswah and Howard, "Where News Could Not Inspire Change," 2085.

41. Elswah and Howard, "Where News Could Not Inspire Change," 2085.

42. Van Meek and Salam quit TRT World in 2017 and 2019, respectively, and returned to Al Jazeera. Garda left TRT World in 2020 but returned three years later. Foster and Hopkins are still with TRT World. Minty was promoted to director of digital of TRT in 2019.

43. Unal, "TRT World CEO Ibrahim Eren."

44. Former TRT World executive, interview with author, March 20, 2021.

45. Former TRT World producer, interview with author, August 5, 2020.

46. The autonomy of public broadcasting in Turkey was established in the 1961 constitution and the 1964 TRT Act. As per these legal frameworks, TRT was to be free from

direct government influence; it would be allowed to access independent revenue sources and would remain free from direct government audits. However, with the increasing political polarization in the late 1960s and the military takeover in 1971, the autonomy of TRT came to an end. The provisions of the 1961 constitution that were considered too liberal were amended, including those concerning the TRT. For a detailed analysis, see Sahin, "Broadcasting Autonomy in Turkey."

47. TRT, *Faaliyet Raporu*, 2019.
48. "International Journalists Quit."
49. Srivastava and Mance, "Turkish TV Station Aims."
50. "TRT'de Kadrolaşma Skandalı."
51. Former TRT manager, interview with author, April 23, 2021.
52. "CHP'den TRT'ye 1422"; "TRT'deki Siyasi Kadrolasma Meclis Gundeminde."
53. Dinc, "TRT World ve TRT'nin Itibarı."
54. Schaffer, "Justice Department Ordered."
55. Elswah and Howard, "Where News Could Not Inspire Change," 2092.
56. Sozeri, "Pelikan Derneği."
57. Sozeri, "Pelikan Derneği."
58. Bulut and Yörük, "Digital Populism"; Karatas and Saka, "Online Political Trolling"; Saka, *Social Media and Politics in Turkey*; Ataman and Coban, "Counter-Surveillance and Alternative New Media."
59. Harding and Letsch, "Turkish Police Arrest 25."
60. Albayrak and Parkinson, "Turkey's Government Forms."
61. There is no publicly available information as to who put together this team and how, but a number of analyses offer some clues. One theory, based on government officials' leaked emails, is that a pro-government NGO operative contacted Erdoğan's son-in-law Berat Albayrak and suggested that "a team of professional graphic designers, coders, and former army officers with training in psychological warfare" could be formed to deliver pro-government messages on X and "counter critical narratives in foreign media outlets." Sozeri, "Pelikan Derneği." Another theory says that it was private individuals with connections to higher echelons of the AKP that proposed to form a social media team to counter Gezi protestors' narratives or that these private individuals engaged in pro-government messaging themselves. Saka, "Social Media in Turkey," 165.
62. Bulut and Yörük, "Digital Populism"; Karatas and Saka, "Online Political Trolling"; Saka, *Social Media and Politics in Turkey*.
63. Saka, "Social Media in Turkey," 168, 176.
64. Grossman, Akis, Alemdaroglu, Goldstein, and Jonsson, *Political Retweet Rings and Compromised Accounts*.
65. Bosphorus Global, "Mission."
66. Bosphorus Global, "Mission." Imposing a simplified center-periphery framework on Turkish history, Bosphorus Global directs attention to the "polarity between state institutions and the people" that emerged during the "transition process of the Ottoman Empire to the Turkish Republic" and has since then resulted in military coups, class elitism, "harsh suppression of Islam," and "cultural representations that blindly imitate the West." In this simplistic interpretation of center-periphery cleavages, Bosphorus Global identifies the center as the military-bureaucratic establishment, the "Westernizing elite" and their economic allies, and recognizes Erdoğan as the one and only "peripheral

actor" that has successfully "moved the periphery to the center." See Bosphorus Global, "Perspective."

67. Bosphorus Global, "Activities."
68. Ünver, "Fact-Checkers and Fact-Checking," 14.
69. Sozeri, "These Fake 'Fact-Checkers.'"
70. Amnesty International, *Amnesty International Report 2016/17*; Human Rights Watch, "Turkey: Protect Rights."
71. Yesil, "Authoritarian Turn or Continuity."
72. Morris, "Law Is Suspended"; Osborne, "Turkey Coup Attempt"; Pownall, "Turkey Could Be Taking."
73. Çolak and Bulur, "Türkiye FETÖ'nün gerçek."
74. "Recep Tayyip Erdoğan."
75. FETÖ is an acronym created by the AKP to refer to Fethullah Gülen and his followers as "Fethullahci Teror Örgütü" (Fethullah-ist terrorist organization).
76. Voices of July 15, (@voicesofjuly15), "Declaration of the July 15."
77. Gülen moved to the United States in 1999, citing medical treatment. In 2000 he was tried in absentia in a Turkish court on charges of antisecular activities. Although he was later acquitted when the AKP came to power, he never returned to Turkey. Gülen received legal residency in the United States in 2002 thanks to endorsement letters written by a former CIA intelligence officer and a former US ambassador. These connections between Gülen and his American supporters have fueled conspiracy theories about Gülen's network being a part of the alleged American plots to destabilize Turkey.
78. The hashtag #TurkeyIsNotAChicken is based on a wordplay that is used to communicate that Turks are not afraid to fight against the putschists and speak their minds against Western media.
79. Voices of July 15 (@voicesofjuly15), "Example of the Western Media" and "It All Started with a Bullet."
80. Sevin, "Digital Diplomacy."
81. Among these accounts were @StreamStreamTR, @failedcoupfacts, and @VoicesofJuly15. The most commonly used hashtags included #TurkeyCoupAttempt, #TerroristGulen, #WhatWouldYouDo, #NeverForgetJuly15, and #TurkeyIsNotAChicken.
82. Yesil, "#TurkeyIsNotAChicken."
83. Broderick, "Turkish Trolls Working for Erdoğan."
84. Amsterdam, "Turkey: Is the Gulen"; Flynn, "Our Ally Turkey"; Klasfeld, "Boom Times."
85. Jones, "Journalist Deniz Yucel."
86. Cav, "Wall Street Journal."
87. Schwartz and Fairclough, "Wall Street Journal Reporter."
88. Scott, "As ISIS Attacks Mount."
89. Çağlar, Akdemir, and Toker, *Uluslararası Medya*.
90. SETA's report is not the only one that analyzes international media bias toward Turkey. For example, TRT World Research Centre published a report on the "politics of [Western] representations, particularly during critical moments and events" in Turkey and their "potential political, economic, social, and even national security ramifications"

on the country. To its credit, though, this report does not single out journalists as SETA did. See Cherkaoui, "Representation of Politics."

91. Durmus, "Int'l Media Fails."
92. Övür, "ABD'li Vakif."
93. "Chrest Foundation Medyascope'a."
94. Soylu, "Turkey to Regulate."
95. Gundogan, "Cumhurbaşkanlığı İletişim."
96. Canefe and Bora, "Intellectual Roots."
97. Öğüt, "PM Erdoğan and AK Party"; Babaoglu, "New Orientalism and the Western Media."
98. Bayraklı, *Orientalism Reloaded*, 5–6.
99. "Eren TRT World'ün Hedeflerini Anlattı."
100. Said, *Orientalism*.
101. Osman, *Television and the Afghan Culture Wars*.
102. Alloul and Markey, "Please Deny," 273.
103. Yanatma, "Dominance, Collaboration, and Resistance," 5–9.
104. Alloul and Markey, "Please Deny."
105. Alloul and Markey, "Please Deny," 273.
106. Yanatma, "Dominance, Collaboration, and Resistance."
107. Deringil, *Well-Protected Domains*.
108. Deringil, *Well-Protected Domains*, 153–54.
109. Makdisi, "Ottoman Orientalism," 772.
110. The channel, called +90 (after Turkey's international telephone country code), provides news and analysis about social and political issues in Turkey.
111. Özkir, "Mainstream Western Media."
112. Özkir, "Mainstream Western Media."
113. Whereas nationalist Islamist circles view Abdülhamid II as the "Almighty Sultan," others refer to him as the "Red Sultan," which is also the moniker used in European press at the time to describe him as a bloody tyrant. In Ottoman historiography, Abdülhamid II is a divisive figure, one that worked to modernize the empire via infrastructure, education, and health projects, on one hand, and ordered the massacre of Assyrian and Armenian subjects of the empire, on the other. Abdülhamid II is also known for suspending the constitution, suppressing the press, and running a notorious spy network. See Bulut and Ileri, "Screening Right-Wing Populism."
114. Armstrong, "Army of Spin."
115. See, for example, the September 2016 issue of *Derin Tarih*, a popular history magazine published by Turkuvaz Media. A few months after the coup attempt, the magazine juxtaposed images of Abdulhamid II and Erdoğan on its cover and published a lead article, "Abdulhamid's Resistance and New Turkey's Resurrection."
116. "Surrounded by Ottoman Soldiers."

Chapter 2. Legitimizing Turkey's Communication Model

1. "Altun'dan Basın Özgürlüğü Mesajı"; Türkiye Cumhuriyeti İletişim Başkanlığı, "Altun Speaks."

2. Stratcom Summit, "Stratcom Acilis Konusmasi." Altun delivered his remarks in Turkish. Translations are mine. The recording of his entire speech is available at Stratcom's YouTube channel, https://youtu.be/buBwbwKMQGA?si=gE6CJCZT1xwMg-CE.

3. Tosun, "Cumhurbaskanligi Iletisim Baskani Altun."

4. TRT World (@trtworld), "It's Our Duty."

5. Türkiye Cumhuriyeti İletişim Başkanlığı, "Director of Communications Altun: Our Main Goal."

6. For analyses of the decline of journalistic autonomy and professionalism during the AKP era, see Akser and Baybars-Hawks, "Media and Democracy in Turkey"; Yesil, *Media in New Turkey*.

7. Committee to Protect Journalists, "40 journalists imprisoned."

8. Akdeniz, "Report of the OSCE Representative"; Yesil, Sözeri, and Khazraee, "Turkey's Internet Policy"; Freedom House, *Freedom in the World*.

9. Parks, Goodwin, and Han, "'I Have the Government"; Yesil and Sözeri, "Online Surveillance."

10. Reporters without Borders, *Türkiye*.

11. Freedom House, *Freedom in the World*.

12. "Altundan Basın Özgürlüğü Mesajı"; Türkiye Cumhuriyeti İletişim Başkanlığı, "Director of Communications Altun: The Struggle for Truth."

13. Benabdallah, *Shaping the Future of Power*, 6.

14. Mirjam and Josua, "How Authoritarian Rulers Seek"; Del Sordi and Delmasso, "Relation between External and Internal Authoritarian Legitimation"; Scartozzi, "Assad's Strategic Narrative."

15. Mirjam and Josua, "How Authoritarian Rulers Seek."

16. See Creemers, "Cyber China"; Guo, "Occupying the Internet"; Zhang, Liu, and Wen, "Nationalism on Weibo"; McKune and Shazeda, "Contestation and Shaping"; Michaelsen, "Transforming Threats"; Pigman, "Russia's Vision of Cyberspace"; Marechal, "Networked Authoritarianism."

17. Chakravartty and Roy rightly criticize this "familiar Eurocentric practice of granting world-historical significance and generalizability to a phenomenon only when it occurs in Europe and North America." Chakravartty and Roy, "Mediatized Populisms," 4073.

18. For a critical analysis of these approaches, see Benkler, Faris, and Roberts, *Network Propaganda*; Lenoir and Anderson, "Introduction Essay."

19. Altun, "Truth Is a Human Right."

20. Türkiye Cumhuriyeti İletişim Başkanlığı, "Director of Communications Altun: Increase."

21. Türkiye Cumhuriyeti İletişim Başkanlığı, "Director of Communications Altun: A Full-Fledged Fight."

22. Windwehr and York, "Turkey's New Internet Law."

23. "Turkish Parliament Passes."

24. This interpretation resurfaced again in January 2021 when X (then Twitter) verified the YPG leader's account with a blue badge. The AKP's spokesman asked why the social media company gave a blue badge to a "terrorist leader" while denying it to Turkish Cypriot leaders.

25. "Turkey's Fahrettin Altun Blasts International Media."

26. Altun (@fahrettinaltun), "Üzülerek belirtmek istiyorum ki" and "İslam'a ve Müslümanlara yönelik nefret söylemlerini."
27. Altun (@fahrettinaltun), "Hoşunuza gitsin ya da gitmesin."
28. Türkiye Cumhuriyeti İletişim Başkanlığı, "Director of Communications Altun: We Will Continue."
29. Sayın, "Dijital Mecralar Komisyonu."
30. Çetinkaya and Güngördü, "When National Laws."
31. Pitel, "Facebook to Defy."
32. Amnesty International. "Turkey."
33. "Turkey Slaps Advertising Ban"; Kozok, "Biggest Social Media Companies"; "Facebook Says Starts Process."
34. "All Social Media Providers"; Human Rights Watch, "Turkey: Dangerous."
35. As part of its so-called struggle against disinformation, in 2022 the Directorate of Communications established the Center for Fight against Disinformation. The center "monitors and counters activities such as psychological warfare, propaganda, perception operations, manipulative content, and domestic and foreign disinformation campaigns" against Turkey. It distributes a weekly disinformation bulletin to "call out specific misinformation and disinformation incidents aimed at our citizens." Altun, "Truth Is a Human Right." In 2023 the directorate also introduced an app that citizens can use to report news and information they suspect to be disinformation. It is called DBS (Dezenformasyon Bildirim Servisi, Disinformation Notification Service) and is available on iOS and Android devices. "Turkey Introduces App."
36. Human Rights Watch, "Turkey: Dangerous, Dystopian New Legal Amendments." The disinformation law also raised concerns because of its criminalization of dissemination of "false information" about Turkey's internal and external security and public order with the intent to instigate panic, fear, or anxiety. Individuals found guilty under the law face imprisonment from one to three years. Voice of America, "Turkish Lawmakers Adopt New Disinformation Law."
37. Media and Law Studies Association, "Reasons for the Government's Anger."
38. Pitel, "Turkey Bans Access."
39. "Turkey Aims to Create." GAFAM is an abbreviation for Google, Amazon, Facebook, Apple, and Microsoft and is generally used in critiques of the power and overreach of Silicon Valley. See, for example, Mirrlees, "Getting at Gafam's 'Power.'"
40. Budnitsky, "Kremlin Tightens Control."
41. McKune and Ahmed, "Contestation and Shaping."
42. Kokas, "Platform Patrol."
43. Kokas, "Platform Patrol."
44. Galloway and Baogang, "China."
45. McKune and Ahmed, "Contestation and Shaping," 3840–41.
46. Budnitsky, "Relational Approach."
47. Shanghai Cooperation Organization was established in 2001 as an intergovernmental political, economic, and security alliance among China, Russia, Kazakhstan, Kyrgyzstan, Tajikistan, and Uzbekistan. In 2017 India and Pakistan joined the SCO as full members. SCO has six dialogue partner countries (Armenia, Azerbaijan, Cambodia, Nepal, Sri Lanka, and Turkey) and four observer states (Afghanistan, Belarus, Iran, and Mongolia).

48. McKune and Ahmed, "Contestation and Shaping."
49. Michaelsen, "Transforming Threats," 3867.
50. Michaelsen, "Transforming Threats," 3867–68. Other states that introduced data localization initiatives and implemented censorship mechanisms to restrict access to information are Bahrain, Egypt, Ethiopia, Kazakhstan, Kyrgyzstan, Myanmar, Pakistan, Saudi Arabia, Singapore, Syria, Sudan, Tajikistan, Thailand, United Arab Emirates (UAE), Uzbekistan, Venezuela, and Vietnam. Deibert and Pauly, "Mutual Entanglement."
51. Yesil, Sözeri, and Khazraee, "Turkey's Internet Policy," 15.
52. "Turkey to Launch Domestic Google."
53. Türkiye Cumhuriyeti Ulaştırma ve Altyapı Bakanlığı, "Ulusal Siber Güvenlik"; Türkiye Cumhuriyeti İletişim Başkanlığı, "Director of Communications Altun: Increase."
54. Türkiye Cumhuriyeti İletişim Başkanlığı, "Director of Communications Altun: We Are Going."
55. See Borenstein, *Plots against Russia*.
56. Üngör, *China Is Playing*.
57. Üngör, *China Is Playing*, 11.
58. Costello, "Russia's Use of Media."
59. TASS Russian News Agency, "Cavusoglu Says."
60. The DoC maintains that it has independently introduced this branding, but Stratcom is intriguingly similar to StratCom COE, which represents the Strategic Communications Centre of Excellence at NATO. See Stratcom, "About."
61. See Stratcom, "Agenda."
62. Türkiye Cumhuriyeti Milli Savunma Bakanlığı (@tcsavunma), "Cumhurbaşkanlığı."
63. Stratcom Summit, "Content."
64. Stratcom Summit, "Stratcom Youth."
65. Stratcom Summit, "About."
66. Stratcom Summit, "Stratcom Youth Speakers." Out of twenty-five speakers, only two were *not* affiliated with Turkish state agencies or progovernment media outlets: a public relations professor from a private Turkish university, and the founder of a communications agency based in Switzerland.
67. The first media forum for OTS members was held in Turkey 2010 but was discontinued until DoC revived it in 2021. See Gokce, "How the Turkic World Is Enhancing Cooperation."
68. "Media Summit in Istanbul"; Türkiye Cumhuriyeti İletişim Başkanlığı, "Türkiye-Africa Media Summit Kicks Off"; Kanat, "Experts Mull Shifting." Also in 2022 the DoC held a one-day event in Nairobi, Kenya, in partnership with the Kenya Media Council. This event catered to sixty journalists and offered comprehensive training sessions centered around fact-checking, combatting disinformation, and crisis management. See Stratcom Summit, "Stratcom Kenya."
69. Türkiye Cumhuriyeti İletişim Başkanlığı, "Director of Communications Altun Speaks."
70. Türkiye Cumhuriyeti İletişim Başkanlığı, "President Erdoğan Sends."
71. Former state official, Ministry of Foreign Affairs, interview with author, October 12, 2021. These publications are produced in Turkish and English by Anadolu Agency and the Directorate of Communications. Some prominent titles include *Africa Rising*,

Turkey's Security Policy, Turkey's Cultural Heritage, FETO's Cup Attempt in Turkey: A Timeline, and *U.N. Reform: A New Approach to International Cooperation*.

72. Republic of Türkiye, "TIKA Gives Support," "TIKA Provides Technical Equipment"; Türkiye Cumhuriyeti Kültür ve Turizm Bakanlığı, "TİKA'dan Afganistan'daki."

73. Borekci and Loffler, "I Want You," 83–84.

74. The War Journalism Program is perhaps the most comprehensive and the most consistently offered one. Spanning a duration of twelve days, it is provided throughout the year and in collaboration with the Turkish General Staff, the Police Academy, and AFAD (Afet ve Acil Durum Yınetimi Başkanlığı, Presidency of Disaster and Emergency Management).

75. "Anadolu Agency Trains."

76. "Başkanın Mesajı."

77. TRT, "UMEP—Uluslararası Medya Eğitim Programi."

78. TRT World Citizen describes J4J as "a movement, not just a program . . . a tool and a platform that opens up new perspectives and a way for youth to build self-esteem and connect with other societies." TRT World Citizen, "Journalism for Juniors."

79. TRT World Citizen, "Journalism for Juniors."

80. TRT Journalism for Juniors (jforjuniors), "J4J educates students" and "J4J teaches youths."

81. Turkish Maarif Foundation (Turkiye Maarif Vakfi in Turkish) was established in June 2016 by the government as the sole organization in charge of providing educational services abroad. After the coup attempt in July 2016, the government began the process of taking over more than two hundred schools that were operated by Gulenists in Africa, Central Asia, and the Balkans. Today, TMF runs 446 educational institutions and thirty-six dormitories in sixty-seven countries, providing education, training, and scholarships for both Turks and the local populace. See Türkiye Maarif Foundation, "Current Status Information." TMF works closely with Turkish embassies and other state agencies, such as TIKA and YEE (Yunus Emre Enstitusu, Yunus Emre Institute). Its educational vision is centered on the "nurturing of a 'good person' with universal moral values, ethics and responsibilities," instilling in students an awareness of "their traditions, culture, and values." Akgün and Özkan, "Turkey's Entrance," 67.

82. Other examples of TRT Journalism for Juniors' activities can be found on X under @jforjuniors.

83. Borekci and Loffler, "I Want You," 85–87.

84. YTB also offers its own training programs to media professionals hailing from South Asia (Bangladesh, India, Pakistan, Sri Lanka, and Nepal and their diaspora members), the Middle East, North Africa, and Central Asia.

85. Musa, "Türkiye, Africa Need"; "Training on Strengthening."

86. Addis, "African Media Representatives"; "YTB, AA ve TRT Ortakligiyla."

87. "YTB, AA ve TRT Ortaklığıyla."

88. Zarifoğlu, "Afrika Medya Temsilcileri."

89. Former official, Ministry of Foreign Affairs, interview with author, October 18, 2021.

90. "Regulatory Authorities and Useful Links."

91. Members of the OIC-IBRAF include Azerbaijan, Afghanistan, Bahrain, Bangladesh, Benin, Burkina Faso, Cameroon, Egypt, Gambia, Guinea, Indonesia, Iran, Iraq,

Jordan, Kirgizstan, Lebanon, Libya, Malaysia, Mali, Mauritania, Morocco, Mozambique, Niger, Pakistan, Palestine, Qatar, Saudi Arabia, Senegal, Somalia, Sudan, Tajikistan, Togo, Turkey, Uganda, and Uzbekistan. See "IBRAF at a Glance." For a detailed discussion of BRAF and OIC-IBRAF, see Kaptan and Karanfil, "RTUK, Broadcasting, and the Middle East."

92. Mutlu, "Project to Bring." Karagöz's statement did not clarify whether the newly proposed Turkic News Agencies Association would replace the existing Association of News Agencies of Turkic Speaking Countries (known as TKA), which was established in Ankara in 1992.

93. Wilkins, "Development and Modernization."

94. Sienkiewicz, *Other Air Force*.

95. Jenks, "Crash Course."

96. Shafer, "Soviet Foundations," 19–34.

97. Post–September 11 development communication is very different from the Cold War–era efforts. Although the primary objective is the assertion of US hegemony, it, nonetheless, "embraces and depends on important levels of local agency." Sienkiewicz, *Other Air Force*, 2. For nuanced and well-researched accounts of American policy makers' approaches to development communication in Afghanistan and the Middle East and the mixed results they yield, see Sienkiewicz, *Other Air Force*; Osman, *Television and the Afghan Culture Wars*.

98. Drefs and Thomass, "Research Findings."

99. Gagliardone, Repnikova, and Stremlau, "China in Africa"; Louisa and Bergin, "Telling China's Story."

100. Madrid-Morales, "Sino-African Media Cooperation," 51.

101. Madrid-Morales, "Sino-African Media Cooperation," 51.

102. Benabdallah, *Shaping the Future*, 8–10.

103. Official at a state entity, interview with author, September 16, 2020. Due to the high-level status of this interlocutor, I am not disclosing where this official works.

104. During the Cold War, a number of newly independent, developing countries chose to remain neutral vis-à-vis the US-led capitalist or the Soviet Union–led communist bloc. Their movement is referred to as the non-aligned movement (NAM).

105. Carlsson, "Rise and Fall of NWICO," 42.

106. Carlsson, "Rise and Fall of NWICO," 44–46.

107. Carlsson, "Rise and Fall of NWICO," 54.

108. Topuz, "Past Witnesses' Present Comments."

Chapter 3. Restoring Justice to Muslims

1. Gul, "Pakistan, Turkey, Malaysia."

2. The symposium has been held annually since 2021. It is jointly organized by the Radio and Television Supreme Council (RTUK), Presidency of Religious Affairs (Diyanet), Erciyes University, Turkish Radio and Television Corporation (TRT), and SETA.

3. Bayar, "Anadolu Agency."

4. In January 2022 Karagöz tweeted that the unit would be called the AA Discrimination Line and said, "We all have to stand against Islamophobia with no excuses, and

there has to be absolute zero tolerance for it." Karagöz (@serdarkaragoz), "We all have to stand." While the English-language initiative has yet to come to fruition, its Turkish counterpart (AA Ayrimcilik Hatti) is currently in use.

5. Karagöz (@serdarkaragoz), "We all have to stand."

6. Another entity that organizes international conferences on Islamophobia is the Center for Islam and Global Affairs (CIGA) at Istanbul Zaim University. CIGA has organized four annual in Istanbul since 2018 with the participation of international scholars. See Center for Islam and Global Affairs, "Islamophobia." The founder of CIGA is Sami Al Arian, an academic who was deported from the United States on terrorism-related charges in 2015. He was later given residency in Turkey and hired by Istanbul Zaim University, an institution known for its close links to nationalist Islamist circles in Turkey.

7. A very brief overview of Turkey's Western-oriented foreign policy is as follows: In the 1920s and 1930s, the newly founded Turkish Republic pursued a noninterventionist foreign policy. However, after World War II it began to align itself with the Western bloc in order to protect its territorial integrity from the neighboring Soviet bloc countries. See Stein, *Turkey's New Foreign Policy*. After the war, Turkey participated in the Marshall Plan in 1947, joined the Council of Europe in 1950 and NATO in 1952, and, thus, confirmed its status as a Western ally and a bulwark against the spread of communism. In the post–Cold War era, Turkey continued to maintain close ties with its Western partners, highlighting its unique position as a bridge between the East and West. In the 1990s it developed a trilateral security relationship with Israel and the United States and became a candidate country for European Union membership. At the same time, it improved its economic relations with its long-neglected Middle Eastern neighbors and rekindled its religious-ethnic ties with the newly independent Turkic states in Central Asia. During the mid-to-late part of the first decade of the 2000s, Turkey's so-called Europeanization process slowed down, and relations with the United States frayed due to the occupation of Iraq and the ensuing instability in the region. Anti-Western, nationalist sentiments in the country increased remarkably, with public opinion polls indicating unfavorable views of both the United States and the European Union. See Grigoriadis, "Friends No More?" For a general discussion of the changes in Turkey's foreign policy during the AKP era, see Baser, "Shift of Axis in Turkish Foreign Policy"; Saraçoğlu and Demirkol, "Nationalism and Foreign Policy Discourse"; Akkoyunlu, "Five Phases"; Özpek and Yaşar. "Populism and Foreign Policy in Turkey under the AKP Rule."

8. Özkan, "Turkey, Davutoğlu, and the Idea of Pan-Islamism"; Saraçoğlu and Demirkol, "Nationalism and Foreign Policy Discourse."

9. Saraçoğlu and Demirkol, "Nationalism and Foreign Policy Discourse," 311. For a detailed analysis of the AKP's deployment of and/or emphasis on Muslim identity and Ottoman heritage in domestic politics, see Uzer, "Glorification of the Past"; Kaya, "Islamisation of Turkey." For a critical discussion of the discourse on uniting Muslims, see Aydin, *Idea of the Muslim World*.

10. Davutoğlu, *Stratejik Derinlik*.

11. Öniş and Kutlay, "Rising Powers"; Ersen, "Rise of New Centers."

12. Although these initiatives were promoted as tantamount to Turkey's status as a great power, they were based on ill-suited decisions and the AKP's general disregard for ethnic, sectarian dynamics in the region. They, therefore, failed to have long-lasting,

positive impacts. See Demïrtaş-Bagdonas, "Reading Turkey's Foreign Policy"; Altunısık and Martin, "Making Sense of Turkish Foreign Policy"; Özkan, "Turkey, Davutoğlu, and the Idea of Pan-Islamism."

13. For a detailed analysis of how the government has used Islam to cultivate relationships with Balkan countries and grow its sphere of influence in the region, see Öztürk, *Religion, Identity, and Power*. For similar efforts in Africa, see Tepeciklioğlu, "Turkey's Religious Diplomacy in Africa."

14. For detailed analyses of Turkey's pivot to Africa and its political, economic, military, and humanitarian dimensions, see Donelli, *Turkey in Africa*; Tepeciklioğlu and Tepeciklioğlu, *Turkey in Africa*.

15. Uzer, "Glorification of the Past," 347.

16. Neo-Ottomanism was first promoted in the 1990s by conservative circles as a remedy to the homogenizing logic and isolationist policies of Kemalism and when Turkey was redefining its place in the world following the collapse of the Soviet Union. During the AKP era, neo-Ottomanism assumed a more central role in foreign policy. See Bargu, "Neo-Ottomanism."

17. See Langan, "Virtuous Power Turkey in Sub-Saharan Africa," 2–4. Because the term is implicated with Ottoman imperialism and generally used to criticize the Erdoğan government's foreign policy as expansionist and irridentist, it has been vehemently rejected by some AKP officials.

18. Kavaklı, "Domestic Politics."

19. The number of TIKA's international offices increased from twelve in 2002 to sixty-two in 2019. See Republic of Türkiye, TIKA, "2019 Annual Report."

20. Among these Islamic NGOs are IHH (İnsani Yardım Vakfi, Humanitarian Aid Foundation), Deniz Feneri, Can Suyu, and Kimse Yok Mu. IHH is perhaps the most well-known due to its involvement in the Gaza aid flotilla incident in 2010. See Celik and Iseri, "Islamically Oriented Humanitarian NGOs."

21. Yabancı, "Work for the Nation," 493.

22. Republic of Türkiye, TIKA, "2019 Annual Report."

23. Beck, "Turkey's Global Soft-Power Push"; "Turkey's President Erdogan."

24. For a detailed examination of Diyanet's transformation under AKP rule, see Gözaydın, "Diyanet and Politics"; Öztürk, "Transformation of the Turkish Diyanet."

25. Öztürk, "Transformation of the Turkish Diyanet."

26. Guo, "Turkey's International Humanitarian Assistance," 126.

27. "Why Yunus Emre."

28. "Islamophobia 101."

29. Council on American-Islamic Relations (CAIR), "Islamophobia 101."

30. "Islamophobia Research and Documentation Project."

31. Kumar, *Islamophobia*, 18–46.

32. Mamdani, *Good Muslim, Bad Muslim*.

33. Kumar, *Islamophobia*, 18–67.

34. The units used for data collection were online news videos (two to five minutes long) on TRT World and news articles on *Daily Sabah*. Keyword-based searches were conducted on TRT World's website, YouTube channel, and iPhone app, and on the *Daily Sabah* website. The terms for content published between January 1, 2021, and October 1, 2021, were "Muslim," "Islam," "Islamophobia," "Islamophobic," "anti-Muslim," "hate

crime," "hate speech," and "discrimination." Identical items were removed; remaining items were then coded with respect to the country in which the anti-Muslim discrimination, exclusion, and/or marginalization occurred. I thank my research assistant, who wishes to remain anonymous, for assistance with data collection and analysis.

35. Türkiye Cumhuriyeti İletişim Başkanlığı, "Turkey Is the Biggest Opportunity."
36. Atlas, "Anadolu Ajansı, İslamofobi."
37. Altun (@fahrettinaltun), "Europe's Hostility."
38. Former foreign producer, TRT World, interview with author, August 5, 2020.
39. Former journalist, *Daily Sabah*, interview with author, December 16, 2021.
40. There are, however, instances of managerial influence regarding the coverage of others topics, such as the coup attempt and Kurdish issue.
41. Former foreign producer, TRT World, interview with author, August 5, 2020.
42. Entman, "Theorizing Mediated Public Diplomacy," 90.
43. Aldridge and Evetts, "Rethinking the Concept"; Donsbach, "Psychology of News Decisions"; Cotter, *News Talk*.
44. Asik, "Politics, Power, and Performativity," 589.
45. Bunce, "Management and Resistance," 892.
46. Bunce, "Management and Resistance," 893.
47. Elswah and Howard, "Anything That Causes Chaos."
48. Foreign journalist, TRT World, interview with author, June 3, 2021.
49. A list of these events can be found by visiting the "Events" page on SETA website at https://www.setav.org/en/activities/ and using the search term "Islamophobia."
50. On *Politics Today*, Islamophobia-related content can be found under the Xenophobia link. See https://politicstoday.org/topics/xenophobia/.
51. To promote these reports, SETA organizes online and offline panels with the participation of editors and authors. See SETAV, *Islamophobia Report*.
52. "Turkey to Prepare Reports."
53. TRT World Forum, "Western Mainstream Media."
54. TRT World Citizen, "Who We Are."
55. TRT World Research Centre, *Am I Not a Child?*
56. TRT World Research Centre, *Women of War*.
57. TRT World Citizen, *Hello Brother*.
58. TRT World Research Centre, *Dignity without Borders*.
59. Presidency of the Republic of Türkiye, "Those Who Are Unfamiliar."
60. "Dünya Beş'ten Büyüktür."
61. Canikligil, "'Dünya 5'ten Büyüktür' Kampanya Oldu."
62. "Birleşmiş Milletler'de Isyan." The video can be viewed at https://www.dailymotion.com/video/x26lkgk. The song was repurposed from the English rock band Muse's "Uprising."
63. Çavuşoğlu, (@MevlutCavusoglu), "As President @RT_Erdoğan Underlined"; Acar, (@AcarUmut), "Current Structure"; Kavakçı Kan, (@RavzaKavakci), "It Is Time"; Altun, (@fahrettinaltun), "Recep Tayyip Erdoğan"; Kalın, (@ikalin1), "It Takes Virtue."
64. The theme of Erdoğan standing in solidarity with fellow Muslims has also been evident in other instances. One such example occurred in 2016 when a Syrian girl named Bana Alabed gained global attention for sharing a series of tweets detailing the siege of her hometown by regime forces. Alabed's mother reached out to Turkish authorities

for assistance, leading to the evacuation of their family and numerous other civilians to Turkey. Subsequently, Erdoğan's office extended an invitation to Alabed and circulated photographs that depicted Erdoğan embracing her and gently holding her face in his hands. See Lila and Masters, "Bana Alabed." Similarly, in 2018 Erdoğan met at his presidential palace with Fawzi Al-Juneidi, a Palestinian teenager. Al-Juneidi had become a symbol of the Palestinian cause after he was blindfolded and forcefully detained by Israeli soldiers during a protest. The meeting presented a significant opportunity for the Erdoğan government to showcase its support for Palestinians enduring hardship under Israeli occupation. See "President Erdoğan Receives Palestinian Teen Fawzi Al-Juneidi."

65. Erdoğan, *Daha Adil Bir Dunya Mumkun*, 3. The book is available in Turkish, English, Arabic, German, French, Russian, and Spanish. It is published by Turkuvaz Medya, and the English translation is available on Amazon.

66. Erdoğan, *Daha Adil Bir Dunya Mumkun*, 3.

67. Al-Ghazzi. "We Will Be Great Again."

68. Al-Ghazzi, "We Will Be Great Again," 50–52.

69. Feinstein and Bonikowski, "Nationalist Narratives and Anti-Immigrant Attitudes"; Risør, "Civil Victimhood."

70. Açıkel, "Kutsal Mazlumlugun Psikopatolojisi"; Bora, *Cereyanlar: Turkiye'de Siyasi İdeolojiler*; Tokdoğan, "Reading Politics through Emotions."

71. Savaş, "Muslim 'Crying Boy,'" 117.

72. Savaş, "Muslim 'Crying Boy,'" 120.

73. Başkan and Taşpınar, *Nation or the Ummah*, 195.

74. Başkan and Taşpınar, *Nation or the Ummah*, 195.

75. Tokdoğan, "Reading Politics through Emotions," 395–96.

76. Verbeek and Zaslove, "Populism and Foreign Policy," 400.

77. Destradi and Plagemann, "Populism and International Relations," 719.

78. Zúquete, "Missionary Politics of Hugo Chávez."

79. Zúquete, "On Top of the Volcano," 510–11.

80. Zúquete, "On Top of the Volcano," 516.

81. Yabancı, "Fuzzy Borders," 102.

82. "China's ICBC to Loan"; Altay, "Why Erdoğan."

83. Westcott and Sarıyüce, "Erdoğan Says."

84. Kakissis, "I Thought It Would Be Safe."

85. "Recep Erdogan Storms."

86. Ertan, "Turkish Government Criticized."

87. Hubbard, "After Erdoğan's Attacks."

Chapter 4. Discrediting the West

1. Deringil, *Well-Protected Domains*, 15.

2. Deringil, *Well-Protected Domains*, 149.

3. Çetinkaya, "Atrocity Propaganda and the Nationalization," 772–73.

4. Çetinkaya, "Atrocity Propaganda and the Nationalization," 774.

5. The term "refugee crisis" is a contested one. It implies that refugees are responsible for their own suffering and conceals the fact that European countries are violating international laws when they stop refugees from entering their territories. The word "crisis"

is also problematic because the number of refugees in Europe or trying to reach Europe corresponds only to a small percentage of the continent's entire population, and, in fact, European countries are wealthy enough to host and protect the refugees. While I agree with these criticisms, I use the term without quotation marks due to stylistic considerations. For a critical analysis of the term, see Trilling, "How the Media"; Ellis, "Don't Call."

6. At its core, civilizationism can be defined as a political framework that highlights the importance of a given civilization in the shaping of domestic politics and international relations. It promotes a sense of exceptionalism, advocating for the superiority or distinctiveness of a particular civilization. For a detailed discussion, see Brubaker, "Between Nationalism and Civilizationism"; Bettiza, Bolton, and Lewis, "Civilizationism and the Ideological Contestation"; Haug and Roychoudhury, "Civilizational Exceptionalism"; Chatterjee and Das, "India's Civilizational Arguments"; Mezhuyev, "Civilizational Realism."

7. Akkoyunlu, "Five Phases."
8. S. B. Çevik, "Narrating Turkey's Story."
9. Kalın, "Kamu Diplomasisi İçin Mola!"
10. Kalın, "Kamu Diplomasisi İçin Mola!"
11. Quoted in Çapan and Zarakol, "Turkey's Ambivalent Self," 275.
12. Dombey, "Erdogan Attacks West's Reaction."
13. Detmer, "Turkey Angry over Morsi Ouster."
14. "Erdoğan'dan Batı'ya."
15. Former official at Ministry of Foreign Affairs, interview with author, May 1, 2021.
16. Official at Ministry of Foreign Affairs, interview with author, May 20, 2021.
17. Kutlay and Öniş, "Turkish Foreign Policy," 1086.
18. Former official at the Office of Public Diplomacy, interview with author, June 5, 2021.
19. Saatçioğlu, " European Union's Refugee Crisis," 174.
20. Makovsky, "Turkey's Refugee Dilemma."
21. Makovsky, "Turkey's Refugee Dilemma."
22. Terry, "EU-Turkey Deal."
23. European Commission, "EU Facility for Refugees."
24. Bilge, "Friend or Foe," 118–20. In contrast to pro-government newspapers, other outlets criticized the AKP's refugee policies and described Syrians as economic and security threats. See Efe, "Corpus-Driven Analysis."
25. International Crisis Group, "Turkey's Syrian Refugees."
26. Karakas, "Is Anti-Refugee Sentiment Growing?"
27. Morgül, Savaşkan, and Mutlu, "İstanbul'da Suriyeli Sığınmacılara Yonelik Algı ve Tutumlar."
28. Sar and Kuru, "İstanbul'da Suriyeli Sığınmacılara Yönelik Tutumlar."
29. "Erdoğan, 1 milyon." One must note that anti-Syrian sentiment in Turkey cuts across political divides with opposition parties of all stripes promising to repatriate Syrians if or when these parties assume office.
30. Gostoli, "Turkish Presidential Run-Off."
31. Indeed, between 2013 and 2016, Turkey ranked second among the top-twenty government contributors of international humanitarian assistance, with the majority of aid delivered to Syrian refugees. In 2020 Turkey became the second-largest donor

country, after the United States, accounting for 26 percent of all global humanitarian aid. Development Initiatives, *Global Humanitarian Assistance Report 2021*. The international press has applauded Turkey's refugee camps for their orderliness, cleanliness, and their "luxuries," such as power lines, streetlights, fire hydrants, and "playgrounds that look like McDonald's Play Places." McClelland, "How to Build." Turkey has also been praised by international organizations for the support programs it provides for Syrian refugees in education, health, and employment. World Bank, "10 Years On." Lastly, SETA and TRT World have organized workshops and prepared information packs and policy reports to promote Turkey's humanitarian efforts. See TRT World Forum, "Setting an Example"; Pekkendir, "Protecting the Most Vulnerable"; Mohydin, "Syrian Refugees"; Coşkun, et al., *Breaking Down Barriers*.

32. Miskimmon, O'Loughlin, and Roselle, *Strategic Narratives*, 2, 5; Oates and Steiner, "Projecting Power," 2.

33. Hinck, Cooley, and Kluver, *Global Media and Strategic Narratives*, 5.

34. Among TRT World content analyzed here are documentaries and episodes of *The Newsmakers* and *Roundtable* that specifically address the refugee crisis and related topics. *The Newsmakers* and *Roundtable* were selected because they are TRT World's flagship discussion programs. *The Newsmakers* features in-depth reports about the major stories of the week and interviews with experts and is broadcast from TRT World's Istanbul studios. It bills itself as a program that offers "debates, context and commentary that disrupt conventional perspectives on international affairs, drive the news agenda and demand accountability from people in power." "The Newsmakers." *Roundtable* is broadcast from TRT World's London studios. It is self-described as a program "with an edge" that offers audiences "fierce debate" and "reflective thinking." "Roundtable." To locate specific episodes of these discussion programs on the refugee crisis, a keyword search was conducted on the TRT World's website and its YouTube channel, using the terms "refugee," "refugees," "migrant," "migrants," "refugee crisis," "migrant crisis," "refuge deal," and "EU refugee deal" for the time period between January 1, 2015 and June 1, 2016, which corresponds to the peak of the refugee crisis and the time of the signing of the EU-Turkey deal. The episodes analyzed, which are available on TRT World's YouTube channel, are as follows: *Roundtable*: "Refugee Crisis"; "Refugee Crisis: Are Rich Nations Shirking Their Responsibility?"; "Migrant Crisis"; "Can Europe's Migration Crisis Be Solved?"; "Refugee Economics"; "Is the Migrant Crisis Dividing Europe?" *The Newsmakers*: "The EU, Turkey, and the Refugee Crisis"; "Hungary's Refugee Crisis"; "EU-Turkey Refugee Deal"; "Refugee Fingerprinting"; "Syria Peace Talks and Refugee Volunteers"; "UK Refugees"; "The Plight of Child Refugees"; "The Other Refugee Route"; "Denmark's Decision"; "Breaking Down the Refugee Deal"; "Last Hours of the 'Jungle.'" For *Daily Sabah* op-eds, a search was conducted on the newspaper's website using the same terms as above during the same time period. The search returned 234 results and op-ed pieces by prominent writers, such as Melih Altınok, İlnur Çevik, Burhanettin Duran, and Haşmet Babaoğlu, were selected for analysis. I thank my research assistant based in Turkey, who wishes to remain anonymous, for conducting these searches.

35. Batha, "Factbox."

36. Simonsen and Bonikowski, "Moralizing Immigration," 1403.

37. Clifford, "How Emotional Frames Moralize," 76.

38. Presidency of the Republic of Türkiye, "'We Have Opened Our Doors.'"

39. Bazian, "Erasure of the Human."
40. İ. Çevik, "Plight of Refugees."
41. Altınok, "Whose 'Barbarism' Is It?"
42. Former reporter at *Daily Sabah*, interview with author, December 16, 2021.
43. See, for example, these episodes available on YouTube: "How Is France Treating Calais Refugees?"; "EU Border Force: Breaking International Law?"; "The Plight of Child Refugees"; "What's a Refugee's Worth in the EU?"
44. TRT World, "Did Europe Turn Its Back on Syria?"
45. TRT World, "What Is a Refugee's Worth in the EU?"
46. TRT World, "Beaten by the Border."
47. "Yayınlarımız Uluslararası Adaletsizliğe Karşı."
48. Karakum, "Uluslararası Basında TRT World'un Rolu Ne?"
49. "Inside America with Ghida Fakhry," emphasis added.
50. Emphasis added.
51. These titles can be found on the TRT World website and its YouTube channels.
52. Bosphorus Global, "Activities."
53. Chronicles of Shame, "Homepage."
54. Crackdown Chronicles, "About Us."
55. Crackdown Chronicles, (@CrackdownReport), "Illegal Surveillance."
56. "No Genocide, Colonialism."
57. Kalın, (@ikalin1), "Milyonları Ölüme Götüren."
58. Henley, "Recep Tayyip Erdoğan."
59. "Fascism Consuming Europe."
60. "Turkey's Erdogan Invokes Holocaust."
61. Henley, "Recep Tayyip Erdoğan."
62. Kluver, Cooley, and Hinck, "Contesting Strategic Narratives."
63. Oates and Steiner, "Projecting Power"; Orttung and Nelson, "Russia Today's Strategy"; Ramsay and Robertshaw, *Weaponising News*; Szostek, "Defence and Promotion."
64. Moore and Colley, "Two International Propaganda Models," 17.
65. Bradshaw, DiResta, and Miller, "Playing Both Sides."
66. Greenberg, "American Spring."
67. "Xinhua Headlines"; "US Government Should Stand."
68. Hernández, "As Protests Engulf the United States."
69. Oates and Steiner, "Projecting Power"; Ramsay and Robertshaw, *Weaponising News*; Szostek, "Defence and Promotion"; Bradshaw, DiResta, and Miller, "Playing Both Sides"; Marsh, "Re-Evaluating China's Global Media Expansion"; Rutland and Kazantsev, "Limits of Russia's 'Soft Power'"; DiResta, Miller, Molter, Pomfret, and Tiffert, "Telling China's Story."
70. Aydin, "Between Occidentalism and the Global Left," 448.
71. Başkan and Taşpınar, *Nation or the Ummah*, 185–86.
72. Z. Çelik, *Europe Knows Nothing*, 13.
73. Ersoy's poem was later adopted as the national anthem of the Turkish Republic. Ersoy is highly respected among nationalist and Islamist circles in Turkey. Erdoğan refers to him as Turkey's "national poet" and the Muslim world's "poet of independence" for his contributions in fostering the "spiritual side of our freedom struggle." Türkiye Cumhuriyeti İletişim Başkanlığı, "President Erdoğan's message."

74. Duran, "Transformation of Islamist Political Thought," 92–94.
75. Çoruk, "Oryantalizm Üzerine Notlar"; Aydin, "Between Occidentalism and the Global Left," 451.
76. Duran and Aydin, "Competing Occidentalisms," 480–81.
77. Duran and Aydin, "Competing Occidentalisms," 485–87.
78. Duran, "Transformation of Islamist Political Thought," 330.
79. Aydin, "Between Occidentalism and the Global Left," 452.
80. Duran and Aydin, "Competing Occidentalisms," 492.
81. Aydin and Duran, "Arnold J. Toynbee," 316–18.
82. Aydin and Duran, "Arnold J. Toynbee," 310, 314.

83. These civilizationist perspectives have been contradicted by other Islamist thinkers such as Ali Bulaç and İsmet Özel. See Dalacoura, "Islamic Civilization."

84. For a discussion of ideological affinities between Kısakürek and Erdoğan, see Singer, "Erdogan's Muse"; Cornell, "Erbakan, Kısakürek, and the Mainstreaming."

85. During the 1990s Davutoğlu served as a professor of political science at the International Islamic University of Malaysia, coinciding with İbrahim Kalın's time there as a graduate student. Davutoğlu and Kalın are also known to have collaborated at both SETA and the Ministry of Foreign Affairs, further solidifying their shared professional history.

86. Dalacoura, "Islamic Civilization," 140–42; Davutoğlu, *Civilizational Transformation*.

87. Dalacoura, "Islamic Civilization," 145–46.
88. Kalın, *Barbar, Modern, Medeni*.

89. Huntington, "Clash of Civilizations." In 1996 Huntington expanded this article into a book, *The Clash of Civilizations and the Remaking of World Order*.

90. Huntington is not alone in presenting an essentialist view of geographic regions and civilizations. Bernard Lewis has, too, embraced the idea of an inherent clash between Islam and the West and attributed challenges faced by Middle East countries to their culture and religion. See Lewis, "Roots of Muslim Rage."

91. Huntington, "Clash of Civilizations."

92. For a summary of critiques that focus on Huntington's methodological fallacy, see Shahi, *Understanding Post-9/11 Afghanistan*.

93. Açıkel, "Critique of Occidental Geist," 74–79.
94. Said, "Clash of Ignorance."
95. Castle, "Recep Tayyip Erdogan."
96. Iğsız, "From Alliance of Civilizations," 692, Ardıç, "Civilizational Discourse."
97. Aydin, "Between Occidentalism and the Global Left," 458.

98. For a comprehensive discussion of the nexus of domestic and foreign policy challenges, see Çınar, "Turkey's 'Western' or 'Muslim' Identity."

99. Al-Ali, *Secularism, Gender*, 26. Contrary to conventional wisdom, Occidentalism is not limited to Muslim polities; it can be found in intellectual traditions of other non-Western contexts, such as Russia and Japan. As historian Cemil Aydin notes, criticisms of the West were also developed by Russian and Japanese intellectuals during mid-to-late nineteenth century when their respective countries were confronted with a changing international order that was predominantly shaped by European powers. See Aydin, *Politics of Anti-Westernism*.

100. Coronil, "Beyond Occidentalism," 57.
101. Coronil, "Beyond Occidentalism," 57.
102. Al-Ali, *Secularism, Gender*, 26.
103. Ahıska, "Occidentalism," 366.
104. "Turkiye Challenges Imperialism, Erdogan Says."
105. Aydıntaşbaş, "New Gaza."
106. Badi, "To Advance Its Own Interests."
107. Dalay, "Turkey, Europe, and the Eastern Mediterranean."
108. "Erdoğan'dan Neo-Osmanlıcı Çıkış."
109. Haug and Roychoudhury, "Civilizational Exceptionalism," 543.
110. Haug and Roychoudhury, "Civilizational Exceptionalism," 541.

Chapter 5. Promoting Turkish History and Civilization

1. "Turkish Day"; "Türkiye Challenges Imperialism."
2. Vömel, "Pathos and Discipline," 498. Developed by Turkish Islamists from the 1950s onwards, this ideal type dominated the religiously inflected literary works of the 1960s and 1970s.
3. Similar historical depictions of Turkish Muslim warriors can be found in Turkish literature, film, and graphic novels of the 1960s and 1970s. For a detailed analysis of films about Turkish warriors fighting against the "infidel" Byzantium, see Bayri, "Contemporary Perception."
4. In media coverage and scholarly literature, Turkish series are generally referred to as "soap operas," "dramas," or "telenovelas." Turkish series do have elements of these different genres, but, as Öztürkmen argues, Turkish series have their own distinctive characteristics. For example, their "musical, textual and visual diversity" is richer than soap operas and telenovelas. Unlike soap operas, they are shot in natural settings and with dialogues performed almost in real time. Because of these differences, Öztürkmen proposes to use the word "dizi" to categorize Turkish series as a separate genre. See Öztürkmen, "Turkish Content."
5. When broadcast domestically in Turkey, each episode runs between 120 and 150 minutes, and a season generally consists of forty to fifty episodes. Turkish series are much longer than their counterparts produced in Latin America, Europe, and the United States, mostly because of Turkish television channels' financial concerns. In 2004 RTUK (Supreme Board of Radio and Television), the main regulatory body in charge of broadcasting, declared that broadcast channels must have at least twenty minutes of airtime between each commercial break. To meet this requirement and maximize advertising revenues, channel executives lengthened program durations. The sheer length of a Turkish series obviously puts immense pressure on production crews for they are compelled to work fifteen to eighteen hours a day on the set. In recent years, the Turkish Actors Union, Turkish Cinema Workers Union, and a number of prominent actors have called on production companies and broadcast channels to treat workers more humanely. For a detailed analysis, see Bulut, "Dramın Ardındaki Emek."
6. Mohamed, "Yesilcam Overtakes"; "Turkish TV Series Continue"; Alexander, "South Africa's e.tv."
7. "SPI/FilmBox Launches."

8. Kraidy and Bergere, "From Dazzle to Diesel."
9. Grater, "How Turkey Has Become"; Yorulmaz, "Turkish Dramas."
10. Vivarelli, "Turkey Experiences Its Own."
11. "Turkey Ranks Second."
12. Whittock, "Germany, France," and "NBC to Remake"; Middleton, "Japan's Nippon TV."
13. Carney, "ResurReaction."
14. Fowler, "Dirt, and the Soap." *Magnificent Century* received similar negative responses in other predominantly Muslim countries. For example, in Indonesia, viewers expressed concern about sexually suggestive material, and clerics condemned the show for promoting hatred toward Islam because of the show's depiction of Suleiman as "a prideful, promiscuous man." Rakhmani and Zakiah, "Consuming Halal Turkish Television."
15. Carney, "Re-Creating History" and "ResurReaction."
16. For a detailed discussion of *Rebellion*'s failure, see Carney, "Re-Creating History," para. 44.
17. Polat, "Ertuğrul Diriliş: Ertuğrul'un Yapımcısı Bozdağ."
18. The docudrama had been greenlighted by Yusuf Kaplan, an Islamist cultural critic and pro-AKP pundit, who at the time was in charge of film and television production for the government-sponsored Istanbul: European Capital of Culture project. See Polat, "Diriliş Ertuğrul'un Yapımcısı."
19. Carney, "Resur(e)recting a Spectacular Hero," 95.
20. "Turkish History-Themed Series."
21. When broadcast on TRT, each episode was approximately two hours long. On Netflix, episodes were edited down to forty minutes. See Nelson, "Ertuğrul."
22. Carney, "Resur(e)recting a Spectacular Hero," 112.
23. Polat, "Diriliş Ertuğrul'un Yapımcısı."
24. Polat, "Diriliş Ertuğrul'un Yapımcısı."
25. Sani, "Yapımcı Bozdağ."
26. "Cumhurbaşkanı Erdoğan: 'Sosyal ve Kulturel.'"
27. Butler, "With More Islamic Schooling." For a detailed discussion of the AKP's religiously oriented education and culture policies, see Lukuslu, "Creating a Pious Generation."
28. "Diriliş Ertuğrul Oyuncuları"; "Diriliş'in Oyuncuları."
29. The narrative of Turks protecting fellow oppressed Muslims can be traced back to two specific films produced in the 2000s. In *Valley of the Wolves: Iraq* (2006) and *Valley of the Wolves: Palestine* (2011), Turks are portrayed as guardians of Iraqis and Palestinians in the face of American and Israeli occupation, respectively. For a detailed analysis, see Yanik, "Valley of the Wolves—Iraq"; Kraidy and Al-Ghazzi, "Turkish Rambo."
30. Although Abdülhamid II was not actually the last emperor of the Ottoman Empire as the English title suggests, he is considered by Islamists in Turkey to be the last truly pious sultan.
31. Ari, "TRT Sayesinde."
32. Ranger and Ranger, "Towards a Resonant Theory."
33. Verovšek, "Collective Memory," 532.

34. Couperus, Tortola, and Rensmann, "Memory Politics," 437.
35. Jaskulowski and Majewski, "Populist in Form."
36. Programming executive at TRT, interview with author, August 5, 2021.
37. These three prominent websites have offered many of the historical dramas with English subtitles since 2018. Historical Fun TV sells monthly, six-month, and yearly subscription plans to users, while Osman Online provides free content in exchange for donations to help Muslims in Gaza and elsewhere.
38. One of the first international fan groups to emerge is the English-speaking Turkish Dramas Appreciation Group. Unlike other groups devoted to historical dramas, it brings together North American- and Europe-based viewers with a focus on the commercially produced romance, family, or crime series.
39. There are debates about what exactly the term "ghaza" implicates, whether it means military raid or holy war. In contemporary Turkey, the expression "May your ghaza be blessed" is used to motivate soldiers and wish them well in military operations. It is also used in everyday language to wish someone good luck in their new endeavor.
40. For a detailed analysis of this narrative, see Bulut and Ileri, "Screening Right-Wing Populism."
41. Mishra, "Putin Isn't Alone"; Salhani, "One More Twist."
42. "Cumhurbaşkanı Erdoğan: Biz Nasıl."
43. See chapter 3 for a detailed discussion of Erdoğan's discourse on achieving justice on behalf of the oppressed Muslims.
44. Ogutcen and Gozelik, "Cumhurbaşkanlığı Sözcüsü Kalın."
45. Ogutcen and Gozelik, "Cumhurbaşkanlığı Sözcüsü Kalın."
46. Çavuşoğlu, "Why Turkey Took."
47. Çavuşoğlu, "Why Turkey Took."
48. Arslan, "Abdülhamid'in hayallerini"; "Sultan Abdülhamid'in Rüyası."
49. Former Anadolu Agency executive, interview with author, June 18, 2021.
50. Executive at TRT, interview with author, August 23, 2021.
51. Bilbassy-Charters, "Leave It to Turkish"; Salem, "Turkey's Image"; Bhutto, "How Turkey's Soft Power."
52. "Turkish Dramas Play Key Role"; TRT World, "Turkey's Soft Power"; Mohydin, "Lasting Appeal."
53. Mohydin, "Turkish Dramas' Impact"; Mohydin "Global Appeal"; "Popular Turkish TV Drama"; "Turkish Language Courses"; TRT World, "Turkey's Soft Power."
54. Yoruk and Vatikiotis, "Soft Power."
55. Kraidy and Bergere, "From Dazzle to Diesel." For other audience analyses of Turkish television, see Wagner and Kraidy, "Watching Turkish Television Dramas"; Anaz, "Geography of Reception"; Yanardağoğlu and Karam, "Fever That Hit."
56. These viewers were recruited from three prominent Facebook pages devoted to Turkish content: Turkish Dramas Appreciation Group English Speaking, the Great Caliph Abdulhamid, and Kuruluş Osman & Ertuğrul Dirilis Fans. Approximately fifty viewers volunteered to talk to me, and in the end, I interviewed fifteen male and twelve female adults. The semi-structured, in-depth interviews (approximately seventy-five to ninety minutes, in English) took place between January and February 2020 and May through July 2021 via Facebook Messenger and WhatsApp. Conventional protocols

for anonymity and confidentiality were followed during the recruitment, interview, and transcription stages. Research participants were all non-Turkish Muslims from countries in the Global South (Afghanistan, Bangladesh, Indonesia, Malaysia, Pakistan, South Africa, or Sri Lanka). Two participants were non-Turkish Muslims that live in the United Kingdom and the United States. For the list of interviewees' demographic information, see appendix in the current volume.

57. Participant 7; participant 22; participant 25, all interview with author.
58. Participant 3, interview with author.
59. Participant 21, interview with author.
60. Participant 3, interview with author.
61. Participant 16, interview with author.
62. Participant 6, interview with author.
63. Participant 2; participant 16, both interview with author.
64. Participant 18, interview with author.
65. Participant 4, interview with author.
66. Participant 27, interview with author.
67. Participant 9, interview with author.
68. Participant 12, interview with author.
69. Participant 2, interview with author.
70. Participant 14, interview with author.
71. Participant 23, interview with author/
72. Participant 18, interview with author/
73. Participant 20, interview with author.
74. Participant 6; participant 9; participant 11; participant 20, all interview with author.
75. Participant 1, interview with author.
76. Participant 17, interview with author.
77. Participant 8, interview with author.
78. Participant 25, interview with author.
79. Participant 23, interview with author.
80. Participant 19, interview with author.
81. Participant 23; participant 19, both interview with author.
82. Participant 10, interview with author.
83. Participant 15, interview with author.
84. I thank Collen Kennedy Karpat for bringing this important point to my attention.
85. El-Behary, "Turkey's Soft Power"; Gambrell, "Turkish Soap Operas"; Saeed, "Saudi Broadcaster MBC."
86. "Egypt Fatwa Bans Ertuğrul." For an in-depth analysis of the tensions between Egypt and Turkey over television dramas, see Kraidy, "Boycotting Neo-Ottoman Cool."
87. Bulos, "Game of Shows."
88. Shaheen, "Ramadan TV Series."
89. Shaheen, "Ramadan TV Series."
90. Makris, "Bishop Anthimos Lashes Turkish Soap Fans."

91. "Radical Groups Campaign."
92. Morina and Buyuk, "Turkish Series about Sultan." For a discussion of the complicated relationship between Balkan audiences and Turkish series in light of the Ottoman legacy in the region, see Amzi-Erdogdular, "Ottomania."
93. Osman, "Building Spectatorial Solidarity," 372. For a general and comprehensive analysis of post–September 11 media portrayals of Arabs and Muslims, see Alsultany, *Arabs and Muslims in the Media*.
94. Osman, "Building Spectatorial Solidarity," 372.
95. Brubaker, "Between Nationalism and Civilizationism," 1193. For a detailed discussion on the nexus of populism and religion, see DeHanas and Shterin, "Religion and the Rise of Populism," and Arato and Cohen, *Populism, Civil Society, and Religion*.
96. Davies, "Trump Says West."
97. Peker, "Religious Populism, Memory, and Violence in India"; Haug and Roychoudhury, "Civilizational Exceptionalism."

Conclusion

1. Tosun, "Cumhurbaşkanlığı İletişim Başkanı."
2. Özkır, "Turk Dis Politikasinda," 39.
3. Mignolo, "Epistemic Disobedience, Independent Thought" and "Epistemic Disobedience and the Decolonial Option."
4. Mignolo, "Epistemic Disobedience and the Decolonial Option," 224.
5. Chakrabarty, *Provincializing Europe*.
6. Spivak, "Can the Subaltern Speak?"
7. Kandiyoti, "Post-Colonialism Compared," 285.
8. TRT World, "What Western Media Gets Wrong."
9. Al-Ali, *Secularism, Gender, and the State*, 32.
10. Fisher-Onar, "Capitulations Syndrome."
11. For analyses of other state-sponsored news outlets with respect to editorial interference, see Wright, Scott, and Bunce, "Soft Power, Hard News"; Elswah and Howard, "Anything That Causes Chaos."
12. Elswah and Howard, "Where News Could Not Inspire Change."
13. Unal, "TRT World CEO Ibrahim Eren."
14. Former TRT World executive, interview with author, September 5, 2022.
15. Former TRT World executive, interview with author, September 5, 2022.
16. Former TRT executive, interview with author, April 13, 2021. For TRT World's "recruitment drive" in Pakistan, see "Turkish State Broadcaster."
17. Foreign producer at TRT World, interview with author, January 18, 2021.
18. Cull, *Public Diplomacy*; Gilboa, "Global Communication and Foreign Policy"; Price, *Free Expression, Globalism*.
19. Rawnsley, "To Know Us Is to Love Us."
20. Toula, "Failure to Launch."
21. See Toula, "Failure to Launch," for a discussion of Chinese and Russian arguments about the Western monopoly on news.

22. Figenschou, "Voice for the Voiceless?" 86.

23. Elswah and Howard, "Anything That Causes Chaos," 625. For a discussion of how RT uses conspiracy theories, see Yablokov and Chatterje-Doody, *Russia Today and Conspiracy Theories*.

24. Repnikova, *Chinese Soft Power*, 23, 27.

25. Eliot Borenstein's *Plots against Russia* offers an in-depth analysis of these dynamics within the context of Russian media and cultural landscapes.

Bibliography

Acar, Umut. (@AcarUmut). "Current structure of the UN Security Council which is basically 5 Countries vs rest of the world weakens UN's Credibility. #WorldIsBiggerThanFive." X, October 5, 2020. https://x.com/AcarUmut/status/1313104827803676684?s=20.

Açıkel, Fethi. "A Critique of Occidental Geist: Embedded Historical Culturalism in the Works of Hegel, Weber, and Huntington." *Journal of Historical Sociology* 19 (2006): 60–83.

Açıkel, Fethi. "Kutsal Mazlumlugun Psikopatolojisi" [The psychopathology of sacred victimhood]. *Toplum ve Bilim* 70 (1996): 153–98.

Addis, Ayele. "African Media Representatives Training Program II (AFMED II): Turkey-Africa Media Training Program Held in Virtual Amid Call for Enhanced Cooperation." *Africa News Channel*, May 26, 2021. https://www.africanewschannel.org/news/african-media-representatives-training-program-ii-afmedii-turkey-africa-media-training-program-held-in-virtual-amid-call-for-enhanced-cooperation/.

"After Protests, Evaluating Turkey's Role as a Democracy." *NPR*, June 5, 2013. https://www.npr.org/2013/06/05/188924496/after-protests-evaluating-turkeys-role-as-a-democracy.

Ahıska, Meltem. "Occidentalism: The Historical Fantasy of the Modern." *South Atlantic Quarterly* 102, nos. 2–3 (2003): 351–79.

Akdeniz, Yaman. "Report of the OSCE Representative on Freedom of the Media on Turkey and Internet Censorship." *OSCE* (Organization for Security and Co-operation in Europe), January 11, 2010. https://www.osce.org/fom/41091.

Akgün, Birol, and Mehmet Özkan. "Turkey's Entrance to International Education: The Case of Turkish Maarif Foundation." *Insight Turkey* 22, no. 1 (2020): 59–71.

Akkoyunlu, Karabekir. "The Five Phases of Turkey's Foreign Policy under the AKP." *Social Research: An International Quarterly* 88, no. 2 (2021): 243–70.

Akser, Murat, and Banu Baybars-Hawks. "Media and Democracy in Turkey: Toward a Model of Neoliberal Media Autocracy." *Middle East Journal of Culture and Communication* 5, no. 3 (2012): 302–21.

Aksoy, Asu, and Kevin Robins. "Thinking across Spaces: Transnational Television from Turkey." *European Journal of Cultural Studies* 3, no. 3 (2000): 343–65.

Akyol, Mustafa. "The Middle East 'Mastermind' Who Worries Erdogan." *Al-Monitor* (Washington, DC), October 31, 2014. https://www.al-monitor.com/pulse /originals/2014/10/turkey-erdogan-middle-east-mastermind.html.

Akyol, Mustafa. "President Erdoğan and the French Riot Police." *Hurriyet Daily News* (Istanbul), May 31, 2016. https://www.hurriyetdailynews.com/opinion/mustafa -akyol/president-erdogan-and-the-french-riot-police-99907.

Al-Ali, Nadje. *Secularism, Gender, and the State in the Middle East: The Egyptian Women's Movement.* Cambridge: Cambridge University Press, 2000.

Albayrak, Ayla, and Joe Parkinson. "Turkey's Government Forms 6,000-Member Social Media Team." *Wall Street Journal*, September 16, 2013. https://www.wsj.com /articles/SB10001424127887323527004579079151479634742.

Aldinç, Burcu. "Türkiye'yi Dünyaya Daily Sabah Anlatacak" [*Daily Sabah* will tell the world about Turkey]. *Sabah* (Istanbul), March 2, 2014. https://www.sabah.com.tr /pazar/2014/03/02/turkiyeyi-dunyaya-daily-sabah-anlatacak.

Aldridge, Meryl, and Julia Evetts. "Rethinking the Concept of Professionalism: The Case of Journalism." *British Journal of Sociology* 54, no. 4 (2003): 547–64.

Alemdaroğlu, Ayça, and Sultan Tepe. "Erdogan Is Turning Turkey into a Chinese Client State." *Foreign Policy*, September 16, 2020. https://foreignpolicy.com/2020/09/16 /erdogan-is-turning-turkey-into-a-chinese-client-state/.

Alexander, Inigo. "South Africa's e.tv Takes Turkish Drama." *C21 Media*, May 1, 2020. https://www.c21media.net/news/south-africas-e-tv-takes-turkish-drama/.

Al-Ghazzi, Omar. "We Will Be Great Again: Historical Victimhood in Populist Discourse." *European Journal of Cultural Studies* 24, no. 1 (2021): 45–59.

Al-Ghazzi, Omar, and Marwan M. Kraidy. "Neo-Ottoman Cool 2: Turkish Nation Branding and Arabic-Language Transnational Broadcasting." *International Journal of Communication* 7 (2013): 2341–60.

Alloul, Houssine, and Roel Markey. "Please Deny These Manifestly False Reports: Ottoman Diplomats and the Press in Belgium (1850–1914)." *International Journal of Middle East Studies* 48, no. 2 (2016): 267–92.

"All Social Media Providers Have Opened Rep Offices in Turkey." *Daily Sabah* (Istanbul), September 27, 2021. https://www.dailysabah.com/politics/legislation/all -social-media-providers-have-opened-rep-offices-in-turkey.

Alsultany, Evelyn. *Arabs and Muslims in the Media: Race and Representation after 9/11.* New York: New York University Press, 2012.

Altas, Mumin. "Anadolu Ajansı, İslamofobi İzleme Birimi Oluşturacak." *Anadolu Ajansı*, May 25, 2021. https://www.aa.com.tr/tr/kurumsal-haberler/anadolu-ajansi -islamofobi-izleme-birimi-olusturacak/2253567.

Altay, Kuzzat. "Why Erdogan Has Abandoned the Uyghurs." *Foreign Policy*, March 2, 2021. https://foreignpolicy.com/2021/03/02/why-erdogan-has-abandoned-the -uyghurs/.

Altınok, Melih. "Whose 'Barbarism' Is It?" *Daily Sabah* (Istanbul), October 10, 2014. https://www.dailysabah.com/columns/melih-altinok/2014/10/10/whose -barbarism-is-it.

Altinordu, Ates. "The Political Incorporation of Anti-System Religious Parties: The Case of Turkish Political Islam." *Qualitative Sociology* 39, no. 2 (2016): 147–71.

Altinordu, Ates. "Uncivil Populism in Power: The Case of Erdoganism." In *Populism in the Civil Sphere,* edited by Jeffrey Alexander, Peter Kivisto, and Guiseppe Sciortino, 74–95. London: Polity, 2020.

Altun, Fahrettin. (@fahrettinaltun). "Europe's hostility towards Muslims and efforts to 'discipline' them is inseparable from the increasingly widespread hostility towards Islam, Turkey and our president Recep Tayyip Erdoğan." X, October 25, 2020. https://twitter.com/fahrettinaltun/status/1320310223089840133?s=20.

Altun, Fahrettin. (@fahrettinaltun). "Hoşunuza gitsin ya da gitmesin, her fırsatta terörün dili, dini, ırkı olmadığını söyleyeceğiz. Bir kere daha gördük ki her alanda olduğu gibi medya ve iletişim alanında da yerli ve milli platformlara ihtiyacımız var. Yaşasın Hakikat!" [Whether you like it or not, we will say at every opportunity that terrorism has no language, religion or race. We see once again that we need local and national platforms in the field of media and communication, as in every field. Long live the truth!]. *X,* July 1, 2021. https://twitter.com/fahrettinaltun/status/14106 67910595502083?s=20.

Altun, Fahrettin. (@fahrettinaltun). "İslam'a ve Müslümanlara yönelik nefret söylemlerini görmezden gelen, terör örgütlerinin kara propagandalarına kolaylıkla alan açan YouTube, Türk diplomatlarımızı şehit eden katil teröristlerle ilgili söylediklerimizin nefret suçu! sayıyor" [YouTube, which ignores the hate speech directed at Islam and Muslims and readily opens space for terrorist organizations' black propaganda, considers what we said about the murderer terrorists who martyred our Turkish diplomats is a hate crime!]. *X,* July 1, 2021. https://twitter.com/fahrettinaltun /status/1410667909073063938?s=20.

Altun, Fahrettin. (@fahrettinaltun). "Recep Tayyip Erdoğan is the leader who fights against oppression and injustice while standing with the oppressed, and truth all over the world. With the prayers of voiceless people for whom he becomes a voice, Erdoğan continues his march tirelessly and undauntedly. #OurVoice Erdogan." *X,* September 24, 2019. https://twitter.com/fahrettinaltun/status/11764967592514 60096?s=20.

Altun, Fahrettin. (@fahrettinaltun). "Üzülerek belirtmek istiyorum ki, Sehit Diplomatlar Sergisinde yaptığım şu konuşma YouTube tarafından sansürlendi. Sozum ona bu konusma, nefret söylemi iceriyormus. Lutfen kulak verin ve siz karar verin. Bu cifte standarttır, bu riyakarlıktır" [I regret to inform you that the speech I delivered at the Martyred Diplomats Exhibition has been censored by YouTube. This speech allegedly contains hate speech. Please listen to it and make your call. This is double standards, this is hypocrisy]. *X,* July 1, 2021. https://twitter.com/fahrettinaltun/status /1410667506595946499?s=20.

Altun, Fahrettin. "Truth Is a Human Right: Türkiye's Stance on the Fight against Disinformation." *Insight Turkey* 25, no. 1 (2023):13–217. https://www.insightturkey .com/commentary/truth-is-a-human-right-turkiyes-stance-on-the-fight-against -disinformation.

"Altun'dan Basın Özgürlüğü Mesajı: 20 yıl Oncesine Kıyasla" [Altun's message about freedom of press: Compared to 20 years ago]. *Cumhuriyet* (Istanbul), January 9,

2021. https://www.cumhuriyet.com.tr/haber/altundan-basin-ozgurlugu-mesaji-20-yil-oncesine-kiyasla-1804797.

Altunışık, Meliha B., and Lenore G. Martin. "Making Sense of Turkish Foreign Policy in the Middle East under AKP." *Turkish Studies* 12, no. 4 (2011): 569–87.

Amnesty International. *Amnesty International Report 2016/17: The State of the World's Human Rights*. Amnesty International, February 22, 2017. https://www.amnesty.org/en/documents/pol10/4800/2017/en/.

Amnesty International. "Turkey: Facebook and Other Companies 'in Danger of Becoming an Instrument of State Censorship.'" *Amnesty International*, January 18, 2021. https://www.amnesty.org/en/latest/press-release/2021/01/turkey-facebook-and-other-companies-in-danger-of-becoming-an-instrument-of-state-censorship/.

Amsterdam, Robert. "Turkey: Is the Gulen Organization a Cult?" *Breitbart*, July 31, 2016. https://www.breitbart.com/national-security/2016/07/31/gulen-organization-cult/#.

Amzi-Erdoğdular, Leyla. "Ottomania: Televised Histories and Otherness Revisited." *Nationalities Papers* 47, no. 5 (2019): 879–93.

"Anadolu Agency Trains over 2,400 Journalists in News Academy Last Year." *Anadolu Agency*, 2023. https://www.aa.com.tr/en/newsacademy/turkey/anadolu-agency-trains-over-2-400-journalists-in-news-academy-last-year/533190.

Anaz, Necati. "The Geography of Reception: Why Do Egyptians Watch Turkish Soap Operas?" *Arab World Geographer* 17, no. 3 (2014): 255–74.

"A News: Turkuvaz Media's English-Language Broadcaster Launched." *Daily Sabah* (Istanbul), April 4, 2017. https://www.dailysabah.com/turkey/2017/04/04/a-news-turkuvaz-medias-english-language-broadcaster-launched.

Arato, Andrew, and Jean L. Cohen. *Populism and Civil Society: The Challenge to Constitutional Democracy*. New York: Oxford University Press, 2022.

Ardıç, Nurullah. "Civilizational Discourse, the 'Alliance of Civilizations,' and Turkish Foreign Policy." *Insight Turkey* 16, no. 3 (2014): 101–22. https://www.insightturkey.com/articles/civilizational-discourse-the-alliance-of-civilizations-and-turkish-foreign-policy.

Arı, Ismail. "TRT Sayesinde Koseyi Donduler" [Thanks to TRT, they struck it rich]. *Birgün* (Istanbul), June 14, 2023. https://www.birgun.net/haber/trt-sayesinde-koseyi-donduler 445234.

Armstrong, William. "Army of Spin." *Foreign Policy*, December 9, 2014. https://foreignpolicy.com/2014/12/09/army-of-spin-turkey-media-erdogan/.

Armstrong, William. "The Sultan and the Sultan." *History Today*. November 8, 2017. https://www.historytoday.com/miscellanies/sultan-and-sultan.

Arnold, David. "Gramsci and Peasant Subalternity in India." In *Mapping Subaltern Studies and the Postcolonial*, edited by Vinayak Chaturvedi, 24–49. London: Verso, 2000.

Arora, Payal. *The Next Billion Users: Digital Life beyond the West*. Cambridge, MA: Harvard University Press, 2019.

"Arrogance Undoes the Turkish Model." *Financial Times*, January 8, 2014. https://www.ft.com/content/e6cc4e26-785c-11e3-831c-00144feabdc0.

Arslan, Faruk. "Abdülhamid'in Hayallerini Erdoğan Gerçekleştirdi" [Erdoğan made Abdulhamid's dreams come true]. *Yeni Akit* (Istanbul), June 20, 2018. https://www

.yeniakit.com.tr/haber/abdulhamidin-hayallerini-erdogan-gerceklestirdi-482801.html.
Aşık, Ozan. "Politics, Power, and Performativity in the Newsroom: An Ethnography of Television Journalism in Turkey." *Media, Culture, and Society* 41, no. 5 (2019): 587–603.
Ataman, Bora, and Baris Coban. "Counter-Surveillance and Alternative New Media in Turkey." *Information, Communication, and Society* 21, no. 7 (2018): 1014-29.
Ataman, Muhittin, and Gloria Shkurti. "Coup d'état Record of the West and the Western Reaction to the July 15 Coup Attempt." In *July 15 Coup Attempt in Turkey: Context, Causes, and Consequences*, edited by Muhittin Ataman, 219–50. Istanbul: SETA, 2017.
Atasoy, Yıldız. *Islam's Marriage with Neoliberalism: State Transformation in Turkey*. Basingstoke, UK: Palgrave Macmillan, 2009.
Atilla, Toygun. "Turkey Issues Arrest Warrant for Former CIA Official Graham Fuller Over Coup Attempt." *Hurriyet Daily News* (Istanbul), December 1, 2017. https://www.hurriyetdailynews.com/turkey-issues-arrest-warrant-for-former-cia-official-graham-fuller-over-coup-attempt-123392.
Aydin, Cemil. "Between Occidentalism and the Global Left: Islamist Critiques of the West in Turkey." *Comparative Studies of South Asia, Africa, and the Middle East* 26, no. 3 (2006): 446–61.
Aydin, Cemil. *The Politics of Anti-Westernism in Asia: Visions of World Order in Pan-Islamic and Pan-Asian Thought*. New York: Columbia University Press, 2007.
Aydin, Cemil. *The Idea of the Muslim World: A Global Intellectual History*. Cambridge, MA: Harvard University Press, 2017.
Aydin, Cemil, and Burhanettin Duran. "Arnold J. Toynbee and Islamism in Cold War Era Turkey: Civilizationism in the Writings of Sezai Karakoç." *Comparative Studies of South Asia, Africa. and the Middle East* 35, no. 2 (2015): 310–23.
Aydıntaşbaş, Aslı. "A New Gaza: Turkey's Border Policy in Northern Syria." *European Council on Foreign Relations*, May 28, 2020. https://ecfr.eu/publication/a_new_gaza_turkeys_border_policy_in_northern_syria/.
Aytac, Erdem, and Ziya Onis. "Varieties of Populism In a Changing Global Context: The Divergent Paths of Erdogan and Kirchnerismo." *Comparative Politics* 47, no. 1 (2014): 41–59.
Babaoğlu, Haşmet. "New Orientalism and the Western Media." *Daily Sabah* (Istanbul), March 7, 2014. https://www.dailysabah.com/columns/hasmet-babaoglu/2014/03/07/new-orientalism-and-the-western-media.
Badi, Emadeddin. "To Advance Its Own Interests, Turkey Should Now Help Stabilize Libya." *War on the Rocks*, May 24, 2021. https://warontherocks.com/2021/05/to-advance-its-own-interests-turkey-should-now-help-stabilize-libya/.
Baer, Marc David. "An Enemy Old and New: The Donme, Anti-Semitism, and Conspiracy Theories in the Ottoman Empire and Turkish Republic." *Jewish Quarterly Review* 103, no. 4 (2013): 523–55.
Bargu, Banu. "Neo-Ottomanism: An Alt-Right Formation from the South?" *Social Research: An International Quarterly* 88, no. 2 (2021): 299–333.
Baritci, Fatih, and Hediyetullah Aydeniz. "Kamu Diplomasisi Aracı Olarak Medya: TRT World Örneği" [Media as a tool of public diplomacy: the example of TRT World]. *Erciyes Iletisim Dergisi* 6, no. 2 (2019): 1551–76.

Baser, Ekrem. "Shift of Axis in Turkish Foreign Policy: Turkish National Role Conceptions before and after the AKP." *American Political Studies Association*, August 27, 2013. https://papers.ssrn.com/sol3/papers.cfm?abstract_id=2301923.

"Başkanın Mesajı: Uluslararası Rekabet Edecek Haberci Yetiştirmek!" [President's message: To train internationally competitive newsmakers]. *Anadolu Ajansı*, 2023. https://www.aa.com.tr/tr/haberakademisi/p/baskanin-mesaji.

Başkan, Birol, and Ömer Taşpınar. *The Nation or the Ummah: Islamism and Turkish Foreign Policy*. Albany: State University of New York Press, 2021.

Bastos, Marco, and Johan Farkas. "'Donald Trump Is My President!' The Internet Research Agency Propaganda Machine," *Social Media + Society* 5, no. 3 (2019). DOI: https://doi.org/10.1177/2056305119865466.

Batha, Emma. "Factbox: How Big Is Europe's Refugee and Migrant Crisis?" *Trust*, November 30, 2016. https://news.trust.org/item/20161130143409-nr3lz.

"Batı Medyasından Eş Zamanlı Algı Operasyonu" [Coordinated influence operation by Western media]. *A Haber*, March 12, 2020. https://www.ahaber.com.tr/dunya/2020/03/12/bati-medyasindan-es-zamanli-algi-operasyonu-bbc-cnn-ve-new-york-times-koronavirus-uzerinden-turkiyeyi-hedef-aldi.

Bayar, Gozde. "Anadolu Agency to Establish Islamophobia Monitoring Unit." *Anadolu Agency*, May 25, 2021. https://www.aa.com.tr/en/corporate-news/anadolu-agency-to-establish-islamophobia-monitoring-unit/2253685.

Baykurt, Burcu, and Victoria de Grazia. *Soft Power Internationalism: Competing for Cultural. Influence in the 21st Century Global Order*. New York: Columbia University Press, 2021.

Bayrakli, Enes. *Orientalism Reloaded: How Western Media Covered the Coup Attempt in Turkey*. SETA, 2016. https://file.setav.org/Files/Pdf/20160809164911_24_perspective.pdf.

Bayri, Buket Kitapci. "Contemporary Perception of Byzantium in Turkish Cinema: The Cross-Examination of Battal Gazi Films with the Battalname." *Byzantine and Modern Greek Studies* 37, no. 1 (2013): 81–91.

Bazian, Hatem. "Erasure of the Human." *Daily Sabah* (Istanbul), August 18, 2016. https://www.dailysabah.com/columns/hatem-bazian/2016/08/18/erasure-of-the-human.

Beck, John M. "Turkey's Global Soft-Power Push Is Built on Mosques." *Atlantic*, June 1, 2019. https://www.theatlantic.com/international/archive/2019/06/turkey-builds-mosques-abroad-global-soft-power/590449/.

Benabdallah, Lina. *Shaping the Future of Power: Knowledge Production and Network-Building in China-Africa Relations*. Ann Arbor: University of Michigan Press, 2020.

Bengi, Hilmi. "Tarihsel Surec Icinde Anadolu Ajansı'nin Ozgun Kurumsal Yapisi (1920–2011)" [Anadolu Agency's original institutional structure throughout time (1920–2011)]. *Ataturk Yolu Dergisi* 13, no. 50 (2012): 299–341.

Benkler, Yochai, Robert Faris, and Hal Roberts. *Network Propaganda: Manipulation, Disinformation, and Radicalization in American Politics*. Oxford: Oxford University Press, 2018.

Bernays, Edward L. *Propaganda: The Public Mind in the Making*. New York: Liveright, 1936.

Bettiza, Gregorio, Derek Bolton, and David Lewis. "Civilizationism and the Ideological Contestation of the Liberal International Order." *International Studies Review* 25, no. 2 (2023): 1–28.

Bhutto, Fatima. "How Turkey's Soft Power Conquered Pakistan." *Foreign Policy*, September 5, 2020. https://foreignpolicy.com/2020/09/05/ertugrul-turkey-dizi-soft-power-pakistan/.

Bilbassy-Charters, Nadia. "Leave It to Turkish Soap Operas to Conquer Hearts and Minds." *Foreign Policy*, April 15, 2010. https://foreignpolicy.com/2010/04/15/leave-it-to-turkish-soap-operas-to-conquer-hearts-and-minds/.

Bilge, Nurhayat. "Friend or Foe: Cultural Fusion Theory and Media Coverage of Syrian Refugees in Turkey." *Communication, Culture, and Critique* 12 (2019): 110–27.

Birge, Lucy, and Precious N. Chatterje-Doody. "Russian Public Diplomacy: Questioning Certainties in Uncertain Times." In *Public Diplomacy and the Politics of Uncertainty*, edited by Pawel Surowiec and Ilan Manor, 171–95. London: Palgrave Macmillan, 2021.

"Birleşmiş Milletler'de İsyan: Dunya Beşten Büyüktür" [Revolt at the United Nations: World is bigger than five]. *HaberTurk* (Istanbul), September 25, 2014. https://www.haberturk.com/dunya/haber/993531-birlesmis-milletlerde-isyan.

Boas, Taylor C. "Weaving the Authoritarian Web: The Control of Internet Use in Nondemocratic Regimes." In *How Revolutionary Was the Digital Revolution: National Responses, Market Transitions, and Global Technology*, edited by John Zysman and Abraham Newman, 361–78. Stanford, CA: Stanford University Press, 2006.

Bokhari, Sonia. "Turkish Drama 'Resurrection: Ertuğrul' and Turkey-Pakistan Relations." *Daily Sabah* (Istanbul), May 20, 2020. https://www.dailysabah.com/opinion/op-ed/turkish-drama-resurrection-ertugrul-and-turkey-pakistan-relations.

Bora, Tanıl. *Cereyanlar: Turkiye'de Siyasi Ideolojiler* [Currents: Political ideologies in Turkey]. Istanbul: Iletisim Yayinlari, 2023.

Bora, Tanıl. "Komplo Zihniyetinin Ornek Ulkesi Turkiye" [Quintessential example of the conspiratorial mindset: Turkey]. *Birikim* 90 (1996): 42–44.

Börekçi, Deniz, and Dieter Loffler. "I Want You to Want Me: Turkey and Africa's Media." In *It Is about Their Story: How China, Turkey, and Russia Influence the Media in Africa*. Konrad Adenauer Stiftung, 2021, 71–112. https://www.kas.de/en/web/medien-afrika/einzeltitel/detail/-/content/it-is-about-their-story.

Borenstein, Eliot. *Plots against Russia: Conspiracy and Fantasy after Socialism*. Ithaca, NY: Cornell University Press, 2019.

Bosphorus Global. "Activities." *Bosphorus Global*, 2023. https://bosphorusglobal.org/en/activities.

Bosphorus Global. "Mission." *Bosphorus Global*, 2023. https://bosphorusglobal.org/en/mission.

Bosphorus Global. "News." *Bosphorus Global*, 2023. https://bosphorusglobal.org/en/news.

Bosphorus Global. "Perspective." *Bosphorus Global*, 2023. https://www.bosphorusglobal.org/en/perspective.

Boyd-Barrett, Oliver. *Media Imperialism*. London: Sage, 2015.

Boyd-Barrett, Oliver. *RussiaGate and Propaganda: Disinformation in the Age of Social Media*. London: Routledge, 2019.

Boyd-Barrett, Oliver, and Shuang Xie. "Al-Jazeera, Phoenix Satellite Television and the Return of the State: Case Studies in Market Liberalization, Public Sphere, and Media Imperialism." *International Journal of Communication* 2 (2008): 206–22.

Boyd-Barrett, Oliver, and Tanner Mirrlees. *Media Imperialism: Continuity and Change.* Lanham, MD: Rowman and Littlefield, 2019.

Bradshaw, Samantha, Renée DiResta, and Carly Miller. "Playing Both Sides: Russian State-Backed Media Coverage of the #BlackLivesMatter Movement." *International Journal of Press/Politics*, February 28, 2022. https://doi.org/10.1177/19401612221082052.

Brady, Anne-Marie. "Authoritarianism Goes Global: China's Foreign Propaganda Machine." *Journal of Democracy* 26, no. 4 (2015): 51–59.

Briant, Emma Louise. *Propaganda and Counter-Terrorism: Strategies for Global Change.* Manchester, UK: Manchester University Press, 2016.

Broderick, Ryan. "Turkish Trolls Working for Erdogan Hijacked American Right-Wing Media—and Rudy Giuliani's Brain." *BuzzFeedNews*, October 18, 2019. https://www.buzzfeednews.com/article/ryanhatesthis/giuliani-turkey-gulen-erdogan-conspiracy-theory.

Brubaker, Rogers. "Between Nationalism and Civilizationism: The European Populist Moment in Comparative Perspective." *Ethnic and Racial Studies* 40, no. 8 (2017): 1191–226.

Budnitsky, Stanislav. "Kremlin Tightens Control over Russians' Online Lives, Threatening Domestic Freedoms and the Global Internet." *Conversation*, June 30, 2022. https://theconversation.com/.

Budnitsky, Stanislav. "A Relational Approach to Digital Sovereignty: e-Estonia between Russia and the West." *International Journal of Communication* 16 (2022): 1918–39.

Bulos, Nabih. "Game of Shows: In the Middle East, TV Programs Launched as Weapons of War." *Los Angeles Times*, December 9, 2019. https://www.latimes.com/world-nation/story/2019-12-09/middle-east-television-shows-turkey-saudi-arabia.

Bulut, Ergin. "Dramın Ardındaki Emek: Dizi Sektöründe Reyting Sistemi, Calişma Koşullarıve Sendikalaşma Faaliyetleri" [Labor behind the drama: ratings system, working conditions, and unionization in television series sector]. *İletisim Dergisi* (2016): 79–100. http://iletisimdergisi.gsu.edu.tr/tr/download/article-file/225468.

Bulut, Ergin, and Erdem Yörük. "Digital Populism: Trolls and Political Polarization of Twitter in Turkey." *International Journal of Communication* 11 (2017): 4093–117.

Bulut, Ergin, and Nurçin İleri. "Screening Right-Wing Populism in 'New Turkey': Neo-Ottomanism, Historical Dramas, and the Case of Payitaht Abdulhamid." In *The Routledge Companion to Global Television*, edited by Shawn Shimpach, 244–55. New York: Routledge, 2020.

Bunce, Mel. "Management and Resistance in the Digital Newsroom." *Journalism* 20, no. 7 (2019): 890–905.

Burns, Nicholas. "The Rise of Turkey as a Superpower." *Boston Globe*, April 27, 2012. https://www.belfercenter.org/publication/rise-turkey-superpower.

Butler, Daren. "With More Islamic Schooling, Erdogan Aims to Reshape Turkey." *Reuters*, January 25, 2018. https://www.reuters.com/investigates/special-report/turkey-erdogan-education/.

Çağlar, Ismail, Kevser Hulya Akdemir, and Seca Toker. *Uluslararasi Medyanin Turkiye Uzantilari* [The extensions of international media outlets in Turkey]. SETA, 2019. https://setav.org/assets/uploads/2019/07/R143Tr.pdf.

Çağlar, Ismail, Mehmet Akif Memmi, and Fahrettin Altun, eds. *15 Temmuz'da Medya: Darbe ve Direnisin Mecrasi*. [Media on July 15: Media of coup and resistance] Istanbul: SETA Kitaplari, 2017. https://setav.org/assets/uploads/2017/07/15TemmuzdaMedyaOzet.pdf.

Canefe, Nergis, and Tanıl Bora. "The Intellectual Roots of Anti-European Sentiments in Turkish Politics: The Case of Radical Turkish Nationalism." *Turkish Studies* 4, no. 1 (2003): 127–48.

Canikligil, Razi. "'Dünya 5'ten Büyüktür' Kampanya Oldu" [The World Is Bigger Than Five is now a campaign]. *Hurriyet* (Istanbul), September 26, 2014. https://www.hurriyet.com.tr/dunya/dunya-5-ten-buyuktur-kampanya-oldu-27276792.

Çapan, Zeynep Gülşah, and Ayşe Zarakol. "Turkey's Ambivalent Self: Ontological Insecurity in 'Kemalism' versus 'Erdoğanism.'" *Cambridge Review of International Affairs* 32, no. 3 (2019): 263–82.

Carlsson, Ulla. "The Rise and Fall of NWICO: From a Vision of International Regulation to a Reality of Multilevel Governance." *The NORDICOM Review of Nordic Research on Media and Communication* 24, no. 2 (2003): 31–67. https://doi.org/10.1515/nor-2017–0306.

Carney, Josh. "Re-Creating History and Recreating Publics: The Success and Failure of Recent Ottoman Costume Dramas in Turkish Media." *European Journal of Turkish Studies* 19, no. 19 (2014). https://doi.org/10.4000/ejts.5050.

Carney, Josh. "Resur(e)recting a Spectacular Hero: Diriliş Ertuğrul, Necropolitics, and Popular Culture in Turkey." *Review of Middle East Studies* 52, no. 1 (2018): 93–114. DOI: https://doi.org/10.1017/rms.2018.6.

Carney, Josh. "ResurReaction: Competing Visions of Turkey's (Proto) Ottoman Past in Magnificent Century and Resurrection Ertuğrul." *Middle East Critique* 28, no. 2 (2019): 101–20.

Castle, Stephen. "Recep Tayyip Erdogan: 'Taking Part in the EU Will Bring Harmony of Civilisations—It Is the Project of the Century.'" *Independent* (London), December 13, 2004. https://www.independent.co.uk/news/people/profiles/recep-tayyip-erdogan-taking-part-in-the-eu-will-bring-harmony-of-civilisations-it-is-the-project-of-the-century-24489.html.

Cav, Filiz G. (@Filiz_Gunduz) "'Wall Street Journal'in temsilcisi katliam gorseli RT'liyor. Turkiye'den derhal sinirdisi edilmeli!!" [Wall Street Journal's Turkey representative RT's images of a massacre. He must be expelled from Turkey immediately!!]. *X*, December 22, 2016. https://twitter.com/Filiz_Gunduz/status/812043102588456960.

Çavuşoğlu, Mevlüt (@MevlutCavusoglu). "As President @RT_Erdogan underlined at his speech at @ChathamHouse, #Turkey will continue to stand against all global injustices. #WorldIsBiggerThanFive." *X*, May 14, 2018. https://twitter.com/MevlutCavusoglu/status/995978118451122176.

Çavuşoğlu, Mevlüt. "Why Turkey Took the Fight to Syria." *New York Times*, October 11, 2019. https://www.nytimes.com/.

"Cavusoglu Says Statements on Russia Meddling in Turkish Election False, Unfair." *TASS Russian News Agency*, May 13, 2023. https://tass.com/world/1616953.

Çelik, Nihat, and Emre İşeri. "Islamically Oriented Humanitarian NGOs in Turkey: AKP Foreign Policy Parallelism." *Turkish Studies* 17, no. 3 (2016): 429–48.

Çelik, Zeynep. *Europe Knows Nothing about the Orient: A Critical Discourse from the East, 1872–1932*. Istanbul: Koç University Press, 2021.

Center for Islam and Global Affairs (CIGA). "Islamophobia." *Istanbul Zaim University*, 2023. https://www.izu.edu.tr/en/ciga/conferences/islamophobia.

Çetinkaya, Doğan. "Atrocity Propaganda and the Nationalization of the Masses in the Ottoman Empire during the Balkan Wars (1912–13)." *International Journal of Middle East Studies* 46, no. 4 (2014): 759–78.

Çetinkaya, Orçun, and Atakan Güngördü. "When National Laws and International Standards Are at Odds: Human Rights Responsibilities of Social Media Platforms under Turkey's New Internet Law." *International Comparative Legal Studies*, September 9, 2021. https://iclg.com/briefing/17140-when-national-laws-and-international-standards-are-at-odds-human-rights-responsibilities-of-social-media-platforms-under-turkey-s-new-internet-law.

Çevik, İlnur. "Plight of Refugees: Europeans Failing the Humanity Test." *Daily Sabah* (Istanbul), September 4, 2015. https://www.dailysabah.com/columns/ilnur-cevik/2015/09/04/plight-of-refugees-europeans-failing-the-humanity-test.

Çevik, Senem B. "Discursive Construction of Syrian Refugees in Shaping International Public Opinion: Turkey's Public Diplomacy Efforts." In *Routledge Handbook of Public Diplomacy*, edited by Nancy Snow and Nicholas Cull, 350–59. London: Routledge, 2020.

Çevik, Senem B. "Narrating Turkey's Story: Communicating Its Nation Brand through Public Diplomacy." In *Middle Powers in Global Governance: The Rise of Turkey*, edited by Emel Parlar Da0l, 213–30. Cham, Switzerland: Palgrave Macmillan, 2018.

Çevik, Senem B. "Turkish Historical Television Series: Public Broadcasting of Neo-Ottoman Illusions." *Southeast European and Black Sea Studies* 19, no. 2 (2019): 227–42.

Chakrabarty, Dipesh. *Provincializing Europe: Postcolonial Thought and Historical Difference*. Princeton, NJ: Princeton University Press, 2000.

Chakravartty, Paula, and Srirupa Roy. "Mediatized Populisms: Inter-Asian Lineages: Introduction." *International Journal of Communication* 11 (2017): 4073–92.

Chatterjee, Shibashis, and Udayan Das. "India's Civilizational Arguments in South Asia: From Nehruvianism to *Hindutva*." *International Affairs* 99, no. 2 (2023): 475–94.

Cherkaoui, Tarek. "Representation of Politics or Politics of Representation? Patterns of Western Mainstream Media Coverage during Turkey's 2018 Elections." *TRT World Research Centre*, 2018. https://researchcentre.trtworld.com/reports/representation-of-politics-or-politics-of-representationpatterns-of-western-mainstream-media-coverage-during-turkeys-2018-elections/.

Cherribi, Sam. *Fridays of Rage: Al Jazeera, the Arab Spring, and Political Islam*. Oxford: Oxford University Press, 2017.

"China's ICBC to Loan $3.6 billion for Turkey's Energy and Transport, Albayrak Says." *Daily Sabah* (Istanbul), July 26, 2018. https://www.dailysabah.com

/economy/2018/07/26/chinas-icbc-to-loan-36-billion-for-turkeys-energy-and-transport-albayrak-says.

Chouliaraki, Lilie. *The Spectatorship of Suffering*. London: Sage, 2006.

Chouliaraki, Lilie. "The Symbolic Power of Transnational Media: Managing the Visibility of Suffering." *Global Media and Communication* 4, no. 3 (2008): 329–51.

"CHP'den TRT'ye 1422 Yeni Personel Yorumu" [CHP comments on TRT's 1422 new personnel]. *Bianet* (Istanbul). September 17, 2019. https://m.bianet.org/bianet/medya/213134-chp-den-trt-ye-1422-yeni-personel-yorumu-kadrolasma.

"Chrest Foundation Medyascope'a Neden Para Yardımı Yapar? Iste Cevabı" [Why does Chrest Foundation donate money to Medyascope? Here is the answer]. *Yeni Akit* (Istanbul), July 23, 2021. https://www.yeniakit.com.tr/haber/chrest-foundation-medyascopea-neden-para-yardimi-yapar-iste-cevabi-1560055.html.

Chronicles of Shame. "Homepage." 2023. https://chroniclesofshame.com/.

Çınar, Menderes. "Turkey's 'Western' or 'Muslim' Identity and the AKP's Civilizational Discourse." *Turkish Studies* 19, no. 2 (2018): 176–97.

Clifford, Scott. "How Emotional Frames Moralize and Polarize Political Attitudes." *Political Psychology* 40, no. 1 (2019): 75–91.

Çolak, Ecenur, and Meltem Bulur. "Turkiye FETO'nun Gercek Yuzunu Dunyaya Anlatti" [Turkey told the world about the real FETO]. *Anadolu Ajansı*, July 14, 2017. http://aa.com.tr/tr/15-temmuz-darbe-girisimi/turkiye-fetonun-gercek-yuzunu-dunyaya-anlatti/861241.

Committee to Protect Journalists. "40 Journalists Imprisoned in Turkey." December 1, 2022. https://cpj.org/data/imprisoned/2022/?status=Imprisoned&cc_fips%5B%5D=TU&start_year=2022&end_year=2022&group_by=location.

Cornell, Svante E. "Erbakan, Kisakurek, and the Mainstreaming of Extremism in Turkey." *Current Trends in Islamist Ideology* 23 (2018): 5–33.

Coronil, Fernando. "Beyond Occidentalism: Toward Nonimperial Geohistorical Categories." *Cultural Anthropology* 11, no. 1 (1996): 51–87.

Çoruk, Ali Sukru. "Oryantalizm Uzerine Notlar" [Notes on Orientalism]. *Sosyal Bilimler Dergisi* 9, no. 2 (2007): 193–203.

Coşar, Simten, and Aylin Ozman. "Centre-Right Politics in Turkey after the November 2002 General Election: Neo-liberalism with a Muslim Face." *Contemporary Politics* 10, no. 1 (2004): 57–74.

Coşkun, Ipek, Celile Eren Ökten, Nergis Dama, Mümine Barkçin, Shady Zahed, Marwa Fouda, Dilruba Toklucu, and Hande Özsarp. *Breaking Down Barriers: Getting Syrian Children into School in Turkey*. SETA, 2017. https://setav.org/en/assets/uploads/2017/09/R90_BreakingBarriers.pdf.

Coşkuntuncel, Aras. "Privatization of Governance, Delegated Censorship, and Hegemony in the Digital Era: The Case of Turkey." *Journalism Studies* 19, no. 5 (2018): 690–708.

Costello, Katherine. *Russia's Use of Media and Information Operations in Turkey: Implications for the United States*. Washington, DC: RAND, 2018. https://www.rand.org/pubs/perspectives/PE278.html.

Cotter, Colleen. *News Talk: Investigating the Language of Journalism*. Cambridge: Cambridge University Press, 2010.

Cottle, Simon. "Taking Global Crises in the News Seriously: Notes from the Dark Side of Globalization." *Global Media and Communication* 7, no. 2 (2011): 77–95.
Couldry, Nick, and Ulises A. Mejias. *The Costs of Connection: How Data Is Colonizing Human Life and Appropriating It for Capitalism.* Stanford, CA: Stanford University Press, 2019.
Couperus, Stefan, Pier Domenico Tortola, and Lars Rensmann. "Memory Politics of the Far Right in Europe." *European Politics and Society* 24, no. 4 (2022): 435–44. DOI: 10.1080/23745118.2022.2058757.
Crackdown Chronicles, "About Us." https://crackdownchronicles.com.
Crackdown Chronicles. (@CrackdownReport). "Illegal Surveillance from the USA, Land of Freedom." *X*, March 7, 2022. https://twitter.com/CrackdownReport/status/1500754820541698049?s=20.
Crackdown Chronicles. (@CrackdownReport). "In Switzerland, one of the 'most livable' countries in the world. Only known examples of racism that has become systematic: Racist tagging against blacks. Violent police checks. Being treated as criminal." *X*, January 27, 2022. https://x.com/CrackdownReport/status/1486675022253019144?s=20.
Creemers, Rogier. "Cyber China: Upgrading Propaganda, Public Opinion Work, and Social Management for the Twenty-First Century." *Journal of Contemporary China* 26, no. 103 (2017): 85–100.
Cull, Nicholas J. *The Cold War and the United States Information Agency: American Propaganda and Public Diplomacy, 1945–1989.* Cambridge: Cambridge University Press, 2009.
Cull, Nicholas J. *Public Diplomacy: Foundations for Global Engagement in the Digital Age.* Cambridge: Polity, 2019.
Cull, Nicholas J. *Selling War: The British Propaganda Campaign against American "Neutrality" in World War II.* Oxford: Oxford University Press, 1996.
"Cumhurbaşkanı Erdoğan: Biz Nasıl Kimsenin Toprağına Göz Dikmiyorsak, Bize Ait Olanlardan da Taviz Vermeyeceğiz" [Just as we do not covet anyone's land, we will not compromise on what belongs to us either]. *Anadolu Agency*, August 26, 2020. https://www.aa.com.tr/tr/turkiye/cumhurbaskani-erdogan-biz-nasil-kimsenin-topragina-goz-dikmiyorsak-bize-ait-olanlardan-da-taviz-vermeyecegiz/1953549.
"Cumhurbaskani Erdoğan: 'Sosyal ve Kulturel Iktidarimiz Konusunda Sikinitilarimiz Var'" [We have problems regarding our social and cultural hegemony]. *Hurriyet* (Istanbul), May 28, 2017. https://www.hurriyet.com.tr/gundem/cumhurbaskani-erdogan-sosyal-ve-kulturel-iktidarimiz-konusunda-sikintilarimiz-var-40472482.
Dağli, Tarik. "Bati Medyasinin Kronik Hastaligi: Turkiye Karsitligi" [Western media's chronic disease: Opposition to Turkey]. *Kriter*, May 2, 2017. https://kriterdergi.com/dosya/bati-medyasinin-kronik-hastaligi-turkiye-karsitligi.
"Daily Sabah Chief Karagoz Tapped to Lead TRT World, Arabic." *Daily Sabah* (Istanbul), October 15, 2018. https://www.dailysabah.com/turkey/2018/10/15/daily-sabah-chief-karagoz-tapped-to-lead-trt-world-arabic.
Dalacoura, Katerina. "'Islamic Civilization' as an Aspect of Secularization in Turkish Islamic Thought." *Historical Social Research* 44, no. 3 (2019): 127–49.
Dalay, Galip. "Turkey, Europe, and the Eastern Mediterranean: Charting a Way out of the Current Deadlock." *Brookings Institute*, January 28, 2021. https://www

.brookings.edu/articles/turkey-europe-and-the-eastern-mediterranean-charting-a-way-out-of-the-current-deadlock/.

Daloğlu, Tülin. "Atalay Claims Jewish Diaspora Was behind Gezi Park Protest." *Al-Monitor* (Washington, DC), July 3, 2013. https://www.al-monitor.com/pulse/originals/2013/07/turkey-protests-gezi-jewish-diaspora-conspiracy.html.

"Darbenin Arkasinda CIA Var" [CIA is behind the coup]. *Sabah* (Istanbul), November 29, 2016. https://www.sabah.com.tr/gundem/2016/11/29/darbenin-arkasinda-cia-var?paging=7.

Davies, Christian, Jamie Grierson, and Patrick Wintour. "Trump Says West Is at Risk, during Nationalistic Speech in Poland." *Guardian* (London), July 6, 2017. https://www.theguardian.com/us-news/2017/jul/06/donald-trump-warn-future-west-in-doubt-warsaw-speech.

Davutoğlu, Ahmet. *Civilizational Transformation and the Muslim World*. Kuala Lumpur: Mahir, 1994.

Davutoğlu, Ahmet. *Stratejik Derinlik* [Strategic depth]. Istanbul: Kure Yayinlari, 2014.

Davutoğlu, Ahmet. "Turkey's Humanitarian Diplomacy: Objectives, Challenges And Prospects." *Nationalities Papers: The Journal of Nationalism and Ethnicity* 41, no. 6 (2013): 865–70.

DeHanas, Daniel Nilsson, and Marat Shterin. "Religion and the Rise of Populism." *Religion, State, and Society* 46, no. 3 (2018): 177–85.

Deibert, Ronald J., and Louis W. Pauly. "Mutual Entanglement and Complex Sovereignty in Cyberspace." In *Data Politics: Worlds, Subjects, Rights*, edited by Didier Bigo, Engin Isin, and Evelyn Ruppert, 81–99. London: Routledge, 2019.

Del Sordi, Adele, and Emanuela Delmasso. "The Relation between External and Internal Authoritarian Legitimation: The Religious Foreign Policy of Morocco and Kazakhstan." *Taiwan Journal of Democracy* 14, no. 1 (2018): 95–116.

Demirtaş-Bagdonas, Özlem. "Reading Turkey's Foreign Policy on Syria: The AKP's Construction of a Great Power Identity and the Politics of Grandeur." *Turkish Studies* 15, no. 1 (2014): 139–55.

Deringil, Selim. *The Well-Protected Domains: Ideology and the Legitimation of Power in the Ottoman Empire 1876–1909*. New York: Tauris, 2011.

Destradi, Sandra, and Johannes Plagemann. "Populism and International Relations: (Un)predictability, Personalisation, and the Reinforcement of Existing Trends in World Politics." *Review of International Studies* 45, no. 5 (2019): 711–30.

Detmer, Jamie. "Turkey Angry over Morsi Ouster." *Voice of America,* July 31, 2013. https://www.voanews.com/a/turkey-angry-over-morsi-ouster/1713848.html.

Deutsch, Jillian. "RT, Sputnik Content Officially Banned across European Union." *Bloomberg*, March 2, 2022. https://www.bloomberg.com/news/articles/2022-03-02/rt-sputnik-content-officially-banned-across-european-union?leadSource=uverify%20wall.

Development Initiatives. *Global Humanitarian Assistance Report 2021. Development Initiatives*, 2021. https://devinit-prod-static.ams3.cdn.digitaloceanspaces.com/media/documents/Global-Humanitarian-Assistance-Report-2021.pdf.

"Dış Basın Cephe Savaşı Veriyor" [Foreign press fighting a battle]. *Yeni Safak* (Istanbul), June 13, 2013. https://www.yenisafak.com/gundem/dis-basin-cephe-savasi-veriyor-531366.

Dinç, Ozden. "TRT World ve TRT'nin Itibarı" [TRT World and TRT's reputation]. *Gercek*, October 5, 2021. https://www.gercek.co.uk/kategori/politika/72102/trt-world-ve-trt-nin-itibari.

"Diriliş Ertuğrul Oyuncuları Fetih Kutlamalarında Şiir Okudu" [Resurrection Ertuğrul actors recite poetry in conquest celebrations]. *Yeni Safak* (Istanbul), May 30, 2016. https://www.yenisafak.com/video-galeri/haber/dirilis-ertugrul-oyunculari-fetih-kutlamalarinda-siir-okudu-2095600.

"Diriliş'in Oyuncuları Erdoğan'ın Uçağında" [Resurrection actors on Erdoğan's plane]. *Yeni Cag*, May 10, 2017. https://www.yenicaggazetesi.com.tr/-163228h.htm.

Dirlik, Arif. "Global South: Predicament and Promise." *Global South* 1, no. 1 (2007): 12–23. http://www.jstor.org/stable/40339225.

DiResta, Renee, Carly Miller, Vanessa Molter, John Pomfret, and Glenn Tiffert. "Telling China's Story: The Chinese Communist Party's Campaign to Shape Global Narratives." *Stanford Internet Observatory*, 2020. https://stacks.stanford.edu/file/druid:pf306sw8941/sio-china_story_white_paper-final.pdf.

Doğantekin, Vakkas. "Twitter Censors Turkey's TRT World amid Syria Operation." *Anadolu Agency*, October 15, 2019. https://www.aa.com.tr/en/operation-peace-spring/twitter-censors-turkeys-trt-world-amid-syria-operation/1614760.

Dombey, Daniel. "Erdogan Attacks West's Reaction to Morsi's Overthrow." *Financial Times*, July 5, 2013. https://www.ft.com/.

Donelli, Federico. *Turkey in Africa: Turkey's Strategic Involvement in Sub-Saharan Africa*. London: Bloomsbury, 2021.

Donsbach, Wolfgang. "Psychology of News Decisions: Factors behind Journalists' Professional Behavior." *Journalism* 5, no. 2 (2004): 131–57.

Drefs, Ines, and Barbara Thomass. "Research Findings about Organisations Engaging in Media Assistance in the Fields of Journalism Training, Civil Society Support, and Good Governance." *MeCoDem (Media, Conflict and Democratization)*, 2015. http://www.mecodem.eu/publications/working-papers.

"DS Editorial Coordinator Atlas Ties the Knot in Istanbul's Emirgan Park." *Daily Sabah* (Istanbul), September 30, 2018. https://www.dailysabah.com/life/2018/09/30/ds-editorial-coordinator-atlas-ties-the-knot-in-istanbuls-emirgan-park.

"'Dünya Beş'ten Büyüktür' Kampanyası Başlatıldı" [The World Is Bigger Than Five campaign kicks off]. *Anadolu Ajansı*, September 25, 2014. https://www.aa.com.tr/tr/dunya/dunya-bes-ten-buyuktur-kampanyasi-baslatildi/116888.

Duran, Burhanettin. "Transformation of Islamist Political Thought in Turkey from the Empire to the Early Republic (1908–1960): Necip Fazil Kisakürek's Political Ideas." PhD dissertation, Bilkent University, 2001.

Duran, Burhanettin, and Cemil Aydin. "Competing Occidentalisms of Modern Islamist Thought: Necip Fazil Kisakürek and Nurettin Topçu on Christianity, the West, and Modernity." *Muslim World* 103, no. 4 (2013): 479–500.

Durmuş, Yusuf Ziya. "Int'l Media Fails to Objectively Approach Turkey Coverage: Report." *Daily Sabah* (Istanbul), July 8, 2019. https://www.dailysabah.com/turkey/2019/07/08/intl-media-fails-to-objectively-approach-turkey-coverage-report.

Efe, Ibrahim. "A Corpus-Driven Analysis of Representations of Syrian Asylum Seekers in the Turkish Press 2011–2016." *Discourse and Communication* 13, no. 1 (2019): 48–67.

"Egypt Fatwa Bans Ertugrul, Turkish Soaps." *Middle East Monitor*, February 12, 2020. https://www.middleeastmonitor.com/20200212-egypt-fatwa-bans-ertugrul-turkish-soaps/.

El-Behary, Hend. "Turkey's Soft Power Threatened after MBC Bans Turkish Dramas." *Egypt Independent*, March 7, 2018. https://egyptindependent.com/turkeys-soft-power-threatened-after-mbc-bans-turkish-dramas/.

Ellis, Izzy Tomico. "Don't Call It the 'Refugee Crisis,' It's a Humanitarian Issue." *Independent* (London), November 13, 2019. https://www.independent.co.uk/voices/refugee-migrant-crisis-humanitarian-greece-syria-turkey-eu-a9201006.html.

Ellul, Jacques. *Propaganda: The Formation of Men's Attitudes*. Translated by Konrad Kellen and Jean Lerner. New York: Knopf, 1968.

El Nawawy, Mohammed, and Adel Iskandar. *Al Jazeera: The Story of the Network That Is Rattling Governments and Redefining Modern Journalism*. New York: Basic Books, 2008.

Elswah, Mona, and Philip N. Howard. "'Anything That Causes Chaos': The Organizational Behavior of Russia Today (RT)." *Journal of Communication* 70, no. 5 (2020): 623–45.

Elswah, Mona, and Philip N. Howard. "Where News Could Not Inspire Change: TRT World as a Party Broadcaster." *Journalism* 23, no. 10 (2022): 2079–95.

Entman, Robert. *Projections of Power: Framing News, Public Opinion, and U.S. Foreign Policy*. Chicago: University of Chicago Press, 2004.

Entman, Robert. "Theorizing Mediated Public Diplomacy: The US Case." *International Journal of Press/Politics* 13, no. 2 (2008): 87–102.

"Erdogan Accuses West of Writing the Script for Turkey Coup." *Telegraph* (London), August 2, 2016. https://www.telegraph.co.uk/.

"Erdoğan: "Bunlar Postmodern Haçlı Seferinin Yeni İşbirlikçileri" [They are the new collaborators of the postmodern crusades]. *Birgün* (Istanbul), January 24, 2018. https://www.birgun.net/haber/erdogan-bunlar-postmodern-hacli-seferinin-yeni-isbirlikcileri-201394.

"Erdoğan, 1 milyon Suriyelinin Gönüllü Geri Dönüşü İçin Hazırlık Yaptıklarını Söyledi" [Erdoğan says preparations are underway for the voluntary expatriation of 1 million Syrians]. *BBC News Türkçe*, May 3, 2022. https://www.bbc.com/turkce/haberler-turkiye-61307585.

Erdoğan, Recep Tayyip. *Daha Adil Bir Dunya Mumkun: Birlesmis Milletler Reformu icin Bir Model Onerisi* [A fairer world is possible: A proposed model for a United Nations reform]. Istanbul: Turkuvaz Kitap, 2021.

Erdoğan, Recep Tayyip. *A Fairer World Is Possible: A Proposed Model for a United Nations Reform*. Istanbul: Turkuvaz Kitap, 2021.

"Erdoğan, 24 Yıl Sonra Aynı Yerde, Cezaevine Girmesine Neden Olan Siiri Okudu" [24 years later, Erdoğan recited the poem that landed him in prison]. *T24* (Istanbul), December 4, 2021. https://t24.com.tr/video/erdogan-24-yil-sonra-ayni-yerde-cezaevine-girmesine-neden-olan-siiri-okudu-ben-o-siiri-nerde-okumustum-burada,43806.

"Erdoğan'dan Batı'ya: Siz Işinize Bakın, Biz Işimizi Biliyoruz" [From Erdoğan to the West: You mind your own business, we know what we are doing]. *Sputnik Turkiye* (Istanbul), August 18, 2016. https://sputniknews.com.tr/20160818/erdogan-kulliye-1024447532.html.

"Eren TRT World'ün Hedeflerini Anlattı" [Eren explained TRT World's goals]. *En Son Haber* (Istanbul), March 17, 2017. https://www.ensonhaber.com/medya/eren-trt-worldun-hedeflerini-anlatti-2017-03-17.

Ergöçün, Gokhan. "Turkey Accounts for 26% for 2019 World Humanitarian Aid." *Anadolu Agency*, July 23, 2020. https://www.aa.com.tr/en/economy/turkey-accounts-for-26-of-2019-world-humanitarian-aid/1919544.

Erşen, Emre. "Rise of New Centres of Power in Eurasia: Implications for Turkish Foreign Policy." *Journal of Eurasian Studies* 5 (2014): 184–91.

Ertan, Nazlan. "Turkish Government Criticized for Creating New Alevi Cultural Agency." *Al Monitor* (Washington, DC), November 9, 2022. https://www.almonitor.com/originals/2022/11/turkish-government-criticized-creating-new-alevi-cultural-agency#ixzz8DNw74yPY.

Ertekin, Aydin Bülend. "Uluslararasi Sistemde Gorsel-Isitsel Medyanin Kamu Diplomasisi ve Kamuoyu Yaratmadaki Onemi: TRT'nin Turkce Disinda Yayin Yapan Kanallari Uzerine Bir Inceleme" [The importance of audio-visual media in public diplomacy in the international system: an analysis of TRT's non-Turkish channels]. *Elektronik Sosyal Bilimler Dergisi* 11, no. 42 (2012): 323–54.

Ertem, Cemil. "Fascism Is Consuming Europe!" *Daily Sabah* (Istanbul), March 22, 2017. https://www.dailysabah.com/columns/cemil-ertem/2017/03/22/fascism-is-consuming-europe.

European Commission. "The EU Facility for Refugees in Turkey." September 2022. https://neighbourhood-enlargement.ec.europa.eu/system/files/2023-08/frit_factsheet.pdf.

European Commission. "EU Member States Granted Protection to More Than 330 000 Asylum Seekers in 2015." April 20, 2016. https://ec.europa.eu/eurostat/web/products-euro-indicators/-/3-20042016-ap.

"European Parliament President Bans Distribution of Daily Sabah at Parliament." *Hurriyet Daily News* (Istanbul), March 23, 2017. https://www.hurriyetdailynews.com/european-parliament-president-bans-distribution-of-daily-sabah-at-parliament-111171.

"Facebook Says Starts Process of Appointing Turkey Representative." *Reuters*, January 18, 2021. https://www.reuters.com/article/us-turkey-facebook/facebook-says-starts-process-of-appointing-turkey-representative-idUSKBN29N18X.

"Fascism Consuming Europe." *Daily Sabah* (Istanbul), March 12, 2017. https://www.dailysabah.com/editorial/2017/03/12/fascism-consuming-europe.

Feinstein, Yuval, and Bart Bonikowski. "Nationalist Narratives and Anti-immigrant Attitudes: Exceptionalism and Collective Victimhood in Contemporary Israel." *Journal of Ethnic and Migration Studies* 47, no. 3 (2021): 741–61.

"15 Temmuz'dan Cerablus'a" [From July 15 to Jarabulus]. *Derin Tarih*, September, 2016. https://www.derintarih.com/editorden/15-temmuzdan-cerablusa/.

Figenschou, Tine Ustad. "A Voice for the Voiceless? A Quantitative Content Analysis of Al-Jazeera English's Flagship News." *Global Media and Communication* 6, no. 1 (2010): 85–107.

Fisher, Aleksandr. "Demonizing the Enemy: The Influence of Russian State-Sponsored Media on American Audiences." *Post-Soviet Affairs* 36, no. 4 (2020): 281–96.

Fisher-Onar, Nora. "The Capitulations Syndrome: Why Revisionist Powers Leverage Post-Colonial Sensibilities toward Post-Imperial Projects." *Global Studies Quarterly* 2, no. 4 (2022). DOI: https://doi.org/10.1093/isagsq/ksac077.

Flynn, Michael. "Our Ally Turkey Is in Crisis and Needs Our Support." *Hill*, November 8, 2016. https://thehill.com/blogs/pundits-blog/foreign-policy/305021-our-ally-turkey-is-in-crisis-and-needs-our-support.

"4'üncü Yasinda 4'üncü Dil" [4th language on the 4th anniversary]. *Sabah* (Istanbul). February 2, 2018. https://www.sabah.com.tr/medya/2018/02/24/4uncu-yasinda-4uncu-dil-daily-sabah-rusca-yayina-basladi.

Fowler, Susanne. "The Dirt, and the Soap, on the Ottoman Empire." *New York Times*, March 17, 2011. https://www.nytimes.com/2011/03/17/world/middleeast/17iht-m17-soap.

Freedom House. "Freedom in the World: Turkey Country Report." *Freedom House*, 2022. https://freedomhouse.org/country/turkey/freedom-world/2022.

Gagliardone, Iginio, Maria Repnikova, and Nicole Stremlau. *China in Africa: A New Approach to Media Development?* Center for Global Communication Studies, University of Pennsylvania, 2010. https://repository.upenn.edu/cgcs_publications/18.

Galloway, Tristan, and He Baogang. "China and Technical Global Internet Governance: Beijing's Approach to Multi-Stakeholder Governance within ICANN, WSIS, and the IGF." *China: An International Journal* 12, no. 3 (2014): 72–93. https://ssrn.com/abstract=2532336.

Gambrell, Jon. "Turkish Soap Operas Latest Casualty of Mideast Conflicts." *CNBC*, March 6, 2018. https://www.cnbc.com/2018/03/05/the-associated-press-turkish-soap-operas-latestcasualty-of-mideast-conflicts.html.

Gao, Jia, Catherine Ingram, and Pookong Kee. *Global Media and Public Diplomacy in Sino-Western Relations*. London: Routledge, 2016.

Genç, Kaya. "Erdogan's Way: The Rise and Rule of Turkey's Islamist Shapeshifter." *Foreign Affairs* 98, no. 5 (2019): 26–35. https://www.foreignaffairs.com/articles/turkey/2019-08-12/erdogans-way.

Gilboa, Eytan. "Global Communication and Foreign Policy." *Journal of Communication* 52, no. 4 (2002): 731–48.

Göçek, Fatih. "Return of the War on Terror: A Comparative Discourse Analysis of TRT World and BBC World News Regarding the Syrian War." *Journal of Communication* 5, no. 2 (2020): 21–38.

Göçek, Fatma Müge. "Postcoloniality, the Ottoman Past, and the Middle East Present." *International Journal of Middle East Studies* 44, no: 3 (2012): 549–63.

Gökçe Gökhan. "How the Turkic World Is Enhancing Cooperation in Media and Communication." *Politics Today*, December 15, 2021. https://politicstoday.org/how-the-turkic-world-is-enhancing-cooperation-in-media-and-communication/.

Gostoli, Ylenia. "Turkish Presidential Run-off Leaves Syrians with Uncertain Future." *Al Jazeera*, May 27, 2023. https://www.aljazeera.com/news/2023/5/27/turkish-presidential-run-off-leaves-syrians-with-uncertain-future.

Gözaydın, İştar. "Diyanet and Politics." *Muslim World* 98, no. 2–3 (2008): 216–27.

Grater, Tom. "How Turkey Has Become a European TV Drama Powerhouse." *Screen Daily*, August 18, 2017. https://www.screendaily.com/news/how-turkey-has-become-a-european-tv-drama-powerhouse/5120941.article.

Greenberg, Nathaniel. "American Spring: How Russian State Media Translate American Protests for an Arab Audience." *International Journal of Communication* 15 (2021): 2547–68.

Grigoriadis, Ioannis N. "Friends No More? The Rise of Anti-American Nationalism in Turkey." *Middle East Journal* 64, no. 1 (2010): 51–66.

Grossman, Shelby, Fazil Alp Akis, Ayca Alemdaroglu, Josh A. Goldstein, and Katie Jonsson. *Political Retweet Rings and Compromised Accounts: A Twitter Influence Operation Linked to the Youth Wing of Turkey's Ruling Party*. Stanford Internet Observatory, Stanford University, 2020. https://cyber.fsi.stanford.edu/io/publication/june-2020-turkey-takedown.

Gül, Ayaz. "Pakistan, Turkey, Malaysia to Jointly Launch Anti-Islamophobia TV." *Voice of America*, September 26, 2019. https://www.voanews.com/a/south-central-asia_pakistan-turkey-malaysia-jointly-launch-anti-islamophobia-tv/6176511.html.

Gündoğan, Barış. "Cumhurbaşkanlığı İletişim Başkanlığından Ulke Dısından Medyanin Fonlanması Ile Ilgili Aciklama" [Statement from the Directorate of Communications regarding the funding of media from outside the country]. *Anadolu Ajansi*, July 21, 2021. https://www.aa.com.tr/tr/gundem/cumhurbaskanligi-iletisim-baskanligindan-ulke-disindan-medyanin-fonlanmasi-ile-ilgili-aciklama-/2311069#.

Guo, Shaohua. "'Occupying' the Internet: State Media and the Reinvention of Official Culture Online." *Communication and the Public* 3, no. 1 (2018): 19–33.

Guo, Xiaoli. "Turkey's International Humanitarian Assistance during the AKP Era: Key Actors, Concepts, and Motivations." *Asian Journal of Middle Eastern and Islamic Studies* 14, no. 1 (2020): 121–40.

Gürpinar, Bulut, and Ömür Aydın. "The Uniformization of Think Tanks in Turkey: The Foundation for Political, Economic, and Social Research (SETA) as a Case Study." *Sage Open* 12, no. 1 (2022). DOI: https://doi.org/10.1177/21582440221086660.

Gutkowski, Stacey. "We Are the Very Model of a Moderate Muslim State: The Amman Messages and Jordan's Foreign Policy." *International Relations* 30, no. 2 (2016): 206–26.

Hacaloğlu, Hilmi. "Basbakan Erdoğan 'dan Bati medyasina elestiri" [Prime Minister Erdoğan criticizes Western media]. *Amerika'nin Sesi*, June 16, 2013. https://www.amerikaninsesi.com/a/basbakan-erdogandan-bati-medya-eletiri/1682948.html.

"Hard Act to Follow, A." *Economist*, August 6, 2011. https://www.economist.com/briefing/2011/08/06/a-hard-act-to-follow.

Harding, Luke, and Constanze Letsch. "Turkish Police Arrest 25 People for Using Social Media to Call for Protests." *Guardian* (London), June 5, 2013. https://www.theguardian.com/world/2013/jun/05/turkish-police-arrests-social-media-protest.

Haşimi, Cemalettin. "Turkey's Humanitarian Diplomacy and Development Cooperation." *Insight Turkey* 16, no. 1 (2014): 127–45.

Haug, Sebastian, and Supriya Roychoudhury. "Civilizational Exceptionalism in International Affairs: Making Sense of Indian and Turkish Claims." *International Affairs* 99, no. 2 (2023): 531–49.

Hendrick, Joshua D. *Gulen: The Ambiguous Politics of Market Islam in Turkey and the World*. New York: New York University Press, 2013.

Henley, John. "Recep Tayyip Erdoğan: 'We Know Dutch from Srebrenica Massacre.'" *Guardian* (London), March 14, 2017. https://www.theguardian.com/world/2017

/mar/14/turkish-sanctions-bizarre-as-netherlands-has-more-to-be-angry-about-dutch-pm.
Herf, Jeffrey. *Nazi Propaganda for the Arab World*. New Haven, CT: Yale University Press, 2017.
Hernández, Javier C. "As Protests Engulf the United States, China Revels in the Unrest." *New York Times*, June 2, 2020. https://www.nytimes.com/.
Hills, Jill. *Telecommunications and Empire*. Urbana: University of Illinois Press, 2007.
Hinck, Robert, Skye Cooley, and Randolph Kluver. *Global Media and Strategic Narratives of Contested Democracy: Chinese, Russian, and Arabic Media Narratives of the US Presidential Election*. New York: Routledge, 2020.
"How Government Attacks on the Press Exacerbated the Devastation of the Earthquakes in Turkey." *CIMA (Center for International Media Assistance)*, March 30, 2023. https://www.cima.ned.org/blog/how-government-attacks-on-the-press-exacerbated-the-devastation-of-the-earthquakes-in-turkey/.
Hubbard, Ben, Elif Ince, and Safak Timur. "After Erdogan's Attacks, Fear Spreads among L.G.B.T.Q. People in Turkey." *New York Times*, June 5, 2023. https://www.nytimes.com/.
Human Rights Watch. "Turkey: Dangerous, Dystopian New Legal Amendments." October 14, 2022. https://www.hrw.org/news/2022/10/14/turkey-dangerous-dystopian-new-legal-amendments.
Human Rights Watch. "Turkey: Protect Rights, Law after Coup Attempt." July 18, 2016. https://www.hrw.org/news/2016/07/18/turkey-protect-rights-law-after-coup-attempt.
Huntington, Samuel. "The Clash of Civilizations?" *Foreign Affairs*, June 1, 1993. https://www.foreignaffairs.com/articles/united-states/1993-06-01/clash-civilizations.
"IBRAF at a Glance." *OIC Broadcasting Regulatory Authorities Forum*, 2022. https://www.oic-ibraf.org/menu/2.
Iğsız, Aslı. "From Alliance of Civilizations to Branding the Nation: Turkish Studies, Image Wars and Politics of Comparison in an Age of Neoliberalism." *Turkish Studies* 15, no. 4 (2014): 689–704.
İnsel, Ahmet. "Becoming a World Economic Power." In *Turkey between Nationalism and Globalization*, edited by Riva Kastoryano, 187–98. New York: Routledge, 2013.
"Inside America with Ghida Fakhry." *Ghida Fakhry*, 2017. http://www.ghidafakhry.com/inside-america.
International Crisis Group. "Turkey's Syrian Refugees: Defusing Metropolitan Tensions." *International Crisis Group*, January 29, 2018. https://www.crisisgroup.org/europe-central-asia/western-europemediterranean/turkey/248-turkeys-syrian-refugees-defusing-metropolitan-tensions.
"International Journalists Quit World Service of Turkey's National Broadcaster." *IPA News*, February 8, 2019. https://ipa.news/2019/02/08/international-journalists-quit-world-service-of-turkeys-national-broadcaster/.
Isani, Aamna Haider. "The Rise of Dirilis: Ertugrul." *News*, May 2020. https://www.thenews.com.pk/magazine/instep-today/662976-the-rise-of-dirilis-ertugrul.
"Islamophobia 101." *Council on American-Islamic Relations (CAIR)*, 2023. https://islamophobia.org/islamophobia-101/.

"Islamophobia Research and Documentation Project." Center for Race and Gender, University of California, Berkeley, 2023. https://crg.berkeley.edu/research/research-initiatives/islamophobia-research-and-documentation-project.

Jamieson, Kathleen Hall. *Cyberwar: How Russian Hackers and Trolls Helped Elect a President: What We Don't, Can't, and Do Know*. Oxford: Oxford University Press, 2018.

Jankowicz, Nina. *How to Lose the Information War: Russia, Fake News, and the Future of Conflict*. London: Bloomsbury, 2020.

Jaskulowski, Krzysztof, and Piotr Majewski. "Populist in Form, Nationalist in Content? Law and Justice, Nationalism, and Memory Politics." *European Politics and Society*, 24, no. 4 (2023): 461–76.

Jenks, John. *British Propaganda and News Media in the Cold War*. Edinburgh: Edinburgh University Press, 2006.

Jenks, John. "Crash Course." *Media History* 26, no. 4 (2020): 508–21.

Jirik, John. "CCTV News and Soft Power." *International Journal of Communication* 10 (2016): 3536–53.

Jones, Timothy. "Journalist Deniz Yucel Sentenced to Almost 3 Years Prison in Turkey." *Deutsche Welle*, July 16, 2020. https://www.dw.com/en/deniz-yucel1-turkey-prison/a-54193689.

Jourde, Cedric. "The International Relations of Small Neo-authoritarian States: Islamism, Warlordism, and the Framing of Stability." *International Studies Quarterly* 51, no. 2 (2007): 481–503.

Jowett, Garth S., and Victoria J. O'Donnell. *Propaganda and Persuasion*. 7th ed. Thousand Oaks, CA: Sage, 2018.

Kakissis, Joanna. "'I Thought It Would Be Safe': Uighurs In Turkey Now Fear China's Long Arm." *NPR*, March 13, 2020. https://www.npr.org/2020/03/13/800118582/i-thought-it would-be-safe-uighurs-in-turkey-now-fear-china-s-long-arm.

Kalın, İbrahim. (@ikalin1). "It takes virtue, determination and leadership to stand up for justice. #WorldIsBiggerThanFive #OurVoiceErdogan." X, September 24, 2019. https://x.com/ikalin1/status/1176549027149701120?s=2.

Kalın, İbrahim. (@ikalin1). "Milyonları ölüme götüren, dünya savaşları çıkartan, kitlesel imha silahları yapan, atom bombası atan, köle ticareti yapan, insanları hayvanat bahçelerinde sergileyen modern barbarlar" [Modern barbarians who killed millions, started world wars, created weapons of mass destruction, dropped atomic bombs, traded slaves, and exhibited people in zoos]. *X*, April 24, 2022. https://twitter.com/ikalin1/status/1518221263508062211?s=20&t=fU9BYZbfRvCiOv2VWKJqGg.

Kalın, İbrahim. *Barbar, Modern, Medeni: Medeniyet Uzerine Notlar* [Barbaric, modern, civilized: notes on civilization]. Istanbul: Insan Yayinlari, 2018.

Kalın, İbrahim. "Kamu Diplomasisi Icin Mola!" [Taking a break for public diplomacy]. *Sabah* (Istanbul), March 27, 2010. https://www.sabah.com.tr/yazarlar/ibrahim__kalin/2010/03/27/kamu_diplomasisi_icin_mola.

Kanat, Kılıç Buğra. "Experts Mull Shifting Int'l Order at Turkiye-Africa Media Summit." *SETA*, May 26, 2022. https://www.setav.org/en/experts-mull-shifting-intl-order-at-turkiye-africa-media-summit/.

Kandiyoti, Deniz. "Post-Colonialism Compared: Potentials and Limitations in the Middle East And Central Asia." *International Journal of Middle East Studies* 34, no. 2 (2002): 279–97.

Kaptan, Yeşim, and Gökçen Karanfil. "RTUK, Broadcasting, and the Middle East: Regulating the Transnational." *International Journal of Communication* 7 (2013): 2232–40.

Karagöz, Serdar. (@serdarkaragoz). "We all have to stand against Islamophobia with no excuses, and there has to be absolute zero tolerance for it. As @anadoluagency we will be monitoring all kinds of discrimination via AA Discrimination Line. Hate crimes against Muslims in Germany are a rising problem." X, January 24, 2022. https://x.com/serdarkaragoz/status/1485708321957031942?s=20.

Karakaş, Burcu. "Is Anti-Refugee Sentiment Growing in Turkey?" *Deutsche Welle*, August 18, 2021. https://www.dw.com/en/refugees-in-istanbul-is-anti-migrant-sentiment-growing-in turkey/a-58890282.

Karakaya, Kerim, and Asli Kandemir. "Turkey Got a $1 Billion Foreign Cash Boost from China in June." *Bloomberg*, August 9, 2019. https://www.bloomberg.com/news/articles/2019-08-09/turkey-got-1-billion-from-china-swap-in-june-boost-to-reserves.

Karakum, Arife. "Uluslararasi Basinda TRT World'ün Rolü Ne?" [What is the role of TRT World in international media?]. *Medium*, January 5, 2020. https://medium.com/@arifekarakum/uluslararasi-basinda-trt-world%C3%BCn-rol%C3%BC-ne-972b3ff0c01.

Karanfil, Gökçen. "Continuities and Changes in the Transnational Broadcasts of TRT." In *Television in Turkey: Local Production, Transnational Expansion, and Political Aspirations*, edited by Yesim Kaptan and Ece Algan, 151–71. Cham, Switzerland: Springer, 2020.

Karataş, Duygu, and Erkan Saka. "Online Political Trolling in the Context of Post-Gezi Social Media in Turkey." *International Journal of Digital Television* 8, no. 3 (2017): 383–401.

Karaveli, Halil. "Erdogan's Journey: Conservatism and Authoritarianism in Turkey." *Foreign Affairs* 95, no. 6 (2016): 121–30.

Kavakçi Kan, Ravza. (@RavzaKavakci). "It Is Time to Unite to Put a Stop to the #Humanrightsviolations against the People of Palestine. #WorldIsBiggerThanFive." X, December 21, 2017. https://x.com/RavzaKavakci/status/943871754564440064?s=20.

Kavaklı, Kerem Can. "Domestic Politics and the Motives of Emerging Donors: Evidence from Turkish Foreign Aid." *Political Research Quarterly* 71, no. 3 (2018): 614–27.

Kaya, Ayhan. "Islamisation of Turkey under the AKP Rule: Empowering Family, Faith, and Charity." *South European Society and Politics* 20, no. 1 (2015): 47–69.

Kessler, Andy. "The Autocrat-and-Mouse Censorship Game." *Wall Street Journal*, April 2, 2014. https://www.wsj.com/articles/andy-kessler-the-autocrat-and-mouse-censorship-game-1396472268?tesla=y.

Kington, Izzy. "TRT World's Live Broadcast Added to Panasonic Offering." *Aircraft Interiors International*, November 22, 2018. https://www.aircraftinteriorsinternational.com/news/inflight-entertainment/trt-worlds-live-broadcast-added-to-panasonic-offering.html.

Kınıkoğlu, Batu. "Evaluating the Regulation of Access to Online Content in Turkey in the Context of Freedom of Speech." *Journal of International Commercial Law and Technology* 9, no. 1 (2014): 36–55.

Kızılkaya, Emre. "AKP's Social Media Wars." *Al-Monitor* (Washington, DC), November 15, 2013. https://www.al-monitor.com/originals/2013/11/akp-social-media-twitter-facebook.html.

Klasfeld, Adam. "Boom Times for Turkey's Lobbyists in Trump's Washington." *Courthouse News Service*, October 31, 2019. https://www.courthousenews.com/.

Kluver, Randolph, Skye Cooley, and Robert Hinck. "Contesting Strategic Narratives in a Global Context: The World Watches the 2016 U.S Election." *International Journal of Press/Politics* 24, no. 1 (2019): 92–114.

Kokas, Aynne. "Platform Patrol: China, the United States, and the Global Battle for Data Security." *Journal of Asian Studies* 77, no. 4 (2018): 923–33.

Konrad, Felix. *From the "Turkish Menace" to Exoticism and Orientalism: Islam as Antithesis of Europe (1453–1914)*. Mainz, Germany: Institut für Europäische Geschichte, 2011.

Kozok, Firat. "Biggest Social Media Companies Are Fined by Turkey under New Law." *Bloomberg*, November 4, 2020. https://www.bloomberg.com/news/articles/202-11-04/biggest-social-media-companies-are-fined-by-turkey-under-new-law.

Kraidy, Marwan M. "Boycotting Neo-Ottoman Cool: Geopolitics and Media Industries in the Egypt-Turkey Row over Television Drama." *Middle East Journal of Culture and Communication* 12, no. 2 (2019): 149–65.

Kraidy, Marwan M., and Clovis Bergere. "From Dazzle to Diesel: Mediating Neo-Ottoman Cool South in Guinea-Conakry." *Public Culture* (forthcoming).

Kraidy, Marwan M., and Omar Al-Ghazzi. "Neo-Ottoman Cool: Turkish Popular Culture in the Arab Public Sphere." *Popular Communication* 11, no. 1 (2013): 17–29.

Kraidy, Marwan M., and Omar Al-Ghazzi. "'Turkish Rambo': Geopolitical Drama as Narrative Counter-Hegemony." *Flow*, November 5, 2013. https://www.flowjournal.org/.

Kreps, Sarah. *Social Media and International Relations*. Cambridge: Cambridge University Press, 2020.

Kristianasen, Wendy. "Turkey's Ailing Sultan." *Le Monde Diplomatique*, September, 2013. https://mondediplo.com/2013/09/06turkey.

Kumar, Deepa. *Islamophobia and the Politics of Empire: 20 Years after 9/11*. London: Verso, 2021.

Kurban, Hakkı. "Başbakan Erdoğan: Olayların İstihbaratını 3 Ay Önce Aldık" [Prime Minister Erdogan: We received intelligence about these events 3 months ago]. *Aksam (Istanbul)*, June 12, 2013. http://www.aksam.com.tr/siyaset/basbakan-erdogan-olaylarin-istihbaratini-3-ay-once-aldik/haber-215118.

Kutlay, Mustafa, and Ziya Öniş. "Turkish Foreign Policy in a Post-Western Order: Strategic Autonomy or New Forms of Dependence?" *International Affairs* 97, no. 4 (2021): 1085–104.

Langan, Mark. "Virtuous Power Turkey in Sub-Saharan Africa: The 'Neo-Ottoman' Challenge to the European Union." *Third World Quarterly* 38, no. 6 (2016): 1399–414.

Lasswell, Harold D. *Propaganda Technique in World War I*. Cambridge, MA: MIT Press, 1971.

Lenoir, Theophile, and Chris Anderson. "Introduction: What Comes after Disinformation Studies." Center for Information, Technology, and Public Life, University of North Carolina at Chapel Hill, January 23, 2023. https://citap.pubpub.org/pub/oijfl3sv.

Letsch, Constanze. "Turkish PM Davutoğlu Resigns as Erdoğan Tightens Grip." *Guardian* (London), May 5, 2016. https://www.theguardian.com/world/2016/may/05/ahmet-Davutoglus-future-turkish-prime-minister-balance.

Lewis, Bernard. "The Roots of Muslim Rage." *Atlantic*, September 1990. https://www.theatlantic.com/magazine/archive/1990/09/the-roots-of-muslim-rage/304643/.

Lila, Muhammad, and James Masters. "Bana Alabed: 7-Year-Old Syrian Girl Meets Turkey's President Erdogan." *CNN*, December 21, 2016. https://www.cnn.com/2016/12/21/middleeast/bana-alabed-erdogan-aleppo/index.html.

Lim, Gabrielle. "Securitize/Counter-Securitize: The Life and Death of Malaysia's Anti-Fake News Act." *Data and Society*, March 25, 2020. https://datasociety.net/library/securitize-counter-securitize/.

Livingston, Steven. *The Terrorism Spectacle*. New York: Routledge, 1994.

Lord, Ceren. *Religious Politics in Turkey: From the Birth of the Republic to the AKP*. Cambridge: Cambridge University Press, 2018.

Louisa, Lim, and Julia Bergin. "Telling China's Story: Reshaping the World's Media." *International Federation of Journalists*, 2020. https://www.ifj.org/fileadmin/user_upload/IFJ_ChinaReport_2020.pdf.

Lowen, Mark. "Fake News in Turkey: Hunting for Truth in Land of Conspiracy." *BBC*, November 15, 2018. https://www.bbc.com/news/world-europe-46137139.

Lüküslü, Demet. "Creating a Pious Generation: Youth and Education Policies of the AKP in Turkey." *Southeast European and Black Sea Studies* 16, no. 4 (2016): 637–49.

Lynch, Marc. *Voices of the New Arab Public: Iraq, Al Jazeera, and Middle East Politics Today*. New York: Columbia University Press, 2006.

Madrid-Morales, Dani. "Sino-African Media Cooperation: An Overview of a Long-standing Asymmetric Relationship." In *It Is about Their Story: How China, Russia, and Turkey Influence the Media in Africa*. Johannesburg: Konrad Adenauer Stiftung, 2021, 9–70. https://www.kas.de/en/web/medien-afrika/einzeltitel/detail/-/content/it-is-about-their-story.

Mahler, Anne Garland. *From the Tricontinental to the Global South: Race, Radicalism, and Transnational Solidarity*. Durham, NC: Duke University Press, 2018.

Makdisi, Ussama. "Ottoman Orientalism." *American Historical Review* 107, no. 3 (2002): 768–96.

Makovsky, Alan. "Turkey's Refugee Dilemma: Tiptoeing toward Integration." *Center for American Progress*, 2019. https://www.americanprogress.org/article/turkeys-refugee-dilemma/.

Makris, A. "Bishop Anthimos Lashes Turkish Soap Fans." *Greek Reporter*, October 30, 2012 https://greekreporter.com/2012/10/30/bishop-anthimos-hits-out-at-turkish-soap-fans/.

Malcolm, Noel. *Useful Enemies: Islam and the Ottoman Empire in Western Political Thought, 1450–1750*. Oxford: Oxford University Press, 2020.

Mamdani, Mahmood. *Good Muslim, Bad Muslim: America, the Cold War, and the Roots of Terror*. New York: Doubleday, 2005.

Manor, Ilan. *The Digitalization of Public Diplomacy*. Cham, Switzerland: Palgrave Macmillan, 2019.

Marechal, Nathalie. "Networked Authoritarianism and the Geopolitics of Information: Understanding Russian Internet Policy." *Media and Communication* 5, no. 1 (2017): 29–41.

Marsh, Vivien. "Re-Evaluating China's Global Media Expansion." *Westminster Papers in Communication and Culture* 13, no. 1 (2018): 143–46.

Martin, Natalie. "Allies and Enemies: The Gulen Movement and the AKP." *Cambridge Review of International Affairs* 35, no. 1 (2022): 110–27.

McClelland, Mac. "How to Build a Perfect Refugee Camp." *New York Times Magazine*, February 3, 2014. https://www.nytimes.com/2014/02/16/magazine/how-to-build-a-perfect-refugee-camp.html.

McKune, Sarah, and Shazeda Ahmed. "The Contestation and Shaping of Cyber Norms through China's Internet Sovereignty Agenda." *International Journal of Communication* 12 (2018): 3835–55.

Media and Law Studies Association (MLSA). "Reasons for the Government's Anger at DW Turkish." *MLSA*, March 25, 2023. https://www.mlsaturkey.com/en/reasons-for-the-governments-anger-at-dw-turkish/.

"Media Summit in Istanbul Brings Together African, Turkish Journalists." *Daily Sabah* (Istanbul), May 25, 2022. https://www.dailysabah.com/turkey/istanbul/media-summit-in-istanbul-brings-together-african-turkish-journalists.

Mercan, Ahmet Furkan. "Afrikalı Medya Temsilcileri AA'yı Ziyaret Etti" [African media representatives visited AA]. *Anadolu Ajansı*. November 11, 2019. https://www.aa.com.tr/tr/kurumsal-haberler/afrikali-medya-temsilcileri-aayi-ziyaret-etti/1642000.

Mezhuyev, Boris. "Civilizational Realism: A Chance to Bring Theory Back in Touch with Real Politics." *Russia in Global Affairs* 16, no. 4 (2018): 31–50.

Michaelsen, Marcus. "Transforming Threats to Power: The International Politics of Authoritarian Internet Control in Iran." *International Journal of Communication* 12 (2018): 3856–76.

Middleton, Richard. "Japan's Nippon TV Buys Turkish Remake of Its Scripted Format 'Mother.'" *TBI-Television Business International*, August 27, 2020. https://tbivision.com/2020/08/27/japans-nippon-tv-buys-turkish-remake-of-its-scripted-format-mother/.

Mignolo, Walter D. "Epistemic Disobedience and the Decolonial Option: A Manifesto." *Transmodernity* 1, no. 2 (2011): 3–23.

Mignolo, Walter D. "Epistemic Disobedience, Independent Thought and Decolonial Freedom." *Theory, Culture, and Society* 26, nos. 7–8 (2009): 159–81.

Mignolo, Walter D. "The Global South and World Dis/Order." *Journal of Anthropological Research* 67, no. 2 (2011): 165–88.

Minty, Riyaad. (@Riy). "Across All Our Languages #Ertugrul Is Now Almost at 1.5 Billion Views and 50 Million+ Unique Viewers on @YouTube." *X*, June 18, 2020. https://twitter.com/Riy/status/1273634491286859776.

Mirjam, Edel, and Maria Josua. "How Authoritarian Rulers Seek to Legitimize Repression: Framing Mass Killings in Egypt and Uzbekistan." *Democratization* 25, no. 5 (2018): 882–900.

Mirrlees, Tanner. "Getting at Gafam's 'Power' in Society: A Structural-Relational Framework." *Heliotrope*, January 2020. https://www.heliotropejournal.net/helio/gafams-power-in-society.

Mirrlees, Tanner. "Not (Yet) the "Chinese Century": The Endurance of the US Empire and Its Culture Industries." In *Media Imperialism: Continuity and Change*, edited by Oliver Boyd-Barrett and Tanner Mirrlees, 305–20. Lanham: Rowman and Littlefield, 2020.

Mishra, Pankaj. "Putin Isn't Alone in His Imperial Fantasies." *Bloomberg*, March 1, 2022. https://www.bloomberg.com/opinion/articles/2022-03-01/ukraine-invasion-putin-shares-imperial-fantasies-with-xi-erdogan.

Miskimmon, Alister, Ben O'Loughlin, and Laura Roselle. *Strategic Narratives: Communication Power and the New World Order*. London: Routledge, 2014.

Mohamed, Nuur. "Yesilcam Overtakes Hollywood and Bollywood in Somalia." *Al Jazeera*, February 20, 2018. http://www.aljazeera.com/indepth/features/yesilcam-overtakes-hollywood-bollywood-somalia-180215054002526.html.

Mohydin, Ravale. "The Global Appeal of Turkish Drama Series: A Case Study in Pakistan." *TRT World Research Centre*, May 21, 2020. https://researchcentre.trtworld.com/reports/the-global-appeal-of-turkish-drama-series-a-case-study-in-pakistan/.

Mohydin, Ravale. "The Lasting Appeal of Turkish Entertainment," *TRT World Research Centre*, May 27, 2020. https://researchcentre.trtworld.com/policy-outlooks/the-lasting-appeal-of-turkish-entertainment/.

Mohydin, Ravale. "Syrian Refugees in Turkey: A Decade of Care." *TRT World Research Centre*, April 29, 2021. https://researchcentre.trtworld.com/featured/syrian-refugees-in-turkey-a-decade-of-care.

Mohydin, Ravale. "Turkish Dramas' Impact on Tourism, Skilled Immigration and Foreign Direct Investment." *TRT World Research Centre*, March 2, 2022. https://researchcentre.trtworld.com/featured/turkish-dramas-impact-on-tourism-skilled-immigration-and-foreign-direct-investment%ef%bf%bc/.

Moore, Martin, and Thomas Colley. "Two International Propaganda Models: Comparing RT and CGTN's 2020 US Election Coverage." *Journalism Practice*, June 13, 2022. DOI: https://doi.org/10.1080/17512786.2022.2086157.

Morgül, Kerem, Osman Savaşkan, and Burcu Mutlu. "İstanbul'da Suriyeli Siğinmacilara Yonelik Algi ve Tutumlar: Partizanlik, Yabanci Karsitligi, Tehdit Algilari ve Sosyal Temas" [Perceptions and attitudes toward Syrian refugees in Istanbul: partisanship, xenophobia, threat perceptions, and social interactions]. *Heinrich Böll Stiftung*, Istanbul, 2021. https://tr.boell.org/sites/default/files/2021-06/Istanbulda%20Suriyeliler%20Raporu%20BASIM.pdf.

Morina Die, and Hamdi Fırat Buyuk. "Turkish Series about Sultan Causes Concern in Kosovo." *Balkan Insight*, March 12, 2018. https://balkaninsight.com/2018/03/12/turkish-series-about-sultan-causes-concern-in-kosovo-03-09-2018/.

Morris, Loveday. "'Law Is Suspended': Turkish Lawyers Report Abuse of Coup Detainees." *Washington Post*, July 24, 2016. https://www.washingtonpost.com/.

Musa, Waliat. "Turkiye, Africa Need to Double Down on Telling, Protecting Her Stories, Says Nwanze." *The Guardian* (Nigeria), June 6, 2022. https://guardian.ng/news/turkiye-africa-need-to-double-down-on-telling-protecting-her-stories-says-nwanze/.

Mutlu, Sefa. "Project to Bring Turkic News Agencies under Single Roof nears Completion." *Anadolu Agency*, May 16, 2022. https://www.aa.com.tr/en/turkey/project-to-bring-turkic-news-agencies-under-single-roof-nears-completion/2588960.

Myers, Steven Lee, and Sheera Frenkel. "How Russian Propaganda Is Reaching beyond English Speakers." *New York Times*, August 9, 2022. https://www.nytimes.com/.

Nas, Alparslan. "Branding and National Identity: The Analysis of 'Turkey: Discover the Potential' Campaign." *Bilig: Turk Dunyasi Sosyal Bilimler Dergisi* 83 (2017): 201–24.

Nefes, Turkay Salim. "Political Parties' Perceptions and Uses of Anti-Semitic Conspiracy Theories in Turkey." *Sociological Review* 61 (2013): 247–64.

Nelson, Alex. "Ertugrul: The 'Turkish Game of Thrones' on Netflix That Redefines 'Epic.'" *INews*, February 21, 2018. https://inews.co.uk/culture/television/ertugrul-turkish-game-thrones-netflix-512666.

"New Disinformation Law Will Be Soon Announced, Turkish Official Says." *Daily Sabah* (Istanbul), April 17, 2022. https://www.dailysabah.com/politics/legislation/new-disinformation-law-will-be-soon-announced-turkish-official-says.

Newman, Dina. "'The Right Kind of Refugees': Racism in the Western Media Coverage of the Conflict in Ukraine." *Media Diversity*, March 2, 2022. https://www.media-diversity.org/the-right-kind-of-refugees-racism-in-the-western-media-coverage-of-the-conflict-in-ukraine/.

"Newsmakers, The." *YouTube*, 2023. https://www.youtube.com/channel/UCiDyg5GUMxZiHiwiQ29Nwhw.

"No Genocide, Colonialism in Turkey's History: FM Çavuşoğlu." *Hurriyet Daily News* (Istanbul). April 15, 2019. https://www.hurriyetdailynews.com/no-genocide-colonialism-in-turkeys-history-fm-cavusoglu-142673

Nye, Joseph S. *Soft Power: The Means To Success In World Politics*. New York: Public Affairs, 2009.

Oates, Sarah, and Sean Steiner. "Projecting Power: Understating Russian Strategic Narrative." *Russian Analytical Digest* 229 (2018): 2–5. https://www.research-collection.ethz.ch/bitstream/handle/20.500.11850/311091/2/RAD229.pdf.

Öğüt, Süheyb. "PM Erdogan and AK Party: The Usual Objects of Racism." *Daily Sabah* (Istanbul), March 3, 2014. https://www.dailysabah.com/opinion/2014/03/03/pm-erdogan-and-ak-party-the-usual-objects-of-racism.

Öğütcen, Büşra Selvi, and Emel Öz Gözellik. "Cumhurbaşkanlığı Sözcüsü Kalın: Türkiye Afrika'da Kazan-Kazan Politikasi İzliyor" [Presidential spokesperson Kalın: Turkey pursues a win-win policy in Africa]. *Anadolu Ajansi*, January 28, 2017. https://www.aa.com.tr/tr/turkiye/cumhurbaskanligi-sozcusu-kalin-turkiye-afrika-da-kazan-kazan-politikasi-izliyor/736665.

Omelicheva, Maria Y. "Islam and Power Legitimation: Instrumentalisation of Religion in Central Asian States." *Contemporary Politics* 22, no. 2 (2016): 144–63.

Öniş, Ziya and Mustafa Kutlay. "Rising Powers in a Changing Global Order: The Political Economy of Turkey in the Age of the BRICS." *Third World Quarterly* 34, no. 8 (2013): 1409–26.

Organization of Turkic States. "Turkic Council Media Forum Was Held under the Theme 'Deep-Rooted Past, Strong Future' in Istanbul." *Organization of Turkic States*, October 24, 2021. https://www.turkkon.org/en/haberler/turkic-council-media-forum-was-held-under-the-theme-deep-rooted-past-strong-future-in-istanbul_2367.

Orttung, Robert W., and Elizabeth Nelson. "Russia Today's Strategy and Effectiveness on YouTube." *Post-Soviet Affairs* 35, no. 2 (2019): 77–92.

Oruç, Saadet. "President Erdoğan as a Target of Western Media." *Daily Sabah* (Istanbul), December 27, 2016. https://www.dailysabah.com/columns/saadet-oruc/2016/12/27/president-erdogan-as-a-target-of-the-western-media.

Osborne, Samuel. "Turkey Coup Attempt: Government Had List of Arrests Prepared before Rebellion, EU Commissioner Says." *Independent* (London), July 18, 2016. http://www.independent.co.uk/news/world/europe/turkey-coup-attempt-erdogan-government-arrests-military-uprising-eu-commissioner-a7142426.html.

Osman, Wazhmah. "Building Spectatorial Solidarity against the 'War on Terror' Media-Military Gaze." *International Journal of Middle East Studies* 54 (2022) 369–75.

Osman, Wazhmah. *Television and the Afghan Culture Wars: Brought to You by Foreigners, Warlords, and Activists*. Urbana: University of Illinois Press, 2020.

Övür, Mahmut. "ABD'li Vakıf, Sol Basını Neden Besliyor?" [Why does a US foundation nurture the leftist press?]. *Sabah* (Istanbul), July 23, 2021. https://www.sabah.com.tr/yazarlar/ovur/2021/07/23/abdli-vakif-sol-basini-neden-besliyor.

Özer, Asya, and Burak Özçetin. "Rewriting History in Contemporary Turkey: Neo-Ottomanism, Islamism, Nationalism, and Militarism in the Republic of Türkiye Directorate of Communications' Historical Videos." *Southeast European and Black Sea Studies* (forthcoming).

Özkan, Behlül. "SETA: From the AKP's Organic Intellectuals to AK-Paratchiks." In *Turkey's New State in the Making: Transformations in Legality, Economy, and Coercion*, edited by Pinar Bedirhanoglu, Caglar Dolek, Funda Hulagu, and Ozlem Kaygusuz, 226–42. London: Zed, 2020.

Özkan, Behlül. "Turkey, Davutoğlu and the Idea of Pan-Islamism." *Survival* 56, no. 4 (2014): 119–40.

Özkır, Yusuf. "Mainstream Western Media Has Lost Its Credibility." *Daily Sabah* (Istanbul), June 12, 2019. https://www.dailysabah.com/op-ed/2019/06/12/mainstream-western-media-has-lost-its-credibility.

Özkır, Yusuf. "The Tiananmens Ignored by the Western Media." *Politics Today*, July 15, 2019. https://politicstoday.org/the-tiananmens-ignored-by-the-western-media/.

Özkır, Yusuf. "Türk Dış Politikasında İletişim Başkanlığının Yeri" [The place of the Directorate of Communications in Turkey's foreign policy]. In *Turk Dis Politikasi Yilligi 2019* [The Annals of Turkish Foreign Policy 2019], edited by Burhanettin Duran, Kemal Inat, and Mustafa Caner, 31–56. Istanbul: SETA Yayinlari, 2020.

Özkır, Yusuf. *Uluslararası Medyada Türkiye Karşıtlığı* [Anti-Turkey stance in international media]. Istanbul: Pruva, 2020.

Özpek, Burak Bilgehan, and Nebahat Tanriverdi Yaşar. "Populism and Foreign Policy in Turkey under the AKP Rule." *Turkish Studies* 19, no. 2 (2018): 198–216.

Öztürk, Ahmet Erdi. *Religion, Identity and Power: Turkey and the Balkans in the Twenty-First Century*. Edinburgh: Edinburgh University Press, 2021.

Öztürk, Ahmet Erdi. "Transformation of the Turkish Diyanet Both at Home and Abroad: Three Stages." *European Journal of Turkish Studies* 27 (2018): 1–14.

Öztürk, Kemal. "Anadolu Agency and the New Media Order." In *Chaos, Complexity, and Leadership*, edited by Santo Banerjee and Sefika Sule Ercetin, 43–46. Dordrecht, Netherlands: Springer, 2014.

Öztürkmen, Arzu. "'Turkish Content': The Historical Rise of the Dizi Genre." *TV/Series* 13 (2018). DOI: https://journals.openedition.org/tvseries/2406.

Parim, Ali, and Cem Cetin. "Bir Kamu Diplomasisi Araci olarak TRT Avaz ve Milliyetcilik" [TRT Avaz as a public diplomacy tool and nationalism]. *Iletisim ve Diplomasi* 5 (2021): 25–55.

Parks, Lisa, Hannah Goodwin, and Lisa Han. "'I Have the Government in My Pocket': Social Media Users in Turkey, Transmit-Trap Dynamics, and Struggles over Internet Freedom." *Communication, Culture, and Critique* 10, no. 4 (2017): 574–92.

Peker, Efe. "Religious Populism, Memory, and Violence in India." *New Diversities* 21, no. 2 (2019): 1–14. https://newdiversities.mmg.mpg.de/wp-content/uploads/2019/12/2019_21-02_03_Peker.pdf.

Pekkendir, Semanur. "Protecting the Most Vulnerable: Refugees in Turkey amidst COVID-19." *TRT World Research Centre*, May 7, 2020. https://researchcentre.trtworld.com/info-packs/protecting-the-most-vulnerable-refugees-in-turkey-amidst-covid-19.

Pigman, Lincoln. "Russia's Vision of Cyberspace: A Danger to Regime Security, Public Safety, and Societal Norms and Cohesion." *Journal of Cyber Policy* 4, no. 1 (2018): 22–34.

Pitel, Laura. "Facebook to Defy New Turkish Social Media Law." *Financial Times*, October 6, 2020. https://www.ft.com/content/91c0a408-6c15-45c3-80e3-d6b2cf913070.

Pitel, Laura. "Turkey Bans Access to US and German Public Broadcasters." *Financial Times,* July 1, 2022. https://www.ft.com/content/49b4e348-304b-453c-9a65-48ee3e155109.

Polat, Cüneyt. "Diriliş Ertuğrul'un Yapimcisi Mehmet Bozdağ: Hersey Bir Ruya ile Basladi!" [Producer of Resurrection Ertugrul, Mehmet Bozdağ: it all started with a dream!]. *Cuneyt Polat*, May 10, 2016. https://www.cuneytpolat.com/mehmet-bozdag-her-sey-bir-ruya-ile-basladi/.

Pomerantsev, Peter. "Authoritarianism Goes Global: The Kremlin's Information War." *Journal of Democracy* 26, no. 4 (2015): 40–50.

"Popular Turkish TV Drama 'Diriliş: Ertuğrul' Inspires Statues in Pakistan." *Daily Sabah* (Istanbul), June 24, 2020. https://www.dailysabah.com/arts/cinema/popular-turkish-tv-drama-dirilis-ertugrul-inspires-statues-in-pakistan.

Pownall, Katy. "Turkey Could Be Taking a Big Step Backwards in Human Rights." *Time*, July 22, 2016. http://time.com/.

Presidency of the Republic of Türkiye. "10 Questions to Understand 15 July Coup Attempt and Fetullah Terrorist Organization." *Presidency of the Republic of Türkiye*, December, 6, 2016. https://www.tccb.gov.tr/en/news/542/66338/10-soruda-15-temmuz-darbe-girisimi-ve-fetullahci-teror-orgutu.

Presidency of the Republic of Türkiye. "Those Who are Unfamiliar with Civilization are Bound to Give into Imitation." *Presidency of the Republic of Türkiye*, October 21, 2017. https://www.tccb.gov.tr/en/news/542/85040/those-who-are-unfamiliar-with-civilization-are-bound-to-give-into-imitation.

Presidency of the Republic of Türkiye. "TRT World's Cameras Should Focus on the Victims." *Presidency of the Republic of Türkiye*, November 15, 2016. https://www.tccb.gov.tr/en/.

Presidency of the Republic of Türkiye. "We Have Opened Our Doors to Millions of People Facing Discrimination and Oppression." *Presidency of the Republic of Türkiye*, February 22, 2021. https://www.tccb.gov.tr/en/news/542/125009/-we-have-opened-our-doors-to-millions-of people-facing-discrimination-and-oppression.
"President Erdoğan Admits Wrong Strategies in Education and Culture." *Hurriyet Daily News* (Istanbul), December 28, 2016. https://www.hurriyetdailynews.com/.
"President Erdoğan Receives Palestinian Teen Fawzi al-Juneidi." *Daily Sabah* (Istanbul), January 18, 2018. https://www.dailysabah.com/politics/2018/01/18/president-erdogan-receives-palestinian-teen-fawzi-al-juneidi.
Price, Monroe E. *Free Expression, Globalism, and the New Strategic Communication*. New York: Cambridge University Press, 2015.
"Prime Minister Erdogan's Strongman Tactics to Turkey's Protests." *Washington Post*, June 3, 2013. https://www.washingtonpost.com/.
Purvis, Andrew. "Recep Tayyip Erdogan." *Time*, April 26, 2004. http://content.time.com/.
"Radical Groups Campaign against Turkish Series in Serbia." *Hurriyet Daily News* (Istanbul), March 29, 2012. https://www.hurriyetdailynews.com/.
Rai, Mugdha, and Simon Cottle. "Global Mediations: On the Changing Ecology of Satellite Television News." *Global Media and Communication* 3, no. 1 (2007): 51–78.
Rakhmani, Inaya, and Adinda Zakiah. "Consuming Halal Turkish Television in Indonesia: A Closer Look at the Social Responses towards Muhteşem Yüzyıl." In *Television in Turkey, Local Production, Transnational Expansion, and Political Aspirations*, edited by Yesim Kaptan and Ece Algan, 245–66. Cham, Switzerland: Springer, 2020.
Ramsay, Gordon, and Sam Robertshaw. *Weaponising News: RT, Sputnik, and Targeted Disinformation*. London: Centre for the Study of Media, Communication, and Power, 2019. https://www.kcl.ac.uk/policy-institute/assets/weaponising-news.pdf.
Ranger, Jamie, and Will Ranger. "Towards a Resonant Theory of Memory Politics." *Memory Studies*, 2022. DOI: https://doi.org/10.1177/17506980221101112.1
Rawnsley, Gary D. "Introduction, International Broadcasting and Public Diplomacy in the 21st Century." *Media and Communication* 4, no. 2 (2016): 42–44.
Rawnsley, Gary D. "To Know Us Is to Love Us: Public Diplomacy and International Broadcasting in Contemporary Russia and China." *Politics* 35, nos. 3–4 (2015): 273–86.
"Recep Erdogan Storms Out of Davos after Clash with Israeli President over Gaza." *Guardian* (London), January 30, 2009. https://www.theguardian.com/world/2009/jan/30/turkish-prime-minister-gaza-davos.
"Recep Tayyip Erdogan: 'Western Leaders Preferred to Leave Turkish People to Themselves.'" *Le Monde* (Paris), August 8, 2016. https://www.lemonde.fr/europe/article/2016/08/08/recep-tayyip-erdogan-western-leaders-prefered-to-leave-turkish-people-to-themselves_4979866_3214.html.
"Regulatory Authorities and Useful Links." *BRAF Black Sea Regulatory Authorities Forum*, 2023. http://braf.info/EN/Menu/3.
"Remarks by President Erdoğan during TRT World Forum 2020." *Hurriyet Daily News* (Istanbul), December 2, 2020. https://www.hurriyetdailynews.com/.
Repnikova, Maria. *Chinese Soft Power*. Cambridge: Cambridge University Press, 2022.

Reporters without Borders. *Türkiye: Reporters without Borders*, 2023. https://rsf.org/en/country-t%C3%BCrkiye.
Republic of Türkiye, Ministry of Culture and Tourism, Turkish Cooperation and Coordination Agency (TIKA). "TİKA Gives Support to Media Organizations." 2013. https://www.tika.gov.tr/en/news/tika_gives_support_to_media_organizations-8620.
Republic of Türkiye, Ministry of Culture and Tourism, Turkish Cooperation and Coordination Agency (TIKA). "TİKA Provides Technical Equipment to a Radio Station in Kenya." 2021. https://www.tika.gov.tr/en/news/tika_provides_technical_equipment_to_a_radio_station_in_kenya-66662.
Republic of Türkiye, Ministry of Culture and Tourism, Turkish Cooperation and Coordination Agency (TIKA). *2019 Annual Report* (Ankara, 2019). https://www.tika.gov.tr/upload/sayfa/publication/2019/TIKAFaaliyet2019ENGWebKapakli.pdf.
Risør, Helene. "Civil Victimhood: Citizenship, Human Rights, and Securitization in Post-Dictatorship Chile." *Anthropological Theory* 18, nos. 2–3 (2018): 271–95.
Roettgers, Janko. "How Turkey's TRT World Wants to Win over US Online Video Viewers." *Variety Daily*, November 22, 2017. https://variety.com/2017/digital/news/trt-world-u-s-viewers-1202621932/.
"Roundtable." *YouTube*, 2023. https://www.youtube.com/channel/UCxE0UJ9cfjUD_FLJkxKaH5w.
Rumelili, Bahar, and Rahime Suleymanoglu-Kurum. "Brand Turkey: Liminal Identity and Its Limits." *Geopolitics* 22, no. 3 (2017): 549–70.
Rutland, Peter, and Andrei Kazantsev. "The Limits of Russia's 'Soft Power.'" *Journal of Political Power* 9, no. 3 (2016): 395–41.
Saatçioğlu, Beren. "The European Union's Refugee Crisis and Rising Functionalism in EU-Turkey Relations." *Turkish Studies* 21, no. 2 (2020): 169–87.
Saeed, Saeed. "Saudi Broadcaster MBC Takes All Turkish TV Shows Off Air." *National*, March 5, 2018. https://www.thenational.ae/.
Şahin, Haluk. "Broadcasting Autonomy in Turkey: Its Rise and Fall, 1961–1971." *Journalism Quarterly* 58, no. 3 (1981): 395–400.
Said, Edward. "The Clash of Ignorance." *Nation*, October 4, 2001. https://www.thenation.com/article/archive/clash-ignorance/.
Said, Edward. *Orientalism*. New York: Vintage, 1979.
Saka, Erkan. *Social Media and Politics in Turkey: A Journey through Citizen Journalism, Political Trolling, and Fake News*. London: Lexington, 2019.
Saka, Erkan. "Social Media in Turkey as a Space for Political Battles: AKTrolls and Other Politically Motivated Trolling." *Middle East Critique* 27, no. 2 (2018): 161–77.
Salem, Paul. *Turkey's Image in the Arab World*. Turkish Economic and Social Studies Foundation, *TESEV*—Turkiye Ekonomik ve Sosyal Etudler Vakfi, 2011. https://www.tesev.org.tr/en/research/turkeys-image-in-the-arab-world/.
Salhani, Claude. "One More Twist in Erdogan's Imperial Mindset." *Arab Weekly*, January 16, 2020. https://thearabweekly.com/one-more-twist-erdogans-imperial-mindset.
Samuel-Azran, Tal. "Al-Jazeera, Qatar, and New Tactics in State-Sponsored Media Diplomacy." *American Behavioral Scientist* 57, no. 9 (2013): 1293–311.

Sancar, Gaye Asli. "Turkey's Public Diplomacy: Its Actors, Stakeholders, and Tools." In *Turkey's Public Diplomacy*, edited by Senem B. Çevik and Philip Seib, 13–42. New York: Palgrave Macmillan, 2015.

Sani, Ahmet Esad. "Yapımcı Bozdağ: Tarih Kitaplarında Yazanlar Sinemaya Yansısın" [Producer Bozdağ: Let what is written in the history books be reflected in the cinema]. *Anadolu Ajansi*, January 16, 2020. https://www.aa.com.tr/tr/kultur-sanat/yapimci-bozdag-tarih-kitaplarinda-yazanlar-sinemaya-yansisin/1704477.

Sar, Edgar, and Nezih Onur. "Istanbul'da Suriyeli Sığınmacılara Yönelik Tutumlar" [Attitudes towards Syrian refugees in Istanbul]. *Istanbul Politik Arastirmalar Enstitusu*, 2020. https://www.istanpol.org/post-i-stanbul-da-suriyeli-sig-nmac-lara-yonelik-tutumlar.

Saraçoğlu, Cenk, and Özhan Demirkol. "Nationalism and Foreign Policy Discourse in Turkey under the AKP Rule: Geography, History, and National Identity." *British Journal of Middle Eastern Studies* 42, no. 3 (2015): 301–19.

Savaş, Özlem. "The Muslim 'Crying Boy' in Turkey: Aestheticization and Politicization of Suffering in Islamic Imagination." In *Visual Culture in the Modern Middle East: Rhetoric of the Image*, edited by Christiane Gruber and Sune Haugbolle, 103–26. Bloomington: Indiana University Press, 2013.

Sayın, Ayşe. "Dijital Mecralar Komisyonu Başkanı Yayman: Ocak'tan Itibaren Ilk Işimiz Sosyal Medya Platformlarıyla Dijital Diplomasi" [Digital media commission chairman Yayman: Our first job starting from January is social media platforms and digital diplomacy]. *BBC Turkce*, December 18, 2020. https://www.bbc.com/turkce/haberler-turkiye-55361310.

Scartozzi, Cesare M. "Assad's Strategic Narrative: The Role of Communication in the Syrian Civil War." *Contemporary Review of the Middle East* 2, no. 4 (2015): 313–27.

Schaffer, Aaron. "Justice Department Ordered Turkish TV Station to Register as Foreign Agent." *Al-Monitor* (Washington, DC), March 19, 2020. https://www.al-monitor.com/.

Schiller, Dan. *Digital Capitalism: Networking the Global Market System*. Cambridge, MA: MIT Press, 1999.

Schiller, Dan. *Digital Depression: Information Technology and Economic Crisis*. Urbana: University of Illinois Press, 2014.

Schiller, Herbert. *Mass Communication and American Empire*. 2nd ed. 1969; Boulder, CO: Westview, 1992.

Schwartz, Felicia, and Gordon Fairclough. "Wall Street Journal Reporter Dion Nissenbaum Returns to U.S. after Being Detained in Turkey." *Wall Street Journal*, December 31, 2016. www.wsj.com/articles/turkish-authorities-detain-wall-street-journal-staff-reporter-dion-nissenbaum-for-2days-1483191134.

Scott, Alev. "As ISIS Attacks Mount, Turkey Steps Up Its War on Free Speech." *Newsweek*, June 7, 2016. https://www.newsweek.com/2016/07/15/zaman-newspaper-turkey-free-speech-477859.html.

Seib, Phillip. *The Al Jazeera Effect: How the New Global Media Are Reshaping World Politics*. Washington, DC: Potomac, 2008.

Seib, Phillip. *Al Jazeera English: Global News in a Changing World*. New York: Palgrave Macmillan, 2016.

Seib, Phillip. "Hegemonic No More: Western Media, the Rise of Al-Jazeera, and the Influence of Diverse Voices." *International Studies Review* 7, no. 4 (2005): 601–15.

Seref, Salih. "TRT 1 Yeni Yayin Donemine Yeni Yapimlarla Cikmaya Hazirlaniyor" [TRT 1 ready for the new broadcast season with new productions]. *Anadolu* Ajansı, July 8, 2021. https://www.aa.com.tr/tr/kultur-sanat/trt-1-yeni-yayin-donemine-yeni-yapimlarla cikmaya-hazirlaniyor/2298362.

Sevin, Efe. "Bridge No More? Turkish Public Diplomacy and Branding under the AKP Government." *E-International Relations*, October 5, 2012. https://www.e-ir.info/2012/10/05/bridge-no-more-turkish-public-diplomacy-and-branding-under-the-akp-government/.

Sevin, Efe. "Digital Diplomacy as Crisis Communication: Turkish Digital Outreach after July 15." *Mexican Journal of Foreign Policy* 113 (2017): 185–207.

Shafer, Richard. "Soviet Foundations of the Post-Independence Press in Central Asia" In *After the Czars and Commissars Journalism in Authoritarian Post-Soviet Central Asia*, edited by Eric Freedman and Richard Shafer, 19–34. East Lansing: Michigan State University Press, 2011.

Shafy, Samiha. "The Rise and Fall of Erdogan's Turkey." *Der Spiegel*, September 24, 2015. http://www.spiegel.de/international/europe/turkey-under-erdogan-is-becoming-politically-riven-a-1054359.html.

Shaheen, Kareem. "Ramadan TV Series Lays Bare Turkey's Colonial Legacy." *News Line Magazine*, March 27, 2023. https://newlinesmag.com/spotlight/ramadan-tv-series-lays-bare-turkeys-colonial-legacy/.

Shahi, Deepshikha. *Understanding Post-9/11 Afghanistan: A Critical Insight into Huntington's Civilizational Approach*. Bristol, UK: E-International Relations, 2017. https://www.e-ir.info/publication/understanding-post-911-afghanistan-a-critical-insight-into-huntingtons-civilizational-approach/.

Sienkiewicz, Matt. *The Other Air Force: US Efforts to Reshape Middle Eastern Media since 9/11*. New Brunswick, NJ: Rutgers University Press, 2016.

Sim, Sukrü, and Fatih Göksu. "A Comparative Discourse Analysis of TRT World and Al Jazeera News Channels on the News Reports of the Syrian War." *Journal of Communication* 57 (2019): 155–72.

Simonsen, Kristina B., and Bart Bonikowski. "Moralizing Immigration: Political Framing, Moral Conviction, and Polarization in the United States and Denmark." *Comparative Political Studies* 55, no. 8 (2022): 1403–36.

Singer, Sean. R. "Erdogan's Muse: The School of Necip Fazil Kisakurek." *World Affairs* 176, no. 4 (2013): 81–88.

Snow, Nancy, and Yahya Kamalipour. *War, Media, and Propaganda: A Global Perspective*. New York: Rowman and Littlefield, 2004.

Soylu, Ragıp. "Turkey to Regulate Foreign Funding of News Media." *Middle East Eye*, July 22, 2021. https://www.middleeasteye.net/news/turkey-regulate-foreign-funding-news-media.

Sözeri, Efe Kerem. "Pelikan Derneği: Berat Albayrak, Ahmet Davutoğlu'nu Neden Devirdi?" [Pelikan Association: why did Berat Albayrak oust Ahmet Davutoğlu]. *Medium*, November 3, 2016. https://medium.com/.

Sözeri, Efe Kerem. "These Fake 'Fact-Checkers' Are Peddling Lies about Genocide and Censorship in Turkey." *Poynter*, May 31, 2017. https://www.poynter.org/.

"SPI/FilmBox Launches Turkish Drama Channel on DStv in Sub-Saharan Africa." *Broadcast Pro*, October 22, 2020. https://www.broadcastprome.com/.

Spivak, Gayatri Chakravorty. "Can the Subaltern Speak?" In *Colonial Discourse and Post-Colonial Theory: A Reader*, edited by Patrick Williams and Laura Chrisman, 67–111. New York: Columbia University Press, 1994.

Srivastava, Mehul, and Henry Mance. "Turkish TV Station Aims to Switch Western Views." *Financial Times*, March 12, 2016. https://www.ft.com/.

Stein, Aaron. *Turkey's New Foreign Policy: Davutoğlu, the AKP, and the Pursuit of Regional Order*. Whitehall Paper 83, Royal United Services Institute for Defence and Security Services. Abingdon, UK: Routledge Journals, 2014.

Stratcom Summit. "About." *Stratcom*, 2021 https://www.stratcomsummit.com/about.

Stratcom Summit. "Agenda." *Stratcom*, 2021. https://stratcomsummit.com/en/events/stratcom-21-agenda-en

Stratcom Summit. "Content." *Stratcom*, 2022. https://stratcomsummit.com/en/events/stratcom-22-content-en.

Stratcom Summit. "Speakers." *Stratcom*, 2021. https://www.stratcomsummit.com/events/stratcom-21/speakers.

Stratcom Summit. "Stratcom Açılış Konuşması-Fahrettin Altun-Hakikat Ötesi Çağda Stratejik İletişim" [Stratcom opening remarks-Fahrettin Altun-strategic communication in the post-truth era]. *YouTube*, December 15, 2021. https://youtu.be/buBwbwKMQGA?si=gE6CJCZT1xwMg-CE.

Stratcom Summit. "Stratcom Kenya." *Stratcom*, 2023. https://stratcomsummit.com/en/events/stratcom-kenya.

Stratcom Summit. "Stratcom Youth." *Stratcom*, 2022. https://stratcomsummit.com/en/events/stratcom-youth-about-en.

Stratcom Summit. "Stratcom Youth Speakers." *Stratcom*, 2022. https://web.archive.org/web/20220526235810/https://www.stratcomsummit.com/events/stratcom-youth/stratcom-youth-speakers.

Stratcom Summit. (@StratcomSummit). "Turkiye Iletisim Modelinin Temelinde Ne Var?" [What are the fundamentals of Turkey's Communication Model?]. *X*, May 8, 2022. https://twitter.com/StratcomSummit/status/1523248478096617475?s=20&t=YIYq-WupqMRkpABjKkcWHw.

"Sultan Abdülhamid'in Rüyası Gerçek Oluyor: Filyos Limanı Yarın Hizmete Giriyor" [Sultan Abdülhamid's dream comes true: Filyos port will open tomorrow]. *Sabah* (Istanbul), June 3, 2021. https://www.sabah.com.tr/galeri/ekonomi/sultan-abdulhamidin-ruyasi-gercek-oluyor-filyos-limani-yarin-hizmete-giriyor.

"Surprisingly European: Mr. Erdogan and His Islamist AK Party Are Not the Obvious People to Take Turkey into the EU." *Economist*, March 19, 2005. https://www.economist.com/.

"Surrounded by Ottoman Soldiers, Erdoğan Toughens Rhetoric against New York Times." *Hurriyet Daily News* (Istanbul), May 30, 2015. https://www.hurriyetdailynews.com/.

Szeto, Winston. "Former Syrian Refugee Cries Foul at 'Racist' Media Coverage of Ukraine War." *CBC*, March 2, 2022. https://www.cbc.ca/.

Szostek, Joanna. "Defence and Promotion of Desired State Identity in Russia's Strategic Narrative." *Geopolitics* 22, no. 3 (2017): 571–93.

Taş, Hakkı. "A History of Turkey's AKP-Gulen Conflict." *Mediterranean Politics* 23, no. 3 (2018): 395–402.

TASS Russian News Agency. "Cavusoglu Says Russia's Claims on Implementation of Grain Deal Not Unfounded." April 28, 2023. https://tass.com/world.1610979.

Tecmen, Ayşe. "The Relations between Public Diplomacy and Nation Brands: An Investigation of Nation Branding in Turkey." *Horizon, 2020, Critical Heritages: Performing and Representing Identities in Europe. Istanbul Bilgi University*, 2018. https://eu.bilgi.edu.tr/media/files/WORKING_PAPER_10–180518–2.pdf.

Telci, Ismail Numan, Ibrahim Efe, Tuncay Kardas, and Ismail Caglar, eds. *15 Temmuz Darbe Girisimi ve Bati Medyasi* [July 15 Coup Attempt and Western Media]. SETA (Istanbul, 2017). https://setav.org/assets/uploads/2017/07/Rapor86.pdf.

Tepeciklioğlu, Elem Eyrice. "Turkey's Religious Diplomacy in Africa." In *Turkey in Africa*, edited by Elem Eyrice Tepeciklioğlu and Ali Onur Tepeciklioğlu, 199–216. London: Routledge, 2021.

Tepeciklioğlu, Elem Eyrice, and Ali Onur Tepeciklioğlu. *Turkey in Africa: A New Emerging Power?* London: Routledge, 2021.

Terry, Kyilah. "The EU-Turkey Deal, Five Years On: A Frayed and Controversial but Enduring Blueprint." *Migration Policy Institute*, April 18, 2021. https://www.migrationpolicy.org/.

Thussu, Daya Kishan. *Communicating India's Soft Power: From Buddha to Bollywood*. London: Palgrave Macmillan, 2013.

Thussu, Daya Kishan. "Globalization of Chinese Media: The Global Context." In *China's Media Go Global*, edited by Daya K. Thussu, Hugo de Burgh, and Anbin Shi, 17–33. London: Routledge, 2018.

Thussu, Daya Kishan. *Media on the Move: Global Flow and Contra-Flow*. New York: Routledge, 2006.

Thussu, Daya Kishan, Hugo de Burgh, and Anbin Shi, eds. *China's Media Go Global*. London: Routledge, 2018.

TIKA. (@tika_english1). "Media Support from TİKA to #Vojvodina, #Serbia." *X*, May 17, 2021. https://twitter.com/tika_english1/status/1394306345541767180?s=20&t=lp4XEWLT8xEktIks04z-AA.

"TIKA Donates Studio Equipment to NAMPA." *Namibia News Digest*, October 26, 2021. https://www.namibianewsdigest.com/tika-donates-studio-equipment-to-nampa/.

Tokdoğan, Nagehan. "Reading Politics through Emotions: Ontological Ressentiment as the Emotional Basis of Current Politics in Turkey." *Nations and Nationalism* 26 (2020): 388–406.

Topçu, Elmas. "Erdogan's AKP Basks in Glow of Loyal Think Tank." *Deutsche Welle*, November 14, 2019. https://www.dw.com/en/erdogans-akp-basks-in-glow-of-think-tank-financed-by-influential-family-dw-finds/a-51258757.

Topuz, Hıfzı. "Past Witnesses' Present Comments." In *From NWICO to WSIS: 30 Years of Communication Geopolitics, Actors, Flows, Structures, and Divides*, edited by Divina Frau-Meigs, Jeremie Nicey, Michael Palmer, Julia Pohle, and Patricio Tupper, 81–86. Bristol, UK: Intellect, 2012.

Tosun, Mehmet. "Cumhurbaşkanlığı İletişim Başkanı Altun: Uluslararası Alanda Bir Avuç Medya Şirketinin Tahakkümüyle Karşı Karşıyayız" [Presidential Director of

Communications Altun: In the international arena, we are faced with the domination of a handful of media companies]. *Anadolu Ajansi*, May 11, 2022. https://www.aa.com.tr/tr/gundem/cumhurbaskanligi-iletisim-baskani-altun-uluslararasi-alanda-bir-avuc-medya-sirketinin-tahakkumuyle-karsi-karsiyayiz/2585408.

Toula, Christopher M. "Failure to Launch: International Broadcasters as Counter-Hegemonic News." *International Journal of Communication*, 16 (2022): 3495–515.

"Training on Strengthening the Role of African Media Kicks off in Istanbul." *Somali National News Agency*, October 23, 2019. https://sonna.so/en/training-on-strengthening-the-role-of-african-media-kicks-off-in-istanbul/.

Traub, James. "Déjà Vu and Paranoia in the Deep State Foreign Affairs." *Foreign Policy*, January 10, 2014. https://foreignpolicy.com/.

Trilling, Daniel. "How the Media Contributed to the Migrant Crisis." *Guardian* (London), August 1, 2019. https://www.theguardian.com/news/2019/aug/01/media-framed-migrant-crisis-disaster-reporting.

TRT (Türkiye Radyo ve Televizyon Kurumu, Turkish Radio and Television Corp.). "External Services Department." *TRT*, 2022. https://trtvotworld.com/.

TRT (Türkiye Radyo ve Televizyon Kurumu, Turkish Radio and Television Corp.). *Faaliyet Raporu 2019* [Annual report 2019]. *TRT*, 2019. https://www.trt.net.tr/kurumsal/2019/#09-finansal-gostergeler.

TRT (Türkiye Radyo ve Televizyon Kurumu, Turkish Radio and Television Corp.). *Faaliyet Raporu 2020* [Annual report 2020]. *TRT*, 2020. https://www.trt.net.tr/pdfs/event-reports/2020.pdf.

TRT (Türkiye Radyo ve Televizyon Kurumu, Turkish Radio and Television Corp.). *Faaliyet Raporu 2022* [Annual report 2022]. *TRT*, 2022. https://www.trt.net.tr/pdfs/event-reports/2022.pdf.

TRT (Türkiye Radyo ve Televizyon Kurumu, Turkish Radio and Television Corp.). "Kilometre Taslari" [Milestones]. *TRT*, 2023. https://www.trt.net.tr/kurumsal/kilometre-taslari.

TRT (Türkiye Radyo ve Televizyon Kurumu, Turkish Radio and Television Corp.). "UMEP—Uluslararasi Medya Egitim Programi" [International media training program]. *TRT*, 2023. https://www.trt.net.tr/umep/.

"TRT'de Kadrolaşma Skandalı" [Politicization of cadres at TRT, scandal]. *Birgün*, May 8, 2016. https://www.birgun.net/haber/trt-de-kadrolasma-skandali-111661.

"TRT'deki Siyasi Kadrolasma Meclis Gundeminde" [Politicization of TRT cadres on the Parliament's agenda]. *Evrensel* (Istanbul), June 14, 2019. https://www.evrensel.net/haber/38120/trtdeki-siyasi-kadrolasma-meclis-gundeminde.

TRT Journalism for Juniors. (@jforjuniors). "J4J educates students on how they can be journalists with only a phone #journalism #journalists #photography #mobilejournalism #inspiring." *X*, July 22, 2022. https://twitter.com/jforjuniors/status/1550408588165775360?s=20.

TRT Journalism for Juniors. (@jforjuniors). "J4J teaches youths how to do journalism with a "human first" mentality. #journalism # journalists #mobilejournalism." *X*, July 21, 2022. https://twitter.com/jforjuniors/status/1550177884970663937?s=20.

TRT Originals Urdu. (@TRTOriginals_Urdu). "Let's get [Pakistan] the world record for most new subscribers in 1 month on YouTube." *X*, May 8, 2020. https://twitter.com/TRTErtugrulPTV/status/1258819302981074951.

"TRT Türk Dünyasına Avaz Avaz Seslenecek" [TRT will call out to Turkic world]. *Hurriyet* (Istanbul), March 22, 2009. http://www.hurriyet.com.tr/gundem/trt-turk-dunyasina-avaz-avaz-seslenecek-11263045.

TRT World. (@trtworld). "It's Our Duty to Re-Establish the Professional and Moral Principles of the Press. Türkiye's Communications Director, Fahrettin Altun, said on combatting the negative effects of digitalisation at the International Media Information Association's awards ceremony in Ankara." *X*, May 8, 2020. https://twitter.com/trtworld/status/1536699979548565505?s=20&t=MnmWVjwpjlzdd5ziBy8iSg.

TRT World. "Beaten by the Border: Croatia." *YouTube*, July 25, 2019. https://www.youtube.com/watch?v=w4JY8Xn-PWA.

TRT World. "Did Europe Turn Its Back on Syria?" *YouTube*, March 15, 2018. https://www.youtube.com/watch?v=5rQzLTpi_NY.

TRT World. "Focal Point: Transit Film." *YouTube*, April 26, 2018. https://www.youtube.com/watch?v=ToWh4J7VRys.

TRT World. "Hopes Denied: An Aegean Tragedy." *YouTube*, February 7, 2021. https://www.youtube.com/watch?v=7uXvAizg5cY.

TRT World. "Hotels." *TRT World*, 2023. https://www.trtworld.com/hotels.

TRT World. Network: Uncovering Facts behind Attempted Coup in Turkey." *YouTube*, July 18, 2019. https://www.youtube.com/watch?v=w4JY8Xn-PWA.

TRT World. "Turkey's Soft Power Goes Global." *YouTube*, November 28, 2020. https://www.youtube.com/watch?v=uYkGJ4NG1k4.

TRT World. "What Is a Refugee's Worth in the EU?" *YouTube*, July 31, 2018. https://www.youtube.com/watch?v=IvXjCFHO77M.

TRT World. "What Western Media Gets Wrong about Türkiye's Elections." *YouTube*, May 28, 2023. https://www.youtube.com/watch?v=XeGOcJXjadc.

TRT World Citizen. (@TRTWorldCitizen). "Field production on smart devices is the most popular #J4J workshop amongst students." *X*, July 9, 2019. https://twitter.com/TRTWorldCitizen/status/1148577546906112000?s=20&t=SvCsn39EWmjxNFNsY73×4Q.

TRT World Citizen. (@TRTWorldCitizen). "Journalism for Juniors (J4J) is a movement, not just a program." *X*, July 30, 2019. https://twitter.com/TRTWorldCitizen/status/1156164894955364354?s=20&t=GtuMW8B_eWaKdW0Iq2hgNA.

TRT World Citizen. "Hello Brother." *TRT World Citizen*, 2022. https://worldcitizen.trtworld.com/hello-brother/.

TRT World Citizen. "Journalism for Juniors." *TRT World Citizen*, 2023. https://worldcitizen.trtworld.com/journalism-for-juniors/.

TRT World Citizen. "Who We Are." *TRT World Citizen*, 2023. https://worldcitizen.trtworld.com/who-we-are/.

"TRT World'den Gorkemli Acilis" [TRT World's spectacular launch]. *TRT Haber*, November 23, 2016. https://www.trthaber.com/haber/yasam/trt-worldden-gorkemli-acilis-284284.html.

TRT World Forum. @trtworldforum. "As part of a week-long series to mark the fourth anniversary of the #July15 coup attempt, #DigitalDebates hosted sessions discussing measures taken by Turkey's government." *X*, July 21, 2020. https://twitter.com/trt0worldforum/status/1285472565004308481?s=20&t=ed_CYrppANjtH_ThUWiJ6Q.

TRT World Forum. "Setting an Example: Turkey's Humanitarian Role." July 10, 2019. https://www.trtworldforum.com/workshop/setting-an-example-turkeys-humanitarian-role/.
TRT World Forum. "Western Mainstream Media and Coverage of the Muslim World." October 4, 2018. https://www.trtworldforum.com/workshop/western-mainstream-media-and-coverage-of-the-muslim-world/.
TRT World Research Centre. *Am I Not a Child? The Neglect of Child Refugees in Europe*. January 30, 2018. https://researchcentre.trtworld.com/policy-papers/am-i-not-a-child-the-neglect-of-child-refugees-in-europe/.
TRT World Research Centre. *Dignity without Borders*. March 4, 2020. https://researchcentre.trtworld.com/policy-papers/dignity-without-borders/.
TRT World Research Centre. "History and Memory: TRT World in the Face of July 15 Coup." July 16, 2019. https://researchcentre.trtworld.com/books/history-and-memory-trt-world-in-the-face-of-july-15-coup/.
TRT World Research Centre. "The Impact of the July 15th Coup Attempt on Turkish State and Society." January 12, 2018. https://researchcentre.trtworld.com/wp-content/uploads/2021/03/The-Impact-of-the-July-15th-Coup-Attempt-on-Turkish-State-and-Society.pdf.
TRT World Research Centre. *Women of War*. December 10, 2018. https://researchcentre.trtworld.com/policy-papers/women-of-war/.
"TRT World Sesini Duyuramayanlarin Sesi Olmak Uzere Kuruldu" [TRT World was founded to be the voice of the voiceless]. *TRT Haber*, October 18, 2017. https://www.trthaber.com/haber/gundem/trt-world-sesini-duyuramayanlarin-sesi-olmak-uzere-kuruldu-338410.html.
"TRT World Test Yayinina Gecti" [TRT World started test broadcasts]. *TRT Haber*, May 18, 2015. https://www.trthaber.com/haber/medya/trt-world-test-yayinina-gecti-185371.html.
"TRT World Turkiye'nin Mesajini Dunyaya Iletecek" [TRT World will disseminate Turkey's message to the world]. *HaberTurk*, May 18, 2015. https://www.haberturk.com/gundem/haber/1080082-trt-world-turkiyenin-mesajini-dunyaya-iletecek.
Tuğal, Cihan. *Passive Revolution: Absorbing the Islamic Challenge to Capitalism*. Stanford, CA: Stanford University Press, 2009.
Tuğal, Cihan. "Towards the End of a Dream? The Erdogan-Gulen Fallout and Islamic Liberalism's Descent." *Jadaliyya*, December 22, 2013. https://www.jadaliyya.com/Details/29981.
Tuncer, Anil Can. "'Asrın Felaketi' Propagandası Hükümetin Elinde Kaldı" [Government failed in its 'disaster of the century' propaganda]. *Diken* (Istanbul), February 13, 2023. https://www.diken.com.tr/asrin-felaketi-propagandasi-iktidarin-elinde-kaldi/.
Tunstall, Jeremy. *The Media Were American*. New York: Oxford University Press, 2008.
Türk, Hikmet Sami. "Anadolu Ajansı Sorunu ve Cozum Yollari" [Anadolu Agency problems and solutions]. *Ankara Universitesi Hukuk Fakultesi Dergisi* 34 (1977): 61–86.
"Turkey Aims to Create 'Local and National' Versions of Tech Giants." *Duvar English* (Istanbul), March 1, 2021. https://www.duvarenglish.com/turkey-aims-to-create-local-and-national-versions-of-tech-giants-news-56447.

"Turkey Introduces App to Combat Online 'Disinformation' In Wake of Major Earthquake." *Turkish Minute* (Istanbul), February 7, 2023. https://www.turkishminute.com/2023/02/07/turkey-introduce-app-to-combat-online-disinformation-in-wake-of-major-earthquake/.

"Turkey Ranks Second in TV Drama Export." *Hurriyet Daily News* (Istanbul), September 30, 2017. https://www.hurriyetdailynews.com/.

"Turkey's Altun Slams DW's 'Fake News' on Ambassadors Crisis." *Daily Sabah* (Istanbul), October 26, 2021. https://www.dailysabah.com/politics/diplomacy/turkeys-altun-slams-dws-fake-news-on-ambassadors-crisis.

"Turkey's Erdogan Calls CNN Reporter 'Agent' for His Coverage of Protests." *Reuters*, June 3, 2014. https://www.reuters.com/article/ us-turkey-cnn/turkeys-erdogan-calls-cnn-reporter-agent-for-his-coverage-of-protests-idUSKBN0EE1J820140603.

"Turkey's Erdogan Invokes Holocaust to Condemn French Crackdown on Radical Islam." *Times of Israel*, October 26, 2020. https://www.timesofisrael.com/turkeys-erdogan-invokes-holocaust-to-condemn-french-crackdown-on-radical-islam/.

"Turkey's Erdogan Tightens His Grip." *Bloomberg Business Week*, April 3, 2014. https://www.bloomberg.com/news/articles/2014-04-03/turkeys-autocratic-leader-reverses-past-democratic-gains.

"Turkey's Fahrettin Altun Blasts International Media for Spreading Fake News." *TRT World*, October 8, 2021. https://www.trtworld.com/magazine/turkey-s-fahrettin-altun-blasts-international-media-for-spreading-fake-news-50590.

"Turkey Slams 'Propaganda Machine' Twitter over Removal of Accounts." *Reuters*, June 12, 2020. https://www.reuters.com/article/china-twitter-disinformation-turkey/turkey-slamspropaganda-machine-twitter-over-removal-of-accounts-idUSL8N2DP2V1.

"Turkey Slaps Advertising Ban on Twitter with New Social Media Law." *Al Jazeera*, January 19, 2021. https://www.aljazeera.com/news/2021/1/19/turkey-slaps-advertising-ban-on-twitter-with-new-social-media-law.

"Turkey's President Erdogan Opens Cambridge 'Eco-mosque.'" *BBC*, December 5, 2019. https://www.bbc.com/news/uk-england-cambridgeshire-50666385.

"Turkey's TIKA Starts 2022 with Nearly 50 New Projects in Pakistan." *Daily Sabah* (Istanbul), January 23, 2022. https://www.dailysabah.com/turkey/turkeys-tika-starts-2022-with-nearly-50-new-projects-in-pakistan/news.

"Turkey to Launch Domestic Google, Gmail Replacements Aligned with Local Culture and Values." *Turkey Blocks*, January 6, 2017. https://turkeyblocks.org/2017/01/06/turkey-building-domestic-search-engine-and-email/.

"Turkey to Prepare Reports on Islamophobia, Racism in the West." *Daily Sabah* (Istanbul), February 2, 2021. https://www.dailysabah.com/politics/diplomacy/turkey-to-prepare reports-on-islamophobia-racism-in-west.

"Turkic-Speaking States to Set Up Joint Media Association." *Daily Sabah* (Istanbul), December 20, 2021. https://www.dailysabah.com/politics/diplomacy/turkic-speaking-states-to-set-up-joint-media-association.

"Turkish Cultural Centre to Be Established in Karachi." *Anadolu Agency*, June 7, 2022. https://tribune.com.pk/story/2360320/turkish-cultural-centre-to-be-established-in-karachi.

"Turkish Day." Flier. Awqaf South Africa, July 2019. In possession of the author.

"Turkish Dramas Play Key Role in 'Soft Power' Says Minister." *Anadolu Agency*, June 12, 2014. https://www.aa.com.tr/en/turkey/turkish-dramas-play-key-role-in-soft-power-says-minister/151723.

"Turkish History-Themed Series Diriliş Ertuğrul Enjoyed in 60 Countries." *Daily Sabah* (Istanbul), March 15, 2017. https://www.dailysabah.com/cinema/2017/03/15/turkish-history-themed-series-dirilis-ertugrul-enjoyed-in-60-countries.

"Turkish Language Courses Flourish in Uganda, Pakistan." *Daily Sabah* (Istanbul), May 12, 2022. https://www.dailysabah.com/turkey/education/turkish-language-courses-flourish-in-uganda-pakistan.

"Turkish Lawmakers Adopt New Disinformation Law." *Voice of America*, October 14, 2022. https://www.voanews.com/a/turkish-lawmakers-adopt-new-disinformation-law-/6790659.html.

"Turkish Parliament Passes 'Disinformation Law' Tightening Control on Internet Media." *Duvar English* (Istanbul), October 14, 2022. https://www.duvarenglish.com/turkish parliament-passes-disinformation-law-tightening-control-on-internet-media-news-61433.

"Turkish State Broadcaster Kicks off Recruitment Drive in Pakistan." *Express Tribune*, November 10, 2015. https://tribune.com.pk/story/988699/turkish-state-broadcaster-kicks-off-recruitment-drive-in-pakistan.

"Turkish TV Series Continue to Grow in Popularity in Ethiopia." *Daily Sabah* (Istanbul), February 7, 2017. https://www.dailysabah.com/arts-culture/2017/02/07/turkish-tv-series-continue-to-grow-in-popularity-in-ethiopia.

"Türkiye-Africa Media Summit to 'Strengthen Our Friendship,' Altun." *TRT World*, May 25, 2022. https://www.trtworld.com/turkey/t%C3%BCrkiye-africa-media-summit-to-strengthen-our-friendship-altun-57423.

"Türkiye Challenges Imperialism, Erdoğan Says." *Hurriyet Daily News* (Istanbul), April 18, 2023. https://www.hurriyetdailynews.com/turkiye-challenges-imperialism-erdogan-says-182484.

Türkiye Cumhuriyeti İletişim Başkanlığı [Republic of Türkiye Directorate of Communications]. "Altun Speaks at The International Strategic Communications Summit." *Republic of Türkiye*, December 2, 2022. https://www.iletisim.gov.tr/turkce/haberler/detay/director-of-communications-altun-speaks-at-the-international-strategic-communications-summit.

Türkiye Cumhuriyeti İletişim Başkanlığı [Republic of Türkiye Directorate of Communications]. "Altun: Today, Our Duty Is to Strengthen Our Joint Channels of Information Creation and Dissemination in the Face of Digital Fascism, Cyber Imperialism, and the Global Fake News Industry." *Republic of Türkiye*, October 22, 2021. https://www.iletisim.gov.tr/turkce/haberler/detay/altun-today-our-duty-is-to-strengthen-our-joint-channels-of-information-creation-and-dissemination-in-the-face-of-digital-fascism-cyber-imperialism-and-the-global-fake-news-industry.

Türkiye Cumhuriyeti İletişim Başkanlığı [Republic of Türkiye Directorate of Communications]. "Biography." *Republic of Türkiye*, 2019. https://www.iletisim.gov.tr/english/baskan.

Türkiye Cumhuriyeti İletişim Başkanlığı [Republic of Türkiye Directorate of Communications]. "Director of Communications Altun: A Full-Fledged Fight against Disinformation Requires Short-, Mid-, and Long-Term Strategic Planning." *Republic of Türkiye*, September 10, 2019. https://www.iletisim.gov.tr/english/haberler/detay/director-of-communications-altun-a-full-fledged-fight-against-disinformation-requires-a-short-mid-and-long-term-strategic-planning.

Türkiye Cumhuriyeti İletişim Başkanlığı [Republic of Türkiye Directorate of Communications]. "Director of Communications Altun: Increase in Tendency towards National Platforms such as BiP and Yaay in the Face of Double Standards on Personal Data Is a Positive Development." *Republic of Türkiye*, January 19, 2019. https://www.iletisim.gov.tr/english/haberler/detay/director-of-communications-altun-increase-in-tendency-towards-national-platforms-such-as-bip-and-yaay-in-the-face-of-double-standards-on-personal-data-is-a-positive-development/.

Türkiye Cumhuriyeti İletişim Başkanlığı [Republic of Türkiye Directorate of Communications]. "Director of Communications Altun: Our Main Goal Is to Build "Türkiye's Communication Model." *Republic of Türkiye*, December 26, 2021. https://www.iletisim.gov.tr/english/haberler/detay/director-of-communications-altun-our-main-goal-is-to-build-turkiyes-communication-model.

Türkiye Cumhuriyeti İletişim Başkanlığı [Republic of Türkiye Directorate of Communications]. "Director of Communications Altun: The Struggle for Truth Is a Form of Resistance and the Rebirth of the Nation." *Republic of Türkiye*, May 11, 2023. https://www.iletisim.gov.tr/turkce/haberler/detay/director-of-communications-altun-the-struggle-for-truth-is-a-form-of-resistance-and-the-rebirth-of-the-nation.

Türkiye Cumhuriyeti İletişim Başkanlığı [Republic of Türkiye Directorate of Communications]. "Director of Communications Altun: We Are Going through a Time When Communication Has Rather a Primary Character." *Republic of Türkiye*, February 9, 2021. https://www.iletisim.gov.tr/turkce/haberler/detay/director-of-communications-altun-we-are-going-through-a-time-when-communication-has-rather-a-primary-character-than-an-auxiliary-one.

Türkiye Cumhuriyeti İletişim Başkanlığı [Republic of Türkiye Directorate of Communications]. "Director of Communications Altun: We Will Continue to Advocate for Palestine on Every International Platform." *Republic of Türkiye*, May 21, 2021. https://www.iletisim.gov.tr/turkce/haberler/detay/director-of-communications-altun-we-will-continue-to-advocate-for-palestine-on-every-international-platform.

Türkiye Cumhuriyeti İletişim Başkanlığı [Republic of Türkiye Directorate of Communications]. "Directorate of Communications Publishes Book Titled 'Cultural Diplomacy and Communication as Türkiye's Soft Power Instrument.'" *Republic of Türkiye*, April 16, 2022. https://www.iletisim.gov.tr/english/haberler/detay/directorate-of-communications-publishes-book-titled-cultural-diplomacy-and-communication-as-turkiyes-soft-power-instrument.

Türkiye Cumhuriyeti İletişim Başkanlığı [Republic of Türkiye Directorate of Communications]. "Director's Message." 2019. https://www.iletisim.gov.tr/english/baskanin-mesaji.

Türkiye Cumhuriyeti İletişim Başkanlığı [Republic of Türkiye Directorate of Communications]. "President Erdoğan Sends Video Message to the Stratcom Summit." *Republic of Türkiye*, December 11, 2021. https://www.iletisim.gov.tr/english/haberler/detay/president-erdogan-sends-video-message-to-the-stratcom-summit.

Türkiye Cumhuriyeti İletişim Başkanlığı [Republic of Türkiye Directorate of Communications]. "President Erdoğan's Message on the Anniversary of the Adoption of the National Anthem." *Republic of Türkiye*, March 12, 2022. https://www.iletisim.gov.tr/turkce/haberler/detay/president-erdogans-message-on-the-anniversary-of-the-adoption-of-the-national-anthem.

Türkiye Cumhuriyeti İletişim Başkanlığı [Republic of Türkiye Directorate of Communications]. "Stratcom Summit '21 by Presidency's Directorate of Communications Kicks Off." *Republic of Türkiye*, December 11, 2021. https://www.iletisim.gov.tr/english/haberler/detay/stratcom-summit-21-by-presidencys-directorate-of-communications-kicks-off.

Türkiye Cumhuriyeti İletişim Başkanlığı [Republic of Türkiye Directorate of Communications]. "Turkey Is the Biggest Opportunity for Western Countries in the Fight against Xenophobia, Islamophobia, Cultural Racism, and Extremism." *Republic of Türkiye*, October 6, 2020. https://www.iletisim.gov.tr/english/haberler/detay/turkey-is-the-biggest-opportunity-for-western-countries-in-the-fight-against-xenophobia-islamophobia-cultural-racism-and-extremism

Türkiye Cumhuriyeti İletişim Başkanlığı [Republic of Türkiye Directorate of Communications]. "Türkiye-Africa Media Summit Kicks Off." *Republic of Türkiye*, May 25, 2022. https://www.iletisim.gov.tr/english/haberler/detay/turkiye-africa-media-summit-kicks-off.

Türkiye Cumhuriyeti Kültür ve Turizm Bakanlığı, Türk İşbirliği ve Koordinasyon Ajansı Başkanlığı (TİKA) [Republic of Türkiye, Ministry of Culture and Tourism, Turkish Cooperation and Coordination Agency]. "TİKA'dan Afganistan'daki Yerel Televizyon Kanalına Destek" [TIKA support to local television channel in Afghanistan]. 2020. https://www.tika.gov.tr/tr/haber/tika_dan_afganistan_daki_yerel_televizyon_kan lina_de stek-58027.

Türkiye Cumhuriyeti Milli Savunma Bakanlığı [Republic of Türkiye Ministry of National Defense. (@tcsavunma). "Cumhurbaşkanlığı @iletisim Başkanlığı tarafından İstanbul'da düzenlenen 'Uluslararası Stratejik İletişim Zirvesi-21' de Türk Silahlı Kuvvetlerimizin DEAŞ terör örgütü ile mücadelesini anlatıyoruz" [We are making a presentation about the fight of our Turkish Armed Forces against the DAESH terrorist organization at the "International Strategic Communication Summit-21" organized by the Presidency @communications Directorate in Istanbul]. *X*, December 12, 2021 https://twitter.com/tcsavunma/status/1470040177854889987?s=20&t=YIYq-WupqMRkpABjKkcWHw.

Türkiye Cumhuriyeti Ulaştırma ve Altyapı Bakanlığı [Republic of Türkiye Ministry of Transportation and Infrastructure]. "Ulusal Siber Güvenlik Stratejisi ve Eylem Planı 2020–2023" [National Cyber Security Strategy and Action Plan]. *Türkiye Cumhuriyeti Ulaştırma ve Altyapı Bakanlığı*, 2020. https://hgm.uab.gov.tr/uploads/pages/strateji eylem planlari/ulusal-siber-guvenlik-stratisisi-ve-eylem-plani-2020-2023.pdf.

Türkiye Maarif Foundation. "Current Status Information." *Türkiye Maarif Foundation*, 2023. https://turkiyemaarif.org/dunyada-maarif.

Ünal, Ali. "TRT World CEO Ibrahim Eren: We Will Tell the Truth Even If It Is Inconvenient or Disturbing." *Daily Sabah* (Istanbul), November 21, 2016. https://www.dailysabah.com/turkey/2016/11/21/trt-world-ceo-ibrahim-eren-we-will-tell-the-truth-even-if-it-is-inconvenient-or-disturbing.

Üngör, Çağdaş. "China Is Playing by Turkey's Media Rules." *Carnegie Endowment for International Peace*, November 9, 2022. https://carnegieendowment.org/2022/11/09/china-is-playing-by-turkey-s-media-rules-pub-88368.

United Nations High Commissioner for Refugees (UNHCR). "Syria Regional Refugee Response: Turkey." *UNHCR*, January 14, 2022. https://data2.unhcr.org/en/situations/syria/location/113.

Ünver, Akın. *Fact-Checkers and Fact-Checking in Turkey*. EDAM-Ekonomi ve Dis Politikalar Arastirma Merkezi (Istanbul), 2020. https://edam.org.tr/wp-content/uploads/2020/06/FactCheckers-and-FactChecking-in-Turkey-H.-Ak%C4%B1n-%C3%9Cnver.pdf.

"US Government Should Stand with Minnesota People: Global Times Editorial." *Global Times*, May 29, 2020. https://www.globaltimes.cn/content/1189972.shtml.

Uzer, Umut. "Glorification of the Past as a Political Tool: Ottoman History in Contemporary Turkish Politics." *Journal of the Middle East and Africa* 9, no. 4 (2018): 339–57.

Uzer, Umut. "Turkey's Islamist Movement and the Palestinian Cause: The 1980 'Liberation of Jerusalem' Demonstration and the 1997 'Jerusalem Night' as Case Studies." *Israel Affairs* 23, no. 1 (2017): 22–39.

Van Herpen, Marcel H. *Putin's Propaganda Machine: Soft Power and Russian Foreign Policy*. London: Rowman and Littlefield, 2015.

Verbeek, Bertjan, and Andrej Zaslove. "Populism and Foreign Policy." In *The Oxford Handbook of Populism*, edited by Cristóbal Rovira Kaltwasser et al., 384–405. Oxford: Oxford University Press.

Verovšek, Peter J. "Collective Memory, Politics, and the Influence of the Past: The Politics of Memory as a Research Paradigm," *Politics, Groups, and Identities* 4, no. 3, (2016): 529–43.

Vivarelli, Nick. "Turkey Experiences Its Own Wave of Peak TV." *Variety*, April 8, 2018. https://variety.com/2018/tv/features/turkey-experiences-its-own-wave-of-peak-tv-1202746009/.

Voci, Paola, and Luo Hui. *Screening China's Soft Power*. London: Routledge, 2017.

Voices of July 15. (@voicesofjuly15). "Declaration of the July 15 #TurkishCoup Attempt #TurkeyFailedCoup." X, July 24, 2016. https://twitter.com/voicesofjuly15/status/756967480032129024?s=20&t=8-w6dmwV6w1gL8r0OgSNAw.

Voices of July 15. "Example of the Western media covering the #coupattempt in #Turkey. You do the math @Independent #MEDIAHYPOCRISY." X, August 2, 2016. https://twitter.com/voicesofjuly15/status/760505571195887617?s=20&t=8-w6dmwV6w1gL8r0OgSNAw.

Voices of July 15. "It all started with a bullet from a coup plotter's gun, yet it's going on through a media coup! #mediacoup #turkey." X, July 25, 2016. https://twitter.com/voicesofjuly15/status/757676053213085696?s=20&t=8-w6dmwV6w1gL8r0OgSNAw.

Volkmer, Ingrid. *The Global Public Sphere: Public Communication in the Age of Reflective Interdependence*. Cambridge: Polity, 2014.

Vömel, Jan-Markus. "Pathos and Discipline. Islamist Masculinity in Turkey, 1950–2000." *Zeithistorische Forschungen—Studies in Contemporary History* 18, no. 3 (2022): 483–509.

Wagner, María Celeste, and Marwan M. Kraidy. "Watching Turkish Television Dramas in Argentina: Entangled Proximities and Resigned Agency in Global Media Flows." *Journal of Communication* 73, no. 4 (2023): 304–15.

Wang, Joseph. *Soft Power in China: Public Diplomacy through Communication*. New York: Palgrave Macmillan, 2011.

"Web Opening Panel: Presentation of the "European Islamophobia Report 2019." *SETA*, June 20, 2020. https://www.setav.org/en/events/web-opening-panel-presentation-of-the-european-islamophobia-report-2019/.

Westcott, Ben, and Isil Sariyuce. "Erdogan Says Xinjiang Camps Shouldn't Spoil Turkey-China Relationship." *CNN*, July 5, 2019. https://www.cnn.com/2019/07/05/asia/turkey-china-uyghur-erdogan-intl-hnk/index.html.

Whittock, Jesse. "Germany, France to Remake Turkish Drama, Netflix Buys Tape." *TBI Television Business International*, March 4, 2014. https://tbivision.com/2014/03/04/germany-france-to-remake-turkish-drama-netflix-buys tape/.

Whittock, Jesse. "NBC to Remake Turkish Drama." *TBI—Television Business International*, September 10, 2014. https://tbivision.com/2014/09/10/nbc-remake-turkish-drama.

Wilkins, Karin Gwinn. "Development and Modernization in the Middle East." In *Handbook of Media and Culture in the Middle East*, edited by Joe F. Khalil, Gholam Khiabany, Tourya Gouaaybess, and Bilge Yesil, 30–36. Hoboken, NJ: Wiley-Blackwell, 2023.

Windwehr, Svea, and Jillian York. "Turkey's New Internet Law Is the Worst Version of Germany's NetzDG Yet." *Electronic Frontier Foundation*, July 30, 2020. https://www.eff.org/deeplinks/2020/07/turkeys-new-internet-law-worst-version-germanys-netzdg-yet.

Winseck, Dwayne R., and Robert M. Pike. *Communication and Empire: Media, Markets, and Globalization, 1860–1930*. Durham, NC: Duke University Press, 2007.

"With Daily Sabah Ban, EP Falls into the Populist Trap." *Daily Sabah* (Istanbul), March 24, 2017. https://www.dailysabah.com/editorial/2017/03/24/with-daily-sabah-ban-ep-falls-into-the-populist-trap.

Wodak, Ruth. "The Discourse-Historical Approach." In *Methods of Critical Discourse Analysis*, edited by Ruth Wodak and Michael Meyer, 63–94. London: Sage, 2001.

Wodak, Ruth. "Politics as Usual: Investigating Political Discourse in Action." In *The Routledge Handbook of Discourse Analysis*, edited by James Paul Gee and Michael Handford, 525–40. London: Routledge, 2012.

World Bank. "10 Years On, Turkey Continues Its Support for an Ever-Growing Number of Syrian Refugees." June 22, 2021. https://www.worldbank.org/en/news/feature/2021/06/22/10-years-on-turkey-continues-its-support-for-an-ever-growing-number-of-syrian-refugees.

Wright, Kate, Martin Scott, and Mel Bunce. "Soft Power, Hard News: How Journalists at State-Funded Transnational Media Legitimize Their Work." *International Journal of Press/Politics* 25, no. 4 (2020): 607–31.

"Xinhua Headlines: Outrage over Racism Combined with COVID-19 Woes Lead to Riots in U.S." *Xinhua*, June 1, 2020. http://www.xinhuanet.com/english/202006/01/c_139105667.htm.

Yabancı, Bilge. "Fuzzy Borders between Populism and Sacralized Politics: Mission, Leader, Community and Performance in 'New' Turkey." *Politics, Religion, & Ideology* 21, no. 1 (2020): 92–112.

Yabancı, Bilge. "Work for the Nation, Obey the State, Praise the Ummah: Turkey's Government-Oriented Youth Organizations in Cultivating a New Nation." *Ethnopolitics* 20, no. 4 (2021): 467–99.

Yablokov, Ilya. "Conspiracy Theories as a Russian Public Diplomacy Tool: The Case of Russia Today (RT)." *Politics* 35, nos. 3–4 (2015): 301–15.

Yablokov, Ilya, and Precious N. Chatterje-Doody. *Russia Today and Conspiracy Theories: People, Power, and Politics on RT*. London: Routledge, 2021.

Yanardağoğlu, Eylem, and Imad N. Karam. "The Fever That Hit Arab Satellite Television: Audience Perceptions of Turkish TV Series." *Identities* 20, no. 5 (2013): 561–79.

Yanatma, Servet. "Dominance, Collaboration, and Resistance: Developing the Idea of a National News Agency in the Ottoman Empire, 1854–1914." *Journalism* 23, no. 2 (2022): 569–85.

Yanık, Lerna. "Valley of the Wolves—Iraq: Anti-Geopolitics Alla Turca." *Middle East Journal of Culture and Communication* 2, no. 1 (2009): 153–70.

"Yayınlarımız Uluslararası Adaletsizliğe Karşı" [Our broadcasts are against international injustice]. *Milliyet* (Istanbul), February 7, 2019. https://www.milliyet.com.tr/gundem/yayinlarimiz-uluslararasi-adaletsizlige-karsi-2823694.

Yenigün, Halil Ibrahim. "The New Antinomies of the Islamic Movement in Post-Gezi Turkey: Islamism vs. Muslimism." *Turkish Studies* 18, no. 2 (2017): 229–50.

Yesil, Bilge. "Authoritarian Turn or Continuity? Governance of Media through Capture and Discipline in the AKP Era." *South European Society and Politics* 23, no. 2 (2018): 239–57.

Yesil, Bilge. *Media in New Turkey: The Origins of an Authoritarian Neoliberal State*. Urbana: University of Illinois Press, 2016.

Yesil, Bilge. "#TurkeyIsNotAChicken: How Pro-Government Netizens Explain the Coup Attempt to Western Audiences." *Middle East Journal of Culture and Communication* 12, no. 2 (2019): 166–84.

Yesil, Bilge, and Efe Kerem Sozeri. "Online Surveillance in Turkey: Legislation, Technology, and Citizen Involvement." *Surveillance & Society* 15, nos. 3–4 (2017): 543–49.

Yesil, Bilge, Efe Kerem Sozeri, and Emad Khazraee. *Turkey's Internet Policy after the Coup Attempt: The Emergence of a Distributed Network of Online Suppression and Surveillance*. Internet Policy Observatory, *University of Pennsylvania*, 2017. https://repository.upenn.edu/internetpolicyobservatory/22.

Yilmaz, Hakan. "Euroscepticism in Turkey: Parties, Elites, and Public Opinion." *South European Society and Politics* 16 (2011): 185–208.

Yilmaz, Zafer. "The AKP and the Spirit of the 'New' Turkey: Imagined Victim, Reactionary Mood, and Resentful Sovereign." *Turkish Studies* 18, no. 3 (2017): 482–513.

Yörük, Zafer, and Pantelis Vatikiotis. "Soft Power or Illusion of Hegemony: The Case of the Turkish Soap Opera 'Colonialism.'" *International Journal of Communication* 7 (2013): 2361–85.

Yorulmaz, Ilgın. "Turkish Dramas Are Rewriting the Global Entertainment Script." *Nikkei Asia*, June 13, 2021. https://asia.nikkei.com/Life-Arts/Arts/Turkish-dramas-are-rewriting-the-global-entertainment-script.

Youmans, William L. *An Unlikely Audience: Al Jazeera's Struggle in America*. Oxford: Oxford University Press, 2017.

"YTB, AA ve TRT Ortaklığıyla Düzenlenen Afrika Medya Temsilcileri Eğitim Programı'nın Üçüncüsü 21 Kasım'da Başlayacak" [The third African media representatives training program organized in partnership with YTB, AA and TRT kicks off on November 21]. *Merhaba Afrika*, November 10, 2022. https://merhabaafrika.com/ytb-aa-ve-trt-ortakligiyla-duzenlenen-afrika-medya-temsilcileri-egitim-programinin-ucuncusu-21-kasimda-baslayacak/.

Yücetürk, Elif. "Tanzimat'tan Cumhuriyet'e Haberleşme: Mültezimlerden Konsorsiyumlara" [Communication from the Tanzimat era to the Republic: From taxmen to consortia]. *Istanbul Universitesi Siyasal Bilgiler Fakultesi Dergisi* 23–24 (2000): 289–302.

Yunus Emre Institute. "Why Yunus Emre." 2020. https://www.yee.org.tr/en/corporate/why-yunus-emre.

Zarakol, Ayşe. *After Defeat: How the East Learned to Live with the West*. Cambridge: Cambridge University Press, 2011.

Zarifoğlu, Ahmet. "Afrika Medya Temsilcileri İstanbul'a geldi, GZT Kesintisiz Muhabbeti 4 Dakikaya Sığdırdı!" [Africa media representatives came to Istanbul, GZT condensed the uninterrupted conversation into 4 minutes]. *GZT* (Istanbul), November 13, 2019. https://www.gzt.com/video/jurnalist/afrika-medya-temsilcileri-istanbula-geldi-gzt-kesintisiz-muhabbeti-4-dakikaya-sigdirdi-2183844.

Zayani, Mohamed. *Al Jazeera Phenomenon: Critical Perspectives on New Arab Media*. New York: Routledge, 2019.

Zayani, Mohamed. "Al Jazeera's Complex Legacy: Thresholds for an Unconventional Media Player from the Global South." *International Journal of Communication* 10 (2016): 3554–69.

Zhang, Xiaoling, Herman Wasserman, and Winston Mano. *China's Media and Soft Power in Africa: Promotion and Perceptions*. New York: Palgrave Macmillan, 2016.

Zhang, Yinxian, Jiajun Liu, and Ji-Rong Wen. "Nationalism on Weibo: Towards a Multifaceted Understanding of Chinese Nationalism." *China Quarterly* 235 (2018): 758–83.

Zhu, Ying, Kingsley Edney, and Stanley Rosen. *Soft Power with Chinese Characteristics: China's Campaign for Hearts and Minds*. London: Routledge, 2020.

Zúquete, José Pedro. "The Missionary Politics of Hugo Chávez." *Latin American Politics and Society* 50, no. 1 (2008): 91–121.

Zúquete, José Pedro. "On Top of the Volcano: Missionary Politics in the Twenty-first Century." *Politics, Religion, & Ideology* 14, no. 4 (2013): 507–21.

Index

Abdülhamid II, 45, 46, 119, 124, 125, 155n5, 159n113, 159n115
AFAD (Disaster and Emergency Management Presidency), 18, 74, 75, 163n74
Africa: and development communication, 66; Gülenists in, 64, 163n81; humanitarian aid for, 19, 83; reception of Turkish television series in, 115; and Turkey's development communication, 12, 58, 60, 61, 62, 63, 64, 67, 131; and Turkey's foreign policy, 60, 61, 64, 71, 72, 73, 74, 93, 113, 124, 125, 126; and Turkey's global communication, 14, 32, 60, 115, 147, 162n68
Africa Media Representatives Training Program (AFMED), 63, 64
AKP (Justice and Development Party): communication policy of, 18, 37, 48, 49, 50, 51, 54, 58, 68, 69; and coup attempt, 38–39, 40; and EU membership, 13, 22, 153n49, 165n7; foreign policy of (*see* Turkey's foreign policy); founding of, 21–22; and Gülen, 27–28, 29, 30, 34; loyalists, 2, 7, 16, 30, 34, 35, 119, 125, 137, 143, 144; in power, 22–23; trolls working for, 37, 40, 157n61; and the West, 19, 92–93, 99, 103, 106–10, 111, 112, 137–38
AK trolls, 37, 40, 157n61
Albayrak, Berat, 16, 29, 30, 36, 157n61
Albayrak, Serhat, 16, 29, 30, 35, 58
Al Jazeera, 5, 9, 17, 33, 35, 145

Al Jazeera English, 9, 31, 144, 146
Altun, Fahrettin, 15, 16, 43, 47, 48, 49, 50, 52, 57, 61, 77, 139
Anadolu Agency (AA), 2, 7, 16, 18, 75, 126, 137, 143, 144; autonomy of, 12, 17; and counter-hegemony, 48, 139; and coup attempt, 39, 40; executives, 30, 45, 65, 70, 77, 101, 139; history and expansion of, 11–12; and international collaborations, 64–65; and Islamophobia, 70; journalism training programs, 48, 58, 62, 63, 69; publications, 162n71
Anadolu Agency News Academy, 62–63
A News, 2, 16, 17, 156n20
anti-Westernism. *See* Turkey's global communication: criticism of the West in; West, and threat source; West: criticism of, during Ottoman Empire; West: Turkey's criticism of
ATV, 30, 35, 119, 120

Balkans: Gülenists in, 64, 163n81; humanitarian aid for, 19, 83; and Ottoman Empire, 45, 91, 107, 126; reception of Turkish television series in, 115, 132, 133; and refugee crisis, 96, 98; and Turkey's development communication, 12, 58, 60, 61, 62, 63, 64, 67, 131; and Turkey's foreign policy, 23, 60, 61, 64, 71, 72, 73, 74, 93, 113, 124, 125, 126; and Turkey's global communication, 12, 13, 14, 32, 60, 115, 147, 162n68 binary oppositions: and Turkey's global communication, 3, 24, 81, 87, 98, 114, 124, 129, 130, 133, 134, 138, 142. *See also* strategic obfuscation

Bosphorus Global, 2, 7, 28, 42, 84, 137, 157n66; and criticism of the West, 103–4; and Fact-Checking Turkey, 37; founding of, 16, 36; political economic structure of, 36; role in influence operations, 37; social media activities of, 36–37, 103

Bozdağ, Mehmet, 117, 118, 119

BRICS (Brazil, Russia, India, China, and South Africa), 56

BBC (British Broadcasting Corporation), 8, 10, 17, 27, 34, 42, 45, 147

Center for Islam and Global Affairs (CIGA), 165n6

Central Asia: and development communication, 66; Gülenists in, 163n81; and Turkey's development communication, 12, 58, 60, 61, 62, 63, 64, 65, 67, 131; and Turkey's foreign policy, 12, 23, 27, 60, 61, 64, 71, 72, 73, 74, 93, 125, 147, 163n81, 165n7; and Turkey's global communication, 12, 13, 14, 32, 60, 99, 115, 147, 162n68. *See also* Organization of Turkic States (OTS)

CGTN. *See* China Global Television Network

Chakrabarty, Dipesh, 140

China, 4, 49, 72, 76, 87, 88, 95; and development communication, 66, 67; and digital sovereignty, 55–57; and global communication, 8, 9, 10, 106, 143, 146, 147; and legitimation strategies, 49–50, 55, 57, 66; and Turkey, 42, 55, 57, 58, 87, 88, 89, 142

China Daily, 9, 10, 83

China Global Television Network (CGTN), 7, 10, 32, 35, 145, 146

China Radio International (CRI), 10, 42, 57, 58

Christchurch mosque attack, 76, 78, 80, 82

civilization/s: alliance of, 111; clash of, 25, 110–11, 134; Turkish Muslim, 107–10, 123, 128, 133; Western, 92, 108–10, 128. *See also* civilizationism; Huntington, Samuel

civilizationism, 92, 107–11, 125, 134, 138, 142, 147, 169n6, 172n83

conspiracy theories: about coup attempt, 40, 158n77; about Gezi Park protests, 15, 27, 123; about Ottoman Empire and Jews, 123, 129, 155n5; about Turkey and Jews, 123, 155n5; about Turkey and the West, 27, 158n77; about Western media, 27, 42–43, 45, 50, 139

counter-hegemony: and Al Jazeera, 5, 146; and Turkey, 1, 2, 3, 46, 67–68, 101, 138–42; and Turkey's global communication; 33, 48, 68, 101, 138, 139, 146; and Turkish television series, 133–35. *See also* NAM (Non-alignment Movement); NWICO (New World Information and Communication Order)

coup attempt, 38; AKP's response to, 38–39; role of Gülen in, 38, 40; and TRT World, 143, 144

Daily Sabah, 2, 7, 18, 24, 36, 43, 59, 60, 75, 106, 126, 137, 144, 147, 156n20; editorial policy of, 17, 30–31, 78; founding of, 28–29; and Islamophobia, 70, 71, 76, 77, 78, 79, 88; and refugee crisis, 98, 99, 100; political economic structure of, 16, 30

data localization, 55, 56, 59

Davutoğlu, Ahmet, 13; and civilizationism, 109–10, 111; and SETA, 109, 172n85; and Turkey's foreign policy, 13, 71, 72, 74, 75, 93, 105, 172n85

Deutsche Welle (DW), 8, 10, 42, 45, 54, 145

development communication, 65–67. *See also* journalism training programs; media assistance

digital sovereignty, 55–57

Directorate of Communications (DoC), 2, 7, 12, 18; activities of, 15, 48, 49, 59, 60, 61, 84, 137, 161n35, 162n71; Center for Fight against Disinformation, 161n35; founding of, 14–15. *See also* Altun, Fahrettin

disinformation, 10, 53, 58, 142; debates about, in the West, 50; instrumentalization of, 5, 31, 47, 48, 49, 50, 51, 68, 139; law, 51, 53; notification service, 161n35

Diyanet (Directorate of Religious Affairs), 23, 73–74, 75, 126

Erbakan, Necmettin, 20, 21

Erdoğan, Bilal, 30, 35, 119

Eren, İbrahim, 34, 35, 43, 143

Establishment: Osman (*Kuruluş: Osman*), 24–25; binary oppositions in, 133–35; and civilizationism, 133–35; and counter-hegemony, 133–35; and political communication, 123–25; plot of, 123; popularity of, 114, 122; production of, 119, 120; reception of, 127–31; representations of Muslims in, 127–28; representations of non-Muslims in, 130–31; and Turkey's foreign policy, 126;

Europe, 3, 5, 12, 50, 55, 62, 66, 73, 95, 121, 134, 140; and Ottoman Empire, 44–45, 46, 124; and refugee crisis, 82, 83, 96, 97, 98, 100, 168–69n5; and Turkey, 13, 15, 21, 22, 29, 31, 93, 94, 95, 96, 99, 108, 153n49, 165n7; and Turkey's global communication, 19, 32, 76, 78, 79, 81, 88, 92, 97, 98, 100, 101, 103, 104, 105, 137; shameful history of, 19, 52, 92, 104–5, 124

European Union (EU), 10, 24, 57, 59, 81, 82, 93, 95; membership of Turkey, 13, 22, 153n49, 165n7; and refugee crisis, 96, 100, 170n34; and Turkey, 15, 21, 31, 96, 165n7

Fact-Checking Turkey (FCT), 37, 38
Foreign Agents Registration Act (FARA), 35
freedom of speech, 48, 53, 55, 61
freedom of press, 31, 48

geopolitics: and global communication, 31, 33, 58, 87, 106, 124, 136, 137, 138
Gezi Park protests, 26, 93; and AK trolls, 36–37, 157n61; conspiracy theories about, 15, 27, 123, 155n5; and Turkey's global communication, 26, 28, 29, 30, 31, 36, 43, 146
global communication: and China, 8, 9, 10, 106, 143, 146, 147; and cultural framework, 5; and foreign policy, 4–5; and geopolitics, 31, 33, 58, 87, 106, 124, 136, 137, 138; and international relations framework, 4–5; and public diplomacy, 2, 4, 5, 35; and Russia, 5, 9, 10, 32, 79, 106, 143, 146, 147. *See also* Turkey's global communication
Global South, as term, 151n2; and development communication, 7, 48, 49, 67–69, 137; and humanitarian aid, 72, 74, 82, 93, 124, 125, 131; reception of Turkish television series in, 127–33; and Turkey's global communication, 1, 5, 33, 58, 61, 115, 124, 126, 137, 138, 142, 146

Gülen, Fethullah, 28, 40, 41, 94, 158n77; and Africa, 64, 163n81; as ally of Erdoğan, 27–28, 29, 30, 34; role of, in coup attempt, 38, 40; as terrorist mastermind, 40, 64
Gülenists, after the coup attempt, 38–39, 136; in Africa, 64, 163n81; in media, 29, 34; in state organs, 28–29; as terrorists, 40, 64, 94, 158n75; and TRT, 34; and TRT World, 34, 144

Huntington, Samuel, 25, 110–11, 134

imperialism: and AKP's foreign policy, 113, 124; Western, 5, 20, 28, 124, 125, 142. *See also* media imperialism
instrumentalization: of colonialism, 3, 7, 19, 52, 92, 104, 110, 124, 138; of disinformation, 5, 31, 47, 48, 49, 50, 51, 68, 139; of fact-checking, 37, 38; of fascism, 48, 52, 105; of history, 19, 52, 92, 104–5, 117–18, 120–21, 124, 125, 126; of the Holocaust, 19, 92, 104, 105; of Islamophobia, 3, 7, 19, 38, 76, 85–90, 104, 137–38, 142; of Nazism, 85, 92, 104, 105; of postcolonialism, 138–40; of post-truth, 5, 24, 49, 50, 59, 68; of refugee crisis, 7, 81, 83, 97, 98, 100, 101; of slavery, 19, 104; of social, racial justice issues in the West, 19, 38, 92, 101, 102, 103, 104, 106, 137; of Srebrenica massacre, 19, 76, 104, 105, 106; of victimhood, 71, 84–86
Iran, 10, 13, 21, 49, 50, 56, 57
Islamophobia: after September 11, 75, 81; as a Western problem, 24, 70, 76–77, 88, 101; definition and history of, 75–76; in Erdoğan's speeches, 70, 76, 84; instrumentalization of, 38, 76, 85–90, 104, 137–38, 142, in Turkey's global communication, 3, 19, 24, 38, 70–72, 76, 77–78, 80–82, 85, 86, 88, 104, 137–38, 142

journalism training programs: and China, 9, 66; and Turkey, 3, 7, 12, 24, 48, 49, 58, 61–64, 137, 163n84, and Western actors, 66

Index 227

justice: in Islam, 85, 129; social and racial, 92, 101, 102, 104, 128; Turkey advocating for, 2, 71, 76, 82, 84, 86, 138; in Turkey's global communication, 81, 124, 138, 139, 142; in Turkish Muslim civilization, 43, 108, 124, 134; in Turkish television series, 123–24, 127, 128, 134

Kalın, İbrahim: and civilizationism, 109–10; and Office of Public Diplomacy, 14; and SETA, 15, 109, 172n85; and Turkey's foreign policy, 93, 105, 172n85

Kandiyoti, Deniz, 140
Kaplan, Hilal, 16, 30, 36, 37
Karakoç, Sezai, 108, 109, 110, 111
Kısakürek, Necip Fazıl, 85, 108, 109, 110, 111, 117
Kurdish question: and AKP, 13, 22, 27, 28, 31, 39, 41, 42, 73, 89, 125, 126; and PKK, YPG, 17, 94, 154n61; and Turkey's global communication, 13, 28, 31, 51

The Last Emperor (*Payitaht: Abdulhamid*), 24–25, 114; binary oppositions in, 133–35; and civilizationism, 133–35; and counter-hegemony, 133–35; negative reception of, in the Balkans, 133; plot of, 124; and political communication, 123–25; popularity of, 122; production of, 114, 119, 120; reception of, 127–32; representations of Muslims in, 127–28; representations of non-Muslims in, 130–31; and Turkey's foreign policy, 126
Lerner, Daniel, 65

Magnificent Century, 115, 116, 117, 118, 121, 133, 174n14
media assistance: and China, 66; and Turkey, 48, 49, 58, 61–62, 67, 69; and Western actors, 65
media imperialism, 24, 43–46, 128, 138–39
memory politics, 120–21. *See also* instrumentalization: of history
Middle East: coverage of, 9, 44; and development communication, 66; Gülenists in, 64, 163n81; humanitarian aid for, 19, 83; and Ottoman Empire, 45, 91, 107, 126; reception of Turkish television series in, 115, 121, 132, 133; and refugee crisis, 95, 96, 98; and Turkey's development communication, 12, 58, 60, 61, 62, 63, 64, 67, 131; and Turkey's foreign policy, 1, 23, 27, 60, 61, 64, 71, 72, 73, 74, 93, 113, 124, 125, 126, 136, 141, 147, 153n49, 165n7; and Turkey's global communication, 12, 13, 14, 32, 60, 99, 115, 147, 162n68

Mignolo, Walter, 140
MTTB (National Union of Turkish Students), 21, 109
missionary politics, 84–86
moral frameworks (term), 92, 98, 99, 100, 102
Muslims: in Kashmir, 76, 80, 81, 82, 129; negative representations of, 44, 82, 127, 128, 130, 133, 134; as oppressed by the West, 1, 68, 81, 82–84, 86, 89, 138, 174n29; in Palestine, 23, 74, 129, 174n29; positive representations of, 127–28; Rohingya, 74, 76, 80, 82; Uighur, 76, 78, 87, 88, 89; as victims, 79, 82, 83, 84–87, 90–91, 100, 129, 142; targeted by Turkey's global communication (*see also* Islamophobia; *Resurrection: Ertuğrul*; *Establishment: Osman*; *The Last Emperor*)

NAM (Non-Aligned Movement), 67–68
nation branding, 153n49
neo-Ottomanism, 72–73
non-Western media, 8–11, 33, 57, 66, 106–7; outlets in Turkey, 42, 57–58. *See also* counter-hegemony
NWICO (New World Information and Communication Order), 67–68, 139

Occidentalism, 112, 172n99
Office of Public Diplomacy (OPD), 7, 14, 93, 95, 109, 136
Organization of Turkic States (OTS), 60
Orientalism, 26, 43–45, 75, 107, 111, 128, 140, 141
Ottoman Empire, 20, 43, 46, 85, 91, 107, 108, 111, 134; conspiracy theories about, 129, 155n5; and European press, 44–45, 139; and image management, 45; and news agency, 11, 45; in Turkish television series, 114, 116, 117, 119, 121, 123, 124, 125, 126, 128, 129; negative perceptions of, 131–33; Orientalist representations of, 45, 107; role of, in Turkey's foreign policy, 71–75, 109, 113

Palestine, 23, 74, 129, 174n29
Palestinian cause, 83, 88, 167–68n64
PKK (Kurdistan Workers' Party), 17, 22, 39, 41, 63, 64, 154n61
populism, 5, 82, 85
postcolonialism: and NAM (Non-Aligned Movement), 67; and NWICO (New World Information and Communication Order), 67, 139; Turkey's instrumentalization of, 138–40. *See also* Chakrabarty, Dipesh; Kandiyoti, Deniz; Mignolo, Walter; Said, Edward; Spivak, Gayatri; subalternity
post-truth, 5, 24, 49, 50, 59, 68, 142
propaganda, 4, 27, 29, 41, 48, 52, 61
public diplomacy, 4, 5, 15, 29, 35, 60, 94, 142. *See also* Office of Public Diplomacy (OPD)

Qatar, 4, 5, 6, 9, 10. *See also* Al Jazeera

refugee crisis, 83, 84, 92, 95–96, 168n5; and Europe, 96, 97, 98; and Turkey's global communication, 19, 32, 76, 78, 79, 81, 88, 92, 97, 98, 100, 101, 103, 104, 105, 113, 137, 170n34
Resurrection: Ertuğrul (*Diriliş: Ertuğrul*), 24–25; binary oppositions in, 133–35; and civilizationism, 133–35; and counter-hegemony, 133–35; government support for, 118–19, 121, 123; negative reception of, in the Middle East, 131–32; plot of, 117, 118; and political communication, 123–25; popularity of, 114, 117, 122; production of, 114, 117, 118, 120; reception of, 127–32; representations of Muslims in, 127–28; representations of non-Muslims in, 130–31
RT (Russia Today), 10, 32, 35, 79, 106, 146
RTUK (Radio and Television Supreme Council), 18, 54, 65, 69, 173n5
Russia: and digital sovereignty and, 55–57; and global communication, 5, 9, 10, 32, 79, 106, 143, 146, 147; and legitimation strategies, 49, 50, 51, 57; and Turkey, 53, 55, 57, 58, 142, 146

Said, Edward, 44, 111
September 11: and clash of civilizations, 111; and development communication, 66, 164n97; and Islamophobia, 75, 81; representations of Muslims after, 44, 127, 133
SETA (Foundation for Political, Economic, and Social Research), 2, 7; activities of, 15–16, 18, 59, 61, 63, 97, 106, 136, 137, 169–70n31; and Ahmet Davutoğlu, 109; founding of, 15; and İbrahim Kalın, 109; reports on international media, 42–43, 58; reports on Islamophobia, 24, 70, 71, 75, 81–82, 88, 89
Shanghai Cooperation Organization (SCO), 56, 161n47
social media: criticism of, companies, 47, 50, 51–52, 57, 61; legal pressures on, companies, 48, 51, 53–54; in Turkey's global communication, 2, 15, 16, 32, 36, 37, 39, 40, 82, 104, 158n81
soft power, 2, 4, 5, 93, 126, 132
Spivak, Gayatri, 140
Sputnik, 10, 35, 42, 57, 58, 106
Srebrenica massacre, 19, 76, 104, 105, 106
Stratcom (Strategic Communication) summits, 59–60
strategic narratives (term), 97
strategic obfuscation, 3, 23, 24, 81, 85, 87, 89, 142. *See also* binary oppositions
subalternity, 37, 140
Syrian refugees in Turkey, 17, 27, 63; humanitarian aid for, 169–70n31; media coverage of, 96, 97, 98, 99; racism toward, 96–97

Tabii, 14, 106, 119
"The world is bigger than five," 55, 83–84, 139
TIKA (Turkish Cooperation and Coordination Agency): and development communication, 58, 62, 63, 69, 137; founding and expansion of, 73; and Turkey's foreign policy, 73, 75, 126, 137, 163n81
Today's Zaman, 29
Topçu, Nurettin, 108, 109, 110, 111
TRT (Turkish Radio and Television Corporation): annual reports of, 32; autonomy of, 34–36, 157n46; executives, 35, 121, 126, 143, 145; Gülenists in TRT, 34; international channels, 12–14, 16, 30, 101; international news sites, 12–14; journalism training programs, 62, 63; streaming platform, 14, 119; television series, 114, 116, 117, 119, 120; YouTube channels of, 114, 122

Index 229

TRT Afrika, 2, 14, 147
TRT Arabi, 2, 13, 35, 136, 147
TRT Avaz, 13
TRT Avrasya, 12–13
TRT Balkan, 2, 14, 147
TRT Deutsch, 2, 14, 35, 102, 147
TRT Français, 2, 14, 139, 147
TRT INT, 12
TRT Journalism for Juniors (J4J), 62–63
TRT Kurdi, 2, 13, 136, 147
TRT Media Academy, 62
TRT Russian, 2, 14, 147
TRT World: after the coup attempt, 143, 144; and Al Jazeera, 17, 31, 33, 35, 146; autonomy of, 17, 34–36, 143; and BBC, 17, 34; and CGTN (China Global Television Network), 35, 146; and counter-hegemony, 33, 68, 101, 139; and *Daily Sabah*, 99–100, 144; documentaries, 32, 70, 71, 78, 80–81, 86, 88, 97, 100–101, 102, 106, 138; editorial policy of, 32, 78, 143–44; executives, 33, 34, 35, 36, 43, 51, 143, 145; and Foreign Agents Registration Act, 35; founding of, 31–32; guests on, 17, 100; and Gülen, 34, 144; hiring practices of, 31, 144–45; and Islamophobia, 70, 71, 75, 76, 78, 79, 80, 81; journalism training programs, 48, 62; and legitimization of AKP policies, 17, 18, 32, 137, 141; and promotion of Turkey, 19, 31, 32, 137, 146; and refugee crisis, 100, 101; and *Resurrection: Ertuğrul*, 122; and RT (Russia Today), 35, 146; and Turkey's foreign policy, 17, 32, 137; as public service broadcaster, 34, 99; personnel, 77–78, 143–45; programs, 31–32, 84, 99, 100, 102, 170n34; as "the voice of the voiceless," 32, 33; and the West, 19, 32, 97, 99, 141, 146; YouTube channel of, 78
TRT World Citizen, 62–63, 81, 82, 89
TRT World Forum, 63, 82, 97
TRT World Research Centre, 71, 81, 82, 97, 158n90
Turkey: as advocating for justice, 2, 3, 46, 71, 73, 83, 84, 133, 138, 142; as benevolent, 89, 96–97, 98, 106, 113, 123, 124, 134, 137–38; as guardian of Muslims, 71, 82–87, 88, 96, 113, 121, 125, 126, 132, 142, 145, 174n29; as model country, 89, 93, 136, 155n3; as rising/great power, 1, 2, 46, 71, 72, 84, 88, 93, 136, 138,

165n12; as superior to the West, 5, 25, 73, 87, 95, 98, 104, 106, 107, 111, 113, 115, 133, 134
Turkey's Communication Model, 47, 48, 60
Turkey's development communication, 3, 7, 12, 24, 48, 49, 58, 61–64, 67, 69, 137, 163n84. *See also* journalism training programs; media assistance
Turkey's foreign policy: and Africa, 1, 61–62, 64, 71, 72, 73, 93, 124, 125; and the Balkans, 1, 13, 61–62, 64, 71, 72, 73, 74, 93, 124, 125; and Central Asia, 1, 13, 61–62, 71, 72, 73, 74, 93, 125; challenges of, 104, 107; and China, 58, 87–88; and Europe, 31, 96, 97, 98, 165n7; as expansionist/irredentist, 3, 112, 113, 125, 141, 166n17; and humanitarian aid, 74, 142, 169n31; and Middle East, 1, 13, 61–62, 71, 72, 73, 124, 125; and Muslims, 2, 71–75, 82–84, 85–88, 121, 138; as neo-Ottomanist, 73; and populism, 86; role of Muslim identity in, 71–75; and Russia, 58; under Davutoğlu, 13, 71–72, 75, 109, 111; and US, 31, 94, 137, 165n7
Turkey's global communication: criticism of the West in, 17, 19, 33, 43–44, 76, 78, 80, 82, 84, 85, 92–95, 103, 106–8, 137–38; and foreign policy, 3, 13, 15, 17, 19, 31, 32, 61, 64, 106, 137, 138, 141; growth of, 11–16, 136, 141; objectives of, 3, 13, 15, 17, 19, 58–61, 87, 113, 126, 136–37, 141, 146; target audience of, 5, 64, 68, 84, 86, 99, 106, 107, 121–22, 125–26, 139. *See also* Anadolu Agency; *Daily Sabah*; Directorate of Communications; Bosphorus Global; SETA; TRT (Turkish Radio and Television Corporation); TRT World
Turkic republics, 12, 13. *See also* Central Asia; Organization of Turkic States (OTS)
Turkish Islamism, 21, 85, 86, 92, 107, 108, 109, 117. *See also* Kısakürek, Necip Fazıl; Karakoç, Sezai; Topçu, Nurettin
Turkish television series: and AKP, 118, 119, 121, 122, 123, 124, 125, 126; criticisms of, 130–31; international sales of, 115–16; instrumentalization of history in, 117–18, 120–21, 125, 126; negative reaction to, 132–33; Ottoman Empire in, 114, 116, 117, 119, 121, 123, 124, 125,

126, 128, 129; plots of, 117, 118, 123, 133; and political communication, 120–22, 126; political economy of, 119–20, 173n5; popularity of, 115; promotion of, 122; reception of, 126–27, 131–32; representations of Muslims in, 127–30; representations of non-Muslims in, 130; and soft power, 126. See also *Resurrection: Ertuğrul; Establishment: Osman; The Last Emperor*
Turkuvaz Media, 29, 30, 35, 58, 159n115
Twitter. *See* X

ummah, 73, 119, 121, 138
United States: and Turkey, 15, 19, 29, 31, 43, 51, 94, 165n7; and Turkey's global communication, 5, 19, 38, 77, 78, 80, 81, 91, 92, 101, 102, 103, 104, 106, 113, 137, 151n4

victimhood, politics of, 71, 84–86. *See also* Muslims: as victims
Voice of America (VoA), 8, 10, 42, 45
Voice of Turkey (VoT), 2, 5, 12, 16, 147

West, the: and China, 9, 55, 106, 146; criticism of, during the Ottoman Empire, 45, 91, 107; decline of, 95, 104, 137–38; and humanity, 98; and hypocrisy, 83, 103–4, 113, 137–38; and Iran, 56; and oppression, 87; and Russia, 55–56, 57, 106, 146, 172n4; shameful history of, 19, 52, 92, 104–5, 124; as term, 151n4; and threat source, 86; Turkey's criticism of, 19, 92, 93, 94, 99, 103, 106–10, 111, 112, 137–38
Westernization, 20, 85, 118
Western media, 54, 68, 101, 142, 146; and coverage of Turkey, 20, 26, 27, 39, 40, 41, 44, 136; hostility toward, 41–43; as Orientalist, 43–44, 141; outlets in Turkey, 42, 58; representations of Muslims in, 44, 82, 127, 128, 130, 133, 134; as threat to Turkey, 27, 42–43, 46, 50, 139; as tool of imperialism, 43–46, 138, 139

X: alternatives to, 56–57; blocking of Turkey-related accounts on, 37, 51, 52; pressured by Turkey, 53; throttling of, 53; Turkey's criticism of, 37, 51–52, 139, 160n24; use of, during the coup attempt, 39–40
Xinhua, 9, 10, 35, 57, 106

YEE (Yunus Emre Institute), 74, 75, 126, 163n81
Yeni Safak English, 2, 16, 17
YPG (People's Defense Units), 17, 64, 94, 137, 154n61, 160n24
YTB (Presidency for Turks Abroad and Related Communities), 62, 63, 64, 74, 75

Index 231

BILGE YESIL is an associate professor of media culture at City University of New York, College of Staten Island. She is the author of *Media in New Turkey: The Origins of an Authoritarian Neoliberal State*.

The University of Illinois Press
is a founding member of the
Association of University Presses.
_____

University of Illinois Press
1325 South Oak Street
Champaign, IL 61820-6903
www.press.uillinois.edu